CORIOLIS

14455 North Hayden Road, Suite 220 • Scottsdale, Arizona 85260

Coriolis: The Training And Certification Destination™

Thank you for purchasing one of our innovative certification study guides, just one of the many members of the Coriolis family of certification products.

Certification Insider Press™ has long believed that achieving your IT certification is more of a road trip than anything else. This is why most of our readers consider us their *Training And Certification Destination.* By providing a one-stop shop for the most innovative and unique training materials, our readers know we are the first place to look when it comes to achieving their certification. As one reader put it, "I plan on using your books for all of the exams I take."

To help you reach your goals, we've listened to others like you, and we've designed our entire product line around you and the way you like to study, learn, and master challenging subjects. Our approach is *The Smartest Way To Get Certified™.*

In addition to our highly popular *Exam Cram* and *Exam Prep* guides, we have a number of new products. We recently launched Exam Cram Live!, two-day seminars based on *Exam Cram* material. We've also developed a new series of books and study aides—*Practice Tests Exam Crams* and *Exam Cram Flash Cards*—designed to make your studying fun as well as productive.

Our commitment to being the Training And Certification Destination does not stop there. We just introduced *Exam Cram Insider,* a biweekly newsletter containing the latest in certification news, study tips, and announcements from Certification Insider Press. (To subscribe, send an email to **eci@coriolis.com** and type "subscribe insider" in the body of the email.) We also recently announced the launch of the Certified Crammer Society and the Coriolis Help Center—two new additions to the Certification Insider Press family.

We'd like to hear from you. Help us continue to provide the very best certification study materials possible. Write us or email us at **cipq@coriolis.com** and let us know how our books have helped you study, or tell us about new features that you'd like us to add. If you send us a story about how we've helped you, and we use it in one of our books, we'll send you an official Coriolis shirt for your efforts.

Good luck with your certification exam and your career. Thank you for allowing us to help you achieve your goals.

Keith Weiskamp
President and CEO

Look For These Other Books From The Coriolis Group:

MCSD Architectures Exam Cram
Donald Brandt

MCSD Visual Basic 6 Desktop Exam Prep
Michael Ekedahl

MCSD Visual C++6 Desktop Exam Prep
James Lacey

*For my loving wife, Debbie, whose encouragement and support enabled me
to pursue writing this book in the first place*
—Keith Morneau

ABOUT THE AUTHOR

Keith Morneau teaches Information Systems technology (Networking, Programming, and Microcomputer Specializations) at Northern Virginia Community College in Annandale, VA, where he is an Assistant Professor. He has over seven years' experience in the computer industry as a computer operator, systems engineer, programmer/analyst, and instructor. Keith has been an active member of the Microsoft Certification Review Board for exam 70-100.

ACKNOWLEDGMENTS

I am very grateful for all the reviewers who provided helpful and thoughtful comments and suggestions during the development of this book:

Ramesh Chandak, Cambridge Technology Partners

Dean Callahan, Computer Learning Center

Duncan McIntosh, International National School of Business

Harold Tonkin, Productivity Point International

Warren Moseley, St. Andrews College

Thanks to my mother, Joan Morneau, for helping and guiding me in the writing of book reports and term papers when I was younger. Without her dedication to teaching me how to write, a book like this would not be possible. Finally, I want to thank my wife, Debbie, for providing insightful comments and suggestions throughout the development of this book and for her help creating the glossary and some solutions in the Instructor's Manual.

CONTENTS AT A GLANCE

TABLE OF CONTENTS

INTRODUCTION

Information systems, including standalone, network, and Internet-based aplications, are being developed to solve a wide range of business problems. The goal of this book is to familiarize you in Information Technology and Computer Science courses about the process of developing information systems using Microsoft technologies. Learning only how to program a language is no longer a minimum requirement for programmers. Programmers must understand hardware and software architectures that support the programming applications, to be competitive and successful in the current marketplace. You must also understand the process of developing complete software systems by using the best of the current tools.

MCSD Architectures Exam Prep is designed to guide the experienced programmer in developing client/server applications using Microsoft Visual Studio 6.0, specifically Visual Basic, Visual SourceSafe, Visual Interdev, Microsoft Transaction Server, Microsoft Message Queue Server, and Microsoft Internet Information Server (IIS) 4.0. You will work through several real-world solutions to problems in the context of the software development life cycle, using the Microsoft Solution Framework (MSF). This book assumes that you have basic programming skills, such as introductory Visual Basic knowledge, including the ability to create VB apps, knowledge of computer systems fundamentals, and user knowledge of Windows 95, Microsoft Office, Internet browsing and HTML, and email systems.

ORGANIZATION AND COVERAGE

MCSD Architectures Exam Prep introduces you to the process of developing information systems and to the advanced programming concepts necessary to solve business problems. Throughout the chapters, you use the Unified Modeling Language (UML) to document the system requirements and design. Microsoft Solutions Framework (MSF) is introduced in Chapter 1 and explored extensively in Chapters 2 through 13. Because these concepts build on one another, you must read the chapters in sequence. For example, you must understand the concepts and complete the procedures and exercises in Chapter 5 before you can perform the tasks in Chapter 6.

Chapter 2 teaches you about basic networking technology. In Chapter 3, you learn about the different Microsoft operating systems and technologies for solving business problems. Chapter 4 teaches students how to create a vision statement during the envisioning phase of MSF. Chapters 5 and 6 teach students how to create requirements using a conceptual model with the use of case scenarios, how to create the logical design from the conceptual design, and how to create the physical design from the logical design in the planning phase.

Chapter 7 explains how to use configuration management tools for managing software projects with Microsoft Visual SourceSafe, and introduces the developing phase of MSF. Chapter 8 shows students how to create data services with SQL Server, specifically SQL and stored procedures. Chapter 9 teaches students how to create business objects in business services, using Visual Basic's ActiveX DLL, Microsoft Transaction Server, and Microsoft Message Queue Server. Chapters 10 and 11 explore how to use Visual Basic to create "traditional" applications, and Visual Interdev to create Web applications.

Chapter 12 explains how to create online Help systems and discusses application localization. Chapter 13 discusses testing software during the stabilizing phase and deploying applications at the end of the stabilizing phase.

Please note there are custom installations and special steps that you must complete to successfully work through this text. These critical instructions are highlighted with a Stop Sign icon. Pay extra attention to all the instructions and information provided whenever the Stop Sign appears in the text.

Using *MCSD Architectures Exam Prep* you learn how to use MSF to build information systems from start to finish. This enables you to experience all phases of the software development life cycle in the classroom, and to gain a deeper understanding of the complexities of developing software applications. Each chapter in this book helps you to build a piece of the system, starting with planning, and ending with product deployment, which is why the chapters must be read in order.

MCSD Architectures Exam Prep is also designed to provide the necessary skills to pass the Analyzing Requirements and Defining Solution Architectures 70-100 Certification Exam, a core requirement of the Microsoft Certified Solutions Developer (MCSD) program. Appendix A discusses the skills needed to use this book, and also supplies a cross-reference matrix to help you match chapters to the topics you will need to study for the exam. Appendix B provides a guide to SQL Server administration functions. It explains how to navigate the SQL Server Enterprise Manager and create, restore, and back up a database. Appendix C outlines the tables included in CTIS, the sample information system used throughout this text. Refer to these tables when you write queries in Chapter 8.

After completing this textbook, you will be able to use Microsoft technologies and write code to solve business problems using a software development process (MSF).

In order to successfully complete this book and prepare adequately for Microsoft Certification Exam 70-100, you must complete each chapter in sequence. For example, you must complete Chapter 1 before Chapter 2, and so on. Completing a chapter includes reading and understanding the material, and performing all the steps and exercises. If you elect to complete Hands-On Projects (which is highly recommended), you must also choose one, and only one, Hands-On Project and work with that same number project throughout the book in the proper sequence.

FEATURES

MCSD Architectures Exam Prep contains numerous features to aid and assist the student's learning:

➤ **Step-by-Step Methodology** This methodology keeps you on track. The text reinforces where you are in the development process and emphasizes how each phase relates to the others. You also learn development concepts and techniques in the context of creating a contemporary application.

➤ **Tips** Tips supply additional information, such as references to materials to enhance the learning experience.

➤ **Summaries** Following each chapter is a summary that recaps the concepts covered in the chapter.

➤ **Review Questions** Each chapter concludes with meaningful, conceptual review questions that test the your understanding of what you learned in the chapter.

➤ **Hands-On Projects** The Review Questions are followed by Hands-On Projects, which provide you with additional practice using the skills and concepts you learned in the chapter. You must work with the same number Hands-On Project throughout the book, following the order of the chapter. If you chose Hands-On Project 1 you must continue doing only Hands-on Project 1 for each chapter.

TEACHING TOOLS

All of the tools for this text are found on the CD-ROM.

➤ **Questions and Project Answers** The CD-ROM that accompanies this book contains answers to the Review Questions and solutions to the Hands-On Projects

➤ **Solution Files** Solution files contain possible solutions to all the problems you are asked to create or modify in the chapters and cases. (Due to the nature of software development, your solutions might differ from these solutions and still be correct.)

➤ **Student Files** Student files, containing all data that you will use for the chapters and exercises in this textbook, are provided on CD-ROM.

➤ **Web Site** (http://www.nv.cc.va.us/home/kmorneau solution_architectures) This Web site contains additional information including technical links, FAQs, and other support information to assist students and instructors using this book.

COURSE TRACKING INFORMATION SYSTEM (CTIS) CASE STUDY

MCSD Architectures Exam Prep guides you in designing and creating an information system to solve a real-world business problem. This book focusses on analyzing, designing, and creating a solution to a grade-tracking problem at a fictitious college. This system is called the Course Tracking Information System (CTIS), and has three main user groups: instructors who track courses and grades for students, students who want to view their assignments and track their grades, and a system administrator who is responsible for maintaining the college labs and any custom software for the college. Each user articulates the problems they want the new system to solve as follows:

Instructor

I currently use an Excel spreadsheet to track my grades. I use worksheets to track categories in my classes. I have one worksheet that tracks the average of each category for each class. I usually use a different workbook for each class. Also, I use different weighted averages for each class. Sometimes, I use the same weighted averages for different classes. Some students register for a number of my classes and their grades are in different workbooks. It's difficult to go back and forth between workbooks to look up a student's progress.

I track assignments in my classes by hand, using a paper-based organizer. I track the description of the assignment, the date assigned, the due date, and the category of the assignment. I consider exams and the final exam as special assignments.

In Excel, I also track my class schedules, such as section, year, and term of the class. I create a separate worksheet for each class.

In the beginning of a semester, I ask students for their personal information such as last name, first name, email address, home phone, and work phone numbers. I also supply my personal information such as last name, first name, phone number, email address, and Web site address.

I would like to automate my grading process by integrating all the information about my classes, students, grades, and assignments. I would like to produce reports such as a final grade report for a class and for an individual student, and reports on the assignments and their due dates. I also would like my students to view their grades and their personal information throughout the semester, and access the assignments they are required to turn in.

Student

When I take classes, I really do not know how I am doing from week to week. I have to call my professors and ask for my grades. Usually, the professors estimate my progress since they don't calculate the average until the end of the semester. I would like to be able to check my grades, class schedule, and assignments when I feel like it. Sometimes I do schoolwork late at night, when I cannot call my classmates to ask them about assignments. I would like access to my class at any time, 24 hours a day, 7 days a week.

System Administrator

I manage the student labs and the instructor's computers on a daily basis. Students and instructors have access to Windows 95/98, Microsoft Office, and Internet Explorer on the desktop. My staff and I are not technically savvy enough to know how to install custom software, and prefer not to. There are several Web servers (running Windows NT) on campus, which faculty, staff, and students can access.

READ THIS BEFORE YOU BEGIN

Installation Requirements and Instructions

Hardware And Software Requirements

Students and professionals who want to get the most from this text should have access to a networked PC running Windows 95/98 or Windows NT 4.0 Workstation or Server. The following table summarizes the minimum requirements and recommendations (in parentheses) for each of these operating systems.

Minimum hardware and software requirements.

Item	Windows 95/98	NT Workstation 4.0	NTServer 4.0
RAM (as much RAM as you can afford)	32 (64) MB	64 (128) MB	64 (128) MB
Disk space (as much disk space as you can afford)	2 (6) GB	2 (6) GB	2 (6) GB
CPU	Pentium	Pentium	Pentium

(continued)

Minimum hardware and software requirements *(continued)*.

Item	Windows 95/98	NT Workstation 4.0	NTServer 4.0
Display Type	SVGA	SVGA	SVGA
Network	Yes	Yes	Yes
Internet Access	Recommended	Recommended	Recommended
Windows NT 4.0 Service Pack 4	N/A	Yes	Yes
SQL Server 7.0 Standard Edition	Yes	Yes	Yes
Microsoft Office	Yes	Yes	Yes
Visual Studio 6.0 Enterprise Edition	Recommended Everything but MSMQ	Recommended Everything but MSMQ	Recommended
Microsoft Front Page	Recommended	Recommended	Recommended

The following sections provide step-by-step instructions for installing SQL Server 7.0 and Visual Studio 6.0 on a Windows 95/98 or Windows NT 4.0 Workstation or Windows NT 4.0 Server box.

These installation instructions assume that you have only installed the operating system (Windows 95/98 or Windows NT) on your computer. The next software you should install is SQL Server 7.0 and Visual Studio 6.0, as instructed below. If you have already installed other software, you may not have to perform some of the following instructions.

Installing SQL Server 7.0 Standard Edition on Windows 95/98 or Windows NT 4.0 Workstation or Windows NT 4.0 Server
If you're working with Windows NT 4.0 Server, you must first install Windows NT Service Pack 4.0 and Internet Explorer 4.01, if you haven't already done so. Then you're ready to install SQL Server 7.0 Standard Edition. The steps below guide you through installations on either Windows 95/98, Windows NT 4.0 Workstation, or Windows NT 4.0 Server.

Before you can install SQL Server 7.0 in Windows NT Workstation and Server, you must install Windows NT Service Pack 4.0 and Internet Explorer 4.01 SP 1.

If you are using Windows 95/98 but have not installed Internet Explorer 4.01 or DCOM95/98, you must complete steps 5 through 7, and can then skip ahead to the "To install SQL Server 7.0" instructions. If the Service Pack and Internet Explorer 4.01 SP 1 are already installed, skip to the "To install SQL Server 7.0" instructions.

To install SQL Server 7.0:

  1. Start Windows or log on to Windows NT as you usually do.

2. Insert the SQL Server 7.0 CD into the CD-ROM drive. If Autoplay is disabled on your machine, then continue to steps 3 and 4. Otherwise, skip to step 5.

3. On the Windows desktop, double-click the My Computer icon.

4. Double-click the CD-ROM drive icon. You see the SQL Server Setup dialog box.

5. For Windows NT only, click the Install SQL Server 7.0 Prerequisites option button.

6. For Windows NT only, click the Windows NT 4.0 option button.

7. For Windows NT only, read the instructions and then click Exit without installing any files. You will install the files in the next set of steps.

To install Windows NT Service Pack 4:

1. Insert the Windows NT 4.0 SP 4 CD into the CD-ROM drive.

2. Click the Service Pack 4 Installation For Intel-based Systems option button.

3. In the Windows NT Service Pack Setup dialog box, click Accept The License Agreement.

4. Click Install. The Windows NT Service Pack installs.

5. When prompted to restart the computer, click OK.

6. Log on to Windows NT as you usually do.

7. If you don't have Internet Explorer 4.01 installed, you may see an informational message from the Service Pack setup. Click No.

8. Remove the Windows NT 4.0 SP 4 CD, and then insert SQL Server 7.0 CD into CD-ROM drive.

9. In the Setup dialog box, click the Install SQL Server 7.0 Prerequisites option button.

10. In the Setup dialog box, click Windows NT 4.0 and then click Launch Setup Wizard.

11. In the Internet Explorer SP1 Active Setup dialog box, click Next.

12. Click I Accept The Agreement if you accept the licensing agreement, and then click Next.

13. In the Installation Option dialog box, click the Full Installation option and then click Next.

14. In the Windows Desktop Update dialog box, click Next to accept the default.

15. In the Active Channel Selection dialog box, click Next to accept the default.

16. In the Destination Folder dialog box, click Next to accept the default. Internet Explorer 4.01 installs.

17. If you receive a Confirm File Replace message, click No To All.

18. When setup is complete, click OK.

19. Click OK again to restart the computer.

To install SQL Server 7.0:

1. Start Windows or log on as you usually do.

2. Double-click the My Computer icon on the desktop, and then double-click the CD-ROM drive icon.

3. In the Setup dialog box, click the Install SQL Server 7.0 Components option button.

4. If you are using Windows NT, click Database Server – Standard Edition. If you are using Windows 95/98 or NT Workstation, click Database Server – Desktop Edition.

5. In the Install Method dialog box, accept the default (Local) by clicking Next.

6. In the Welcome dialog box, click Next.

7. In the Software License Agreement dialog box, click Yes.

8. In the User Information dialog box, click Next.

9. For Windows NT Server, in the Setup Type dialog box, type your 10 digit CD-Key.

10. For Windows NT Server, in the Product ID dialog box, click OK.

11. In the Setup Type dialog box, click Next.

12. For Windows NT Server, in the Services Account dialog box, type your username and password, if necessary, in the Service Settings section and then click Next.

13. In the Start Copying Files dialog box, click Next.

14. For Windows NT Server, in the Choose Licensing Mode dialog box, click Continue.

15. For Windows NT Server, in the Per Server Licensing dialog box, click I Agree That …, and then click OK. If you see any messages, click Close to continue.

16. If you see a message regarding workstation services, click OK.

17. When setup is complete, click Finish.

18. In Windows 98, click Exit in the Microsoft SQL Server Setup Screen.

19. Remove the CD from the CD-ROM drive.

20. Log on to Windows, if necessary.

21. Double-click the SQL Server icon on the taskbar.

22. In Windows 98, click the Start/Continue button to start SQL Server.

23. In Windows 98, check the box labeled Auto-Start Service When OS Starts.

24. Click the Close button to close the SQL Server Service Manager.

To create the CTIS database to be used in this book:

1. On the Windows desktop, click the Start button. Point to Programs, then Microsoft SQL Server 7.0, and click Enterprise Manager.

2. Double-click to expand the Microsoft SQL Servers folder.

3. Double-click to expand the SQL Server Group folder.

4. Double-click to expand your Server folder. (If you do not know your server name, right-click Network Neighborhood on the Windows desktop. Click the Identification tab; your Server name is the Computer name.)

5. Right-click Databases, and then click New Database on the shortcut menu.

6. In the Name text box, type "CTIS" and click OK to create the CTIS database. CTIS is the database you will use in this book to assist you in creating the CTIS system.

7. Click the Close button to close the SQL Server Enterprise Manager.

Installing Visual Studio 6.0 Enterprise Edition On Windows NT 4.0 Server Or Windows 95/98 Or Windows NT 4.0 Workstation

After you install SQL Server 7.0, install Visual Studio 6.0.

To start installing Visual Studio 6.0:

1. Start Windows or log on as you usually do.

2. Insert the Visual Studio 6.0 Disk 1 into the CD-ROM drive.

3. In the Installation Wizard for Visual Studio 6.0 Enterprise Edition, click Next.

4. In the End User License Agreement dialog box, click I accept the agreement, and then click Next.

5. In the User ID dialog box, type the Product ID Number, and then click Next.

6. If you see another dialog box, click the Custom button, and then click Next.

7. In Windows 98, click Next in the Choose Custom Install Folder dialog box.

8. If you see the Welcome dialog box, click Continue. Verify the Product ID, and then click OK.

9. To install Microsoft Virtual Machine for JAVA, click Next in the Microsoft Virtual Machine for JAVA dialog box. Microsoft Virtual Machine for JAVA installs.

10. When the installation is complete, click OK to reboot your machine.

11. Start Windows or log on as you usually do.

12. If you haven't installed DCOM 98 (for Windows 95/98 only), click Next in the Install DCOM98 dialog box. DCOM98 installs.

13. When the installation is complete, click OK to reboot your machine.

14. Start Windows or log on as you usually do.

15. To install Visual Studio 6.0 Enterprise Edition, click Next in the Visual Studio Installation Wizard.

16. In the Choose Common Install Folder dialog box, click Next.

17. In the Visual Studio 6.0 Enterprise Setup dialog box, click Continue.

18. In the Product ID dialog box, click OK.

19. In the Custom dialog box, click Select All, and then click Continue.

20. For Windows NT, click OK in the Setup Environment Variables dialog box.

21. In the Use The New Visual Source Safe Database Format dialog box, click Yes if you need to use the new Visual Source Safe Database format. Visual Studio 6.0 Enterprise Edition installs.

22. For Windows NT, click OK in the Debug Symbols dialog box.

23. For Windows 95/98, click OK in the Setup Environment Variables dialog box.

24. When installation completes, click Restart Windows.

To install Microsoft Developer Network (MSDN) Documentation for Visual Studio 6.0:

1. If necessary, log on to Windows as you usually do. If necessary, start the Setup program by clicking the Start button, clicking Run, typing D:Setup, where D is the letter of your CD-ROM drive, and then clicking OK.

2. In the Install MSDN dialog box, click Next.

3. Insert the MSDN Library CD Disk 1 into the CD-ROM drive, and click OK.

4. In the MSDN library dialog box, click Continue.

5. If you see the Name and Organization Information dialog box, enter your name and the name of your organization and then click OK.

6. In the Product ID dialog box, click OK.

7. In the License Agreement dialog box, click I Agree.

8. Use Windows Explorer to make sure you have more than 800 MB of space on your hard drive, and then, in the MSDN library dialog box, click the Full button to install the full library. The MSDN library installs.

9. When you see the setup message, insert the MSDN library Disk 2 in the CD-ROM drive and click OK.

10. When the MSDN library installation is complete, click OK.

INFORMATION SYSTEMS FUNDAMENTALS

AFTER READING THIS CHAPTER AND COMPLETING THE EXERCISES, YOU WILL BE ABLE TO:

➤ Identify the difference between data and information

➤ Define the term *information system*

➤ Define the user of the information system

➤ Define the purpose of the Microsoft Solutions Framework

➤ Describe the seven models in the Microsoft Solutions Framework

Information systems are increasingly important to the success of a business. Planning, building, and managing information systems requires an organized and coordinated effort by a project team. This team must have good management, analytical, design, programming, testing, and troubleshooting skills. The team uses these skills to develop a technology infrastructure, hardware, software, and information management standards, and policies and procedures describing business operations.

As a computer programmer, you must understand the fundamental concepts involved in creating and managing an information system, including being a member of a project team and understanding how the system fits into the business operation.

CHAPTER OVERVIEW

This chapter provides an overview of the Microsoft Solutions Framework (MSF), Microsoft's guidelines for planning, building, and managing information systems. MSF includes two tracks: software development, where the focus is on enterprise development projects, and infrastructure deployment, where the focus is on hardware, software, and communications projects. This book focuses on the software development track. For more information on the infrastructure deployment track, refer to Microsoft's Web site at *www.microsoft.com*.

INFORMATION SYSTEM FUNDAMENTALS

An information system uses data, people, processes, and information technology—a combination of hardware, software, and telecommunications—to help run daily operations, solve problems, and make decisions in a business. Figure 1.1 shows the information system process.

An information system receives input, processes the input, and then supplies the output. The user supplies the input, or data, the information system processes. *Data* is raw facts that have no meaning on their own. The information system refines data into information.

For example, let's say a sales department's data entry clerk enters customer orders into a sales information system. At the end of the day, the clerk's manager requests a daily report from the sales information system. The manager looks at the report to see how the sales department did today and compares their performance to last week's on the same day. In this example, the clerk is the user. He or she enters data, which consists of the customer orders. The orders have no meaning by themselves, but processed in a report, they become information that means something to the manager.

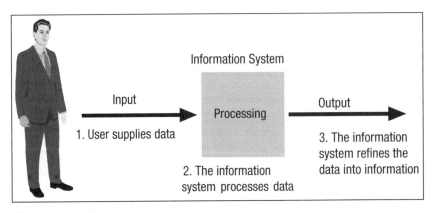

Figure 1.1   Information system process.

Data And Information

The purpose of an information system is to process data into meaningful information. While inaccurate information can easily cause lasting harm, accurate information can give a business a competitive edge. Therefore, a successful information system must deliver helpful, accurate information.

Users

The user works with an information system to accomplish tasks. Users include managers, secretaries, engineers, data entry clerks, and vice presidents. Because an information system must satisfy their needs and solve their problems, users should be part of the design team. By explaining their tasks and goals, users define the initial concept of the information system. Users should also review the system to suggest changes during development.

MICROSOFT SOLUTIONS FRAMEWORK

Microsoft created its Solutions Framework from the best practices of Microsoft's product teams and information technology group. MSF is a flexible series of models that guides information systems professionals in planning an enterprise architecture that adapts to industry change, in building business-driven applications, and in managing the computing environment. These guidelines specifically recommend how businesses should integrate people, processes, hardware, software, and communications technology into their organization. See Figure 1.2 and Table 1.1.

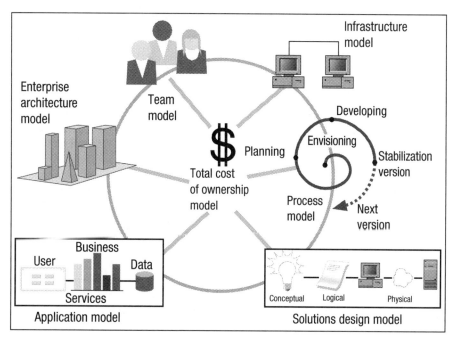

Figure 1.2   Microsoft Solutions Framework.

Table 1.1 Microsoft Solutions Framework models.

Model Name	Purpose of Model	What Model Recommends
Enterprise Architecture model	Incorporate technology into the business	Create the business, application, information, and technology architectures
Team model	Build effective teams	Define the roles of each team member in an enterprise development project
Infrastructure model	Manage the logistics of deploying systems	System management, help desk, and communications work together to deploy a system
Total Cost of Ownership model	Document and manage project	Calculate project costs, minimize these costs, and improve costs your return on investment
Process model	Manage the phases of system development	Develop an information system in the following phases: • Envisioning phase: defining the vision of the project • Planning phase: assembling a team, and developing cost and schedules for a project • Developing phase: defining, designing, and creating the product • Stabilization phase: testing and deploying the product
Solutions Design model	Design to provide solutions for business needs	Specific suggestions for building effective information systems. Consider the suggestions during the developing phase of the process model by analyzing the system from the following perspectives: • Conceptual perspective: what the system will supply for services • Logical perspective: how the system will supply the services logically • Physical perspective: how to create the system from the logical perspective
Application model	Design for usability and flexibility	Applications should include: • User services: a presentation layer that interacts with the user • Business services: the application logic and business rules of the application • Data services: the way data is stored and retrieved in the application

You can use some or all of these models in any logical order when developing information systems. For example, use the Enterprise Architecture, Team, Infrastructure, and Total Cost of Ownership models to provide an infrastructure and manage an information system. After you complete the tasks of the Team,

Process, and Enterprise Architecture models to distribute a product, you can use MSF's Infrastructure model to determine which human resources are needed to manage the information system, and the Total Cost of Ownership model to identify all the actual and hidden costs of developing an information system.

Enterprise Architecture Model

Use the Enterprise Architecture model to plan the infrastructure—all the resources needed to support a computing system, such as technology, operating procedures, staff, and management—as well as the system and processes that business applications use to distribute information throughout the organization.

Before you plan an information system project, set up a technology infrastructure—the hardware, software, and communications technologies that provide the underlying base for a business—to support business activities. As the business needs change, the technology infrastructure must also change. Describing the business, application, and information architectures also lets you plan and manage systems by anticipating and accommodating change. These four architectures—business, application, information, and technology—are detailed in the following sections.

Business Architecture

The business architecture model describes the overall operation of the business, including the business processes. These are informal or formal rules or procedures for running the business. They describe the functions an organization performs, such as filling out an order form, buying software, contracting work to outside sources, or writing a proposal. To implement a successful information system based on business needs, you must completely understand the business architecture.

Application Architecture

The application architecture model describes the interface, service, and application standards the business should set:

➤ **Interface standards** Provide agreements on how information systems interact with each other. For example, let's say two vendors support different email systems. If these two systems are to exchange messages, each system must send and receive messages in a format that is recognized and supported by both systems.

➤ **Service standards** Supply the supported business services, including reusable items such as dialog boxes or math routines. For example, let's say two projects were developed several months apart. The first project created an Open dialog box and a Save As dialog box. The second project used both dialog boxes.

➤ **Application standards** Show how an application looks, feels, and interacts with a user. For example, when you are using Microsoft Word and want to save a document, a Save dialog box appears. If you want to open a document, an Open dialog box appears. Both dialog boxes look, feel, and act very similarly. Application standards provide a consistent look and feel to any application.

Information Architecture

The information architecture model defines the standards for running business processes and operations. These standards identify acceptable data models, define data management and security policies, and explain information consumption and production.

Technology Architecture

The technology architecture model supplies the standards for providing and distributing hardware, software, and networking resources. It also describes the standard hardware, operating systems, and networking configurations, development tools, and application software. These guidelines ensure that everyone is using the same architecture.

Team Model

The people who plan, develop, and manage the information system contribute significantly to the success of the system. In the Team model, they play six possible roles, as illustrated in Figure 1.3.

The Team model shows how to structure development teams to ensure high-quality, cost-effective solutions. Team members play defined roles on the project and focus on the specified vision of the product. Each role is explained in detail in the following sections.

Figure 1.3 The six roles of the Team model.

Product Management

Product management supplies a vision for the product, acquires customer requirements, develops and maintains the business case (the reason for developing this product), and manages the customer's expectations. The product management team also researches the market for potential products, and recommends products and services to program management.

Program Management

Program management must deliver the right product or service at the right time, within the budget. They manage the budgets, schedules, and risks, and develop informal or formal proposals when the product management team requests them.

Development

Development creates plans, specifications, schedules, architecture, designs, and code. They also test and debug the product or service. The development team builds a product or service that meets the needs of the customer or user and complies with the specification. Development must also stay within budget and schedule tasks.

The development team includes systems analysts, programmer/analysts, and programmers. Systems analysts serve as the liaison between the user and the development team and between the testing and development teams. They develop and test the specifications to meet the needs of the users. Programmer/analysts design and create the product or service that fully conforms to the specification. Programmers work with the systems analysts and the programmer/analysts to produce the system.

Testing

The testing team includes the systems analysts and testers who works with the product or service to make sure it complies with the specification.

Logistics Management

The logistics team distributes the product or service after it has been developed and tested. Logistics rolls out the new or upgraded product or service to the operations and support groups.

User Education

User education trains users and ensures product quality to help reduce overall maintenance costs of the product or service. They also advocate the user perspective to the other teams to help make the product easier to understand and use.

Infrastructure Model

The infrastructure includes all the resources needed to support a computing system, such as technology, operating procedures, staff, and management. Use the Enterprise Architecture model to plan the infrastructure. Use the Infrastructure model to manage the logistics of deploying systems. This model defines the roles of logistics management, as shown in Figure 1.4.

This model expands logistics management into three roles:

➤ **System management** System managers maintain the hardware and software systems so the business operates with little interruption. The system management team includes system administrators, network administrators, and other support people. The system administrators and network administrators set up and maintain the computers and network software.

➤ **Help desk** The help desk staff supports the users of the information systems by answering questions and solving problems.

➤ **Communications** These people coordinate voice, video, and data communications. The communications team normally consists of network engineers who design, implement, and maintain network communications.

Total Cost Of Ownership Model

While planning, building, and managing the information system, developers must also document and manage related costs. The Total Cost of Ownership (TCO) model defines all project costs, and explains how to minimize those costs and improve your return on your computing investment.

In the planning phase, the model describes how to calculate the benchmarks, cost baselines, return on investment (ROI), and validation. In the building phase, the model calculates ROI for both new and upgraded systems. In the

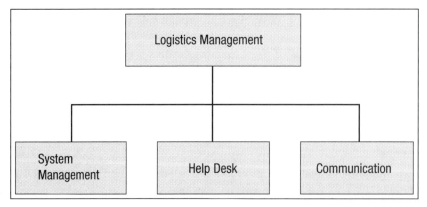

Figure 1.4 Three roles of logistics management in the Infrastructure model.

managing phase, the model estimates the total by calculating the following costs:

➤ Hardware and software costs of desktops, servers, network devices, and upgrades

➤ Support costs of maintenance, disaster recovery, help desk, administration, and training

➤ Development costs in building the system

➤ Management costs of network, systems, and data management

➤ End-user costs of training, peer support, and general experimentation

➤ Downtime or other costs of planned and unplanned outages for applications development and testing

➤ Telecommunications fees of leased lines and other communications expenses

A comprehensive TCO strategy minimizes hidden costs and improves the return on investment of the information system.

Software Development Life Cycle Overview

Managers of information systems use a software development life cycle to keep teams organized, help them stay within budget and on schedule, and deliver products or services that meet business needs. In today's information technology environment, a product or service remains a work in progress and is never "finished." Microsoft has found that an interactive approach to developing products and services has greater long-term success because it recognizes that creating and delivering these products and services involves a process of change. Because most enterprise architectures are too large to tackle at once, an interactive approach lets you release multiple versions to create a new product from the current one. A *version* is a set of requirements built into a product or service and delivered to the customer. Creating smaller working subsets of the total enterprise architecture is better than delivering a whole system that doesn't work.

An interactive approach also keeps the development team focused on releasing versions and working toward *milestones*, which are significant events in the development process, and are defined in the four phases of the Process model explained below.

Process Model

The MSF Process model provides guidelines for planning projects, defining their boundaries, controlling available resources, and scheduling. These tasks are accomplished in four phases: envisioning, planning, developing, and stabilizing. Each phase ends in a milestone. See Figure 1.5.

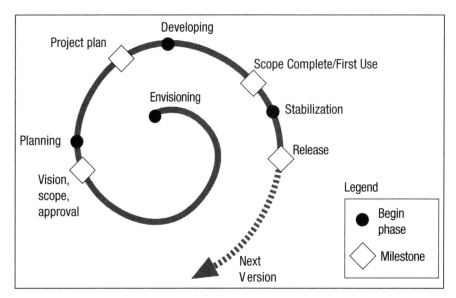

Figure 1.5   Four phases of the MSF Process model.

Envisioning Phase

During the envisioning phase, you ensure that the business develops products and services that meet its current and future needs. The envisioning phase ends with a milestone of vision, scope, and approval.

Once a project gains approval, a development team assembles to define the product or service. They create a vision statement, which articulates the goals of the product or service and provides clear direction to the development team. The project scope defines the limits for a version of a product or service, allowing for incremental development. When the team completes the vision statement and project scope and receives approval for the product or service, the envisioning phase ends.

Planning Phase

The next stage in the Process model is the planning phase, when the customers and development team agree on the requirements of the project. During this phase, systems analysts and users usually negotiate the purpose and content of the product or service. The systems analyst makes sure that what the user requests is within the scope of the version. This phase provides an opportunity to reassess risk, establish user priorities, and finalize the schedule and resource assignments. The planning phase ends in the Project Plan Approved milestone, which includes the updated schedule and the *functional specification*, a document that defines the product or service. The systems analyst negotiates the functional specification with the user or the customer.

Developing Phase

During the developing phase, the developers, programmer/analysts, and programmers use the functional specification and designs to create the product or service within the approved schedule. The development team sets several intermediate milestones, each involving a full test, debug, and fix cycle. The development phase ends in a milestone called Scope Complete/First Use, when users and the development team assess the product or service functionality. The team reaches this milestone when they complete all the work associated with a release. The team also provides a rollout and support plan, and defers any new requirements not within the scope for this version to the next version.

Stabilization Phase

During the stabilization phase, software testers check the system for compliance to the requirements and for bugs, and systematically and thoroughly test the product or service. The users might also test the system themselves to validate that it meets their needs. The stabilization phase ends in a Release milestone, when the testers and the users indicate that the system meets the requirements and is ready for distribution.

After the stabilization phase, the logistics management team and, if necessary, the development team, release and support the version. When the project team meets to work on the next version of the software, they start at the envisioning phase to include any changes or new requirements that did not make it into the current release.

Solutions Design Model

During the planning phase of the Process model, use the Solutions Design model to design business-oriented solutions driven by a specific business need, such as automating time cards, expense reports, or entry of financial data. This model consists of three perspectives: conceptual design, logical design, and physical design. These perspectives can be completed either simultaneously or in phases.

> ➤ **Conceptual design perspective** Developers use a conceptual design perspective when they fully understand the user's needs and produce a set of models to illustrate this understanding. These conceptual design models are like an architect's sketches that include a site plan, elevations, floor plans, cutaway drawings, and other pictures or drawings. The models illustrate the view of the system for the user. For example, if a team develops an email system, they use a series of screen illustrations to show the steps users follow to create and send email messages.

> ➤ **Logical design perspective** After conceptual design, developers use a logical design perspective to represent their view of the system. The logical

design models are like an architect's sketches for the client that show their view of the building. For example, a team may add illustrations that show the system's internals.

➤ **Physical design perspective** After logical design, the system builders use a physical design perspective to create plans. These plans include details about the physical environmental constraints, such as how much RAM and hard drive space the system needs, and what needs to be done to convert the logical illustrations into an application. Physical design plans are like the detailed plans a contractor draws for the builder and subcontractors.

Application Model

The Application model describes how to develop applications using three services: user, business, and data. In general, a *service* is a unit of application logic that defines an operation or function or that transforms data. Services include enforcing business rules, performing calculations or manipulating data, and exposing operations that enter, modify, delete, or view information.

When you perform *user services*, you create the user interface of a traditional GUI application, a web-based application, or an application embedded in Microsoft Office. *Business services* supply business rules that transform data into information and usually interact with the user services. *Data services* provide the mechanism for manipulating data. This mechanism must let users easily and intuitively enter, modify, and delete information. Data services usually interact with the business services, using a database management system (DBMS). The Solutions Design model works with the Application model to create the design with these three services in mind.

CHAPTER SUMMARY

An information system consists of data, people, processes, and information technology for supporting the day-to-day operations and the problem-solving and decision-making needs of a business. The Microsoft Solutions Framework (MSF) provides a series of models for planning, building, and managing an information system. Use this framework to deliver the right product or service on time and within budget.

Successful application development projects follow a software development life cycle, as described in the MSF Process model. This model makes sure the development team delivers a system that meets the user's needs on schedule and within the budget. The Process model also keeps the development team in check, preventing the project from getting out of control.

The Solutions Design model describes how to look at the design from conceptual, logical, and physical design perspectives. The conceptual design perspective lets you view the system through the eyes of the user. The logical design perspective sees the system through the eyes of the developer and the user. The physical design perspective views the system in terms of the physical environment of the product or service.

The Application model describes how to split the application into three services: user, business, and data. The user services provide the user interface. The business services supply business rules and interact with the user services. The data services manage the data and interact with business services.

All MSF models consider that projects are developed incrementally, allowing for constant change, and recommend an interactive approach to design, development, and deployment.

REVIEW QUESTIONS

1. _____ is raw facts that has no meaning on their own.
   a. Information
   b. Data
   c. A user
   d. none of the above

2. _____ is refined and processed _____ that has meaning.
   a. A user/data
   b. Information/data
   c. Data/user
   d. Data/information

3. The _____ interacts with an information system to enter or retrieve information.
   a. systems analyst
   b. developer
   c. user
   d. tester

4. Which model defines the technology infrastructure for delivering services to support business activities?
   a. Enterprise Architecture
   b. Infrastructure
   c. Business Architecture
   d. Team

5. The _____ model describes the overall operation of a business.

   a. Infrastructure

   b. Team

   c. Business architecture

   d. Enterprise Architecture

6. The _____ model explains how to structure development teams to ensure delivery of quality solutions.

   a. Infrastructure

   b. Team

   c. business architecture

   d. Enterprise Architecture

7. What are the six roles of the Team model? What are the responsibilities of each role?

8. What is the TCO model? Why is it important?

9. What is the Infrastructure model? What are the responsibilities of each role in the Infrastructure model?

10. A(n) _____ approach is based on arriving at a future state from the current state through multiple versions.

    a. interactive

    b. recursive

    c. waterfall

    d. none of the above

11. A(n) _____ is a set of requirements that is built into a product or service and delivered to the customer.

    a. analysis

    b. design

    c. version

    d. none of the above

12. The _____ phase is responsible for ensuring that the business develops products and services that meet current and future needs.

    a. developing

    b. planning

    c. stabilizing

    d. envisioning

13. During the _____ phase, the customers and the development team agree on the requirements of the project.

    a. developing

    b. envisioning

    c. planning

    d. stabilizing

14. The _____ phase is when the developers, programmer/analysts, and programmers use the functional specification to design and implement the product or service.

    a. stabilizing

    b. planning

    c. developing

    d. envisioning

15. The _____ phase is when the software testers check the system for compliance to the requirements and test it for bugs.

    a. stabilizing

    b. planning

    c. developing

    d. envisioning

16. The Solutions Design model consists of three perspectives: _____, _____, and _____ design. Choose all that apply.

    a. physical

    b. conceptual

    c. logical

    d. requirements

17. A _____ is a unit of application logic that implements an operation or function, or transforms data.

    a. data

    b. business

    c. service

    d. user

18. The service that supplies the user interface to the application is called
_____ services.

    a. business

    b. user

    c. data

    d. service

19. The service that supplies the data management services to the application is
called _____ services.

    a. user

    b. business

    c. data

    d. service

HANDS-ON PROJECTS

Project 1.1
On the Internet, research two or more information systems that were
developed to solve a specific problem. Give examples of different information
systems and the problems they solved.

Project 1.2
Microsoft has developed several software packages that help automate office
tasks for users such as secretaries and administrative assistants. What are some of
these products and what part of the business do these products help? What are
some of the benefits of using these products?

Project 1.3
Microsoft has developed several software packages that help automate
application development. Briefly explain these products. What are some of these
tools and what are their target markets?

Project 1.4
Microsoft has developed several packages that support data management. Briefly
explain these products.

Project 1.5
Interview a user of an information system. What is this person's job title? What
are this person's tasks? What does this person use the information system for?
Does the system support this person's job? Why, or why not? What would this
person like the system to do to help in his or her current job?

Project 1.6

Visit Microsoft's Web site *http://www.microsoft.com/msf* to research companies that have successfully used MSF. What information systems were developed using MSF? What were the results of using MSF? What problem was the information system solving?

Project 1.7

Research the Internet to find issues involved in using the Total Cost of Ownership model to develop information systems. Why is TCO important for developing information systems? Cite examples of what is being done to lower the TCO in businesses.

Project 1.8

Research the Internet to find information on help desks. What is a help desk? Give some examples of help desks.

Project 1.9

Interview a programmer who works as part of a development team. What company does this programmer work for? Does this company follow a standard development process for all projects? If so, what is the programmer's role in this process? Does the programmer follow a schedule? Does this company have a standard Application model?

Project 1.10

During the stabilization phase of the MSF Process model, software testers test the product or service to make sure it functions as advertised. Research the Internet to find software-testing tools that assist testers in their jobs. A prominent company in this area is Mercury Interactive.

Project 1.11

During the planning phase of the MSF Process model, project managers develop budgets and schedules. Research the Internet for project management tools that assist in developing budgets and schedules. Microsoft also has developed a tool to assist in project management. What tool has Microsoft developed to assist in project planning?

CHAPTER TWO

NETWORKING TECHNOLOGY

> **AFTER READING THIS CHAPTER AND COMPLETING THE EXCERCISES, YOU WILL BE ABLE TO:**
>
> ➤ Describe a communications system and its four components
>
> ➤ Describe a network, network resources, and network services
>
> ➤ Describe clients, peers, and servers
>
> ➤ Identify the different types of networks
>
> ➤ Identify advantages and disadvantages of server-based networks versus peer-based networks
>
> ➤ Describe the layers in the Open Systems Interconnection (OSI) model
>
> ➤ Describe a protocol
>
> ➤ Identify the different protocols in the TCP/IP suite
>
> ➤ Identify the functions and features required in a client/peer machine
>
> ➤ Identify the functions and features required in a server machine

Chapter 1 discussed how to use the Microsoft Solutions Framework outlines to plan, build, and manage information systems. Before you can start planning an information system, however, you need to create and deploy the technology *infrastructure,* the underlying hardware, software, and communications technologies in an organization. Without an infrastructure, you cannot start the process of planning, building, and managing information systems. As you will learn in this chapter, clients, servers, peers, and networks are critical components of a technology infrastructure.

CHAPTER OVERVIEW

Chapter 1 provided an overview of information systems and showed how to use the Microsoft Solutions Framework (MSF) to plan, build, and manage those systems. To effectively communicate information, most information systems use a *network*, a group of two or more computers and other devices linked together to share resources. This chapter introduces the fundamentals of networks, and outlines the hardware you need to create one. Chapter 3 discusses network software, and Chapters 4–16 cover how to create network applications in more detail.

Throughout this book, you will learn how to plan, build, and manage information systems, using a college environment as a hypothetical example. This chapter focuses on the hardware, software, and networking technology needed to support a sample college lab. Figure 2.1 shows an example of a college lab.

The college lab consists of twisted-pair (RJ-45) cables that connect to a wall plate from the client computers that students use. The *clients*, specialized computers that request resources, connect through a network to the *server*, a specialized computer that supplies resources. The network wiring closet manages all the communications equipment for a lab. The wiring closet contains stackable *hubs*, special network devices that connect all the clients, servers, and printers. The clients and servers in the lab use a network printer for printing services.

NETWORKS

Networks are a specialized form of communications system; they transfer information. Figure 2.2 illustrates the components in a communications system.

Communication has four components:

➤ **Transmitter** A device that sends information to another device

➤ **Receiver** A device that receives information from another device

➤ **Medium** The bounded (cables) or unbounded (air) mechanism for connecting the transmitter to the receiver

➤ **Information or data** The message transferred from the transmitter to the receiver as electrical pulses

All communications systems, including networks, consist of the four components. An example of a communications system is the telephone. The handset is the transmitter and receiver. The medium is the cable that connects the phone to the telephone jack. Voice signals, such as words and other sounds, are the information. A network is also a communications system. The computer

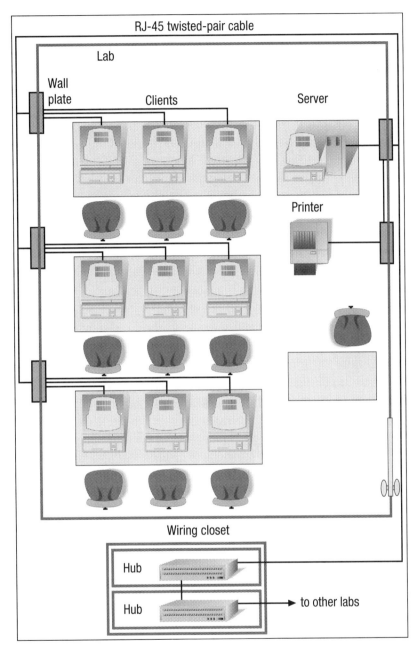

Figure 2.1 Example of a college lab.

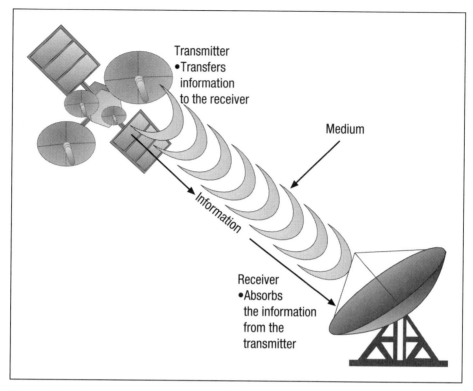

Figure 2.2 Components in a communications system.

is the transmitter and receiver. The medium is the cable that connects the computers together. *Bits*, a combination of zeros and ones, are the information.

A specialized form of electronic communication is called *data communication*, which transfers information in binary form between two computer devices. These devices can be printers, modems, and faxes, for example. Because the purpose of a network is to share resources, any network user has access to a printer, for example, not just the person sitting in front of the computer to which the printer is attached. Networked computers can also share other resources:

➤ Fax modems

➤ Scanners

➤ Floppy disks

➤ Hard disks

➤ CD-ROMs

➤ Tape backup units

➤ Plotters

➤ Almost any device that can be connected to a computer

Network computers have three roles:

➤ **Peers** Provide both presentation management and service functions. Peers also provide network resources.

➤ **Clients** Perform presentation management tasks such as requesting information or filling out electronic forms.

➤ **Servers** Supply services. *Services* are tasks that a network server performs, such as email, Web, Internet, and printer connections; database access; and back-up, network, communications, security, and file management software. Servers also provide network resources.

Network services and the purpose of each are listed below:

➤ **Communications services** Allow different systems to communicate with each other.

➤ **Email services** Let you exchange electronic mail.

➤ **Internet services** Let you transfer files and other information via the Internet.

➤ **Web services** Let you use a Web browser and Web server to access the World Wide Web, a system of Internet servers that support specially formatted documents. You can click hotspots in these documents to jump to other documents, as well as graphics, audio, and video files. Not all Internet servers are part of the World Wide Web.

➤ **Printer services** Let you set up a printer that anyone connected to the network can use.

➤ **Database services** Store and retrieve information such as accounting and financial data.

➤ **Back-up services** Create back-up copies of information on a routine basis.

➤ **Network Management services** manage network resources from a central location.

➤ **Security services** Restrict access to the network by unauthorized users.

➤ **File services** Allow anyone with access to a server to store and retrieve files.

On the basis of the roles of the computers attached to them, networks are divided into three types:

➤ **Server-based** (also called client/server) **networks** Contain clients and the servers that support them.

➤ **Peer** (also called peer-to-peer) **networks** Have no servers and use the network to share resources among independent computers.

➤ **Hybrid networks** Networks that also have peers sharing data. Most networks are actually hybrid networks.

The advantages of server-based networks are:

➤ Strong central security

➤ Central file storage, which allows all users to work from the same set of data and provides easy backup of critical data

➤ Ability to pool available hardware and software, lowering costs through resource sharing

➤ Ability to share expensive equipment, such as laser printers

➤ Optimized dedicated servers, which are faster than peers when sharing network resources

➤ Less intrusive security, since a single password allows access to all shared resources on the network

➤ Freeing of users from the task of managing shared resources

➤ Easy management of many users

➤ Central organization, which keeps the data accessible

The disadvantages of server-based networks are:

➤ Expensive dedicated hardware

➤ Expensive network operating system software and client licenses

➤ Need for a dedicated network administrator (usually required)

Peer networks are defined by a lack of central control over the network. Peer networks include no servers; users simply share disk space and resources, such as printers and faxes, as they see fit.

The advantages of peer networks are:

➤ No extra investment required in server hardware or software

➤ Easy setup

➤ No network administrator involved

➤ Users can control resource sharing

➤ No reliance on other computers for their operation

➤ Lower cost for small networks

The disadvantages of peer networks are:

➤ Additional load on computers because of resource sharing

➤ Inability to handle as many network connections as servers can

➤ Lack of central organization, which can make data hard to find

➤ No central point of storage for file archiving

> Users must administer their own computers

> Weak and intrusive security (if any at all)

> Lack of central control, which makes working with large peer networks difficult

NETWORK ARCHITECTURES

The last section presented network communication, peers, clients, and servers. This section discusses the two main types of network architectures:

> local area networks (LAN)

> wide area networks (WAN)

Local Area Networks (LANs)

A *LAN* links computers that are geographically close together and shares the information of many users, ranging from a group in a single room, to a group within a building. Different types of computers, such as clients, servers, and peers, are connected together in a LAN.

LANs consist of different *topologies*, physical arrangements of network devices (Figure 2.3):

> **Star** All computers in a network connect to a central hub. A *hub* is a special device that manages the communication between devices on the network and uses a special cable called twisted-pair. (Figure 2.3a).

> **Bus** All computers tap into the network with a T-connector. Each end of the bus is a terminator (50 ohms) and uses a special cable called coax (Figure 2.3b).

> **Ring** All computers connect to the network in a circular fashion. (Figure 2.3c).

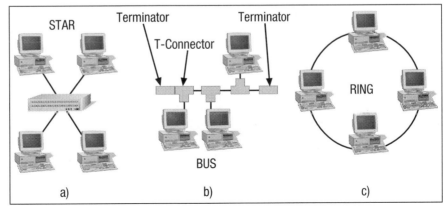

Figure 2.3 LAN topologies.

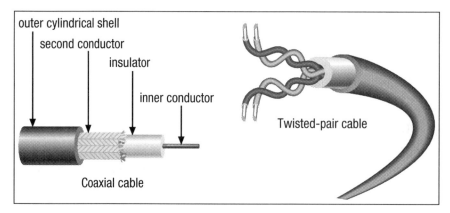

Figure 2.4 LAN cable types.

Figure 2.4 illustrates the different LAN cable types.

Figure 2.1 showed how the clients, server, and printer connect to a hub in the wiring closet of a college's network. The college uses an Ethernet type of LAN, a widely used LAN protocol that traditionally uses a bus or star topology.

Wide Area Networks (WANs)

A WAN shares information among users separated by a long distance. *WANs* are two or more local area networks connected by telephone lines or radio waves.

For example, the sample college has several satellite campuses in the area. If you wanted to connect these satellite campuses together, you could contact your local service provider and discuss the options for connecting them in a WAN.

The Internet

The world's largest public WAN is the Internet. Individuals and corporations use the Internet to share information. Today, connecting private LANs to the Internet provides individuals and corporations with an inexpensive WAN. The most popular ways to interact with other people or computers are sending and receiving electronic mail and using the World Wide Web, where you use a browser that requests different types of resources from a Web server.

For example, let's say a college decides to connect its students to the Internet. The college can connect to the Internet directly through a regional network provider called a network access point (NAP). Examples of NAPs are SprintLink (NJ), MAE East (DC), MAE West (CA), Ameritech (IL), and PacBell (CA). The college can also connect to the Internet through an Internet service provider (ISP). There are thousands of ISPs in the country. Refer to the

Internet and search for ISP to find one in your area. Each option requires connectivity through a local service provider.

Corporate Intranets

Intranets let corporations supply Internet services over their LANs. The Internet is a very insecure environment for connecting corporate LANs. Intranets are private internets with the security to protect a corporation's assets.

For example, the sample college decides to support several Web servers for use on their local network to create an intranet. This intranet will supply information such as faculty and course information.

PROTOCOLS

In the last section, you investigated the available types of networks. These networks require rules of information exchange between two or more computers. Protocols supply these rules to transfer data between computers. *Protocols* are a set of rules governing data organization and transmission.

Most protocols apply to three distinct phases:

➤ **Connection setup phase** The protocol must initiate a connection between computers on the network just as a telephone uses ringing to request a connection to another telephone. When the connection is set up, the protocol creates a virtual communications path between computers. A *virtual communications path* is a medium that exists logically but does not exist physically.

➤ **Data transfer phase** Once the connection is set up, the protocol allows the data to be transferred between computers. After the data is transmitted, the receiving computer decides whether to accept the data or reject the data. This is called *handshaking*.

➤ **Connection release phase** Once the data transfer is complete, the protocol allows the computers to terminate the connection.

Each protocol used in a network incorporates a layered design approach. Why a layered approach?

➤ Each layer contains related functions.

➤ The technology in each layer can be changed without affecting the whole protocol.

➤ Layers provide for a gradual growth of the underlying network.

➤ A layered design hides the details of each layer from the others, to allow for better maintenance.

Open Systems Interconnection (OSI) Model

The OSI model was adopted by the International Organization for Standardization (ISO) as a standard in 1978. This standard is not a real protocol in any network but a model used to compare commercially developed protocols. Figure 2.5 shows the seven layers of the OSI model.

Physical Layer

The physical layer specifies the mechanical (cables, wire) and electrical interfaces to the medium used to transmit data. This layer transmits bits (a series of ones and zeros) to and receives bits from the communications medium.

Data-link Layer

The data-link layer controls access to the physical layer by organizing bits into logical frames of information. This layer provides low-level error detection and recovery between nodes, packages bits into frames, and unpackages frames back into bits.

Network Layer

The network layer routes data across the network. First the transport layer (described below) takes message strings and breaks them into smaller units, called segments. The network layer then separates segments into packets (the unit of information for a network), assembles packets into segments, and routes packets through complex networks. Complex networks are called internetworks or internets. In an internet, each network segment is assigned a logical network address, which is managed at the network layer.

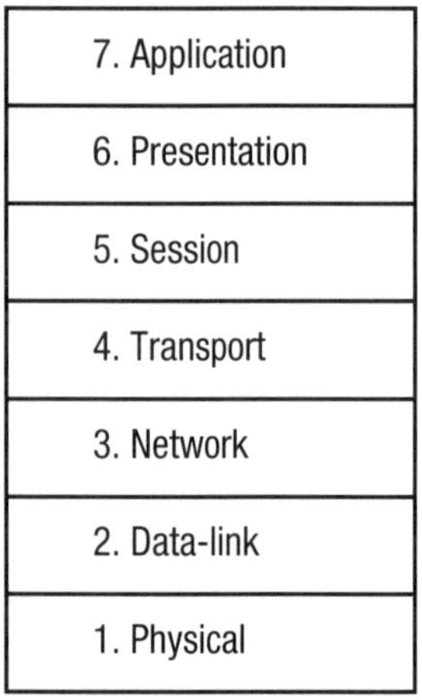

| 7. Application |
| 6. Presentation |
| 5. Session |
| 4. Transport |
| 3. Network |
| 2. Data-link |
| 1. Physical |

Figure 2.5 OSI model.

Transport Layer

The transport layer takes message strings and breaks them into smaller units (segments) that can be handled by the network layer. This layer maintains accuracy in data communications, provides error recovery, and regulates data flow (it serves as a traffic cop). This layer ensures reliable data delivery between processes running on the source and destination computers.

Session Layer

The session layer manages the dialog between application programs on different computers to share data by establishing, synchronizing, and terminating communications. If two people want to converse, for example, they establish rules of conversation. They might agree to converse in French, observing rules of courtesy to communicate their messages in an orderly manner. At the end of the conversation, they engage in a polite exchange to establish that they expect no further messages. Similarly, when establishing a session, the computers negotiate the protocols, communication modes, error checking and recovery, and other communication issues. When the computers no longer need to communicate, they follow a procedure to discontinue the session in an orderly manner.

Dialogs can be in *full-duplex* mode, transmitting and receiving at the same time, or *half-duplex* mode, transmitting and receiving alternately.

Presentation Management Layer

The presentation management layer formats data for proper output. This layer converts data format and code, for example, from ASCII (PC) to EBCDIC (IBM mainframe) when transmitting, and from EBCDIC to ASCII when receiving.

Application Layer

The application layer works directly with the user. This layer provides a uniform interface between end-user applications and the network, specifies the communication interface with the user, and manages communication among computer applications.

Transmission Control Protocol/Internet Protocol (TCP/IP)

Network protocols allow two or more computers to communicate on the network. Computers must communicate using the same language, so network computers use protocols to accomplish this. A very widely-used protocol that is a de facto, commercially accepted standard is TCP/IP. The Internet, for example, uses TCP/IP for communication. Figure 2.6 illustrates how TCP/IP transmits data between computers on a network.

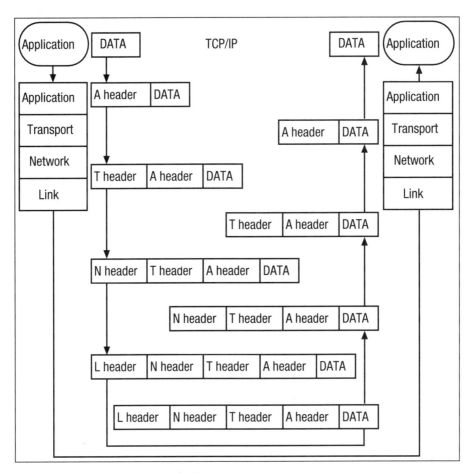

Figure 2.6   How TCP/IP works between computers.

TCP/IP consists of four layers:

➤ **Link** Also called the physical layer (similar to the OSI model's physical and data-link layers).

➤ **Network/internetwork** (similar to the OSI model's network layer).

➤ **Transport** (similar to the OSI model's transport layer).

➤ **Application** (similar to the OSI model's application layer).

When an application interacts with the application layer of TCP/IP, it passes data. The application layer adds a header to the data. The application layer passes the header plus the data to the transport layer. It requests the transport layer to transmit the data to a specific machine. A source port number represents the application requesting a data transmission and lets the transport layer know which application requested the transmission. The application requests a connection with a destination application, which is also represented by a destination port number.

The transport layer accepts multiple requests from applications, multiplexes them, and forwards the requests one at a time onto a single connection. Depending on the transport layer protocol, it either creates a logical connection between two computers or just forwards the data to the next layer. The transport layer adds a header to the data and forwards the header plus the data to the network layer.

The network layer adds a network header and determines the route of the data on the basis of the destination. The network layer uses a logical address called an IP address, which a network administrator manages. The network passes the header plus the data to the link layer.

The link layer handles the physical transmission of the bits of the data and adds a header to the data for handshaking purposes. The destination computer takes the data transmitted from the source and forwards the data without the link header to the network layer.

The network layer removes the header and, if the machine is the destination, it then forwards the data to the transport layer or retransmits the data through the link layer. The transport layer removes its header and forwards the data to the correct application based on the destination port number. The application layer receives the data, removes its header, and acts upon the data either by displaying the data or by displaying a message.

Link Layer

The link layer consists of a hardware interface called the network interface card (NIC) and the software interface to the NIC, called a *device driver*. The device driver consists of the software that interacts with the hardware and a network access protocol. A *network access protocol* allows networked computers to communicate using NICs. Examples of network access protocols are Ethernet and token ring.

Ethernet is a bus-based protocol that lets computers compete for access to the network. If two or more computers communicate at the same time, then each computer "backs off" for a random amount of time.

Token ring is a ring-based protocol that allows for a token to be passed between computers. The token allows a computer to transmit information. The absence of a token prevents computers from transmitting.

Network/Internetwork Layer

The network layer consists of a protocol called *Internet Protocol* (IP), which routes packets through the network. The IP consists of several parameters: The first parameter is the IP address, which is a logical 32-bit address that identifies a computer on the network. It consists of four octets (an octet is 8 bits) in dotted decimal notation, such as 199.1.1.1. Each IP address consists of a *network ID*, which describes the network, and a *host ID*, which describes the actual networked computer. The second parameter is a *subnet mask*, which tells the computer which part of the IP address is the network ID and which part is the subnet ID. It helps determine whether a computer is on the local network or a remote network.

Transport Layer

The transport layer acts as the traffic cop, regulating computers on a network. The transport layer has two main protocols: the Transmission Control Protocol (TCP) and the User Datagram Protocol (UDP). TCP uses a connection-oriented mechanism to let computers communicate. TCP sets up and maintains a connection between computers to deliver packets of information. UDP uses a connectionless-oriented mechanism. It forwards packets between computers but does not set up a connection. UDP provides "best effort unreliable service," meaning that it does not guarantee delivery of the packet to the destination. TCP does guarantee delivery of the packet. The Internet uses both TCP and UDP.

Application Layer

The application layer supplies application programs that can communicate over the network, set up sessions between computers, and format data for transmission. Examples of application level protocols are File Transfer Protocol (FTP), Telnet, Domain Name System (DNS), Hypertext Transport Protocol (HTTP), Network News Transport Protocol (NNTP), and Simple Mail Transport Protocol (SMTP). FTP lets you copy files from one computer to another on the network. Telnet lets you log on to and administer a remote machine. DNS is a protocol that resolves computer names to IP addresses. HTTP allows a Web browser to talk to a Web server. NNTP allows access to Internet news servers. SMTP lets you send and receive email on a network.

CLIENTS AND PEERS

In the last section, you investigated different networking technologies, including LANs, WANs, and different protocols. This section describes the physical hardware and software functions in clients/peers and servers, which are the transmitting and receiving devices on a network. Figure 2.7 shows the network as the interconnecting mechanism between clients/peers and servers.

Clients And Peers

The client computer is the frontline computer, one that actually interacts with the user. The client requests services from the server, such as email, Web, and database services. In most client/server systems, the client computer either has

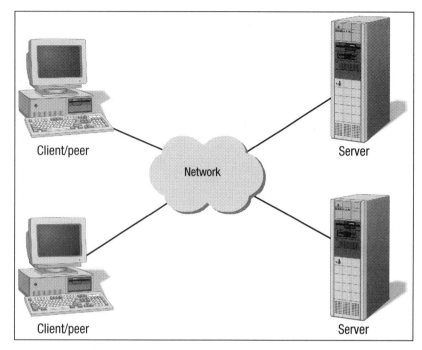

Figure 2.7   Client/server network architecture.

presentation management and application logic or only presentation management. Peer computers implement both presentation management and application logic.

Presentation Management

Presentation management tasks include:

➤ Handling the details of displaying information on the computer screen: windows, dialog boxes, text, graphics, and anything else that appears on the screen

➤ Processing user input

Application Logic

Application logic is the part of the program that makes decisions about the data, such as whether it's valid or should be sent to the database. Application logic also includes business logic that implements policies and procedures, depending on the needs of the business.

When a client implements some application logic, it is called a *fat* client. When a server implements all application logic, the client is called a *thin* client. Most networks now place application logic on the server.

How To Choose A Client/Peer Computer

Choosing the appropriate client/peer computer that meets the needs of the business is a challenging task. Be sure to look for the features listed below:

➤ **Multitasking** The computer must be able to run multiple applications at the same time

➤ **Lots of memory** You should have as much RAM as you can afford

➤ **Local disk storage** The computer should have its own disk drive to run the applications (client/server packages plus the desktop packages). Use the largest hard drive you can afford.

➤ **Processor** The most current and fastest processor you can afford

➤ **Bus architecture** Two or more Peripheral Component Interconnect (PCI) expansion slots

➤ **Video display** Super VGA with 2 MB video card

➤ **Mouse** A must for Graphical User Interface (GUI)

➤ **Printer** A shared printer available through the network

➤ **Sound card** Multimedia application support

➤ **CD-ROM** A must because most applications will soon be available only on CD-ROM

➤ **Network interface card (NIC)** Connects the computer to a LAN directly

➤ **Modem** Connects the computer to a LAN remotely

➤ **Software** Applications such as Microsoft Office

➤ **Operating system** Client operating system, such as Microsoft Windows 98 or Microsoft Windows NT

When setting a budget for a client/peer computer, buy the most RAM, hard disk space, and processor speed you can afford, in that order. RAM is the most valuable feature. The more RAM you have, the better the performance. Next, buy the most hard drive space you can, since applications require a lot of hard disk space. Finally, buy the fastest processor you can afford.

Operating Systems

An *operating system* is an interface that allows a user to interact with the computer's hardware and software. You can use several Microsoft operating systems on a client/peer computer. Microsoft Windows 98 and Microsoft Windows NT 4.0 are the two most popular operating systems loaded on a client/peer personal computer. These Microsoft operating systems and others are discussed in detail in Chapter 3.

SERVERS

The server is a behind-the-scenes machine that supplies services to clients. A server can have one or more processors, and can be scaled from a few to thousands of users.

How To Choose A Server Computer

 You need to meet specific requirements to select the appropriate hardware and software for a server computer. Chapter 3 describes the different software applications that run on a server computer.

Servers must be faster, bigger, and more powerful than client computers. Look for the features listed below when choosing a server computer.

➤ **Multitasking** Must be able to run multiple applications at the same time

➤ **Lots of memory** The largest amount of RAM you can afford

➤ **Local disk storage** Should have its own disk drive to run the applications (client/server plus the desktop packages). The largest amount of disk space you can afford

➤ **Processor** One or more state-of-the-art processors

➤ **Bus architecture** Two or more Peripheral Component Interconnect (PCI) expansion slots and small computer systems interface (SCSI) controllers

➤ **Video displays** Super VGA with 2 MB video card

➤ **Mouse** A must for GUIs

➤ **Printer** A shared printer available through the network

➤ **Sound card** Multimedia application support

➤ **CD-ROM** A must because most applications will soon be available only on CD-ROM

➤ **Network interface card (NIC)** Connects the computer to a LAN directly

➤ **Modem** Connects the computer to a LAN remotely

➤ **Operating system** Server operating system, such as Microsoft Windows NT 4.0

In addition, the server should be able to do the following:

➤ Scale as the demands on the server increase, such as when the number of users increases, or the size of the hard disk space expands

➤ Increase memory. When new users are added, memory demands increase.

➤ Add processors to handle increased workload

➤ Add disk storage

➤ Recover from failures. Servers particularly need fault tolerance, such as the ability to save data on two hard drives.

➤ Receive services in a timely manner with a service and support contract. An on-site contract with a 24-hour turnaround is common.

Kinds Of Servers

Servers can play one or more of the following roles on the network:

➤ **File servers** Retrieve and store files and folders on the server from the client

➤ **Mail servers** Send and retrieve email stored on the server

➤ **Print servers** Print to network printers off the server

➤ **Database servers** Access data from a server using a database management system

➤ **Application servers** Access common applications from a server

➤ **Web servers** Browse the Internet and intranet from the client

Servers can also play other roles, depending on the needs of the business.

CHAPTER SUMMARY

This chapter presented an overview of client, peers, servers, and networks, which are part of a technology infrastructure. A network is a communications system consisting of two or more computers linked together. Network computers have three roles: peer, client, or server, and provide a variety of services, including communication, email, Internet, Web, printing, database, backup, network management, file, and security. The two main types of networks are local area networks (LAN) and wide area networks (WAN). The Internet is the world's largest public WAN. Intranets are special networks that let corporations supply Internet services over their LANs.

Protocols supply the rules of information exchange in a network. TCP/IP is a standard protocol that the Internet uses for communication. The Open Systems Interconnection (OSI) model lets you compare commercially developed protocols.

Before planning an information system, a business creates and deploys the technology infrastructure, including the network. With an infrastructure in place, project teams can start planning information systems, including operating system and application software. Chapter 3 presents Microsoft operating systems and application tools in more detail.

REVIEW QUESTIONS

1. If you have a transmitter, medium, and information or data, you have a communications system.

   a. true

   b. false

2. The purpose of a network is to let computers and users share resources.

   a. true

   b. false

3. Full-duplex means that you can:

   a. transmit only

   b. transmit and receive at the same time

   c. transmit and receive during different cycles

   d. receive only

4. The layer of the OSI model that routes data is:

   a. application

   b. network

   c. transport

   d. data-link

5. The OSI model was proposed by which organization?

   a. ANSI

   b. IEX

   c. ISO

   d. IEEE

6. The layer of the OSI model that packages data into frames is:

   a. network

   b. data-link

   c. session

   d. physical

7. The layer of the OSI model responsible for user interaction is:

   a. physical

   b. data-link

   c. application

   d. network

8. The layer of the OSI model that transmits data between connections is:

    a. session

    b. physical

    c. data-link

    d. network

9. The layer of the OSI model that establishes and maintains the electrical and mechanical connections is:

    a. network

    b. transport

    c. physical

    d. data-link

10. What are network resources?

    a. devices you can use through the network

    b. tasks that a network server performs

    c. graphical user interface

    d. back-end processes

11. What are network services?

    a. devices you can use through the network

    b. back-end processes

    c. graphical user interface

    d. tasks that a network server performs

12. A protocol is defined as:

    a. a hardware entity

    b. the transfer of data between dissimilar devices

    c. rules for implementing network hardware

    d. rules describing the organization and transmission of data between computer devices

13. Handling the details of displaying information on the computer screen is called:

    a. GUI

    b. presentation management

    c. application logic

    d. none of the above

14. Implementing the policies and procedures according to the needs of a business is called:

  a. GUI

  b. application logic

  c. presentation management

  d. none of the above

15. The user's interface to the information system is called the:

  a. server

  b. network

  c. client

  d. none of the above

16. The supplies services to clients.

  a. client

  b. server

  c. network

  d. none of the above

17. When a server implements all application logic, the client is called a _____ client.

  a. fat

  b. chubby

  c. thin

  d. none of the above

18. When a client implements some application logic, it is called a _____ client.

  a. chubby

  b. fat

  c. thin

  d. none of the above

19. The type of server that can retrieve and store files and folders is called a _____ server.

  a. database

  b. mail

  c. print

  d. file

20. The type of server that can send and retrieve email is called a _____ server.
    a. file
    b. mail
    c. print
    d. database

HANDS-ON PROJECTS

Project 2.1
This chapter supplied two examples of communications systems. Give two more examples of a communications system and list the transmitter, receiver, medium, and information or data being transmitted.

Project 2.2
Networks share resources such as printers, fax modems, and scanners. Other resources are listed on page 25. Pick three resources and explain their functions.

Project 2.3
Network applications usually consist of two components: a client and a server. Explain the two components in an e-mail system and a Web system. Also, explain the protocols used in both systems.

Project 2.4
Using the Internet, research the Ethernet and token ring topologies. A topology is the physical architecture of a network. Explain the protocols used and the different ways the network access protocols are used.

Project 2.5
The OSI model can be used to compare commercially available protocols on the market. TCP/IP is the most widely used protocol in the world. Compare and contrast the OSI model and the TCP/IP protocol.

Project 2.6
Use the Internet to research the IPX/SPX protocol. IPX/SPX is another popular protocol in the marketplace. Explain what IPX/SPX is, where it is used, and what the different layers are, and compare and contrast this protocol and the OSI model.

Project 2.7
The Web site *http://www.tucows.com* consists of thousands of shareware and freeware applications that run on top of TCP/IP. The File Transfer Protocol

2

(FTP) is a very popular mechanism for copying files between computers on the Internet. Find several FTP packages and explain what they are and how they're used.

Project 2.8

Use the Internet or standard industry periodicals such as *Computer Shopper* to research client machines for a typical college lab. Report on 2–3 clients and include the manufacturer, the features of the clients, and the price of the clients.

Project 2.9

Use the Internet or standard industry periodicals such as *Computer Shopper* to research server machines for a typical college lab. Report on 2–3 servers and include the manufacturer, the features of the servers, and the price of the servers. (*Hint*: Report on servers manufactured by Compaq, Dell, and Gateway.)

Project 2.10

Several services were explained in this section. Pick one service and explain its function in detail.

Project 2.11

Visit the Microsoft Web site at *http://www.microsoft.com* to research the features of Windows 98, Windows NT 4.0, and Windows NT. Compare and contrast the different operating systems supported by Microsoft.

MICROSOFT OPERATING SYSTEMS AND APPLICATION DEVELOPMENT TOOLS

AFTER READING THIS CHAPTER AND COMPLETING THE EXERCISES, YOU WILL BE ABLE TO:

➤ Describe basic operating system components

➤ Describe the basic features and components of Windows CE, Windows 98, Windows NT Workstation, and Windows NT Server

➤ Choose the best operating system to benefit a variety of customers

➤ Identify Microsoft technologies and their uses in developing applications

➤ Identify Microsoft's applications technology

➤ Describe and identify Microsoft technologies, including Office, BackOffice, and Visual Development tools

➤ Choose the development tool best suited to particular situations

Microsoft's operating systems dominate both the client and server operating system markets. As a computer programmer, you must master Microsoft's operating system technologies to write effective applications.

When you write an application, you write programs for end users, such as database, word processor, and spreadsheet programs. If you write an application for a Microsoft environment, such as Windows, it cannot run without Microsoft's operating system. Programmers interested in developing applications for business should know when and how to use Microsoft technologies such as Microsoft BackOffice, Component Object Model, Distributed Component Object Model, and Universal Data Access. Understanding when and how to use these Microsoft technologies gives you a solid foundation to be able to plan, maintain, and manage information systems.

CHAPTER OVERVIEW

In Chapter 2, you investigated networking technologies and requirements. This chapter focuses on a single client computer or a single server computer. These computers run a wide range of operating systems supplied by Microsoft. The first part of the chapter examines the different Microsoft operating systems and their applications. The second part surveys Microsoft application development tools and helps you determine which tool to use in different scenarios.

This chapter also uses the example of the technological needs of a contemporary college campus. A college needs to deploy Web applications that support the college catalog, class schedules, instructor schedules, class syllabi, and career services, for example. College students also need computer labs for completing course work and communicating with others on campus. As you investigate Microsoft development technologies, you will learn how to use these technologies in a college environment.

OPERATING SYSTEMS FUNDAMENTALS

An operating system (OS) uses software to help control computer resources such as a mouse, keyboard, and monitor, to execute applications, and to act as an interface between a user and the computer system. Figure 3.1 shows the components in a computer operating system.

The hardware of the computer system consists of a system unit, monitor, keyboard, and mouse. The system unit houses the microprocessor, primary memory such as random access memory (RAM), secondary memory such as a hard drive, and a system bus, which lets all components in the system unit communicate with each other.

The *kernel*—the heart of the operating system that supplies software services—includes device drivers and a resource manager, which supplies scheduling services, such as those listed below:

➤ **Multithreading** A Windows application is composed of one or more processes. A *process* is a running application with its own address space and resources. It consists of one or more *threads*, which are the smallest pieces of a program that can be scheduled for execution. For example, Microsoft Word allows you to create a document while it is checking your spelling and grammar. The spelling and grammar checker are examples of threads.

➤ **Preemptive multitasking** The kernel gives each process a certain amount of time to run. When that time expires, the operating system "swaps out" the old process and parcels out a block of time so another process can run, and so on, so that each process has an equal chance to run.

➤ **Cooperative multitasking** Processes yield control to other applications in the operating system.

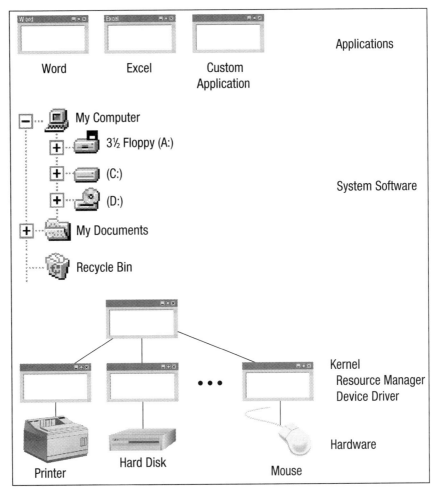

Applications

Word   Excel   Custom
Application

System Software

Kernel
Resource Manager
Device Driver

Hardware

Printer   Hard Disk   Mouse

Figure 3.1   The computer system structure.

A *device driver* acts as a software intermediary between the OS and the hardware.
For example, the printer driver lets the OS communicate directly with the
printer. A *resource manager* schedules when the OS uses various hardware
components. For example, when two applications request access to the hard
drive, the resource manager shares the access between the two applications.
System software includes utilities for accomplishing common tasks such as file,
directory, memory, and user interface management. For instance, the DOS DIR
command allows you to display the files and directories on the hard drive.
Applications are programs that users run to complete common tasks such as
sending and receiving email, creating and printing documents, and managing
information. Applications are not a part of an operating system.

INTRODUCTION TO MICROSOFT WINDOWS OPERATING SYSTEMS

In the last section, you investigated components of a generic operating system. Microsoft provides operating systems that fit any type of business need. Figure 3.2 shows Microsoft's operating systems for the hardware platforms currently available.

Microsoft provides the following client operating systems:

➤ Windows CE

➤ Windows 98

➤ Windows NT Workstation

 Each client operating system can play the role of a server, if necessary, though they are not designed to act like servers. In a peer-to-peer environment, all operating systems act as both a client and a server. Each server operating system can be used as a client operating system. However, for a typical user, this is an expensive solution.

Windows NT Server is Microsoft's server operating system. You can transfer many of the techniques and skills you use when developing applications for one operating system to another. Each system is described in detail in the following pages.

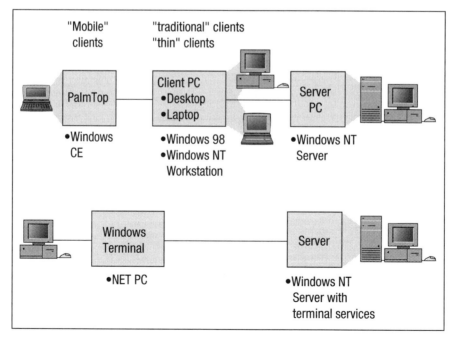

Figure 3.2 Microsoft Windows operating systems.

Windows CE

Windows CE runs on embedded computing architectures, such as:

➤ Palmtop computers

➤ Hand-held computers

➤ Electronic organizers

These embedded computing architectures are good for people who need a basic electronic organizer on a portable computer, personal digital assistant, or other small computing device, because they work outside of a standard office. Students might use these devices to stay organized throughout a semester. An instructor might use these devices to keep track of students, grades, assignments, and schedules.

Windows CE provides the following features:

➤ Support for a wide range of processors such as NEC, Philips, and Toshiba MIPS 39xx and 4xxx, Motorola PowerPC, Hitachi SH3, AMD, and Intel x86 (486 and above)

➤ Modular operating system

➤ Support for communication between input and output devices through various device drivers

Windows CE can support a wide range of processors because the Original Equipment Manufacturer (OEM) Adaptation Layer (OAL) provides software between the hardware and the kernel that allows an OEM to adapt its hardware to Windows CE.

Windows CE also supplies built-in device driver support for the keyboard, touch panel, notification LED, display, audio, battery drivers, bounded and unbounded communications ("terrestrial" LAN and wireless LAN technologies), serial devices, and PC Cards.

Windows CE is a modular operating system because it is composed of separate components you can connect together. The advantage of modular architecture is that you can replace or add any component (module) without affecting the rest of the system. When you are creating applications, your goal is to create modular programs that act just like Windows CE.

Windows CE has a multithreaded, preemptive multitasking kernel. This support helps ensure that your applications run smoothly in Windows.

All Windows operating systems, including Windows CE, contain a Registry that stores hardware and software configuration information. They also supply an application programming interface (API) called Win32. Windows CE uses a subset of the Win32 API that supplies functions, messages, and structures to the programmer. For example, you can configure the Win32 graphical device interface (GDI) for gray-scale, LCD, color VGA, or no display. The Win32 user application provides the user interface and regulates the interaction between the input and output devices to the appropriate device drivers.

Windows CE also supports all standard communications architectures. The Windows CE shell includes a minimum amount of software for launching, switching, and embedding applications. It includes the Pocket Internet Explorer and a limited version of Microsoft Office. This means you can create documents and spreadsheets, and perform other office tasks in Windows CE just as in Windows 98 and Windows NT. This makes using Windows CE devices a lot more manageable. Windows CE also lets you write applications for the international marketplace; it supports internationalization and localization, which means it recognizes different languages. It uses *Unicode*, an international character format, for localizing the operating system.

Choose Windows CE as an operating system when you want to program hand-held computing devices using a basic knowledge of Microsoft Windows architecture.

Windows 98

While Windows CE runs on embedded computing architectures, Windows 98 runs on a standard PC configuration supported by thousands of vendors. Windows 98 is Microsoft's consumer-oriented client operating system. For example, students and instructors use Windows 98 on their home computers and in college computer labs, as in the example in this chapter. Figure 3.3 shows the Windows 98 architecture.

Windows 98 provides the following features:

➤ Support for thousands of hardware platforms from many vendors

➤ Backward compatibility to Windows 95, Windows 3.1, and DOS (meaning that new and old applications can run in Windows 98)

Windows 98 is a 32-bit operating system that supports multitasking and multithreading. As with Windows CE, this means you can run more than one program, and different parts of the same program, at the same time. Unlike Windows CE, however, Windows 98 supplies two methods of multitasking, cooperative and preemptive, which makes it more powerful. In preemptive multitasking, the operating system assigns time to each program. With cooperative multitasking, applications yield control to other applications in the operating system.

One way that Windows 98 is more powerful than Windows CE is that it provides support for 32-bit device drivers such as the keyboard, mouse, disk

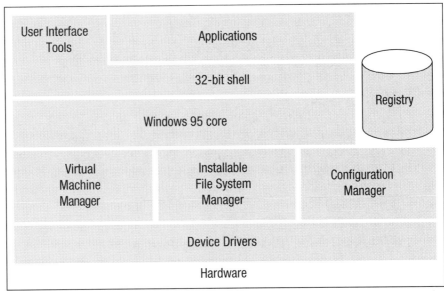

Figure 3.3   Windows 98 architecture.

devices, display adapters, modems, and fax machines. The ability of the Windows configuration manager to automatically detect and install device drivers is called *Plug and Play*. The configuration manager also provides the resources each hardware device needs. The virtual machine manager provides the resources each application and system process needs.

Like Windows CE, Windows 98 contains a *Registry*, which stores hardware and software configurations. As a programmer, you will need to store application-specific information in the Registry.

Unlike Windows CE, Windows 98's file manager lets you use multiple file systems, and supports the ability to read and write to floppy disks, hard disks, and CD-ROM drives, using structures such as the virtual file allocation table (VFAT) and CD-ROM file system (CDFS). Windows 98 also supports long filenames of up to 255 characters.

Unlike Windows CE, Windows 98 supports the full Win32 API. For example, the Windows 98 core consists of user, GDI, and kernel interfaces. The user component manages the user interface and information from input devices to all systems and applications. The GDI interface manages what appears on the screen, and provides graphics support for printers and other output devices. The kernel provides the operating system functionality, including file services, virtual memory management, and program and task scheduling. Because Windows 98 has virtual memory management, it can allocate more memory than the computer actually has. To do so, it uses the hard drive to swap applications out of primary memory into secondary memory (hard drive). Windows 98 also has built-in support for networks, whether local or remote.

Windows NT

Microsoft designed Windows 98 to be used at home or in a small office, not in a large, corporate environment. Windows NT Workstation and Windows NT Server are Microsoft's business-oriented operating systems. Although it looks and works much like Windows 98, the underlying architecture is completely different.

Windows NT includes the following features:

➤ 32-bit operating system

➤ Limited support of hardware, unlike Windows 98

➤ Built-in security, unlike Windows 98

➤ Multithreaded preemptive multitasking kernel

Figure 3.4 shows the Windows NT architecture.

Windows NT architecture consists of two modes: user and kernel. Processes run in the user mode. It also includes code that runs in its own address space, and uses APIs to access system services. This lets applications written for Windows 98 use the enhancements Windows NT provides.

Kernel mode, or Windows NT executive, has direct access to hardware and memory, including all addresses of user mode processes. This means that Windows NT applications can also run on Windows 98. Kernel mode hides the details of the underlying hardware architecture from the application. Creating software this way makes it easy to maintain and update your code.

The hardware abstraction layer (HAL) consists of a library of kernel mode functions that either Microsoft or the hardware manufacturer provides. HAL is a software layer that hides the details of the hardware from the Windows NT operating system. This allows you to port Windows NT to other hardware platforms without rewriting any applications.

The microkernel works very closely with the HAL to schedule threads that run on one or more processors. The microkernel keeps all processors busy, and provides preemptive multitasking and multithreading services. Unlike Windows 98, the Windows NT microkernel supports symmetric multiprocessing (SMP), the ability of Windows NT to host multiple processors. This means Windows NT can make the most efficient use of your computing resources and speed up your applications.

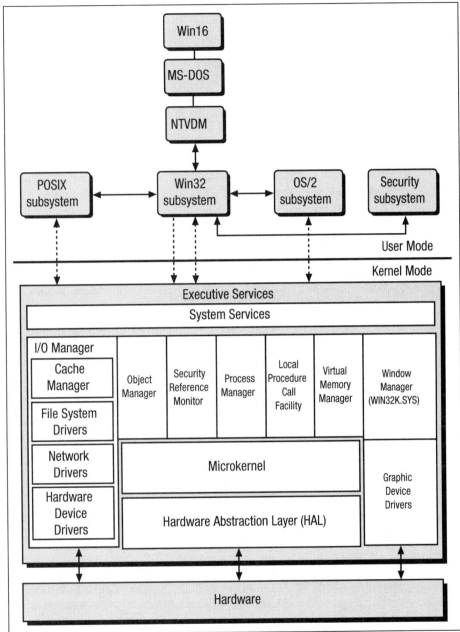

Figure 3.4 Windows NT architecture.

The I/O manager regulates all input and output and the communication between device drivers. The I/O manager also supports different file systems such as the file allocation table (FAT) and Windows NT file system (NTFS). NTFS includes file system security, Unicode, recoverability, long filenames, and Portable Operating System Interface for UNIX (POSIX). Windows 98 does not support file system security, recoverability, or POSIX, which makes it a more unstable, less dependable environment for businesses.

Windows NT helps prevent the loss of information. The object manager provides rules for retaining and naming objects, and for setting object security. Objects are software components such as directory, process and thread, and file objects. The object manager lets you create software components that can enhance Windows NT. The security reference monitor component ensures that no one can access a computer's resources without the proper authorization. It supplies the logon process and the security subsystem. Other operating systems, such as Windows 98, do not have a logon process or security subsystem.

The Windows NT process manager creates, deletes, and tracks process and thread objects. It schedules processes and thread objects on another available processor. The local procedure call facility manages distributed applications by supplying a communications mechanism between remote processes. This means you can write software that communicates across the network from two different machines.

The virtual memory manager physically organizes primary and secondary memory. The Windows manager controls the user interface of Windows NT, and has 32-bit user32 and GDI32 components. The graphics device drivers manage the communication between GDI and graphic hardware devices such as monitors, printers, and fax machines.

Windows NT is Microsoft's most robust operating system. It is designed to be a versatile, business-oriented system that protects information assets from external tampering.

Windows NT Workstation
Windows NT Workstation is Microsoft's business-oriented client operating system. It runs Windows on a standalone machine, a network machine in a peer-to-peer environment, or a workstation in a Windows NT Server domain.

Windows NT Server
Windows NT Server is Microsoft's business-oriented server operating system. The most reliable and secure of Microsoft's operating systems, it runs business applications such as mechanical and electronic design automation, architecture

planning, custom software development, accounting and finance, investment trader workstations, and real-time systems.

Windows NT Server With Terminal Services

Windows NT Server with Terminal Services is Microsoft's newest member of the Windows NT family. A business can use it to centralize all their network processing to the server. Today, a client machine stores all the applications users need to do their work. Maintaining these systems can be costly. With Windows NT Server with Terminal Services, network administrators can manage Windows applications from the server, which means they can administer and control Windows terminals and the network more completely and efficiently, saving a business extensive maintenance costs. Before a business can take advantage of Windows NT terminal services, however, it must invest in Windows terminals or use existing machines as Windows terminals. Windows terminals let network administrators manage Windows-based applications centrally from the server. Some Windows terminals have no hard disk, floppy disk drive, CD-ROM drive, or expansion slots. Others contain an internal hard disk, sealed cases, a minimum of 16 MB of RAM, and a 133-MHz or better CPU. *Thin client* is another term used for Windows terminals.

Choosing The Right Operating System

Choosing the right operating system to meet the needs of a business is a daunting task. Table 3.1 shows the current situation and the choice of operating systems.

Table 3.1   Choosing the right operating system.

Current Computer	Use This Operating System	Recommended Computer
486 DX class or higher that lacks application or hardware support in Windows NT	Windows 98	Same as current computer
Pentium 133 class or higher that has application or hardware support in Windows NT	Windows NT Workstation	Same as current computer
486 DX class or less	Windows NT Workstation or Windows NT Server	Pentium-class machine with Terminal Services
Text-based dumb terminal	Windows NT Server Terminal Server Edition	Windows terminals

(continued)

Table 3.1 Choosing the right operating system *(continued)*.

Current Computer	Use This Operating System	Recommended Computer
Process model	Manage the phases of system development	Develop an information system in the following phases: • Envisioning phase: defining the vision of the project • Planning phase: assembling a team, and developing cost and schedules for a project • Developing phase: defining, designing, and creating the product • Stabilization phase: testing and deploying the product
Solutions Design model Consider the suggestions during the developing phase of the process model by analyzing the system from the following perspectives: • Conceptual perspective: what the system will supply for services • Logical perspective: how the system will supply the services logically • Physical perspective: how to create the system from the logical perspective	Design to provide solutions for business needs	Specific suggestions for building effective information systems.
Application model	Design for usability and flexibility	Applications should include: • User services: a presentation layer that interacts with the user • Business services: the application logic and business rules of the application • Data services: the way data is stored and retrieved in the application

INTRODUCTION TO MICROSOFT APPLICATIONS TECHNOLOGY

Microsoft not only supplies the operating systems for any business need, but also the application technology architecture to support special needs. Both Microsoft BackOffice and Microsoft Office are suites of software tools designed to meet business needs; Office provides these tools on the client, while BackOffice provides them on the server.

Microsoft Technologies are a series of technologies that supply distributed application development support, such as Component Object Model (COM), Distributed Component Object Model (DCOM), ActiveX, and Universal Data Access (UDA).

While Microsoft Technologies provide the foundation for creating distributed applications, Microsoft Visual Tools are a series of application development tools for creating scalable and distributed applications. Microsoft Visual Tools include Visual C++, Visual Interdev, Visual J++, Visual FoxPro, and Visual Basic. The Microsoft Visual Tools are placed under one umbrella called Microsoft Visual Studio.

Microsoft BackOffice

Each Microsoft BackOffice server application that runs on Windows NT Server offers unique business solutions to different types of problems. The following are the components of BackOffice:

➤ **Internet Information Server (IIS)** IIS is a Web server that supplies Web resources to Web browsers such as Microsoft Internet Explorer.

➤ **Microsoft Exchange Server** Exchange Server is an email server with integrated groupware that allows people to interact electronically.

➤ **Microsoft SQL Server** SQL Server is a highly reliable, scalable client/ server database management system (DBMS).

➤ **Microsoft Proxy Server** Proxy Server is a secure way of bringing Internet services to every desktop in an enterprise.

➤ **Microsoft Systems Management Server (SMS)** SMS is a client/server system that allows administrators to centrally manage all computers in an enterprise.

➤ **Microsoft Systems Network Architecture Server (SNA)** SNA is a gateway system that lets PCs communicate seamlessly over a network with an IBM mainframe running the SNA protocol.

➤ **Microsoft Transaction Server** Transaction Server supplies a mechanism to develop and deploy high-performance, scalable, and reliable distributed applications on a network.

➤ **Microsoft Site Server**   Site Server manages a Web site environment that features an electronic catalog, online order processing, and creation of dynamic product and price promotions.

➤ **Microsoft Message Queue Server (MSMQ)**   MSMQ allows you to create applications that communicate asynchronously using messages.

Microsoft Office

Each Microsoft Office client application that runs on Windows NT and Windows 98 offers powerful business office solutions. Microsoft Office can also use Visual Basic for Applications (VBA) to extend its functionality. Microsoft Office includes the following applications:

➤ **Word**   Word is a word processing application for creating, printing, and managing electronic communication.

➤ **Excel**   Excel is a spreadsheet application for calculating and reporting numeric information such as finances and statistics.

➤ **PowerPoint**   PowerPoint is a presentation management application for creating and giving business presentations.

➤ **Access**   Access is a personal database management system for storing and retrieving business data.

➤ **Outlook**   Outlook is a personal information manager for organizing your time, schedules, contacts, and email.

➤ **FrontPage**   FrontPage is used for creating and managing Web sites.

➤ **Project**   Project is a project management tool for creating project schedules and milestones.

➤ **Publisher**   Publisher is desktop publishing software that creates and manages documents such as newsletters and brochures.

Microsoft Technologies

Microsoft Technologies provide the "plumbing" to create reliable, scalable, and high-performance distributed applications. Microsoft technologies include the following:

➤ **Component Object Model (COM)** and **Distributed Object Model (DCOM)**   COM and DCOM are software architectures that you can use to distribute software across the network, either locally or remotely. COM, also known as object linking and embedding (OLE), supplies the foundation for reusing software functionality from one product to another. For example, Microsoft created a Word and Excel COM object so that you can use Excel spreadsheets in Word. For example, you can embed an Excel spreadsheet in a Word document. When you double-click the spreadsheet object, the Excel functionality appears, so that you can update the spreadsheet in Word. COM objects reside on a single machine. DCOM objects are similar to COM objects, except that you can distribute a DCOM object anywhere on the network. When a machine requests a DCOM object, it looks up the object in the Registry and runs its related application either locally or on the remote machine, depending on the application. Chapter 9 shows you how to create different types of COM and DCOM objects using ActiveX technology, which is a wrapper around COM and DCOM. Because they are language-independent, you can create COM and DCOM objects using any Microsoft Visual Tool. You can choose the development tool that meets your needs and feel confident that you can create COM and DCOM objects when needed.

➤ **ActiveX** ActiveX is a set of rules for how applications should share information. It hides the details of COM and DCOM from the programmer to supply software components on a network you can access from anywhere in any computer language.

➤ **Universal Data Access (UDA)** UDA provides access to a variety of information sources including relational and object-relational (those storing images, audio, video, and data) sources, and nonrelational sources, such as files. Object Linking and Embedding Database (OLE DB) technology is a component of UDA that lets users access data from the source. The manufacturer of the data source provides an OLE DB interface layer that programmers use to access the data. For example, when you want to access SQL Server, Microsoft provides an OLE DB driver so you can access SQL Server databases. Open Database Connectivity (ODBC) uses structured query language (SQL) to supply an application programming interface between a relational database management system and an application. ActiveX Data Objects (ADO) is a software layer on top of OLE DB and ODBC that exposes a standard set of properties and functions that applications use to interact with different data sources.

Choosing The Right Applications Technology

Now that you've investigated several types of applications technology, you should understand which technology to use in different circumstances. Table 3.2 illustrates the scenarios.

Table 3.2 Choosing the right applications technology.

Scenario	Use These Applications Technologies
E-commerce application (lets you buy and sell over the Internet)	IIS—provides access to the application on the server Exchange Server—provides e-mail service SQL Server—provides the database to store the e-commerce transactions Proxy Server—provides an added layer of security to protect your internal network Transaction Server—provides a transaction service for ActiveX components Site Server—provides the e-commerce infrastructure to buy and sell over the Internet MSMQ—provides fault tolerance and load balancing to your applications
Central management of clients	System Management Server (SMS) — provides the infrastructure to centrally manage computers in the enterprise
Mainframe access to data	SNA—provides the gateway functionality needed to communicate with a mainframe computer
Web application	IIS—provides access to the application on the server Exchange Server—provides email service SQL Server—provides the database to store the data Proxy Server—provides an added layer of security to protect your internal network Transaction Server—provides a transaction service for ActiveX components MSMQ—provides fault tolerance and load balancing to your applications
Traditional data application	SQL Server—provides the database to store the data Transaction Server—provides a transaction service for ActiveX components MSMQ—provides fault tolerance and load balancing to your applications

Microsoft Visual Studio

In the last section, you learned about the different applications technologies Microsoft provides. Programmers use Microsoft Visual Studio to build scalable and distributed applications; it includes the following tools:

3

➤ **Visual Basic (VB)** VB offers the fastest and easiest way to create applications for Microsoft Windows. VB provides rapid application development (RAD), database integration, visual modeling using Microsoft Visual Modeler, Internet application development, and ActiveX development. VB is currently the premier applications development tool.

➤ **Visual C++** With Visual C++, programmers can create applications and system software using the C++ language. Visual C++ provides database integration, ActiveX development, cross-platform development, and high-performance application development. Visual C++ is currently the premier systems development tool.

➤ **J++** With J++, programmers can create Java applications you can run on any platform that supports Java. J++ can compile Java programs in native Microsoft Windows. Visual J++ provides database integration, ActiveX development, Internet applications development, and cross-platform application development. Visual J++ is becoming a foremost Windows application development tool because it provides better performance than Visual Basic and Visual FoxPro, the most popular Java-based application development tool.

➤ **Visual FoxPro** Programmers can use Visual FoxPro to create data-centered Windows applications. FoxPro provides database integration and ActiveX development.

➤ **Visual InterDev** Using Visual InterDev, programmers can create and manage Web-based projects. Visual InterDev provides Active Server Pages (ASP) to create server-side applications that run with IIS. It also includes tools for managing Web sites, including those that combine images and sounds and create sound files.

➤ **Server development tools** You can use server development tools such as the Windows NT Option Kit, which includes Transaction Server, SQL Server, the latest version of IIS, Personal Web Server for Windows 98 (a stripped-down version of IIS that runs on Windows 98, used for development purposes only), MSMQ, and many other tools.

Choosing The Right Development Platform

After surveying Visual Studio tools, you're ready to learn how to choose the right tool for a particular circumstance. Table 3.3 shows the features you may want in a development tool and the products that support those features.

Table 3.3   Choosing a development tool.

Feature	Visual Studio Tool
Create reusable software components	Visual Basic, Visual C++, Visual J++
Create cross-platform binary-compatible programs that support MIPS, Alpha, and PowerPC processors	Visual C++
Create cross-platform network applications (write once, run in lots of places)	Visual J++
RAD projects	Visual Basic
Create browser-independent applications	Visual InterDev, FrontPage
Create Microsoft Internet Explorer browser applications	Visual Basic
Create client/server applications	Visual Basic, Visual J++, Visual InterDev, Visual FoxPro
Create database applications	Visual Basic, Visual C++, Visual J++, Visual InterDev, Visual FoxPro
Create Internet applications	Visual Basic, Visual J++, Visual InterDev, FrontPage

COLLEGE CASE STUDY

Now that you've reviewed Microsoft's operating systems and application development tools, you can put your knowledge to work in the college computer lab example. Colleges today need computer labs to teach various technologies and support the college administration. Unfortunately, colleges have difficulty finding the funds to support and administer full labs. You need to consider lower-cost alternatives when working in a college environment.

In the last chapter, you investigated the networking technologies used in the computer labs. What is the best operating system for the lab? Most colleges are currently upgrading the computers in their labs from 486-based computers to Pentium computers. With Microsoft NT Server with Terminal Services, some colleges can keep the 486s and turn them into Windows terminals. The only cost to the college would be to buy a server computer for the lab. This may cost 30% to 40% less than upgrading the entire lab to Pentium computers. This would lower a college's total cost of ownership for their labs, and would centralize the management of all applications onto the server.

Another alternative is to install Windows 98 on all machines in the lab. Although this would be the least expensive solution, it creates maintenance difficulties. Each computer would have to be maintained individually. Instead, install SMS on a Windows NT Server to support the client configurations in a central location.

3

In both scenarios, you need to have Microsoft Office on all lab computers to allow students to do homework and projects.

College administrations supply college catalogs, class schedules, and instructor schedules to their students, instructors, and staff. Currently, most colleges do most of this by hand. To transfer these applications to a network, you need to install several Windows NT Servers, providing the following services:

➤ **IIS** Provides for support for accessing Web applications on the server

➤ **Exchange Server** Provides email access for students, instructors, and college staff

➤ **SQL Server** Provides database storage for catalogs, course schedules, and other information (Access is not appropriate for these types of requirements because it is a personal database management system for a single instructor.)

➤ **Proxy Server** Provides secure Web access for all students, faculty, and staff

➤ **SMS** Provides centralized management of all computers on the campus network

➤ **SNA** Provides mainframe access to a Windows network. Most colleges currently store information on mainframes today.

➤ **Transaction Server** Provides for high-performance, scalable applications

➤ **Site Server** Provides a mechanism for allowing students to register and pay for classes remotely from home

➤ **MSMQ** Provides a fault-tolerant, load-balancing application environment on the server. If used correctly, it stops a single server from being the bottleneck.

Choosing a development tool means you should identify your development expertise and choose the appropriate tool that would meet the requirements of the team. Because you need to support many Web services, Visual Basic technologies are the best choice when creating a college lab, because they allow for rapid application development and are the easiest of all languages to learn. Use Visual Basic to create the software components, Visual InterDev to create the Web application, and FrontPage to design the Web pages. If a college already has expertise in C++ or Java, then you could choose those development tools over Visual Basic.

On the client computer side, most colleges choose Windows 98 because it is a less expensive alternative to Windows NT Workstation. You can run Microsoft Office on the clients, so that faculty and staff can create documents and reports, and send and receive email. Software developers should create software both in a server environment and on Windows 98, since it will be on all desks at the college.

CHAPTER SUMMARY

Microsoft meets all of your business needs from operating systems to applications technologies. Microsoft supplies client operating systems such as Windows CE, Windows 98, and Windows NT Workstation. They also provide server operating systems such as Windows NT Server. Microsoft's applications technology offers solutions to basic business problems, and allows you to address special problems through custom software development. The business tools in Microsoft BackOffice run on a Windows NT Server, whereas those in Microsoft Office run on all Windows platforms. Microsoft technologies, such as COM, DCOM, and UDA, provide a foundation for creating scalable and distributed applications. Microsoft Visual Studio provides the programmer with a series of tools for any development environment or project.

REVIEW QUESTIONS

1. The _____ use(s) software to help control the resources of a computer, such as a mouse, keyboard, and monitor, to execute applications, and to act as an interface between a user and the computer system.

    a. kernel

    b. operating system

    c. device drivers

    d. none of the above

2. Which one of the following is not a client operating system?

    a. Windows NT Server

    b. Windows NT Workstation

    c. Windows CE

    d. Windows 98

3. Which one of the following is not a server operating system?

    a. Windows NT Server with Terminal Services

    b. Windows CE

    c. Windows NT Server

    d. none of the above

4. A(n) _____ is the smallest piece of a program that can be scheduled for execution.

    a. application

    b. program

    c. thread

    d. process

3

5. A(n) _____ is a running application.
    a. activeX DLL
    b. program
    c. process
    d. thread

6. Multitasking is the ability of the operating system to:
    a. run more than one application at a time
    b. halt applications
    c. run only one application at a time
    d. none of the above

7. Preemptive multitasking is the ability of the operating system to:
    a. give each process a certain amount of time to run, and then swap it out with another process
    b. give the process the ability to yield control to another process
    c. give each process no time to run
    d. none of the above

8. Which part of the WIN32 API supplies a series of functions, messages, and structures to the programmer to capitalize on the power of the Windows family?
    a. KERNEL
    b. WIN32 API
    c. USER
    d. GDI

9. Which is responsible for the graphics on the screen?
    a. USER
    b. WIN32 API
    c. KERNEL
    d. GDI

10. Which is responsible for the user interface and user interaction in the WIN32 API?
    a. KERNEL
    b. GDI
    c. WIN32 API
    d. USER

11. Which Microsoft operating system runs on a palmtop computer?
    a. Windows CE
    b. Windows 98
    c. Windows NT Workstation
    d. Windows NT Server

12. The _____ is responsible for Windows NT preemptive multitasking and multithreading.
    a. hardware abstraction layer
    b. object manager
    c. microkernel
    d. kernel

13. The ability of Windows NT to support multiple processors is called _____.
    a. MMP
    b. SMP
    c. MPP
    d. none of the above

14. _____ is a suite of tools to help meet server business needs.
    a. Microsoft Visual Studio
    b. Microsoft Office
    c. Microsoft BackOffice
    d. none of the above

15. _____ is a suite of tools to help meet client business office needs.
    a. Microsoft Visual Studio
    b. Microsoft BackOffice
    c. Microsoft Office
    d. none of the above

16. _____ is a suite of tools to help develop custom software applications.
    a. Microsoft Visual Studio
    b. Microsoft BackOffice
    c. Microsoft Office
    d. none of the above

3

17. Which Microsoft technology provides the "plumbing" to create reliable, scalable, and high-performance distributed applications?
    a. Microsoft Visual Studio
    b. COM/DCOM
    c. ActiveX
    d. none of the above

18. Which Microsoft development tool provides a rapid application development (RAD) environment?
    a. Microsoft Visual Basic
    b. Microsoft Visual J++
    c. Microsoft Visual InterDev
    d. Microsoft Visual C++

19. Which Microsoft development tool provides cross-platform binary-compatible programs that support various processors?
    a. Microsoft Visual Basic
    b. Microsoft Visual C++
    c. Microsoft Visual InterDev
    d. Microsoft Visual J++

20. Which Microsoft development tool provides Web site management?
    a. Microsoft Visual J++
    b. Microsoft Visual C++
    c. Microsoft Visual InterDev
    d. Microsoft Visual Basic

HANDS-ON PROJECTS

Project 3.1
Use Intel's Web site or Microsoft's Web site to research the Net PC specification (Windows Terminal). Report on the features of the Net PC. Research several vendors and price different Windows terminals.

Project 3.2
Microsoft claims that Windows NT Workstation provides the lowest total cost of ownership of all desktop operating system products. Use Microsoft's Web site to research this claim.

Project 3.3
ActiveX is Microsoft's component technology. Visit *www.activex.com* to research two or three ActiveX components developed for use with the Internet.

 ### Project 3.4
Compare and contrast Windows NT Workstation and Windows 98.

 ### Project 3.5
Compare and contrast Windows NT Workstation and Windows NT Server.

 ### Project 3.6
Compare and contrast Windows CE and Windows 98.

PLANNING A PROJECT AND ANALYZING BUSINESS REQUIREMENTS

AFTER READING THIS CHAPTER AND COMPLETING THE EXCERCISES, YOU WILL BE ABLE TO:

➤ Define the envisioning phase of the software development life cycle, including the deliverables and activities

➤ Describe risk and risk management strategies

➤ Describe and define Unified Modeling Language (UML)

➤ Define and identify UML diagrams

➤ Define the planning phase of the software development life cycle, including deliverables and activities

➤ Define and identify Use Cases

➤ Describe and learn how to create Use Case diagrams and sequence diagrams

➤ Define business, security, process, performance, maintainability, extensibility, availability, human factors, existing system interface, and scalability requirements

➤ Define and describe project schedules

➤ Define return on investment (ROI)

Successful information systems project teams take the time to create a plan and develop a vision. A common vision keeps project teams focused on delivering the right product or service within budgetary and time constraints. Project teams use the boundaries or features of the software to define the goals of the project. Planning keeps the teams organized and makes sure they meet these goals by including measurable checkpoints during project phases.

A systems analyst works with the product development team to create the vision and plan of the project. As an entry-level programmer, you need to be aware of the systems analyst's role in a project, especially if your aim is to mature in an organization and become a systems analyst. You also need to understand the role of a programmer in a team environment, and that there is more to programming than writing code. As a member of a team, you must learn how to work with the team if you want to survive as a programmer in today's marketplace. The days of writing code in the corner by yourself are gone.

CHAPTER OVERVIEW

Chapters 2 and 3 focused on the technological infrastructure of a company, including its hardware, software, and communications technology. This chapter examines how to plan an information system project and analyze business requirements during the envisioning and planning phases of MSF's Process model. This chapter focuses on the envisioning phase and the conceptual design part of the planning phase of MSF. This chapter also describes how to determine the conceptual design and use UML diagramming techniques to capture the requirements. Conceptual design describes the user's interaction with the system that is independent of any system design. Chapter 5 covers the logical design process, which focuses on the Application model of MSF, and Chapter 6 covers the physical design process, which focuses on system design.

This chapter and other subsequent chapters use a hypothetical project called the Course Tracking Information System (CTIS). CTIS is a system that tracks an instructor's course schedule and assignments, student information, and grades.

ENVISIONING PHASE

Because a common vision helps to ensure project success, the MSF Process model recommends you include an envisioning phase in every project to develop its vision and scope. You should also assign team roles, analyze return on investment, and assess risk. During the envisioning phase of CTIS, for example, product management articulates the vision and scope with the help of systems analysts and users. The vision and scope include the problem statement or business objectives, vision statement, functions or features, user profiles, and solution concept. Each element of the vision and scope is explained below.

The problem statement articulates the problem the system will solve and provides the motivation for the project. For CTIS, the problem statement is as follows:

Professors deal with hundreds of students on a semester basis. In most cases, professors manually track assignments, grades, and student information in a grade book. Any time a student needs to know his or her standing in a class, the professor must calculate the student's grades. Students must also track the assignments and their due dates. If they miss a class, they also miss assignments given in class. The goal is to create a system that gives the professors the flexibility to electronically track assignments, grades, and student information. The system must also let students find out the assignments, when they are due, and what their grade is at any point during a semester.

The vision statement defines the long-term vision and establishes focus on the product. For CTIS, the vision statement of the project is as follows:

To create course-tracking software that students can easily use to view their grades for a particular course anytime, anywhere, and anyplace, and that instructors can use to track assignments, students, and students' grades.

The scope states the boundaries and features of the project. The scope of CTIS is that it will manage student and course information. Specifically, it will store, display, and retrieve course information and student assignments, grades, and other information. It will also generate student, grade, and assignment reports.

4

The vision and scope also include user profiles to identify the people who will typically use this product. People who will use CTIS fit the following profiles:

➤ Users will be students and professors with a wide range of computer experience.

➤ Users will work with CTIS from home computers over slow links and school computers over fast links.

➤ Users will converse with the system in English.

➤ Users will come from various educational backgrounds. Some users will be students with no formal college education, while others will have advanced degrees.

The solution concept outlines the approach that will provide the basis for planning the project. People will use CTIS in the following circumstances:

➤ Students log on to CTIS and retrieve their assignments, grades, syllabus, and grading policy for a particular course, and update their student information.

➤ Instructors log on to CTIS to post grades, store and retrieve students' names, view student information, and store and retrieve assignments for a particular course. Instructors configure each course they teach by entering students' names, determining the grading policy, and posting the course syllabus. At the end of a term, CTIS calculates final grades for each student in a course.

When deciding on the vision and scope, the systems analyst considers existing off-the-shelf applications, anticipated changes in the environment, expected lifetime of the proposed solution, the schedule, budget, and trade-offs. For instance, the systems analyst would envision the CTIS project as follows. When considering existing applications, the systems analyst would discover that some existing systems fulfill the requirements for CTIS. These systems let you track student grades and assignments and register and store course information. However, these systems are fragmented, cannot talk to each other, cannot be networked, and can only be used by the instructor. They therefore do not meet the objectives of CTIS.

The systems analyst anticipates that CTIS users will work at home or at school. CTIS will therefore let students and instructors use any type of machine and connect to the network at any speed. The expected lifetime of CTIS is five to ten years and will be upgraded as technology changes. Once the product manager and user sign off on the vision and scope document, then the project reaches the vision/scope approved milestone, which ends the envisioning phase.

Team Roles

During the envisioning phase, each team member has a specific responsibility to the project. Table 4.1 illustrates the team roles and responsibilities during the envisioning phase.

Return On Investment (ROI)

An important concept in planning a project is the rate of return on investment (ROI) of the product or service. The goal in designing information systems is to save or make money for a company. You need to show how the company will realize savings or profit by using the system you want to build. If you cannot convince management of a high ROI on the system being built, then you may not receive permission to build the system. You need to develop a ROI estimate for the next five years.

Over the next five years, the return on investment is equal to the net present value of the benefits of the system divided by the initial investment plus the operating costs. The initial investment and operating costs include the hardware, software, communications, and other services, and the labor cost, including the project team. The quantifiable benefits include the following:

➤ **Product and process improvements** How much time will this product or service save the users?

Table 4.1   Team roles and responsibilities during the envisioning phase.

Team Role	Responsibility
Product management	Creates and approves the vision/scope document
Program management	Defines design goals and the solution concept
Development	Creates prototypes (proof of concept) of difficult technical topics; researches and provides feedback to project on technical implications of the technical scope
User education	Defines user performance support issues, creates user profiles, and provides training strategies
Testing	Defines the testing and acceptance criteria of the project
Logistics management	Determines the long-term management and technical support implications

➤ **Cost reduction/avoidance** How much money will this product or service save?

➤ **Enhanced revenue/competitive advantage** How much money will this product or service generate in the next five years?

The systems analyst must project the average cost savings or avoidance for a five-year period following the initial investment. This information is valuable in determining whether developing the product or service is a worthwhile endeavor.

Risk Assessment

Risk is the possibility of suffering a failure. For example, a failure could be a schedule slip, cost overrun, product instability, or inability to meet the vision and objectives. Although risk is a part of the daily activities of a project, and you can make significant progress by taking risks, you can also suffer setbacks. Therefore, managing risk must be a part of the project management process from the beginning to the end of the project. The different categories of risk are listed below:

➤ Mission and goals

➤ Decision drivers

➤ Organizational management

➤ Customer/end user

➤ Budget/cost

➤ Schedule

➤ Project characteristics

➤ Development process

➤ Development environment

➤ Personnel

➤ Operational environment

➤ New technology

Table 4.2 shows the potential risks and their possible consequences.

Risk Management Strategies

Project teams assess risk once a month or during milestone meetings. They use this information to make decisions that minimize any risk. Managers can take a *reactive management strategy*, which means the project team reacts to consequences of risks as they happen, or they can take a *proactive management strategy*, which means the project team uses an objective, measurable process to anticipate and manage any risks.

Table 4.2 Possible consequences of risk.

Project Consequences	Explanations
Cost overruns	Defining unrealistic goals causes the project to exceed the budget.
Schedule slips	Underestimating the length of a task causes the project to miss deadlines.
Inadequate functionality	Failing to include functionality creates an unusable system.
Canceled projects	Exceeding the budget and schedule in the project forces upper management to cancel the project.
Sudden personnel changes	Resignation of key co-workers from the project means the project is understaffed, which causes schedule slips.
Customer dissatisfaction	Not satisfying the customer's needs results in project cancellation and leaves customers dissatisfied.
Loss of company image	Failing to produce what you promised causes a loss of company image.
Demoralized staff	Unrealistic expectations from the customer and management make the project members demoralized.
Poor product performance	Sluggish and slow response times in systems make the product perform poorly.
Legal proceedings	Failure to fulfill the contract you have with the customer may cause them to sue.

The best managers use both strategies to minimize and prevent risks. This does not guarantee that risk will never occur, but helps you avoid the consequences of risk. For example, a common risk category is the project schedule. If it seems that a deadline will not be met, the manager may remove functionality or extend the schedule. This is a reactive strategy, because the manager reacts to a missed deadline by removing functionality from the product. A proactive approach, on the other hand, avoids the consequence of the risk by anticipating the problem. For example, a manager may add development resources early in the project to avoid missing later deadlines.

The Proactive Risk Management Process

Figure 4.1 illustrates the proactive risk management process.

The steps in the proactive risk management process are:

1. **Identify and analyze** Clearly identify the risk with the following information:

   ➤ **Risk identifier** The name of the risk used for tracking and reporting

   ➤ **Risk source** Focus area (custom software development, software deployment, infrastructure deployment, enterprise architecture

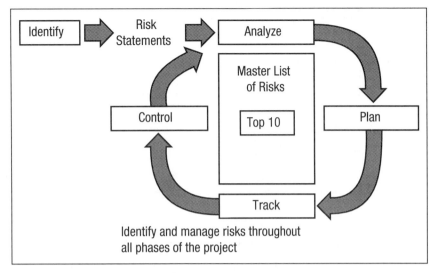

Figure 4.1   The proactive risk management process.

planning) and risk factor (project fit, political influences, organizational stability, or project size)

➤ **Risk condition**   A statement that describes the condition that could cause a loss or failure in the project

➤ **Risk consequence**   A statement that describes the potential loss or failure

➤ **Risk probability**   A percentage greater than zero and less than 100 that represents the likelihood of the loss

➤ **Risk impact classification**   The impact is financial, strategic, technical, or legal

➤ **Risk impact**   The impact of the failure represented in dollar value or on a scale of one to ten, where ten is the largest magnitude

➤ **Risk exposure**   The overall threat to the project, balancing the likelihood of the actual loss with the magnitude of the impact

➤ **Risk context**   A paragraph containing background material that clarifies the risk

➤ **Related risks**   A list of risk identifications that are interrelated with other risks

Periodically categorize and examine the top 10 risks to make sure you are managing the risk properly.

2. **Plan**   Keep the following four key areas in mind during risk action planning:

➤ **Research**   Investigate and gather information about the risk.

➤ **Accept** Accept the consequences of the risk.

➤ **Manage** Minimize the impact of the risk, if possible.

➤ **Avoid** Avoid the risk by changing the scope, schedule, or other factors. You can also avoid risk by applying resources. Find alternatives for risks that are beyond the control of the project team. Transfer the risk by using different hardware, moving a software feature to a new release, or subcontracting the work to an experienced team member.

3. **Tracking** The project team tracks the risk and the actions taken to avoid it.

4. **Control** The project team controls the risk, corrects any problems with the plans, responds to events, and improves the risk management process.

Unified Modeling Language (UML) Overview

UML is an object-oriented modeling language that uses graphical notation to help document a software project, and is especially helpful after you've completed the envisioning phase and are ready to begin the planning phase. Microsoft's development tools use UML, although it is only one of many techniques for documenting a software project. Project members can use UML to communicate with graphics and exchange information. UML uses objects to model the project's solution environment.

Objects are tangible entities that have a state and a behavior. *State* groups the values of all properties. *Properties*, also called *attributes*, are information that describes an object. For example, a ball is an object that has size, color, and other properties. *Behavior* defines all the actions of an object. *Operation* is another name used for each behavior. An *operation* is triggered by an external stimulus such as an event or message. For example, a ball's behavior or operations include bouncing and rolling. The action of a person throwing the ball to the floor creates an external stimulus that causes the ball to bounce.

James Rumbaugh, Grady Booch, and Ivar Jacobson created the UML object-oriented modeling language in the 1990s. Companies around the world adopted UML, and it became a standard in 1997. UML consists of nine types of diagrams:

➤ **Use Case diagrams** Capture the functions of a system from a user's point of view. Conceptual design provides the Use Case diagrams that define what the user requires of the system.

➤ **Sequence diagrams** Capture the interaction between objects. Conceptual and logical design uses sequence diagrams to define the interaction between classes and objects in a system.

➤ **Collaboration diagrams** Capture the structure of objects, links, and interactions, and are similar to sequence diagrams.

➤ **Class diagrams** Capture the static structure of the objects and the relationships between objects. Logical design uses class diagrams to define the properties and operations of different classes in a system. Classes are templates and provide the foundation for objects. For example, a person class describes different properties and operations of a person. One object, Keith, inherits the person's class structure the defined properties and operations. An object is an instance of a class.

➤ **Object diagrams** Capture objects and their relationships. They show the interaction between the real objects in a system. Logical design can also use object diagrams.

➤ **Statechart diagrams** Capture the behavior of a class. Logical design can also use statechart diagrams.

➤ **Activity diagrams** Capture the operation as a set of actions. Logical design can also use activity diagrams.

➤ **Component diagrams** Capture the physical representation of the objects in an application. Components package one or more classes together so they can be reused across applications. Components provide the foundation for the classes to be used in an application. Physical design uses component diagrams.

➤ **Deployment diagrams** Capture the deployment of objects on different hardware. Physical design uses deployment diagrams.

This chapter focuses on Use Case diagrams to document user requirements and Sequence diagrams to document the conceptual design perspective. These diagrams will be defined when they are used in this chapter. Other chapters focus on the other UML diagramming techniques.

PLANNING PHASE

After the vision/scope approved milestone, the planning phase begins. The planning phase consists of conceptual, logical, and physical design. Conceptual design provides the project team with the user's view of the project. Systems analysts use scenarios (or they use cases) to document the user's view. Logical design provides the project team with the classes or objects that include the properties, operations, and interactions between objects.

Chapter 5 describes the logical design process. Physical design provides the components that are candidates for the application. Chapter 6 describes the physical design process. During the planning phase, the project team delivers the functional requirements and project schedule. The planning phase ends when management approves the functional specification, risk management plan, project plan, and master project schedule; this is called the project plan approved milestone. As you analyze the project requirements, answer the following questions:

➤ **What are the legal issues involved with this project?** Some industries, such as education and telecommunications, are highly regulated. Because the project must comply with local, state, and federal laws, you might have to meet with lawyers to discuss your project. Lawyers can recommend ways to stay in compliance. Be sure to document these recommendations. In the case of CTIS, you must consider student privacy issues. CTIS needs to guarantee the privacy of student grades, restricting access to grades to the student to whom the grades are assigned.

➤ **What are the current business practices?** Systems analysts must be aware of the current business practices, which might include (1) special policies and procedures to follow during the phases of the software development life cycle, (2) who needs to be involved in the project, (3) who needs to sign off on project documentation, and (4) other practices. For example, CTIS must involve the system administrators and lab technicians in the project. The school management must also sign off on the project.

➤ **What is the current organizational structure?** The current organizational structure defines who reports to whom, and who needs to be informed about project decisions. In CTIS, the system administrators and lab technicians are responsible for computer systems at the college level and need to be aware of any decisions that affect their responsibilities.

➤ **What are the budgetary constraints for this project?** All projects have a budget that determines which requirements will be supported in each version of the project. You need to know the estimated budget for the project because project decisions are usually based on the budget. Because college budgets are small and limited, CTIS needs to keep the costs low and the total cost of ownership to a minimum.

➤ **What are the current implementation and training methodologies?** When planning the project, consider which programming language is standard in the business and what deliverables are required at each phase. When a project is delivered, what procedures are required to train users? Some companies have policies that define the length of training. In CTIS, the training for students is the responsibility of the professor. The training for professors is the responsibility of the product development team.

➤ **What are the quality control requirements?** To make sure that the project delivers a high-quality product, each project team must meet specified quality control requirements. For example, a company might require different levels of testing to verify that the product meets project requirements. Some companies test the system and verify that it meets requirements, then test user acceptance, and ask users to verify the product's acceptability before delivering the product. This testing is usually done by an independent organization. The testing for CTIS involves internal testers and professors who will use the system. The testing organization will involve the professors, since they will be the primary CTIS users.

➤ **What are the customer's needs for this project?** The most important part of creating requirements is making sure that the user's or customer's needs are met. You can do this by involving the user in the project.

Team Roles

During the planning phase, each team member has a specific responsibility to the project, as they do during the envisioning phase. Table 4.3 illustrates the team roles and responsibilities during the planning phase.

Use Cases

The systems analyst and user work together to document the needs of the user. The systems analyst defines *Use Cases* to document the user's needs. Use Case diagrams document the system functionality. Use Cases consist of *actors*, which are *roles* a user plays when interacting with the system, the system, and *scenarios*, or the functional interaction between the user and the system. The following is a list of the categories of actors, which represent the interfaces to the system (user interfaces and system to system interfaces):

➤ **Primary actors** Represent roles for using the main functions of the system.

➤ **Secondary actors** Represent roles for using the maintenance and management functions of the system.

➤ **Other system actors** Represent systems that interact with the main system.

Table 4.3   Team roles and responsibilities during the planning phase.

Team Role	Responsibility
Product management	Creates the conceptual design and defines the marketing plan and schedule
Program management	Creates the logical design, functional specification, and master plan and schedule
Development	Creates the physical design, development plan, and schedule, and works with program management on logical design, functional specification, master plan, and schedule
User education	Creates user performance support design, user educational plan, and schedule
Testing	Evaluates conceptual, logical, and physical design, and creates testing plan and schedule
Logistics management	Evaluates conceptual, logical, and physical design, and creates logistics plan and schedule

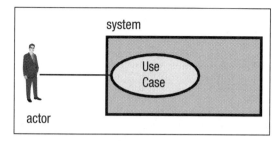

Figure 4.2   UML representation of a Use Case.

For example, in the CTIS system, the primary actors are the instructor and the student, because they interact with the system most often. The secondary actor is the system administrator, who maintains and manages CTIS. In UML, an actor is represented by a stick figure, and a system is a black box. A Use Case is an ellipse. The interaction between an actor and a Use Case is a straight line. Figure 4.2 illustrates the graphical elements used in Use Case diagrams.

Scenarios (i.e., Use Cases) provide the following advantages:

➤ Provide a context for all requirements from the user's point of view

➤ Facilitate common understanding between the team and the user

➤ Serve as a basis for estimates

➤ Facilitate objectivity and consistency in evaluating the user's suggestions

➤ Can be easily prototyped

➤ Organize projects to meet the functional specification

➤ Enable traceability throughout the software development life cycle

Functional Requirements

The functional requirements define what the system will do. When determining what tasks the system will automate for the user, start by evaluating the system's environment. This includes a platform and the hardware, the software, and communications infrastructure to support the system. Chapters 2 and 3 supplied the necessary information for this part of the requirements. Once you determine the environment, consider how the environment may change. For example, the environment in CTIS will probably change every one to two years, so your system must be flexible enough to accommodate these changes.

Next, determine the type of problem your system will solve, such as a messaging problem or communications problem. A solution to a messaging problem occurs when a client computer sends a request message to a server and the server responds with a response message. A solution to a communications problem occurs when a client application sets up a communications link to a server application and you determine the rules that allow the client application and server application to talk to each other. Most applications, including CTIS, solve messaging problems.

You can create the functional requirements for security, workflow process, performance, system maintainability, extensibility, human factors, existing system interface, and scalability. As a systems analyst gathering requirements, you can use several fact-finding and information-gathering instruments and techniques:

4

➤ **Sampling of existing documentation, forms, and databases** Use procedure documents, standards, and other documentation to discover how the user does his or her job. Internet research can also be useful in gathering requirements. Use this technique when the system needs to use building standards.

➤ **Research and site visits** Shadow users as they perform their jobs. Use this technique to observe firsthand how users complete common tasks.

➤ **Observation of work environment** As you shadow users, observe how they work, how they interact with co-workers, and where they perform tasks. Use this technique to understand how users perform their jobs and in what order they complete common tasks.

➤ **Users as teachers** Let users teach you how they do their jobs. Use this technique to reveal inefficiencies, opportunities, and undocumented information relating to the job.

➤ **User surveys** Develop questionnaires to determine requirements. If you are upgrading to a new system, use this technique to learn what users like and dislike about the old system.

➤ **Interviews** Interview the users and managers and document their answers to determine how users do their tasks in detail. Be sure to review and test your interview questions first.

➤ **Facilitated sessions** Hold sessions with participants from various groups involved in the project, to focus on a single functional area in detail. Use this technique to gather information about how each person works in the business and how each interacts with the others in the system. This helps you explore how and why tasks are accomplished.

➤ **Focus groups** Use group interviewing techniques to gather information about attitudes and opinions. Use this technique only if you are a trained interviewer and you want to gather attitudes towards the proposed system. You can also gather useful information on user needs.

➤ **Help desks** Interview members of help desks to see what problems the users are having with current products or services. Use this technique to learn the problems users are having with other systems, so that you can avoid them in the new system.

Security Requirements

When you gather requirements for CTIS or any other system, evaluate existing security policies and how much security the system requires. Answer the following questions to evaluate security needs:

➤ **Do you have enough logon security at the operating system level for this type of system?** If you are using Windows 98 or Windows CE, no real security is built into the system. If you are using Windows NT 4.0 or 2000, you can integrate the system security into the Windows NT 2000 security subsystem. In the case of CTIS, let's say you decide to shadow one of your college professors to see how he grades his students. You notice that he works on a Windows 98 computer system, even though Windows 98 is not very secure. Because operating-system-level security cannot protect instructor and student information, CTIS requires application-level security. This prevents unauthorized access to application functions, such as instructors posting grades. Operating-system-level security only prevents access to parts of the operating system, not to pieces of an application.

➤ **Does this system need another level of logon security at the application level?** If the system does not provide enough security at the operating system level, then you may also need extra security when users log on to the application. Because CTIS needs application-level security, develop an authentication Use Case for CTIS. Figure 4.3 illustrates the authentication Use Case. Figure 4.3(a) shows the UML representation of the Use Case diagram, which includes an actor (the instructor) and a Use Case (authentication). Figure 4.3(b) shows the sequence diagram of the instructor and the system. The Instructor and System boxes are the objects in the Use Case that interact with each other. The vertical lines represent a timeline of the events of the Use Case. The arrow lines represent the messages transmitted between each object and the next, in time. In CTIS, these messages are logon and authorization: the instructor initiates the Use Case by logging on to the system with a username and password, and the system verifies the user and authorizes him or her into the system. Figure 4.3(c) shows a table representing the Use Case. Table 4.4 defines the different row headings in the table. The Use Case table illustrates the successful and unsuccessful course of the Use Case. The successful course of the Use Case presents the step-by-step process of what happens during the logon process. The unsuccessful course of the Use Case presents the step-by-step process of what happens when the Use Case is not successful and must repeat.

➤ **What are the existing mechanisms for security policies?** Windows 2000 includes security that CTIS will use as much as possible. SQL Server and Access also have their own built-in security. Each of these mechanisms

4

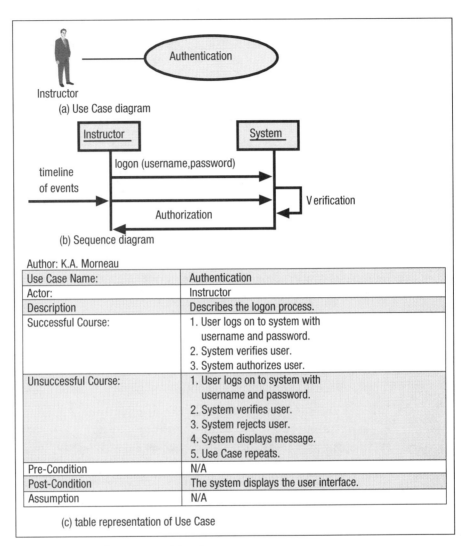

Figure 4.3 Authentication Use Case.

will be used to protect access to the OS and to the data stored in a DBMS. Additional software will be written when Windows 2000 and the DBMS's security are not enough for CTIS.

➤ **What is the level of risk in the application?** Consider the level of risk that is acceptable in your application. CTIS will contain application, operating system, and information security built into the application. CTIS must prevent students from accessing other students' information or gaining instructor rights.

Table 4.4 Use Case row heading descriptions.

Row Element	Description
Author	The author of the Use Case
Actors	The actors who trigger the Use Case
Description	The definition of the Use Case
Successful course	The successful process of the Use Case
Unsuccessful course	The unsuccessful path a Use Case could take
Precondition	What is required before this Use Case is triggered
Postcondition	What happens when the Use Case is finished
Assumptions	The assumptions needed to understand the Use Case

➤ **What is the physical scope of the application?** Consider where this application will exist, such as on a single machine in one location, on multiple machines regionally, or on multiple machines globally. For example, CTIS will run on the Internet, but will reside on local machines.

➤ **How is fault tolerance being built into the application?** Using MSMQ, the application will support fault tolerance. For example, if the server fails while processing a transaction, MSMQ keeps all messages until the server returns to process each message. CTIS, for example, will supply MSMQ services in the application.

➤ **What is the security context for the application?** Applications have several security options. You can use application security to manage security at the application level. You use the operating system security to permit access to the computer. You can also use information security to limit access to the database. CTIS will use all three security options.

➤ **If this system requires another level of logon security, what are the different roles of the users? Does this system need a system administrator, guests, and clients? Does this system need group security?** List all the users of the system and their roles. CTIS requires three types of users: system administrator, instructor, and student. Users will log on to the system with a username and password. CTIS will then check that they belong to either the instructor or student group. Group security based on instructor and student classifications will simplify assigning rights to the application. This allows the application to take two paths: one for the instructors and one for the students, so each can use CTIS in a different way.

➤ **Does this system need to support logging?** *Logging* means the system can write events to a log file to track certain error conditions in the software. For example, CTIS will log errors in a file.

➤ **Does this system need to support auditing?** *Auditing* means the application can write certain security events to a file to track what users do in the system. For example, CTIS will support auditing to track users' movements.

➤ **Does this system need to support physical security?** Physical security is putting the computer under lock and key. CTIS will not require physical security.

➤ **How do security requirements change the existing environment?** Determine whether the security requirements enhance or detract from the current system environment. The security requirements for CTIS, for example, enhance the current environment by adding additional software that works in conjunction with the operating system.

Logging and auditing requirements need to be added to the authentication Use Case and other Use Cases. Hands-on Project 4 will provide you with experience in meeting logging and auditing requirements.

Workflow Process Requirements

As you are gathering requirements, consider the parts of the user's job that the project is automating. Answer the following questions:

➤ **What procedures do the users follow when doing their jobs?** Observe users as they work and note the tasks they perform. For example, as you continue to shadow your professor, focus on how he or she prepares for a new semester and assigns grades. Through observation and questioning, you notice that in the beginning of a semester, the professor creates a syllabus for each course he or she teaches. The syllabus documents the grading policy, which is different for each course. As the new semester approaches, the professor receives a form for each course he or she teaches, in which grades for each assignment can be recorded. On the first day of class, the professor brings 3×5 index cards on which students will enter their name, home phone number, work phone number, email address, and reason for taking the course.

➤ **What forms do users complete to do their jobs?** Examine the paper-based forms users complete as part of their jobs. The professor, for example, records grades in a grade book, including the date of the grade, the course title, the name of the student, and the actual grade.

You create several Use Cases based on the above information, including those for creating, updating, and deleting course information and student assignments; grades; and general information; generating student grades by course; and viewing student information by student; and course information.

Figure 4.4 illustrates the Create Course Information Use Case.

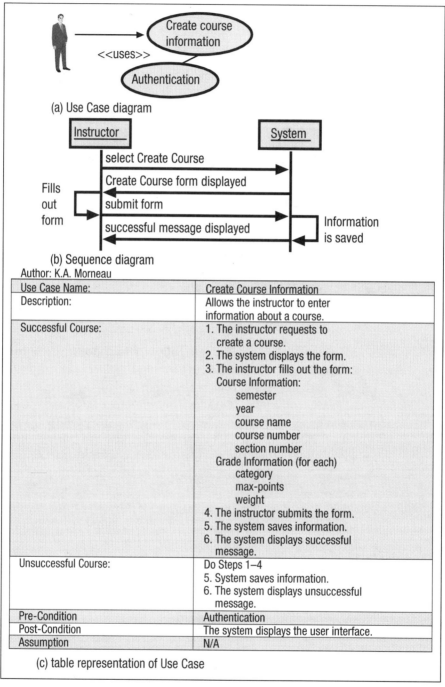

(a) Use Case diagram

(b) Sequence diagram

Author: K.A. Morneau

Use Case Name:	Create Course Information
Description:	Allows the instructor to enter information about a course.
Successful Course:	1. The instructor requests to create a course. 2. The system displays the form. 3. The instructor fills out the form: Course Information: semester year course name course number section number Grade Information (for each) category max-points weight 4. The instructor submits the form. 5. The system saves information. 6. The system displays successful message.
Unsuccessful Course:	Do Steps 1–4 5. System saves information. 6. The system displays unsuccessful message.
Pre-Condition	Authentication
Post-Condition	The system displays the user interface.
Assumption	N/A

(c) table representation of Use Case

Figure 4.4   Create Course Information Use Case.

Figure 4.4(a) shows the diagram for the Create Course Information Use Case. This links to Use Case authentication. To be able to create a course, the user must log on and must be a part of the instructor group. Figure 4.4(b) shows the sequence diagram for the Use Case. The link contains the <<uses>> label. This label says that the Create Course Information Use Case includes the behavior of the Authentication Use Case. <<Uses>> is called a *stereotype*. A stereotype allows the UML modeler to classify the links.

Performance Requirements

When designing a system, consider how quickly it can perform. Sluggish systems can cause problems and give the user the impression that the system is flawed. You can measure the level of performance your system needs by answering the following questions:

> ➤ **How many users will be using the system at any one time?** Estimate the number of users who will be using the system at once. This estimate helps you design the system to allow for scalability. Designing for scalability is described in Chapter 5. For example, as you shadow the professor, you notice that he or she teaches 5 classes, with an average class size of 25 students. This means he or she teaches an average of 125 students per semester. The system must also support 125 students on average.

> ➤ **Is the bandwidth adequate for the type of system being developed?** The bandwidth of a system is the amount of data the system can handle before experiencing delays. A lack of bandwidth causes poor system performance. A multimedia application requires more bandwidth than a data-based application. Because CTIS is a data-based system, it doesn't need as much bandwidth as a multimedia application. A professor's machine is connected to the school's network via Ethernet, which provides sufficient bandwidth for CTIS. However, if you were developing a multimedia system that required streaming of video to each machine, then Ethernet might not be adequate. Bandwidth for Ethernet is 10 Mbps and is shared among all computers connected to the network. To support video, you need to implement a minimum of a dedicated 100 Mbps Ethernet to each user's desktop. The ideal situation for the support of streaming video is to support asynchronous transfer mode (ATM) to the desktop.

> ➤ **During peak times, what is the acceptable response time of the system?** Talk to or observe users to determine how quickly your system should respond to their requests during peak usage. For example, for CTIS, you could observe different labs on campus to decide what response times are acceptable to students. With a stopwatch in hand (start the watch when the user requests a resource in a Web browser, and stop the watch when the

browser finishes displaying the resource), time several students working in different applications. Let's say you notice that response times of 5 to 10 seconds do not disturb the students. If the system takes more than 10 seconds to respond, the students exhibit signs of frustration and impatience. The maximum response time should therefore be 10 seconds during peak times.

➤ **During nonpeak times, what should the average response time be?** Talk to or observe users to determine how quickly your system should respond to their requests during nonpeak usage. For example, you may decide from your sampling of students' computer usage that five seconds or less is acceptable for an average response time.

➤ **What are the barriers to performance?** Determine what prevents you from delivering optimal performance. For CTIS, your observations on campus lead you to several conclusions. The higher the number of students using computers during peak times, the more the system performance degrades. You also notice that students using Pentium computers experience better performance than students using 486 machines. You conclude that the hardware platform and the number of students using the system at one time significantly influence system performance.

➤ **Are any existing response time standards already in place?** Check the existing system documentation to see if others have already provided response time standards.

Maintainability Requirements

After evaluating performance requirements, consider how users will maintain your system. You need to consider:

➤ **Application distribution** How will you distribute the system? Will you use disks, CDs, or a Web site, for example? What is the easiest and most economical way to distribute the application?

➤ **Maintenance expectations** How many people will support this system by answering users' questions and solving problems? What level of expertise does the support staff need? Are there any third-party maintenance agreements for this system?

➤ **Life cycle of application** How long will users work with this system?

For example, CTIS will be a hybrid between a traditional and a Web-based application. Because you're already using the Web, you can also use it to distribute the software. This will minimize costs because you don't need a supply of disks or CDs or related labor for loading the application onto the media. One person will support the application.

Extensibility Requirements

Software development is a process of change. Because you develop a system in cycles—you code to add functionality, test, then code again—systems must be extensible. CTIS, for example, employs an object-oriented analysis and design methodology, which supplies techniques to make sure you can easily add functionality to a system.

Availability Requirements

After you determine the extensibility requirements, you need to also determine how available you want the system to be. You need to consider the following:

➤ **Hours of operation** When should the system be available? Determine when users need to access the system. For example, CTIS needs to be available 24 hours a day, 365 days a year.

➤ **Level of availability** Where and how will the system be available? Determine how users can physically access the system. For example, users can access CTIS from anywhere with a Web browser and an Internet connection.

➤ **Geographic scope** Where will the users be using the system—locally, regionally, or globally? Will people be using the system within an organization or city, within a county, state, or country, or around the world? CTIS will be accessed locally, since most colleges and universities support students at a local level. But CTIS will also be available regionally and globally if necessary.

➤ **Impact of downtime** If the system goes down for any period of time, what are the consequences of this risk? Determine the consequences to the users if the system is not working. For example, downtime of CTIS is not a life or death situation and causes only minor irritation to students.

Human Factors Requirements

In designing systems, whether hardware or software, you need to consider how people interact with the system and how to make the environment for the user as pleasant as possible. Consider the following human factors requirements:

➤ **Target audience and accessibility** For whom is the system designed— regular users, visually impaired, hearing impaired, or other types of users? "Regular" users can respond to visual and auditory cues without assistance. Other users may need audible instructions or text provided in large print. The first version of CTIS supports regular users who do not have special needs.

➤ **Localization** Will this application be used in other countries? If so, then what different languages need to be supported? If people in other countries will use the application, you must translate the commands and use icons appropriate for the culture, for example. CTIS, however, supports only the English-speaking world in the first version.

➤ **Roaming users** Will users access this system from a single machine or from many machines? Users like to use any computer from any location to interact with a system. The system needs to keep track of user settings no matter where the user logs on. CTIS, for example, will be used from any machine anywhere.

➤ **Help** What level of online help do your users need? Determine whether your users need beginning, intermediate, or advanced information about the system. A system often has all types of users. For example, CTIS supports novice, intermediate, and experienced users. Help will be structured for all types of users.

➤ **Training requirements** Will your users need special training to use this application? If your application uses a unique interface or requires other specialized knowledge, the users may need application training. Because CTIS will use a standard Windows interface, training will be minimal.

➤ **Physical environment constraints** What types of computers do your users work with? How fast are their connections to the network? Determine whether your system can run on the computers and network connections your users have. For example, CTIS students use all types of Pentium computers and also access the college network from home, using a modem or a faster connection. This is suitable for CTIS.

Existing System Interface Requirements

An existing application may be a legacy application or an upgrade. Typically, legacy applications run on a mainframe computer. When using a legacy application to develop a new application, consider the following:

➤ **What are the current legacy applications?** Should the new application interface with the legacy applications? If it should, then identify the existing format and location of the data. Also, consider how to connect to existing data sources. If you are working with mainframe data, consider the interface between the Windows applications and the mainframe application. What protocols are used? What software connects the mainframe to a LAN (e.g., a Systems Network Architecture, or SNA, server)? The new application must adhere to the data formats already in place in the legacy application.

➤ **Will the new application replace the legacy application?** If yes, then must you convert the existing data to the new format? You may need a special data conversion program to convert the data from the old legacy system to the new one.

➤ **What is the impact of the technology migration from the legacy system to the new system?** Consider the impact of technology migration when converting from the old system to the new system. Users must be retrained to use the new system. The support staff must be retrained in the new technology. Existing data might have to be converted to the new database. The biggest issue in migrating into new technologies is properly training everyone involved.

Scalability Requirements

As the application grows, make sure you design for scalability, the ability to add more users without degrading the performance of the system. You must consider the following:

➤ **What is the estimated growth in the number of users for this application?** Estimate the number of people using the application each year or quarter for the next five years. This number often changes significantly from the first to the fifth year, although it can remain constant. For example, the number of users in CTIS is always the same as the number of students a professor has. On average, a professor can have over 100 students, but you don't expect many more than that.

➤ **What is the estimated growth of the organization?** Estimate how many people you need to maintain and support the system. For example, as more professors start using this application, the technical support staff will need to grow. You estimate that you need a support person for every campus department as the usage of the system grows.

➤ **What is the estimated growth of the data in this application?** If the data in the application will accumulate from year to year, you need to archive the data to keep the performance high. As a professor uses CTIS every semester, for example, the amount of accumulated data will grow arithmetically. The ability to archive old data from every semester is a critical element in the application.

➤ **What is the estimated life of this application?** Estimate how often you will update the application. For example, CTIS will be upgraded yearly and functionality added as requested by the users.

Project Schedule

As part of the planning process, you must schedule project phases, activities, and tasks. Most projects define a work breakdown structure (WBS). A *WBS* is a hierarchical breakdown of the project into phases, activities, and tasks, as in the following outline:

1.0   Envisioning Phase

1.1   Activity 1 of Envisioning Phase

    1.1.1   Task 1 of Activity 1

    1.1.2   Task 2 of Activity 1

1.2   Vision/Scope Approved Milestone

2.0   Planning Phase

2.1   Activity 1 of Planning Phase

   2.1.1   Task 1 of Activity 1

   2.1.2   Task 2 of Activity 1

2.2   Project Plan Approved Milestone

3.0   Developing Phase

3.1   Activity 1 of Developing Phase

3.2   Scope Complete/First Use

4.0   Stabilization Phase

4.1   Activity 1 of Stabilization Phase

4.2   Release Milestone

In this outline, the four phases in MSF (Envisioning, Planning, Developing, and Stabilizing) are the top-level phases in the WBS. Each phase is divided into activities. Systems analysts create the activities, which are divided into tasks. Usually, the developers identify the tasks they need to perform, in order to accomplish an activity, and then estimate the time needed for each task. Tasks are usually split into 40-hour increments. Milestones signal the end of a phase. A *Gantt chart* is a simple schedule that shows the phases, activities, and tasks in a calendar. Figure 4.5 shows an example of a Gantt chart with phases and activities.

Each phase is a summary task on the Gantt chart. Triangles mark the start and end dates of the phase. A rectangular bar represents an activity and/or a task. A diamond represents a milestone.

Planning Phase Deliverables

The planning phase ends when the systems analyst delivers a requirements statement, a risk management plan, a master project plan, and a master project schedule. The functional specifications include the following information:

➤ Vision/Scope summary

➤ Background information

➤ Top 10 risk list

➤ Design goals, usability goals, constraints, and exceptions

➤ Proposed system objectives

➤ Proposed system Use Case diagrams

➤ Proposed system sequence diagrams

➤ Proposed infrastructure (hardware, software, and communications platform)

➤ Proposed schedule (Chapters 4, 5, and 6)

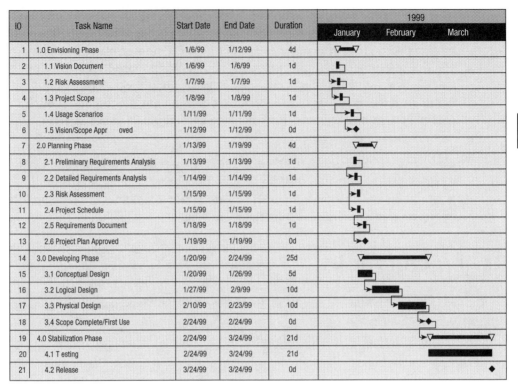

IO	Task Name	Start Date	End Date	Duration	1999		
					January	February	March
1	1.0 Envisioning Phase	1/6/99	1/12/99	4d			
2	1.1 Vision Document	1/6/99	1/6/99	1d			
3	1.2 Risk Assessment	1/7/99	1/7/99	1d			
4	1.3 Project Scope	1/8/99	1/8/99	1d			
5	1.4 Usage Scenarios	1/11/99	1/11/99	1d			
6	1.5 Vision/Scope Approved	1/12/99	1/12/99	0d			
7	2.0 Planning Phase	1/13/99	1/19/99	4d			
8	2.1 Preliminary Requirements Analysis	1/13/99	1/13/99	1d			
9	2.2 Detailed Requirements Analysis	1/14/99	1/14/99	1d			
10	2.3 Risk Assessment	1/15/99	1/15/99	1d			
11	2.4 Project Schedule	1/15/99	1/15/99	1d			
12	2.5 Requirements Document	1/18/99	1/18/99	1d			
13	2.6 Project Plan Approved	1/19/99	1/19/99	0d			
14	3.0 Developing Phase	1/20/99	2/24/99	25d			
15	3.1 Conceptual Design	1/20/99	1/26/99	5d			
16	3.2 Logical Design	1/27/99	2/9/99	10d			
17	3.3 Physical Design	2/10/99	2/23/99	10d			
18	3.4 Scope Complete/First Use	2/24/99	2/24/99	0d			
19	4.0 Stabilization Phase	2/24/99	3/24/99	21d			
20	4.1 Testing	2/24/99	3/24/99	21d			
21	4.2 Release	3/24/99	3/24/99	0d			

Figure 4.5   A sample Gantt chart.

➤ Features and services description

➤ Logical design documents (Chapter 5)

➤ Physical design documents (Chapter 6)

The systems analyst creates the risk management plan, a master project plan, and a master project schedule. The systems analyst also starts creating the functional requirements, which become the main focus of the planning phase. Chapter 5 describes the logical design process and the deliverables of the logical design process. Chapter 6 describes the physical design process and the deliverables of the physical design process.

CHAPTER SUMMARY

This chapter provides an introduction to the envisioning and planning phases of the software development process. During the envisioning phase, you articulate the project vision, which keeps project teams focused on delivering the right product or service within budget and on time. In the project vision, the boundaries or features define the goals of the project. The planning phase helps to ensure the success of an information system project. Planning keeps the project teams organized and creates measurable checkpoints during the project phases. If your team does not define the vision or plan adequately, you can jeopardize the project from the onset. With a good vision and plan, you can measure your success at every stage of the project. Risk assessment is also an important part of the software development process and must be a part of project management. Risk management, if performed correctly, minimizes the consequences of failure.

Use the UML diagrams to help you create the planning documentation. UML is one of many techniques that can be used in creating systems. It provides graphical documentation techniques to assist you in communicating the project information to your users and development team.

REVIEW QUESTIONS

1. Develop the vision and scope of a project during the _____ phase.
    a. stabilization
    b. planning
    c. developing
    d. envisioning

2. List the requirements and create a schedule for the project during the _____ phase.
    a. stabilization
    b. envisioning
    c. planning
    d. developing

3. The envisioning phase results in a _____ milestone.
    a. Project Plan Approved
    b. Vision/Scope Approved
    c. Release
    d. Scope Complete/First Use

4. The planning phase results in a _____ milestone.
    a. Release
    b. Vision/Scope Approved
    c. Project Plan Approved
    d. Scope Complete/First Use

5. _____ is the possibility of suffering a failure.

    a. Product

    b. Project

    c. Risk

    d. none of the above

6. What object-oriented modeling language supplies a graphical notation to assist in documenting a project?

    a. UML

    b. Objects

    c. Classes

    d. none of the above

7. _____ are tangible entities that consist of state and behavior.

    a. Objects

    b. Classes

    c. Diagrams

    d. none of the above

8. _____ are pieces of information that describe an object.

    a. Operations

    b. Attributes

    c. Properties

    d. both b and c

9. _____ define(s) the actions of an object.

    a. Operations

    b. Behavior

    c. Properties

    d. Attributes

10. The systems analyst defines _____ to document users' needs.

    a. roles

    b. operations

    c. objects

    d. Use Cases

4

11. Actors are _____ a user plays when interacting with the system.
    a. objects
    b. operations
    c. Use Cases
    d. roles

12. _____ means that an application writes certain security events to a file to track users and what they do in the system.
    a. Lack of security
    b. Logging
    c. Auditing
    d. Security

13. _____ means that an application writes certain events to a log file to track certain error conditions.
    a. Lack of security
    b. Logging
    c. Auditing
    d. Security

14. A(n) _____ defines a hierarchical breakdown of the project in phases, activities, and tasks.
    a. activity
    b. phase
    c. task
    d. Work Breakdown Structure (WBS)

15. A _____ is a simple schedule chart that shows the phases, activities, and tasks outlined against a calendar.
    a. schedule chart
    b. Gantt chart
    c. WBS
    d. none of the above

16. A(n) _____ diagram shows the interaction between the actors and the system.
    a. object
    b. Use Case
    c. Sequence
    d. none of the above

HANDS-ON PROJECTS

Project 4.1
Investigate the various methods of gathering requirements. Discuss the advantages and disadvantages of each technique.

Project 4.2
Risk management is an important part of the software development process. Identify 3–5 risks of CTIS, using the risk form as described in the proactive risk management process.

Project 4.3
On the Internet, research areas where projects fail. Explain how different companies are avoiding risky ventures in software development.

Project 4.4
Update the Use Cases in this chapter to add security and logging requirements.

Project 4.5
Use Case diagrams, sequence diagrams, and Use Case tables are important in documenting user requirements. Your instructor is your customer in determining the Use Cases in this Hands-on Project. Involve your instructor by asking probing questions, as presented in this chapter. From your conversations with your instructor, create Use Case diagrams, sequence diagrams, and Use Case tables for the following Use Cases in CTIS:

   a. Update course information

   b. Delete course information

   c. Create student information

   d. Update student information

   e. Delete student information

   f. Create student assignment

   g. Update student assignment

   h. Delete student assignment

   i. Create student grade

   j. Update student grade

   k. Delete student grade

   l. Generate student grades by course

m. View student information

n. View grade information by student

o. View course information

p. Any other Use Cases that are needed to support your instructor's needs

Project 4.6

Project schedules are an important part of tracking the progress of a project. Update the CTIS project Gantt chart and add 40-hour tasks to the schedule for each phase and activity. Add additional activities as necessary.

CHAPTER FIVE

DESIGNING AN INFORMATION SYSTEM LOGICALLY

AFTER READING THIS CHAPTER AND COMPLETING THE EXERCISES, YOU WILL BE ABLE TO:

➤ Describe application types including single-tier, two-tier, three-tier, and *n*-tier

➤ Describe and define graphical user interfaces

➤ Define the tasks and the interim milestones involved in the logical design phase

➤ Define and describe the UML class diagrams and sequence diagrams

➤ Learn how to create class diagrams, logical data models, and user interface prototypes

➤ Learn how to use Visual Modeler to create the object diagrams and logical data models

➤ Define business rules for classes or between classes

➤ Define and describe databases, database management systems, and relational databases

➤ Define rows, columns, fields, relations, and tuples

➤ Define relationships between tables and classes

➤ Learn techniques for creating the user interface, logical data model, and class diagram

➤ Learn the importance of logical design reviews to the developing phase

During a development project, project teams continuously update three design frameworks as necessary. To clarify the conceptual design, the project team communicates with the users to define the problem and the underlying functionality needed to solve the problem. To define the logical design, the team specifies the system's organization, structure, and syntax. To determine the physical design, the team uses the logical system components to define the physical structure of the system. They take the objects defined in the logical design and map them into their physical implementation.

Your job as a system designer is to take the scenarios and the functional requirements and turn them into a logical and physical system design. Use Cases act as your guide for determining the system functions. You must create an object design that details the different objects in the system, the services the objects will define, the user interface sketches, and the logical data model.

CHAPTER OVERVIEW

In the last chapter, you developed a vision, scope, and plan for an information system project. The plan is considered a work in progress for the developing phase, which is when you conceive of the conceptual, logical, and physical design. Although the physical design was created in the planning phase, the conceptual and logical design continues in the developing phase. This chapter focuses on the logical design, using CTIS as an example, and explains how to use UML class diagrams and sequence diagrams to visualize that design. It first examines the Application model, which provides the theory for the logical design, and then shows you how to use specialized tools to implement the logical design.

APPLICATION MODEL

The Application model defines a standard way of designing applications. The Application model consists of the following services, as described in Chapter 1:

➤ **User services** Provide an interface to the system, such as a graphical user interface, menu-driven interface, or command-driven interface

➤ **Business services** Provide the application logic or business rules that link the user services and the data services

➤ **Data services** Manipulate data and ensure its integrity. Allow users to insert, update, delete, and query data without knowing where it is located, how it is implemented, or how it is accessed

Breaking up the application into three services allows for:

➤ **Parellelism in software development**, allowing team members to work together on the user, business, and data services. Also, parallelism encourages the team to divide the software development into smaller manageable pieces, which minimizes risk.

➤ **Better software reuse** because business services create components that other teams can use.

➤ **Increased flexibility** in supporting multiple user services such as traditional applications and newer Web applications

➤ **Consistency across software development teams** because all teams create applications using the three services.

➤ **Ability to adapt to ever-changing client and server technologies** because the three services isolate technological changes from each other. For example, if you want to implement a Web-based interface instead of a "traditional" GUI interface, then you can rewrite only the user services portion of the three-tier model. This lets you change the system as the technology changes.

Single-tier, two-tier, three-tier, and *n*-tier types of applications represent ways to physically deploy user, business, and data services. Collaborative and console applications are two other common types of applications.

Single-Tier Applications

Single-tier applications are personal applications that define the user, business, and data services on a single machine. Examples of single-tier applications are word-processing applications such as Microsoft Word and spreadsheet applications such as Microsoft Excel. Figure 5.1 shows the single-tier application functions.

The characteristics of single-tier applications are listed below. Each characteristic is explained in detail in the following pages.

➤ Graphical user interfaces (GUI)

➤ Presentation logic

➤ Business logic

➤ Database management system

➤ Data access logic

Graphical User Interfaces (GUI)

A GUI takes advantage of the computer's graphics capabilities to make an application easier to use. Users view and manipulate icons and other graphical objects to enter information into the computer, interpret displayed information, and generally interact with the application.

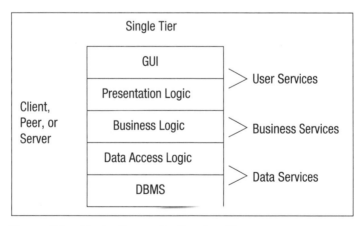

Figure 5.1   Single-tier application functions.

A GUI, such as Microsoft Windows or the one supplied by Apple Macintosh, supplies the following:

➤ **Consistency** All GUI applications perform common functions in the same way. For example, the user can access a menu the same way in any application. Their menu commands also perform similar functions, such as printing or opening a file or exiting a program.

➤ **Predictability** The user can predict what a GUI application will do because of its What-You-See-Is-What-You-Get (WYSIWYG) design. For example, if the user formats a paragraph of text on the screen, it prints in the same format.

➤ **Object-orientation** The user works with a mouse or other pointing device to move a pointer on the screen and select objects, such as buttons or icons (small pictures that represent commands, files, or windows).

➤ **Windows organization** GUI applications operate within windows on the screen so that more than one application can run at the same time. When an application needs to collect information from the user, it can use a special window called a dialog box.

GUI applications can use windows in a number of ways. This chapter introduces two ways: the single-document interface (SDI) and the multiple-document interface (MDI). For more detailed information on creating SDI and MDI applications, including menus, toolbars, status bars, and other SDI and MDI functions, see Chapter 10.

A single-document interface (SDI) is an application that uses a single window. Figure 5.2 shows an example of Notepad, which is an SDI application. All the commands and the user workspace are included in a single window.

A multiple-document interface (MDI) is an application that uses multiple windows. Figure 5.3 shows an example of Microsoft Word, which is an MDI application. The MDI application uses a single primary window, called the parent window, that contains a set of related document, or child, windows.

Here's a list of what each window component does and how to use the components to manipulate windows:

➤ **Title bar** Displays the title of the application. You can reposition a window to any location on the screen by dragging its title bar

➤ **Menu bar** Contains menus of commands for using the application

➤ **Status bar** Displays appropriate status information, such as current page number and the date and time

➤ **Toolbar** An optional collection of buttons that the user can click to quickly perform common commands, such as opening a file or printing a document

Figure 5.2   Example of an SDI application.

➤ **Client area**   Where the application displays its information or a form for user entry

➤ **Control menu**   A menu of commands that affect the window itself, such as Minimize, Restore, or Close

➤ **Minimize button**   Clicking this button shrinks the application to an icon

➤ **Maximize button**   Clicking this button enlarges the window so that it fills the entire screen

➤ **Close button**   Clicking this button exits the application

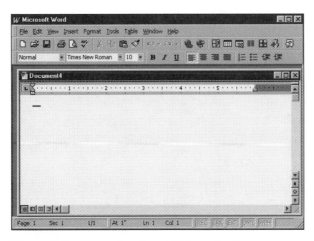

Figure 5.3   Example of an MDI application.

Most GUI applications provide menus that let the user select commands from a list of options. To select a menu command, the user clicks the menu name, such as File or Edit, to see a list of related commands. The user then clicks a command, such as New, Open, or Copy, to select it. To make menus consistent from one application to another, GUI applications use standard menu commands. The exact commands depend on the GUI you're using. Table 5.1 lists some of the standard menu commands for Microsoft Windows.

Table 5.1 Standard menu commands for Windows applications.

Menu	Command	What It Does
File	New	Creates a new document
	Open	Opens an existing document
	Save	Saves changes to an open document
	Save As	Saves the current document under a new name
	Save All	Saves all currently open documents
	Close	Closes an open document
	Print	Prints a document
	Print Preview	Displays a document exactly as it will appear on the printed page
	Exit	Quits an application
Edit	Undo	Reverses the user's last action
	Cut	Deletes the selected objects from the current location and stores them on the Clipboard
	Copy	Copies the selected objects to the Clipboard
	Paste	Pastes the contents of the Clipboard at the cursor location
	Paste Special	Pastes the contents of the Clipboard at the cursor location as an embedded or linked object
	Find	Finds text
	Replace	Replaces one text string with another
Window	New Window	Creates another window for the current file
	Tile	Arranges open windows side by side
	Cascade	Arranges open windows so they overlap
	Arrange	Arranges open windows so that they don't overlap
Help	Contents	Displays the Help table of contents
	Search	Searches for help on a specific topic
	Index	Displays an index of all help topics
	About	Displays information about the program, including a copyright notice

Users who cannot use a mouse can access menu commands by using keyboard shortcuts. The underlined letters for each menu in the menu bar specify a shortcut. Pressing Alt+F, for instance, selects the File menu. Other keyboard shortcuts are listed next to menu options. For example, Ctrl+Z is Edit-Undo, Ctrl+X is Edit-Cut, Ctrl+C is Edit-Copy, and Ctrl+V is Edit-Paste.

Commands followed by an ellipsis open a dialog box. Figure 5.4 shows an example of a dialog box.

The Open dialog box allows users to select files with the mouse or by typing the name and extension of a file.

A *workbook* is a type of application interface. The workbook organizes views of your data into sections within the workbook's primary window, using tabs instead of child windows. Microsoft Excel is an example of this interface (see Figure 5.5).

A *project* is a special MDI application interface that provides a framework where objects reside in a window but do not contain child windows. The child windows are independent windows that appear on the toolbar. This technique works like a control panel so that the project window controls the contents of its window. For example, when the project window closes, the child windows contained in the project window also close.

Presentation Logic

Another characteristic of single-tier applications is that they use presentation logic. *Presentation logic* determines the interaction of the application with the user, including menus, tool bars, status bars, and dialog boxes.

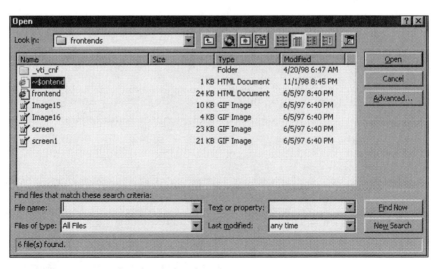

Figure 5.4   Example of a dialog box.

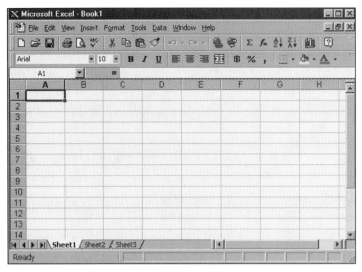

Figure 5.5   Example of a workbook-type application interface (Excel).

Business Logic

Business logic is another characteristic of a single-tier application that defines the application's components, including objects, services, attributes, and interfaces that supply the business rules for the data. (Business logic takes data and refines it into information.)

An object encapsulates attributes, services, and interfaces. *Encapsulation* is the process of packaging attributes and services that are hidden from the external world (*information hiding*). An *interface* is a contract that defines how an object will be exposed to the external world. *Components* are like black boxes that have interfaces so that users can interact with them. For example, when driving your car, you have a steering wheel, brakes, accelerator, and dashboard that displays speed and distance. The steering wheel, brakes, accelerator, and a dashboard are the interfaces to the car. You don't need to know how the engine works or how it is built to drive the car. Components work on this same concept. You can access a component through its interfaces even if you have no idea how the object is built. Software developers can therefore reuse software components in multiple projects. The attributes and the services in the component are internal representations of objects and are hidden from the programmer.

To create components, Microsoft supplies ActiveX technology. You can use it to create two types of components: in-process servers and out-of-process servers. An in-process server shares the same memory space as the container application. An ActiveX dynamic-link library (.dll) hosts an in-process server. An out-of-process server runs in its own memory space separate from the application. An ActiveX executable (.exe) hosts an out-of-process server. Both in-process and out-of-process servers are COM and/or DCOM components. (See Chapter 9 for more information about COM and DCOM.)

Database Management System (DBMS)

In addition to GUIs, presentation logic, and business logic, another characteristic of single-tier applications is that they may use a database management system (DBMS). A *DBMS* uses stored procedures to insert, update, delete, and query data. A *stored procedure* defines a task that operates on the database. For example, one operation might enter data into a database. A stored procedure would supply the necessary steps to complete the data–entry task. A DBMS also stores and manages data in the database. Microsoft provides three database management systems: Access, FoxPro, and SQL Server.

Microsoft Access and Microsoft FoxPro are personal database management systems. You use Access for small databases; that is, those less than 1 GB. Neither Access nor FoxPro are suitable for large databases that many people must access twenty-four hours a day, seven days a week. Access and FoxPro are used on client computers and server computers (as a mapped drive), but do not use the processing power of the database server. Instead, when using Access and FoxPro, the server is considered a file server. Microsoft SQL Server, however, is designed to create and maintain large databases that can span terabytes of disk storage. SQL Server is also a client/server database management system specifically intended to run on a database server.

Consider the following when choosing a data storage architecture:

➤ **Volume of data** Choose the appropriate DBMS depending on the system's future storage requirements. If you need to convert data to a new DBMS, plan for more than adequate space to store the converted data. If you need less than 1 GB of storage space, use Access or FoxPro. If you need more than 1 GB of storage space, use SQL Server.

➤ **Number of transactions and users** If many users will access the database at the same time, each performing many transactions, then SQL Server is the ideal choice. If only a few users will perform a few transactions, then choose FoxPro or Access. Remember to consider future growth when determining the number of users and transactions.

➤ **Scope of business requirements** If you need to store data in less than 10 tables, and each table contains only a few fields, then Access or FoxPro are appropriate. If you need to store data in more than 10 tables, use SQL Server.

➤ **Extensibility requirements** When you are designing a system, plan for the future growth of the system. SQL Server allows you to scale a DBMS as your needs grow. If you know that the database you are creating is not going to grow substantially, then use Access or FoxPro.

➤ **Reporting requirements** If you need to quickly generate a wide variety of reports, use SQL Server. If you only need to occasionally produce several reports, then use Access or FoxPro.

In summary, consider SQL Server as your database management system if you know that your database, number of users, and scope of the business requirements will grow, the system will be extended, and you will often produce many reports. SQL Server is ideal for large databases, such as tracking the product, customer, and order information for a large company. On the other hand, if you know that the size of the database will not change often, and the number of users is small, then use Access or FoxPro. For example, Access or FoxPro are ideal for maintaining and tracking personal contact information or meetings, conferences, and other events.

Data Access Logic

The *data access logic* interacts with a database management system. It supplies the ability to insert, update, delete, and query data without knowledge of the underlying database management system. Data access logic can also use ActiveX components. Microsoft supplies universal data access technologies to support data access logic, including open database connectivity (ODBC), ActiveX data objects (ADO), and object linking and embedding database connectivity (OLE DB).

Two-Tier Applications

While a single-tier application consists of a single application, two-tier applications split into two components: a client-side application and a server-side application. For example, an email system consists of two components: one that allows you to enter the mail message and another that delivers the message to a recipient. These applications reside on two separate computers. Figure 5.6 illustrates the two-tier applications and their functions.

Figure 5.6a shows the first and oldest type of two-tier applications, called the fat client/thin server approach. The term *fat* applies to the machine that contains the business logic. The fat client provides GUI, presentation logic, and business logic functions. The thin server provides data access logic and database management system functions.

Figure 5.6b shows the second type of application, called the thin client/fat server. The *thin client* provides GUI and presentation logic functions. The *fat server* provides business logic, data access logic, and database management system functions.

The DBMS usually includes the fat server functions as stored procedures. The current practice is to use ActiveX components to implement a portion of the fat server functions. This allows your application to support thousands of users and to move application functionality to a different machine if the current machine cannot handle the workload.

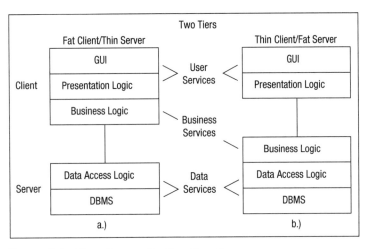

Figure 5.6   Two-tier application functions.

Three-Tier Applications

Just as two-tier applications consist of two components residing on two computers, three-tier applications consist of three components—a client application, an application server application, and a database server application—residing on three separate computers. Figure 5.7 shows the functions of the three-tier applications.

The client application provides GUI and presentation logic functions.

The application server also supplies business logic and data access logic functions.

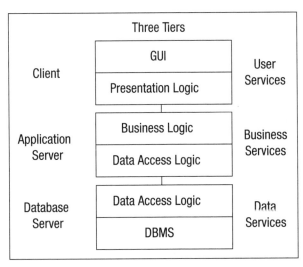

Figure 5.7   Three-tier application functions.

ActiveX components that use MTS reside on the application server. The database resides on the database server. The database server provides data access logic and database management system functions.

N-Tier Applications

While three-tier applications provide three services on three machines, *n*-tier applications are Internet/intranet applications that provide the three services on three or more computers. Figure 5.8 shows the functions of *n*-tier applications.

The client computer includes a browser and user services. The *browser* can be Microsoft Internet Explorer, Netscape Communicator, or another third-party browser. Figure 5.9 shows an example of an Internet/intranet application.

User Services run on the client but are stored on the application/Web server. User services include:

➤ **Hypertext Markup Language (HTML)** Pages that include forms and form elements (supported by most types of browsers). Some browsers support different HTML elements.

➤ **Dynamic HTML (DHTML)** Pages that include forms, form elements, ActiveX components, and scripts (supported by Microsoft Internet Explorer and Netscape Navigator).

➤ **Active Server Pages (ASP)** Pages that include running server-side scripts, using an IIS Web server (supported by all types of browsers).

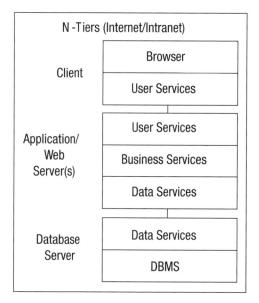

Figure 5.8 *N*-tier application functions.

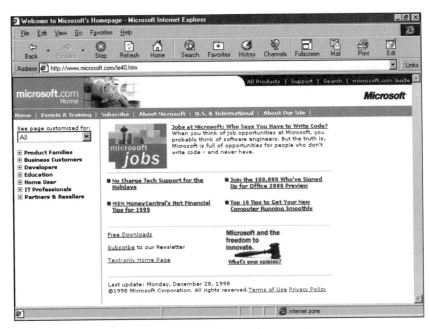

Figure 5.9   Example of an Internet/intranet application.

The application/Web server provides user, business, and data services. (Although the client executes user services, the server stores these services.)

The functions on the application Web server communicate through a Web server to ActiveX components or through MTS to ActiveX components. Figure 5.10 shows the different Microsoft technologies utilized through IIS. This server stores the Internet/intranet applications, HTML forms, and ActiveX components.

The browser handles all requests for services through IIS and ASP. IIS and ASP handle connectivity to the database through data access components. To support transaction processing, you create special ActiveX components that you access through ASP in MTS. Chapter 9 explains how to create MTS ActiveX components using Visual Basic. You can use MTS components to access the database using data access components (e.g., ADO). Also, using IIS and ASP, you can use MSMQ alone or with MTS to create scalable, fault-tolerant applications. Chapter 9 explains how to use MSMQ to create fault-tolerant, scalable applications. Microsoft provides many mechanisms for creating distributed applications. Evaluate each technology and decide which one is best for you. Refer to Chapter 4 for details.

The database server provides data services and database management system functions.

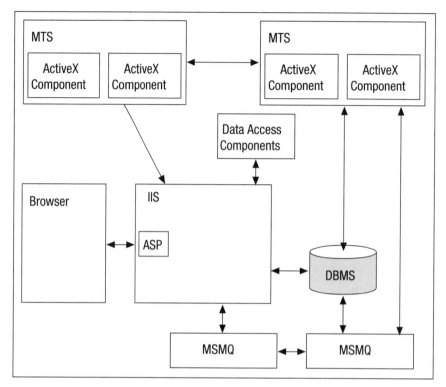

Figure 5.10 Internet/intranet applications via IIS.

Collaborative Applications

A *collaborative application* collects, organizes, distributes, and tracks vital information so groups can easily work together. Once you make an application public (by storing it in a public folder on a network, for example), it becomes a collaboration, even if you designed it for personal use. An effective collaboration application uses an environment that streamlines workflow so that colleagues can interact efficiently, find and share information, collaborate on documents, and publish information to the company intranet or Internet. Applications for workflow and sales automation, document collaboration and publishing, email scheduling, and discussion and news groups are examples of collaborative applications.

Console Applications

Console applications are text-based applications that interact with the user from the command line. Users type on the keyboard to enter text commands, which appear on the console. Examples of console applications are FTP and Telnet. Before GUIs were developed, all applications ran at the command line. If you need to create a simple application and do not want to maintain the overhead of GUI applications, then console applications are a good choice. Otherwise, console applications are obsolete and should not be used in developing user applications.

Choosing The Right Application Type

The previous sections discussed the different types of applications in the marketplace. You decide when to use which application type and for what scenario. Table 5.2 illustrates different scenarios and possible solutions.

Table 5.2   Scenarios and potential solutions.

	Scenario	Solution	Cost And Design Trade-Offs
Single-user	Secretary needs an application that tracks his working hours and whom to charge for those hours.	Single-tier application. The secretary needs an application that runs only on his machine.	Two-, three-, and n-tier solutions are not cost-effective for a single user.
Small group	A manager needs to track his employees, the number of hours they work, and the customers charged. His group never will be larger than 10 employees.	Two-tier application. The load can be handled on a single server without any problems. The system will not grow; therefore this solution is the best for this situation.	Three-tier and n-tier solutions require a minimum of three machines, which for small teams is not cost-effective. Also, dedicated support personnel are usually not an option for small groups.
Large or growing group	A manager needs to track her employees, the number of hours they work, and the customers charged. This manager works with hundreds of employees. The manager hopes to sell this application to other departments in the future.	A two-tier application is not adequate for a large number of users. The load is handled all on a single server and will become a bottleneck in the future if the user population grows.	If managers try to ease the bottleneck by adding RAM and hard disk space, administrative costs could spiral exponentially.

(continued)

Table 5.2 Scenarios and potential solutions *(continued).*

Scenario	Solution	Cost And Design Trade-Offs
	A three-tier solution is adequate. It allows components to be distributed across many servers; therefore if a server becomes a bottleneck, the administrator can move components to different servers. This solution is very flexible.	The three-tier solution requires that an application be installed either manually or automatically onto a client machine. This means more support personnel are involved, which adds more administrative costs in managing the system.
	An n-tier solution is also adequate. It lets you distribute components across many servers, and lets people use browsers and Web servers. This infrastructure is already in place in most businesses, making this the most flexible solution.	The n-tier solution requires you to store the application on the Web server, where everyone has access via a browser. Changes to the program are published directly on the server, and the browsers automatically use the changed application the next time it is accessed. This results in lower administrative costs in managing this system.

When you create applications that run on single-, two-, three-, or *n*-tiers, you will use the three-services approach to developing software. You can emulate the tiers on a single machine for development purposes. It is not recommended in practice to emulate the tiered approach on a single machine in a production environment, unless you are building a small application. If the environment grows, you must move these components to different machines.

As you can see, a three-tier or *n*-tier solution is not appropriate for all types of scenarios. A single-tier solution is adequate for single-user applications. A two-tier solution is adequate for small groups. A three-tier or *n*-tier application is best for large user groups that require maximum flexibility in arranging application components.

For example, consider the case of CTIS, the system college professors and students use to report and check course information, including grades and assignments. CTIS needs extreme flexibility in its solution for a large number of users. Because CTIS is available on a campus network and the Internet to a large group of users, and because it is updated weekly, it needs the flexibility that an *n*-tier application can offer.

LOGICAL DESIGN OVERVIEW

In the last section, you surveyed deployment techniques in system development. You also saw the different services of an application. By understanding how an application is deployed, you gain an appreciation for the complexity involved in designing and creating a system. You will revisit these techniques as you are designing the system architecture of CTIS.

Your next step is the logical design which, along with the conceptual design and physical design, is part of the planning phase. The logical design process consists of the following tasks (not necessarily in order). Each task is explained in detail in the following pages.

➤ Identify objects, services, attributes, and interfaces and define the composition of the product

➤ Define the business rules

➤ Create the UI prototypes

➤ Create the logical data model

➤ Create the logical design with a tool such as Microsoft Visual Modeler

➤ Validate, test, and redesign

Identifying Objects, Services, Attributes, And Interfaces, And Defining The Composition

The logical design defines the parts of the system, the organization of the parts, and the relationship of the parts. Figure 5.11 shows the system hierarchy. The term that UML uses for this breakdown of the system into subsystems and parts is *packages*.

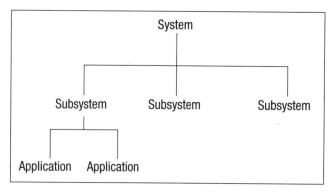

Figure 5.11 The system hierarchy.

At the top of the hierarchy is the complete system. The system consists of subsystems, and the subsystems consist of applications. The system, subsystems, and applications are all modules. *Modules* are groups of services (operations) and data, and include objects, services, attributes, and interfaces. Figure 5.12 shows the system hierarchy for CTIS.

In this illustration, the system is CTIS. The subsystems are course management, student management, grades management, and assignment management. Each subsystem defines the functions for each application.

While you are determining the subsystems, you should consider the following concepts:

➤ **Abstraction: Classification** Classifying objects that have similar attributes and services into a generic object. For example, an animal's attributes include eyes, ears, nose, and four legs. When you see a dog, you classify it as an animal because it shares these attributes.

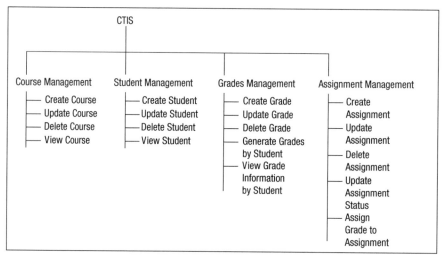

Figure 5.12 The system hierarchy for CTIS.

➤ **Encapsulation** Hiding attributes and operations from the outside world. Interfaces supply access to the object.

➤ **Cohesion** Cohesion concerns how closely related attributes and services are to each other. For example, you would not want to create a single object that is really two distinct objects. For example, if you create a single object that consists of car attributes and human attributes, then you could not change just the human attributes without affecting the car attributes. If the human attributes change, the whole object changes. The idea is to create objects that have attributes and operations that belong to a single logical idea. A single object that contains multiple attributes and operations that do not relate to each other has low cohesion, which is not good. You strive for high cohesion in object design, whereby all attributes and operations relate to each other, not to multiple things.

➤ **Coupling** Coupling concerns how closely related the external interfaces are to each other. Developers need loose coupling to allow the designer the freedom to develop solutions. For example, you need to support multiple user interface designs. You want to keep the interfaces flexible in order to support all kinds of interfaces. If you only support one type of interface, then you have tight coupling, which means you have to design a new object for every new interface. The goal is to design an object that can be used by all types of interfaces.

➤ **Replaceable implementation** The internal structure of the object should be able to change without affecting the entire system and the object's interface. For example, let's say you are using Microsoft Access for a DBMS, but need to change to SQL Server. If the object's implementation is hidden from the external world, then changes to the internal structure do not affect the system.

➤ **Composition** and **customization** Using the objects in different arrangements can solve a variety of problems. For example, CTIS expects that the instructors calculate student grades. From the instructors' perspective, the objects needed would be students and grades. They don't need instructor objects. This requires one arrangement of objects. If the requirements change to allow the system administrator to calculate students' grades, the arrangement of objects will also change. Since a system administrator needs to know about instructors, the objects needed would be instructors, students, and grades. In this case, the system administrator needs to know more information than an instructor needs. This ability to support the different composition of objects is important in the logical design. The system administrator needs to know the instructor, the students, and the grades, in order to calculate grades. The instructor needs to know only the students and the grades. The two different views of object composition depend upon the user and the requirements of the system.

A well-designed system logically classifies objects, encapsulates its operations, and has high cohesion, loose coupling, replaceable implementation, and a flexible composition. Keep these objectives in mind when designing the objects in your system.

The first step in designing objects is to identify them. Nouns used in the Use Case scenarios are clues for identifying objects. For example, in CTIS, instructor, student, class, schedule, assignments, and grades are examples of nouns. But nouns can also identify a role, organizational entity, system, or subsystem, such as manager, vice president, and accounting department. So look for only nouns in their simplest form that do not represent a role, organizational entity, system, or subsystem. For classification purposes, you can use those nouns that contain other nouns, such as an accounting department, which is a container for accountants, secretaries, and cost analysts.

A level of abstraction higher than an object is a class. A *class* describes the attributes, operations, and interfaces of an object. An object is an instance or implementation of a class. For example, Keith, an object, inherits all the features of the **person** class. Figure 5.13 shows the UML representation of a class.

The first compartment is the name of the class. The second compartment is the list of attributes and associated data types. The third compartment is the list of services and their arguments. Services are the minimum capability of a class. An attribute shows an initial value, which is the default value the attribute takes on. In the previous section, you learned that an object needs an interface to the outside world and also needs to encapsulate attributes and services. The visibility of the class attributes or services (operations) is one of the following:

➤ **+ (Public)** The + defines the interface of the class, which is what the outside world uses to access the class.

➤ **# (Protected)** The # defines the attributes and/or operations visible to any subclasses.

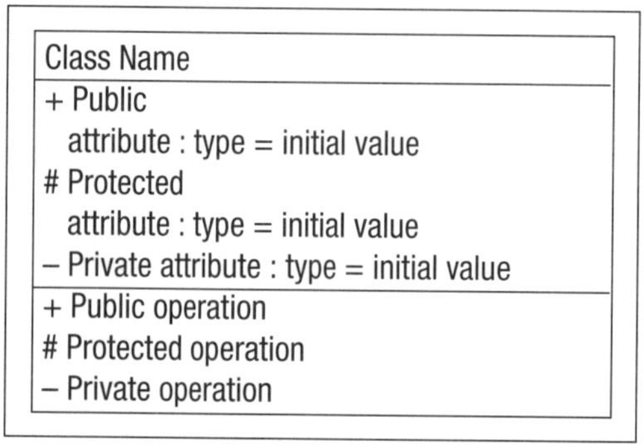

```
┌─────────────────────────────────────────┐
│ Class Name                               │
├─────────────────────────────────────────┤
│ + Public                                 │
│    attribute : type = initial value      │
│ # Protected                              │
│    attribute : type = initial value      │
│ – Private attribute : type = initial value│
├─────────────────────────────────────────┤
│ + Public operation                       │
│ # Protected operation                    │
│ – Private operation                      │
└─────────────────────────────────────────┘
```

Figure 5.13 UML representation of a class.

➤ **– (Private)** The – encapsulates the attributes and/or operations, hiding them from the outside world. This element hides the implementation of the class.

Scanning the authentication Use Case for CTIS, let's say you find the following nouns: instructor, student, username, password, and system. You determine that "**instructor**" and "**student**" are classes because they describe the attributes, operations, and interfaces of an object. You must include information on these two classes in the system. Next, define the attributes of the classes you want to include. For the **student** class, you need to track the username, last name, first name, home phone number, work phone number, email address, and password. You have already gathered this information from your Use Cases. For the instructor class, you need to track the username, last name, first name, phone number, email address, Web address, and password. The final noun, "system," is an object related to the **instructor** and **student** classes. A system noun is an organizational entity that consists of other objects. Instructor and student objects relate to the system because the system uses those objects to complete different tasks. You decide to call the system *login* because its purpose is logging in. Attributes of login are username, password, and usertype, because users must enter this information before using the system. Usertype is the type of user, which contains the value instructor or student. Services are usually the verbs in the Use Case scenarios. Login has one service called verifyuser. **Verifyuser** is a procedure that checks whether the username and password are valid. Figure 5.14 illustrates the UML class representation of instructor, student, and login.

The minus sign in front of an attribute in UML makes the attribute private. Figure 5.14 shows that the classes, attributes, and services are private. In good object-oriented design, all attributes are private. The goal of object-oriented

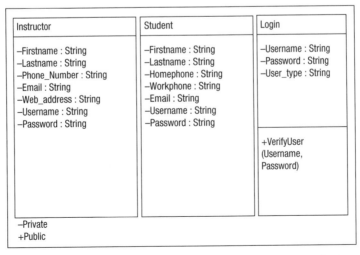

Figure 5.14 UML class representation of instructor, student, and login.

design is to encapsulate the attributes and operations. This hides the implementation of the object from the outside world. Private attributes hide the implementation of the object and give you the freedom to change the attributes when necessary. The problem is how to access these attributes. *Access modifiers* provide a special service that returns the contents of an attribute and assigns a value to the attribute. Figure 5.15 shows the addition of the get and set access modifiers on the attributes. You use a <<get>> stereotype on a service to retrieve the contents of an attribute. You use a <<set>> or <<let>> stereotype on a service to assign a value to the attribute.

Let's say you decide to focus on the login process for now. Recall from the earlier section that you need to split the logical design into user, business, and data services. Under user services, you create a login form class that contains two attributes: username and password. The services contain ok and cancel. Under business services, you use the login class from Figure 5.15, but you decide to add another interface attribute to the class. This new private attribute is called IsValid of type **Boolean**. Therefore, IsValid is true if the user is found, or false if it is not found. Also, you decide to add two events (valid and invalid) to the class. *Events* are actions an object receives, such as clicking or double-clicking. The login object raises a valid event with a usertype argument when the system finds a user, or raises an invalid event when it does not find a user. Because some applications do not support events, the IsValid interface uses an attribute to store information indicating whether or not a user exists, when an application does not support events. Applications that support events can use the **Valid** and **InValid** events interface.

Your next step in the logical design process is to determine the relationships or associations among classes in the system. The best way to show objects and their associations is through the use of UML class diagrams. These diagrams show the static structure of the system, including the attributes, services, interfaces, and associations. Figure 5.16 shows the completed login class diagram.

Instructor	Student	Login
-Firstname : String -Lastname : String -Phone_Number : String -Email : String -Web_address : String -Username : String -Password : String	-Firstname : String -Lastname : String -Homephone : String -Workphone : String -Email : String -Username : String -Password : String	-Username : String -Password : String -User_type : String
+<<get>> FirstName() : string +<<set>> FirstName(name : string) . . . +<<get>> Password() : string +<<set>> Password(pass : string)	+<<get>> FirstName() : string +<<set>> FirstName(name : string) . . . +<<get>> Password() : string +<<set>> Password(pass : string)	+Verify User (username, password) +<<get>> Username() : string +<<set>> Username(name : string) . . . +<<get>> Usertype() : string +<<set>> Usertype(pass : string)

Figure 5.15 Addition of access modifiers to classes.

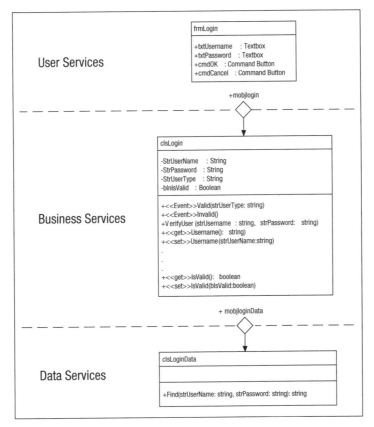

Figure 5.16   UML class diagram for login.

You should use descriptive nouns for each class name and attribute. The name should help you remember both the data type and purpose. One popular naming convention is to use the first three characters of the class name and attribute to represent the data type or type of object. Table 5.3 lists the data type and the three-character prefix for Visual Basic technologies.

Associations or relationships are represented by links in Figure 5.16. The links between the classes **frmLogin** and **clsLogin**, and between **clsLogin** and **clsLoginData** are aggregation relationships. An *aggregation* makes one class a part of another class. For example, an engine and a steering wheel are parts of a car. Class **clsLogin** is a part of the **frmLogin** class. Class **clsLoginData** is a part of the **clsLogin** class. The diamond on the link represents the whole class. The arrow on the aggregation link limits the navigation of the class. The arrow states that the **clsLogin** class is a part of the **frmLogin** class, but **frmLogin** is not a part of the **clsLogin** class. The name +objLogin on the aggregation link supplies a role name for the part **clsLogin**. Each role of an association has a multiplicity value that indicates how many objects of one class link to how

Table 5.3   Data types (also called object types) and their three-character prefixes.

Data Type	Prefix
Byte	byt
Boolean	bln
Currency	cur
Date	dtm
Double	dbl
Integer	int
Long	lng
Object	obj
Single	sng
String	str
Variant	vnt
Class	cls
Form	frm
Collection	col

many objects of another class. Figure 5.16 states that class clsLogin has one object that links to one object of class clsLoginData. Other multiplicity associations include:

➤ 1   One and only one

➤ 0..1   Zero or one

➤ M..N   From M to N (many to many)

➤ ★   From 0 to any positive integer

➤ 0..★   Same as above

➤ 1..★   From 1 to any positive integer

Once you have successfully created a class diagram, your job is to create a sequence diagram that illustrates the interaction among all classes in the system for the login process. Figure 5.17 shows the sequence diagram for the login process.

Defining The Business Rules

Your job is to create an object design from your functional specification. With an object design in place, you need to define the business rules on the classes. Table 5.4 defines the business rules for the class diagram in Figure 5.16.

The business rules define required data fields (mandatory), limits on the size, valid values, or other rules against the attributes.

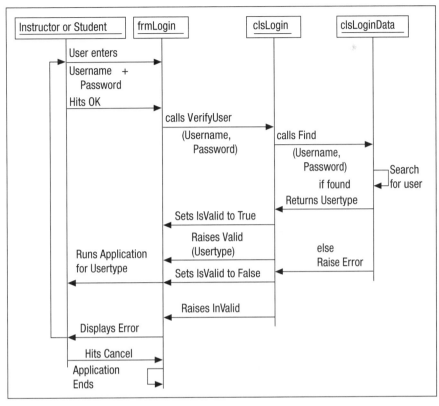

Figure 5.17   Sequence diagram of the login process.

Table 5.4 Business rules for the login process.

Class	Attribute	Business Rule
frmLogin	txtUserName	Mandatory field (cannot be blank) Maximum length is 35 characters
	txtPassword	Mandatory field Maximum length is 35 characters
clsLogin	blnIsValid	True, if username and password are found. Otherwise, false
	strUserName	Mandatory Maximum length is 35 characters. Must be unique; two users cannot have the same username
	strPassword	Mandatory Maximum length is 35 characters Must contain numbers and letters
	strUserType	Mandatory Maximum length is 10 characters Must contain Instructor, Student, or SystemAdmin

Creating The User Interface Prototypes

Your next step in the logical design process is to create the user interfaces for your class diagrams. Figure 5.16 introduces several user interface objects under user services. Figure 5.18 shows some of the important user interface objects, also called *controls*.

Table 5.5 lists the important user interface objects and their descriptions.

You are responsible for making sure that the user interface meets the needs of the user. You must also check that you follow standard GUI design guidelines.

GUI Design Tips

Although GUI design takes place during the logical design phase when you are creating the user services objects, you prototype GUIs during the physical design phase.

Sketching The User Interface

After you lay out and organize the interface, you're ready to sketch the user interface for the login process. Figure 5.19 shows the sketch of your login form.

You decide to use two labels, two text boxes, and two command buttons.

Figure 5.18 User interface objects.

Table 5.5   User interface object descriptions.

Interface Object	Description
Text box	Used to type data such as name, address, quantity
Label	Identifies the information to be typed
Check box	A box that can be checked or unchecked to select a yes/no or on/off type of option
Radio button	Usually one of a set of buttons from which only one can be selected; when you click a radio button, the one previously selected becomes unselected
Drop-down list (combo)	A space-saving list box in which the list doesn't appear until the user clicks the down arrow
List box	Used to select an option from a list of possible choices
Command button	A button that triggers an action; most interfaces have an OK and Cancel button, and some have additional buttons

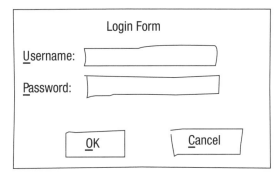

Figure 5.19   Sketch of login form.

Layout and Organization of Your Interface in the following way:

➤ Organize the user interface so that the information flows either vertically or horizontally, with the most important information always located in the upper-left corner of the screen.

➤ Group related controls together, using either white space or a frame.

➤ Either center the command buttons along the bottom of the screen or stack them in the upper-right corner. Use no more than six command buttons on a screen. Place the most commonly used command button first.

➤ Use meaningful captions in command buttons. Place the caption on one line, and use from one to three words only. Use book title capitalization for command button captions.

> ➤ Label each control on the user interface. The labels should be from one to three words only, and entered on one line. Align each label on the left, and use sentence capitalization.

> ➤ Align the labels and controls in the user interface to minimize the number of different margins.

Creating The Logical Data Model

After sketching the user interface, your next step in the logical design process is to create a logical data model from your class diagrams. A logical data model is a representation of your database structure. A *database* is an organized collection of information. Examples of databases are phone books, address books, sales information over the last year, and your stock portfolio.

Relational Databases

Relational databases store data in two-dimensional tables that consist of rows and columns, and use SQL (Structured Query Language) to insert, update, delete, and select data from tables.

A *table (relation)* is a two-dimensional structure made up of *rows (tuples)* and *columns (attributes)*.

Table 5.6 shows an example of the CITIES table that stores information about cities, states, and zip codes.

 Table names should be specified in uppercase and are plural.

A *column* or *field* is a basic category such as CITY, STATE, or ZIP. A *row* or *record* is a set of columns or a collection of related data items. In relational database management systems, records are also called tuples. The rows of the CITIES table are Dunedin, FL, 34698; Fairfax, VA, 22030; Centreville, VA, 20121; and Nashua, NH, 03062. The CITIES table has the following characteristics:

> ➤ **Each row is unique**. Because no two rows are the same, you can easily find and change information in the table.

> ➤ **The order of the rows is unimportant.** You can insert or select rows in any order.

> ➤ **The columns in a table describe, or are characteristics of, an entity**. An *entity* is a person, place, object, event, or idea for which you want to store and process information.

Table 5.6   Example of CITIES table.

CITY_ID	CITY	STATE	ZIP
1	Dunedin	FL	34698
2	Fairfax	VA	22030
3	Centreville	VA	20121
4	Nashua	NH	03062

A *key* uniquely identifies each row in a table. There are two types of keys:

Primary keys ensure that each row in a table is unique. A primary key must be minimal and must not change in value.

 Typically, a primary key is a number that is a one-up counter. Why a number? A number processes faster than an alphanumeric character. In large tables, this will make a difference.

 Column names are specified as all uppercase. Keys are named as in the following: <TABLE_NAME(singular)>_ID in all uppercase and are defined as numbers.

A *foreign key* is a column of one table that corresponds to a primary key in another table. Together, they allow two tables to join together. Tables 5.7 through 5.10 illustrate an example of primary key and foreign key relationships of the CITIES and ADDRESSES tables.

Table 5.7   CITIES primary key and foreign key.

Primary Key	Foreign Key
CITY_ID	

Table 5.8   CITIES table.

CITY_ID	CITY	STATE	ZIP
41	Dunedin	FL	34698
2	Fairfax	VA	22030
3	Centreville	VA	20121
4	Nashua	NH	03062

Table 5.9   ADDRESSES primary key and foreign key.

Primary Key	Foreign Key
ADDRESS_ID	CITY_ID

Table 5.10 ADDRESSES table.

ADDRESS_ID	STREET_ADDRESS	CITY_ID
1	6504 Sharps Dr	3
2	6506 Sharps Dr	3

The foreign key CITY_ID of the ADDRESS table is joined to the primary key CITY_ID of the CITY table. The ADDRESS table and CITY table above show how you relate two tables together. To relate two tables together, a foreign key of one table must match a primary key in another table. The tables can have a one-to-one, one-to-many, or many-to-many relationship.

Two tables have a *one-to-one relationship* when each row in one table has at most one matching row in another table. For example, there's a one-to-one relationship between the CAPITALS table and the STATES table. Table 5.11 and 5.12 illustrate a one-to-one relationship. The foreign key of the CAPITALS table, STATE_ID, matches the primary key in the STATES table.

Two tables have a *one-to-many relationship* when a row in one table has many matching rows in a second table. The second table matches only one row of the first table. Table 5.13 shows the one-to-many relationship between the STATES table and the ZIP_CODES table. The STATES table has a primary key, STATE_ID, that matches the multiple foreign key, STATE_ID, in the ZIP_CODES table.

Two tables have a *many-to-many relationship* when one row in the first table matches many rows in the second table, and one row in the second table matches many rows in the first table. Tables 5.14 through 5.15 show the many-to-many relationship between the CLASSES table and the STUDENTS table.

A many-to-many relationship is not allowed in relational databases. The tables with the many-to-many relationship require a third table called an intermediate table that stores the relationships. Tables 5.16 through 5.18 illustrate the use of

Table 5.11 CAPITALS table.

CAPITAL_ID	CAPITAL	STATE_ID
1	Richmond	1
2	Concord	2

Table 5.12 STATES table.

STATE_ID	STATE
1	VA
2	NH
3	FL

Table 5.13   ZIP_CODES table.

ZIP_CODE_ID	ZIP_CODE	STATE_ID
1	20121	1
2	20122	1

Table 5.14   CLASSES table.

CLASS_ID	CLASS	STUDENT_ID
1	Geometry	1
1	Geometry	2
3	Probability	2
3	Probability	1
5	Linear Algebra	2

Table 5.15   STUDENTS table.

STUDENT_ID	NAME
1	Keith
2	Debbie
3	Karl
4	Kathy
5	Joan

Table 5.16   CLASSES table.

CLASS_ID	CLASS
1	Geometry
3	Probability
4	Statistics
5	Linear Algebra

Table 5.17   SCHEDULES table.

SCHEDULE_ID	CLASS_ID	STUDENT_ID
1	1	1
2	1	2
3	3	2
4	3	1
5	5	2

the third table. In this case, there is a many-to-many relationship between STUDENTS and CLASSES. A third table called SCHEDULES was set up to store the relationships to provide two one-to-many relationships.

Table 5.18   STUDENTS table.

STUDENT_ID	NAME
1	Keith
2	Debbie
3	Karl
4	Kathy
5	Joan

Referential integrity checks the relationship of data contained in one table. Referential integrity addresses the following questions:

➤ What happens when you delete a row from a customer table that has referenced data for that customer in the invoices table?

➤ What happens when you insert a row into a table that has no primary key? Primary keys are normally NOT NULL and require something in that column.

➤ What happens when you enter string information into a number column type?

Relational Database Design

You now have the tools to create a logical data model of the login process. Follow the steps listed below when designing the logical data model.

1. List the major tables and what each table will include. Figure 5.14 shows the different objects and their attributes for the instructor, student, and login objects. When you *massage*, or translate, the objects, they become relations. Figure 5.20 shows the UML object diagram for the login process. The username and password attributes were moved to the users class.

2. Add the primary keys and the foreign keys, and then change the names to follow standard naming conventions of the object model. Figure 5.21 shows the logical data model that adds a primary key to the INSTRUCTORS, STUDENTS, and USERS tables and changes the names.

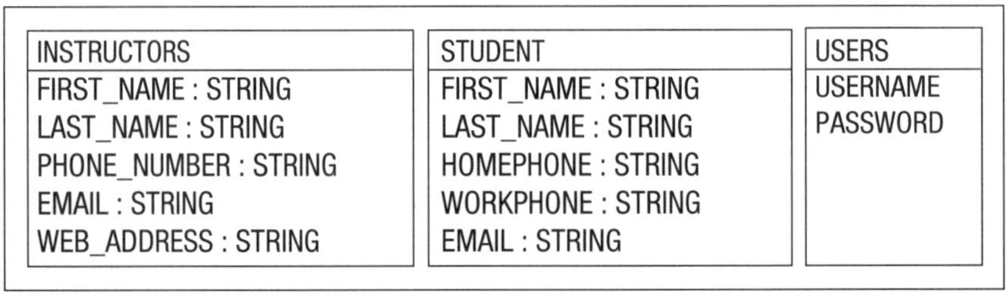

INSTRUCTORS	STUDENT	USERS
FIRST_NAME : STRING	FIRST_NAME : STRING	USERNAME
LAST_NAME : STRING	LAST_NAME : STRING	PASSWORD
PHONE_NUMBER : STRING	HOMEPHONE : STRING	
EMAIL : STRING	WORKPHONE : STRING	
WEB_ADDRESS : STRING	EMAIL : STRING	

Figure 5.20   Logical data model (UML object diagram) of the login process.

3. *Normalize* the data, which means eliminating redundant information and other problems with database design from the logical data model. There are three normal forms to help remove problems with database design:

➤ **First normal form** A table is in first normal form if all columns in the table contain atomic values, which means a column contains only one item of data. For example, if the INSTRUCTORS table has a FULL_NAME column name, then break the FULL_NAME into FIRST_NAME and LAST_NAME columns.

➤ **Second normal form** A table is in second normal form if it is in first normal form and every column in the table depends on the entire key, not just part of the key. For example, a table might contain a first name, last name, and phone number. The primary key for this table is on first name and last name. This causes a problem when you add a second phone number for a person with a last name and first name— you can't, because first name and last name must be unique.

You evaluate your data model and determine that you could separate the phone numbers from the email and Web addresses in the INSTRUCTORS and STUDENTS table. But you cite the reason explained in Step 4 below for not breaking up the tables.

➤ **Third normal form** A table is in third normal form if it is in first and second normal forms and if every column in the table depends on the entire primary key, and none of the non-key columns depend on each other. For example, let's say you create a table that has first name, last name, job title, and pay rate as the columns, and your company pay rates depend on job titles. This table would be a problem. You would need to create a table of job titles and pay rates and another table for employees, because pay rates depend on job titles, NOT on the employee name.

You decide to cite the reason explained in Step 4 below for not touching your data model.

4. Evaluate your normalization and consider denormalizing for performance. For example, separating the phone number, email, and Web address would create unnecessary extra tables.

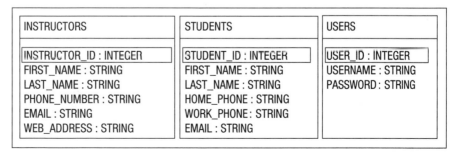

INSTRUCTORS	STUDENTS	USERS
INSTRUCTOR_ID : INTEGER	STUDENT_ID : INTEGER	USER_ID : INTEGER
FIRST_NAME : STRING	FIRST_NAME : STRING	USERNAME : STRING
LAST_NAME : STRING	LAST_NAME : STRING	PASSWORD : STRING
PHONE_NUMBER : STRING	HOME_PHONE : STRING	
EMAIL : STRING	WORK_PHONE : STRING	
WEB_ADDRESS : STRING	EMAIL : STRING	

Figure 5.21   Updated logical data model.

5. Create associations between the tables in the logical data model. Figure 5.22 shows the addition of the relationships between tables.

6. The relationships among the USERS and INSTRUCTORS and STUDENTS tables are one-to-one relationships. You add two foreign keys, INSTRUCTOR_ID and STUDENT_ID to the USERS table.

7. Determine the referential integrity (business rules) on your logical data model. Table 5.19 defines the business rules on your logical data model.

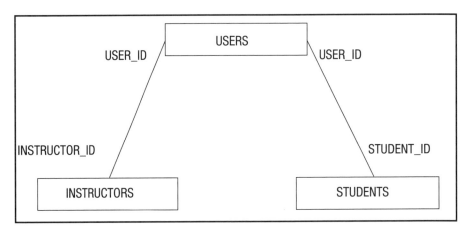

Figure 5.22   Logical data model relationships.

Table 5.19   Business rules against the logical data model.

Relation	Column	Business Rule
USERS		For every user, there must be at least one instructor or student
	USERNAME	Mandatory Maximum length is 35 characters
	PASSWORD	Mandatory Maximum length is 35 characters
INSTRUCTORS	INSTRUCTOR_ID	Mandatory Must be a one-up counter
	FIRST_NAME	Mandatory Maximum length is 35 characters
	LAST_NAME	Mandatory Maximum length is 35 characters
	PHONE_NUMBER	Mandatory Maximum length is 10 characters
	E-MAIL	Maximum length is 200 characters
	WEB_ADDRESS	Maximum length is 200 characters

(continued)

Table 5.19 Business rules against the logical data model *(continued)*.

Relation	Column	Business Rule
STUDENTS		HOME_PHONE or WORK_PHONE must be filled in
	STUDENT_ID	Mandatory Must be a one-up counter
	FIRST_NAME	Mandatory Maximum length is 35 characters
	LAST_NAME	Mandatory Maximum length is 35 characters
	HOME_PHONE	Maximum length is 10 characters
	WORK_PHONE	Maximum length is 10 characters
	E-MAIL	Maximum length is 200 characters

Implementing The Class Diagrams Using Microsoft Visual Modeler

Visual Modeler is an object-oriented analysis and design tool for creating UML class diagrams and generating the application framework in either Visual C++ or Visual Basic. It bridges the gap between object-oriented analysis and design and coding applications. Visual Modeler provides support for *round-trip engineering*, the ability to reverse-engineer Visual C++ or Visual Basic or to generate Visual C++ and Visual Basic code. Figure 5.23 illustrates the round-trip engineering support for Visual Basic.

Visual Modeler contains a model editor that allows you to build UML class diagrams. The analysis and design (A&D) Model generates Visual Basic Code through its code generation utility. The Visual Basic source code filters through

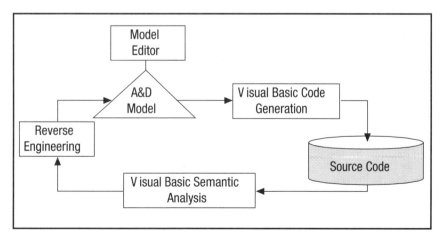

Figure 5.23 Visual Modeler round-trip engineering process.

a Visual Basic Semantic Analysis process and the Reverse Engineering tool to generate an A&D Model. Thus, the term used is round-trip engineering.

The design process allows a developer to generate an application framework to start coding. Once the code is completed, the developer can reverse-engineer the code to keep the model and the code up to date. The biggest issue with most modeling tools has been the lack of support for keeping a model up to date after the code is completed.

The Visual Modeler Environment

Visual Modeler lets you create models by adding new UML class diagrams, component diagrams, and deployment diagrams to define your model. You use class diagrams during the logical design phase. You use component diagrams during the physical design phase. You use deployment diagrams during the physical design phase to show where the components will reside. You can add, edit, or delete classes, attributes, and services to or from your diagram. You can also add new diagrams or edit old diagrams. Models then can be code-generated, and redesigned from Visual Modeler to either Visual C++ or Visual Basic. The Visual Modeler environment is made up of several windows in which you can perform your modeling tasks. Figure 5.24 illustrates the Visual Modeler environment.

These windows have several purposes:

➤ **Title bar**   Contains the name of the file and the name of the current diagram.

➤ **Menu bar**   Contains commands used to create, edit, delete, and generate code, and to reverse-engineer existing code, in Visual Modeler models.

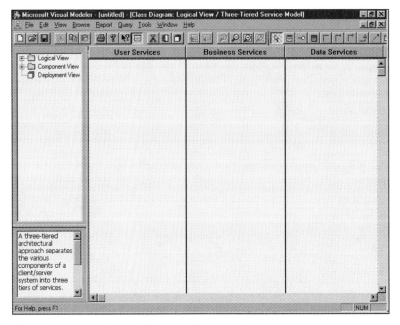

Figure 5.24   Visual Modeler environment.

➤ **Toolbar** Contains buttons providing quick access to menu commands. Visual Modeler can display the standard toolbar, diagram toolbox, documentation window, browser window, and diagram window. You can hide the toolbars and windows by selecting the View menu, and then checking only the toolbars and windows you want to display.

➤ **Browser window** Shows all the packages, objects, attributes, and services in a hierarchical fashion. The interface is similar to the folder tree of Windows Explorer. Click the right mouse button in this window to create new packages, objects, attributes, services, and associations.

➤ **Documentation window** Displays the documentation or specification of a package, object, attribute, service, or association as you supply it.

➤ **Diagram window** Provides the three-tier application model, which allows you to create and edit UML class diagrams. This is where you add your classes, attributes, services, and associations.

When Visual Modeler starts, it creates a new model with two top-level packages, Logical View and Component View. It also creates a deployment diagram in the Browser window. The Diagram window defaults to the three services of the application model of the Logical View package.

Creating, Opening, And Saving Model Diagrams

The diagrams in a model don't save themselves automatically. Rather, you must save these diagrams, using the File menu or the corresponding toolbar buttons. The File menu includes four commands that create, open, and save the model.

The New and Open commands create a new model and open an existing model, respectively. The Save and Save As commands save a model and assign a new file name, respectively.

Because Visual Modeler does not automatically save the model, remember to choose the Save command to save the model regularly. Also, it is a good idea to keep a backup copy of your models in case your current model becomes corrupted or is accidentally deleted. Too many people lose days and weeks of hard work because they do not maintain current backups.

When creating Visual Modeler diagrams, it is a good idea to use Visual Source Safe to track the different versions of the models. You will learn to use Visual Source Safe in Chapter 7.

Visual Modeler's models have a unique three-letter file extension (.mdl).

To open an existing Visual Modeler model file:

1. Click the Start button on the taskbar. Point to Programs|Microsoft Visual Studio 6.0|Microsoft Visual Studio 6.0 Enterprise Tools and then click Microsoft Visual Modeler. The location of Microsoft Visual Modeler on the Start menu may vary depending on where it was installed on your system. The Microsoft Visual Modeler environment screen appears.

2. Click Open from the File menu. Use the Look in: combo box to locate the Chapter_05 folder on the CD. The model filename course appears. Click the file and click Open to load the model.

3. Click the Maximize button on the diagram window to make it full size.

Once you load a model file, you can add classes, attributes, services, and associations to the class diagram. You can also create a new model file and create the classes, attributes, services, and associations. The New command on the File menu creates a new model.

To create and save a model:

1. Click New on the File menu. If a dialog box appears asking you whether or not to save changes, click No.

2. When the new model appears, point to Create, and then click Class on the Tools menu. The mouse cursor turns into a cross.

3. In the Business Services section of the Diagram Window, click the left mouse button. A class element appears with the NewClass name highlighted.

4. Change the name to clsLogin and click the left mouse button in the white space of the window.

5. Click Save on the File menu. The Save As dialog box appears. Use the Look in combo box to locate the Chapter_05 folder. In the File name text box, type in the file name createsave. Click Save to save the model.

Exploring Help

Visual Modeler provides an extensive Help system that documents all the menu commands and class diagram elements you can use in your models. The Visual Modeler Help system has the same characteristics as other Windows Help systems.

Click the Visual Modeler Help Topics command on the Help menu to open the Help Topics dialog box. Highlight an object and then press the F1 key to see context-sensitive help. The Help Topics dialog box includes up to three tabs:

➤ **Contents** Provides a table of contents. The contents list books, or major topics. Each book contains other books or reference pages. Double-click a page to open a Help topic.

➤ **Index** Lists keywords for finding Help topics. It contains a text box where you can enter keywords to search for. As you type characters, the index matches the text. Double-click a topic name to see that Help topic. You can also find keywords by using the vertical scroll bar.

➤ **Find** Lets you search for specific words and phrases in help topics.

The Visual Modeler Help system is an invaluable resource when you are modeling systems.

Creating Classes, Attributes, Services, And Associations

5

To use Visual Modeler to create classes and add attributes, services, and associations to an existing model, use the Create command on the Tools menu. The Create submenu includes the following options for creating UML class diagrams:

➤ **Class** Select this command to create UML classes. When the mouse pointer changes to a cross, you can place the object in any of the three services by clicking the left mouse button. You can then accept or change the name of the class.

Visual Basic generates a class module when using a class.

➤ **Class Utility** Select this command to create a set of methods that provide additional functions for classes.

Visual Basic generates a code module when using a class utility.

➤ **Association** Select this command to create a bidirectional semantic connection between two classes. This semantic connection creates a relationship between classes on a class diagram.

➤ **Aggregation** Select this command to create a whole/part relationship between two classes. You can restrict navigation to either bidirectional (no arrow) or unidirectional (with arrow).

➤ **Generalization** Select this command to classify one class as the parent and another class as the child.

➤ **Package** Select this command to group similar classes into one package. You can use this to specify the subsystems of your system.

Select the Package command to logically segment parts of the model. Visual Basic and Visual C++ ignore packages during code generation.

➤ **Note and Note Anchor** Select these commands to supply a note to a class and to connect a note to the element it affects, respectively. You will use this to clarify the elements on a class diagram.

➤ **Text** Select this commend to add a title, subtitle, or other notes directly to the model. You will use this to label important parts of the model.

After the classes are on the page, you can use the browser to find the class of choice and double-click to add attributes and services (or properties and methods, as Visual Modeler calls them), or you can double-click directly on the class of choice. Figure 5.25 shows the Class Specification dialog box for the **clsLogin** class.

The Class Specification dialog box shows several tabs on the window. Each tab specifies a specific purpose in designing classes.

➤ **General** Shows the class name, any stereotypes (Class Module is common in Visual Basic), and any documentation (i.e., comments).

➤ **Methods** Enables you to add, update, and delete class methods. Right-click to insert a method in the grid control (a spreadsheet-like data entry section). Use the Methods tab to add stereotypes to the methods, the signature (name) of the method, and the return type of the method. Double-click a method in the grid (or list) section to see the Method Specification dialog box. Figure 5.26 shows the Method Specification dialog box.

Use the General tab on the Method Specification dialog box to select a name, return type, stereotype, an export control, and supply documentation of a method. By selecting the Argument tab, you can add arguments to the method. Click OK or Cancel to return to the Class Specification dialog box with the Methods tab selected.

➤ **Properties** Allows you to add, update, and delete class attributes. Right-click to insert a property. You can add stereotypes to the methods, the name

Figure 5.25   Class Specification dialog box.

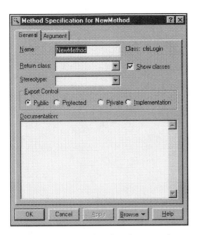

Figure 5.26   Method Specification dialog box.

of the property, the data type, and the initial value of the attribute. Double-click a property in the list to see the Property Specification dialog box, shown in Figure 5.27.

The Properties Specification dialog box allows you to enter or select the name, data type, initial value, export control, and documentation of a property.

➤ **Relations** Allows you to update and delete class relations and change the role name of the relation. Double-click a relation in the list, and the Association Specification dialog box appears, as shown in Figure 5.28.

You can change the association name and the roles on the links, and create documentation for the association.

First create associations on the diagram, then use the Relations tab to update or delete information.

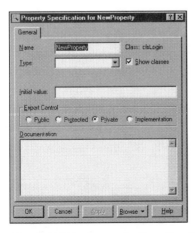

Figure 5.27   Property Specification dialog box.

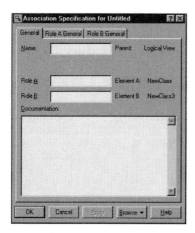

Figure 5.28 Association Specification dialog box.

You must use the Class Specification dialog box or the browser to remove properties, methods, relations, and classes from the diagram. You cannot select a class and/or association on the diagram and remove it. (Visual Modeler only removes the graphic from the screen, not from the model.)

To open an existing Visual Modeler model file:

1. Click Open from the File menu. Use the Look In combo box to locate the Chapter_05 folder. The model filename createsave appears. Click the file and click Open to load the model. Save changes when prompted.

2. Click the Maximize button on the diagram window to make it full size, if necessary.

At this point, your model contains a single class called **clsLogin**. You need to add more classes, and some attributes, services, and associations, for this model to have meaning.

To create a new class and associate it with another class:

1. Click the Class element on the toolbox. Your mouse pointer changes to a cross. Click the data services section. A new class appears with the class name highlighted. Change the class name to **clsLoginData**. Click the white space of your model.

2. Click the Aggregation element on the toolbox. Your mouse pointer changes to an up arrow. Click the clsLoginData class and hold down the left mouse button. Drag the mouse to the clsLogin class and release the mouse button.

3. Double-click the aggregation you just created and add the name objLoginData to the Role A text box. Click the OK button.

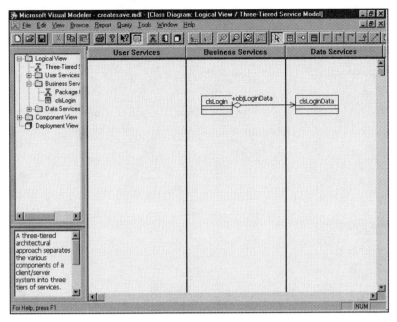

Figure 5.29   Creating a new class with an association.

4. Click the objLoginData role name and drag it slightly to the right. The results are shown in Figure 5.29.

To add properties and methods to a class:

1. Double-click the **clsLogin class**. Visual Modeler's Class Specification dialog box appears with the class name highlighted.

2. Click the Methods tab, and then add a public Valid method with a stereotype of Event with a single argument, **strUserType**. Click OK.

3. Click the Properties tab, and then add a private property **strUserName** of type **String**. Click OK.

4. Save the model. Refer to Figure 5.30 to add the remaining properties and methods to **clsLogin** and **clsLoginData** as shown in the figure.

Validating, Testing, And Redesigning The Logical Design

Once your model is complete, the next step in the logical design process is to validate, test, and redesign your object models. You decide to schedule a logical design review with the following people:

➤ **Reviewers** Reviewers evaluate the design in detail, log errors and issues, and attend design reviews to suggest changes.

➤ **Moderator** The moderator keeps the group focused on logging issues and suggestions, not on fixing problems.

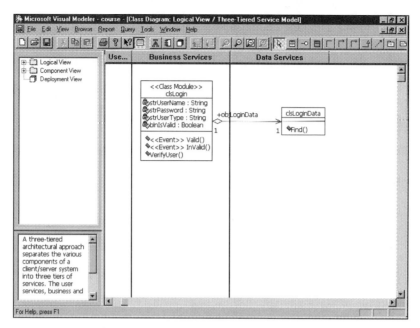

Figure 5.30   Adding properties and methods to a class.

➤ **Recorder** The recorder documents issues and suggestions. This person is responsible for reporting on the review.

The purpose of the design review is to validate the logical design among your team members, diagnose problems with the design, train fellow team members on your part of the project, detect issues with the requirements and catch flaws early in the process.

After the design review, your job is to redesign your logical design and hold another logical design review for approval.

Chapter Summary

During the planning phase, you complete the conceptual, logical, and physical design of a system. The three distinct design views evolve over time. Development teams must work from the conceptual design to the logical design to the physical design, to ensure that the system meets all the users' needs.

This chapter presented the essential techniques in logical design. The first part of the chapter illustrated the different application types (single-tier, two-tier, three-tier, and *n*-tier) for creating the information system. Logical design consists of three services: user, business, and data services. The next part of the chapter showed how to identify objects, services, attributes, and interfaces, define the business rules, create the user interface prototypes, create the logical data model, and validate, test, and redesign the logical design. You can use Microsoft Visual Modeler to create the logical design. Visual Modeler is used for round-trip engineering of information systems.

You need to consider the logical design carefully. Logical design affects the following:

➤ **Performance** Design your system using the three services and tiers, or it could be slow and sluggish, which irritates users. A properly designed system can adapt to changes in performance by increasing RAM and hard disk space or by moving components to other machines. System administrators monitor the system and adjust settings as necessary. Unfortunately, monitoring performance is currently a manual process and requires manual intervention.

➤ **Extensibility** Remember that software development is a process of change, and you need to keep the logical design flexible to allow for future growth. The services and tier models assist in allowing for extensibility.

➤ **Scalability** Make sure that when you are at the logical design stage, your system can scale as the need of the system grows. Component development assists in allowing systems to scale.

➤ **Availability** Make sure that the logical design makes your system available on an as-needed basis. All tiers let your system be available as much as possible.

➤ **Security** Consider security a top issue while you are designing the system, to make sure that people using the system cannot access data they do not have a right to know. Using an integrated security approach that incorporates OS security, application security, and database security is crucial in making your systems secure. You will investigate different security mechanisms during the development phase.

As you are working in your team, make sure that each item above is carefully thought out and that some sort of process is in place to handle such issues. Being proactive is better than finding a problem when it is too late. The next step in the development process is to create the physical design for the information system.

REVIEW QUESTIONS

1. The MSF Application model consists of the following services. Choose all that apply.

    a. User

    b. Interface

    c. Data

    d. Business

2. _____ applications define the Application model services on a single machine.
   a. N-tier
   b. Three-tier
   c. Single-tier
   d. none of the above

3. _____ presents a graphically consistent look and feel to the user.
   a. Application logic
   b. A GUI
   c. Presentation logic
   d. none of the above

4. When a program collects information from the user, it uses a special window called a(n) _____.
   a. SDI window
   b. MDI window
   c. dialog box
   d. none of the above

5. Notepad is an example of a(n) _____ application.
   a. dialog
   b. SDI
   c. MDI
   d. none of the above

6. Word is an example of a(n) _____ application.
   a. MDI
   b. dialog
   c. SDI
   d. none of the above

7. _____ use the concept of a work area to manage the objects they contain.
   a. Projects
   b. SDI applications
   c. MDI applications
   d. Workspaces

8. _____ logic deals with the interaction of the application with the user.
   a. Data access
   b. Presentation
   c. Application
   d. Business

9. _____ logic defines the components, which include objects, services, attributes, and interfaces that define the business rules for the data.

   a. Data access
   b. Business
   c. Presentation
   d. Application

10. _____ logic interacts with a database management system.

   a. Presentation
   b. Application
   c. Business
   d. Data access

5

11. The _____ supplies the necessary functionality to insert, update, delete, and query information in a database.

   a. application logic
   b. presentation logic
   c. business logic
   d. DBMS

12. _____ applications split the functionality into two components: the client and the server.

   a. Single–tier
   b. Two–tier
   c. N–tier
   d. none of the above

13. _____ is a term that applies to the machine that contains the business logic.

   a. Fat
   b. Thin
   c. Medium
   d. none of the above

14. _____ applications split the functionality into three components: the client, the application server, and the database server.

   a. Single–tier
   b. Two–tier
   c. N–tier
   d. Three–tier

15. _____ applications are Internet/intranet applications that provide the three services on three or more computers.

   a. Two-tier

   b. Single-tier

   c. Three-tier

   d. *N*-tier

16. The term that UML uses for the breakdown of the system into subsystems and parts is _____.

   a. objects

   b. services

   c. classes

   d. packages

17. The _____ design defines the parts of the system, the organization of the parts, and the relationship of the parts.

   a. conceptual

   b. physical

   c. logical

   d. none of the above

18. _____ concerns how closely the attributes and services are related to each other.

   a. Abstraction

   b. Coupling

   c. Cohesion

   d. Encapsulation

19. _____ concerns how closely the external interfaces are related to each other.

   a. Abstraction

   b. Cohesion

   c. Coupling

   d. Encapsulation

20. _____ is the hiding of the attributes and operations from the outside world.

   a. Encapsulation

   b. Coupling

   c. Abstraction

   d. Cohesion

21. User interface objects are also called _____.

    a. classes

    b. objects

    c. controls

    d. none of the above

22. A(n) _____ is an organized collection of information.

    a. database

    b. object

    c. service

    d. class

23. A(n) _____ is a two-dimensional structure made up of rows and columns.

    a. service

    b. database

    c. relation

    d. attribute

24. A(n) _____ is a basic category such as CITY, STATE, and ZIP.

    a. field

    b. service

    c. relation

    d. attribute

25. A(n) _____ uniquely identifies each row in a table.

    a. field

    b. key

    c. entity

    d. relation

26. _____ ensure that each row in a table is unique.

    a. Fields

    b. Foreign keys

    c. Columns

    d. Primary keys

27. A _____ is a column of one table that corresponds to a primary key in another table.

    a. column

    b. foreign key

    c. field

    d. primary key

28. _____ is the process of eliminating redundant information and other problems with database design.

   a. Normalization

   b. Removal

   c. Normal

   d. none of the above

HANDS-ON PROJECTS

Project 5.1

Investigate the following applications and determine whether they are single-tier, two-tier, three-tier, or *n*-tier applications.

   a. Microsoft Excel

   b. Microsoft Outlook (specifically the email system)

   c. Microsoft PowerPoint

   d. The World Wide Web

   e. An application that uses MTS on an application server

   f. The FTP system

   g. The Telnet system

Project 5.2

Investigate the following applications and determine whether each is an SDI or MDI application.

   a. Microsoft Excel

   b. Microsoft PowerPoint

   c. Notepad

   d. Calculator

   e. Internet Explorer

   f. Paint

   g. Wordpad

Project 5.3

Label the parts of the window in Figure 5.31.

Project 5.4

Examine the Notepad application and explain the function of each submenu and each command in the submenus.

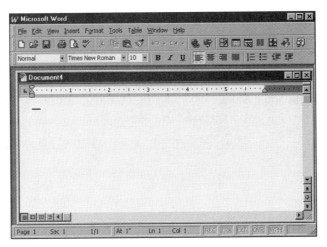

Figure 5.31 An MDI application.

Project 5.5

Compare and contrast single-tier, two-tier, three-tier, and *n*-tier applications. Explain the different functions for each type of application.

Project 5.6

Create a schedule for the logical design process and any interim milestones for course, student, grades, and assignment management subsystems.

Project 5.7

Create a class diagram in Visual Modeler for the course management subsystem from the conceptual design model (Use Case scenarios). You will be creating the business services for the course management subsystem.

a. Open the course model.

b. In the Browse menu, use the Class Diagram command to create a new class diagram and name it Course Management.

c. Identify the classes, attributes, services, and interfaces for the course management subsystem.

d. Create the object diagram.

e. Identify and create the relationships between classes in the class diagram.

f. Identify the business rules in a table like Table 5.19.

g. Save the model.

Project 5.8

Create sketches of the user interface for the course management subsystem.

a. From the class diagram, sketch forms that you need in order to enter, update, and delete data in the class diagram.

b. Sketch any other forms needed to support the requirements.

Project 5.9

Create the logical data model from the class diagram using Visual Modeler for the course management subsystem.

a. Open the course model.

b. In the Browse menu, use the Class Diagram command to create a new class diagram and name it CTIS Logical Data Model.

c. Follow the logical data model design steps as presented in the chapter.

d. Create the object diagram.

e. Identify and create the relationships between classes in the logical data model.

f. Save the model.

Project 5.10

Create a class diagram in Visual Modeler for the student management subsystem from the conceptual design model (Use Case scenarios). You will be creating the business services for the student management subsystem.

a. Open the course model.

b. In the Browse menu, use the Class Diagram command to create a new class diagram and name it Student Management.

c. Identify the classes, attributes, services, and interfaces for the student management subsystem.

d. Create the object diagram.

e. Identify and create the relationships between classes in the class diagram.

f. Identify the business rules in a table like Table 5.19.

g. Save the model.

Project 5.11

Create sketches of the user interface for the student management subsystem.

a. From the class diagram, sketch forms that you need in order to enter, update, and delete data in the class diagram.

b. Sketch any other forms needed to support the requirements.

Project 5.12

Update the logical data model from the class diagram using Visual Modeler for the student management subsystem.

a. Open the course model.

b. In the Browse menu, use the Class Diagram command to open the CTIS Logical Data Model diagram.

c. Follow the logical data model design steps as presented in the chapter.

d. Create the object diagram.

e. Identify and create the relationships between classes in the logical data model.

f. Save the model.

Project 5.13

Create a class diagram in Visual Modeler for the grades management subsystem from the conceptual design model (Use Case scenarios). You will be creating the business services for the grades management subsystem.

a. Open the course model.

b. In the Browse menu, use the Class Diagram command to create a new class diagram and name it Grades Management.

c. Identify the classes, attributes, services, and interfaces for the grades management subsystem.

d. Create the object diagram.

e. Identify and create the relationships between classes in the class diagram.

f. Identify the business rules in a table like Table 5.19.

g. Save the model.

Project 5.14

Create sketches of the user interface for the grades management subsystem.

a. From the class diagram, sketch forms that you need in order to enter, update, and delete data in the class diagram.

b. Sketch any other forms needed to support the requirements.

Project 5.15

Update the logical data model from the class diagram using Visual Modeler for the grades management subsystem.

a. Open the course model.

b. In the Browse menu, use the Class Diagram command to open the CTIS Logical Data Model diagram.

c. Follow the logical data model design steps as presented in the chapter

d. Create the object diagram.

e. Identify and create the relationships between classes in the logical data model.

f. Save the model.

Project 5.16

Create a class diagram in Visual Modeler for the assignment management subsystem from the conceptual design model (Use Case scenarios). You will be creating the business services for the assignment management subsystem.

a. Open the course model.

b. In the Browse menu, use the Class Diagram command to create a new class diagram and name it Student Management.

c. Identify the classes, attributes, services, and interfaces for the student management subsystem.

d. Create the object diagram.

e. Identify and create the relationships between classes in the class diagram.

f. Identify the business rules in a table like Table 5.19.

g. Save the model.

Project 5.17

Create sketches of the user interface for the assignment management subsystem.

a. From the class diagram, sketch forms that you need in order to enter, update, and delete data in the class diagram.

b. Sketch any other forms needed to support the requirements.

Project 5.18

Update the logical data model from the class diagram using Visual Modeler for the assignment management subsystem.

a. Open the course model.

b. In the Browse menu, use the Class Diagram command to open the CTIS Logical Data Model diagram.

c. Follow the logical data model design steps as presented in the chapter.

d. Create the object diagram.

e. Identify and create the relationships between classes in the logical data model.

DESIGNING AN INFORMATION SYSTEM PHYSICALLY

> **AFTER READING THIS CHAPTER AND COMPLETING THE EXERCISES, YOU WILL BE ABLE TO:**
>
> ➤ Define the application type (e.g., single-tier, two-tier, three-tier, or *n*-tier) for CTIS
>
> ➤ Define and describe the user interfaces in an application type
>
> ➤ Map the classes created in the logical design to components in the physical design
>
> ➤ Define the physical data model for Microsoft Access and Microsoft SQL Server
>
> ➤ Complete the project plan, the functional requirements, the risk assessment plan, and the master schedule

The development team is responsible for prototyping the user interfaces, mapping the classes created in the logical design to components in the physical design, and creating the physical database design. The physical design lays out the application environment the development team uses to estimate the schedule and finish the project plan, functional requirements, and risk assessment. During physical design, the development team determines the solution environment of the application. The physical design results in the Project Plan Approved milestone that consists of project plan, functional requirements, master schedule, and risk assessment approvals.

During physical design, you are responsible for completing the application design, project plan, functional requirements, master schedule, and risk assessment. You also need to create user interface prototypes, components, and the physical database design. Then you set up physical design reviews to validate your physical design.

CHAPTER OVERVIEW

In the last chapter, you examined the logical design process and applied it to the login process in CTIS. This chapter examines the physical design process and how to apply it to the login. You will use the component and deployment diagrams of UML to document the physical design, using Microsoft Visual Modeler.

PHYSICAL DESIGN

During the physical design part of the planning phase, you will accomplish the following tasks (you and others can complete these tasks in any order):

➤ Define the application architecture

➤ Prototype the user interfaces

➤ Determine the components from the logical design

➤ Create the physical database design from the logical database design for Microsoft Access and Microsoft SQL Server

➤ Complete the project plan, risk assessment, functional requirements, and master schedule

You can accomplish these tasks in any order that makes sense to you. You can also perform some of these tasks simultaneously.

Application Model

In the last chapter, you investigated single-tier, two-tier, three-tier, and *n*-tier application types. You decided that CTIS should use the *n*-tier application type. Chapter 5 also defined the application model as including user, business, and data services. Figure 6.1 illustrates CTIS application architecture.

The *front end* of CTIS consists of a browser, either Microsoft Internet Explorer or Netscape Communicator. To keep the user services independent of browser implementation, you can use active server pages (ASP). Most browsers do not support Visual Basic script on the client. The only way to write Visual Basic script is to use it on the server. ASPs are special Web pages containing Visual Basic scripts that run on the Web server (IIS). These scripts generate HTML you can view on the browser. On the application and Web server, you can use MTS ActiveX components, which let you manage components on the Web server or move them to another server if necessary. On the *back end*, you can use either Microsoft Access or Microsoft SQL Server. In this book, you will design for both Microsoft Access and Microsoft SQL Server, to experience the subtle differences between these database management systems. In actual practice, you need to choose one during the planning phase. ActiveX data objects (ADO) via ODBC or OLE DB will access the back end and the databases. Microsoft prefers that you use OLE DB rather than ODBC, but both are currently supported.

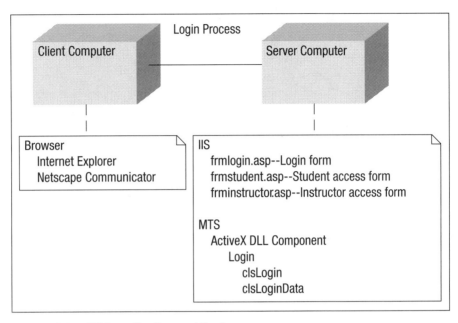

Figure 6.1   CTIS application architecture.

You can use Visual Modeler to show the above information in a deployment diagram, which describes the application and hardware components needed for the login process. A three-dimensional box represents a node in a UML deployment diagram. A *node* is a networked device. A line represents a connection between nodes.

To create a deployment diagram for the CTIS login process:

1. Click the Start button on the taskbar. Point to Programs | Microsoft Visual Studio 6.0 | Microsoft Visual Studio Enterprise Tools and then click Microsoft Visual Modeler 6.0.

2. Click Open from the File menu. Use the Look In combo box to locate the Chapter_06 folder. The model filename course appears. Click the file and click Open to load the model; maximize the window, if necessary.

3. Double-click Deployment View in the browser. A blank screen in the Diagram window appears.

4. Click the node icon on the toolbar. The mouse pointer turns into a cross. Click the diagram on the left. A three-dimensional box appears with New Node text highlighted. Change the name to Client Computer. Resize the box to see the complete name.

5. Click the node icon on the toolbar. The mouse pointer turns into a cross. Click the diagram on the right. A three-dimensional box appears with New Node highlighted. Change the name to Server Computer. Resize the box to see the complete name.

Remember, if you need to delete an object on the diagram, right-click it in the Browser window and then choose Delete.

6. Click the connection icon on the toolbar. The mouse pointer turns into an up arrow. Click the Client Computer box, and hold down the left mouse button. Drag to draw a line to the Server Computer box, and then release the mouse button. You created a logical link between the client computer and the server computer. A logical link represents the fact that the application that runs on the client connects to an application that runs on the server. They are not physically connected on the network.

7. Click the Textbox icon in the toolbar. Then, click on top of the connection line and enter Login Process.

8. Click the Note icon and then click under the Client Computer node.

9. Click the Anchor Note To Item option.

10. Click Client Computer and hold down the left mouse button. Then, drag to the Note icon and release the mouse button.

11. Click the Pointer icon, then double-click the Note icon and enter:

    Browser

    Internet Explorer

    Netscape Navigator

12. Complete the diagram to match Figure 6.2.

13. From the File menu, click Save to save the model.

When you're finished, the deployment diagram should look like Figure 6.2.

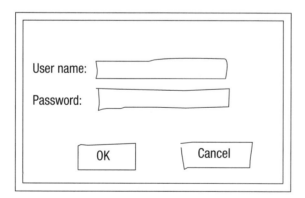

Figure 6.2   Completed deployment diagram.

Prototyping The User Interfaces

You can prototype the user interfaces during physical design using one of Microsoft's Visual Studio tools, or you can place them on storyboards—large sheets of paper bound to a board—which usually sits on an easel.

If you prototype the user interfaces with Visual Studio, you can demonstrate the user interface flow to the users even if they are in another location. Though it is best to meet face to face, you can set up electronic conferences with Microsoft NetMeeting and share the prototyped user interfaces with the users to discuss how they will work. During the conferences, the users can suggest changes to make the interface work for them.

If you prototype the user interfaces with storyboards, you can demonstrate the user interface flow to the users in the same location. Set up a meeting to discuss the interface flow with the users and ask them to suggest how to improve the interface.

Let's say you decide to use storyboards for CTIS. You invite a group of users to a conference and show them the login process. Figure 6.3 shows the login form.

ID	Task Name	Start Date	End Date	Duration	1999 Jan Feb Mar Apr May Jun
1	1.0 Envisioning Phase	1/6/99	1/12/99	4d	
2	1.1 Vision Document	1/6/99	1/6/99	1d	
3	1.2 Risk Assessment	1/7/99	1/7/99	1d	
4	1.3 Project Scope	1/8/99	1/8/99	1d	
5	1.4 Usage Scenarios	1/11/99	1/11/99	1d	
6	1.5 Vision/Scope Approved	1/12/99	1/12/99	0d	
7	2.0 Planning Phase	1/7/99	2/2/99	18d	
8	2.1 Conceptual Design	1/7/99	1/14/99	6d	
9	2.2 Logical Design	1/15/99	1/22/99	6d	
10	2.3 Physical Design	1/25/99	2/1/99	6d	
11	2.4 Risk Assessment	1/25/99	1/29/99	5d	
12	2.5 Project Schedule	1/25/99	1/29/99	5d	
13	2.6 Project Plan/Requirements Document	2/1/99	2/1/99	1d	
14	2.7 Project Plan Approved	2/2/99	2/2/99	0d	
15	3.0 Developing Phase	2/1/99	4/2/99	44d	
16	3.1 User Services	2/1/99	4/1/99	44d	
17	3.2 Business Services	2/1/99	4/1/99	44d	
18	3.3 Data Services	2/1/99	4/1/99	44d	
19	3.4 Database Implementation	2/1/99	4/1/99	44d	
20	3.5 Scope Complete/First Use	4/2/99	4/2/99	0d	
21	4.0 Stabilization Phase	3/1/99	6/3/99	68d	
22	4.1 Testing	3/1/99	6/2/99	68d	
23	4.2 Release	6/3/99	6/3/99	0d	

Figure 6.3 Storyboard view of the login form.

As you show them the login form, discuss what will happen in CTIS. The following steps occur during the login process:

1. Users launch their browser of choice and request the CTIS application on the Web server.

2. The CTIS application displays the login form.

3. Users enter their username and password.

4. CTIS verifies that the user has been added to the system.

5. If the user is a member of the system and is an instructor, the instructor functionality is displayed. If the user is a member of the system and is a student, the student functionality is displayed. Otherwise, an error message is displayed.

Packaging Components Using Microsoft Visual Modeler

The next step in the physical design is to package the classes from the logical design into components. *Components* contain one or more classes from the logical design and instructions to the development team on how to package them. The packaging options are in-process server (.dll) or out-of-process server (.exe), which are types of ActiveX components. Since you are using MTS, you use the in-process server (.dll) option. MTS runs processes as part of the MTS environment and controls resources for the in-process server. An out-of-process server controls its own resources, meaning MTS cannot manage memory as necessary.

The login process draws from user services, business services, and data services. Your goal is to create a package that allows for absolute flexibility in using different user services. You decide that the **clsLogin** business service class and the **clsLoginData** data service class will be packaged together into an Active X dll component because you are using MTS. By packaging the clsLogin and clsLoginData, you can allow CTIS to use different types of user interfaces. Use Visual Modeler to show how to create a component for the login process.

Why not choose the user service class? This class is a logical representation of an ASP Web page, and not a true class. Your job is to package classes that are closely related to each other into a single component that will be reused in other projects.

To create a component diagram for the CTIS login process:

1. Click the **+** sign next to Component View in the Browser.

2. Right-click components view in the Browser, then point to New, and click Component to create a new component. Visual Modeler creates a new

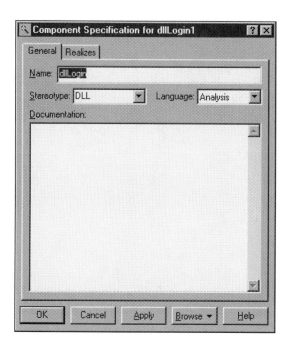

Figure 6. 4   Component Specification window.

component with the name highlighted. Change the name to
<<DLL>>dllLOGIN and press Enter.

3. Double-click the dllLogin component. The Component Specification for
the dllLogin window appears (Figure 6.4).

4. Enter the following text in the Documentation text box:

    The login component packages the business service class clsLogin and data
    service class clsLoginData.

5. Click the Realizes tab. Figure 6.5 shows the information on the Realizes
tab. The Realizes tab is for assigning logical classes to physical components.

6. Right-click clsLogin in the Realizes tab and then click Assign. A red
checkmark appears in the icon next to clsLogin.

7. Right-click clsLoginData in the Realizes tab and then click Assign. A red
checkmark appears in the icon next to clsLoginData. Figure 6.6 shows the
results of packaging clsLogin and clsLoginData into the dllLogin
component.

8. Click the OK button.

9. Save the model.

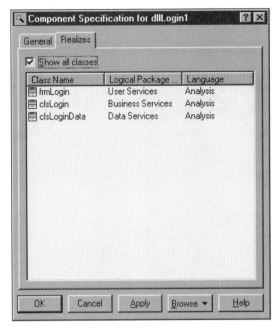

Figure 6.5 Realizes tab.

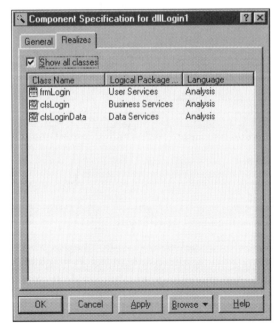

Figure 6.6 Packaging of clsLogin and clsLoginData.

Creating The Physical Data Model From The Logical Data Model

This book shows the physical design for both Microsoft Access and Microsoft SQL Server. Chapter 4 outlines the differences between Access and SQL Server and explains which DBMS is suitable for which scenario. In the real world, you use one or the other. You need to be aware of both database management systems when designing your systems.

In Chapter 5, you defined the logical data model independently of a database management system. In this chapter, you define the physical data model that depends upon the database management system you're using. You will look at the physical database design for Microsoft Access and Microsoft SQL Server. Microsoft Access, as you recall, is a personal database management system used for small databases of less than 1GB. Microsoft SQL Server is a client/server database management system used for small and large databases that require reliable and maintainable data for mission-critical applications.

Physical Database Design With Microsoft Access

As you create the physical design, consider the data types in Microsoft Access. In the logical design, you used data types that are independent of database implementation. Now your job is to convert those logical data types into data types supported by the DBMS. Table 6.1 summarizes all the field data types available, their uses, and their storage sizes.

Table 6.1   Field data types in Microsoft Access.

Data Type	Uses
Text	Use for text or combinations of text and numbers, such as names, addresses, and phone numbers. Size of text data type is up to 255 characters. A character is a byte of information. The FieldSize property determines the size of the field up to 255 bytes.
Memo	Use for lengthy text and numbers, such as notes or descriptions. Size of memo data type is up to 65,535 characters (64KB).
Number	Use for numeric data except for money (use the Currency type). The FieldSize property determines the specific Number type. The size is either 1, 2, 4, or 8 bytes. Use the long (4 bytes) FieldSize for foreign keys.
Date/Time	Use for dates and times. The size is 8 bytes.
Currency	Use for currency values and money to avoid rounding off errors during calculations. This data type is accurate to 15 digits to the left of the decimal point and 4 digits to the right. The size is 8 bytes.

An important decision in the physical design of database applications is the selection of data types. If you choose the wrong data type or field size, the system will be sluggish and you'll waste disk space. For small databases, this is not an issue. For a medium to large database, however, the lack of performance will be noticeable to you and your users.

The next step in deriving the physical database design from the logical database design is to determine the tables, the columns in each table, the data type for each column, and any constraints on the column. A *constraint* is a business rule against the column or the table. Table 6.2 illustrates the physical database design for the login process.

Recall that a *primary key* is the column that makes the rows in the table unique and is usually a one-up counter.

Recall that *normalization* is the process of splitting data up into multiple tables to remove redundant pieces of information. A *foreign key* is the column that joins two or more tables back together again.

A *NULL* value in a column contains nothing.

Table 6.2 is derived from the business rules table and the logical data model from Chapter 5.

Physical Database Design For SQL Server

In the last section, you investigated how to create the physical database design for Microsoft Access. Now you need to investigate the data types used in SQL Server. Table 6.3 summarizes the data types, their uses, and their storage sizes.

You should use varX data types when available, because they require the least amount of space on the hard disk. For example, if you want to assign your first name to a data type, assign varchar instead of char.

Table 6.3 is derived from the business rules table and the logical data model from Chapter 5.

Table 6.2 Microsoft Access physical design of the login process.

Table Field	Data Name	Field Name	Type Size	Constraint
INSTRUCTORS	INSTRUCTOR_ID	AUTONUMBER	LONG INTEGER	NOT NULL (cannot be blank)
	FIRST_NAME	TEXT	35	NOT NULL
	LAST_NAME	TEXT	35	NOT NULL
	PHONE_NUMBER	TEXT	10	NOT NULL
	E_MAIL	TEXT	255	
	URL	TEXT	255	
STUDENTS	STUDENT_ID	AUTONUMBER	LONG INTEGER	NOT NULL
	FIRST_NAME	TEXT	35	NOT NULL
	LAST_NAME	TEXT	35	NOT NULL
	HOME_PHONE	TEXT	10	Either home or work phone number must be filled in
	WORK_PHONE	TEXT	10	Either home or work phone number must be filled in
	E_MAIL	TEXT	200	
USERS	USER_ID	AUTONUMBER	LONG INTEGER	NOT NULL
	USERNAME	TEXT	35	NOT NULL
	PASSWORD	TEXT	35	NOT NULL
	STUDENT_ID	NUMBER	LONG INTEGER	FOREIGN KEY
	INSTRUCTOR_ID	NUMBER	LONG INTEGER	FOREIGN KEY
	PASSWORD	TEXT	35	NOT NULL
	STUDENT_ID	NUMBER	LONG INTEGER	**FOREIGN KEY
	INSTRUCTOR_ID	NUMBER	LONG INTEGER	**FOREIGN KEY

6

Table 6.3 Data types in SQL Server.

Data Type	Uses	Size
int	Whole numbers from –2,147,483,648 to 2,147,483,647	4 bytes
smallint	Whole numbers from –32,768 to 32,767	2 bytes
tinyint	Whole numbers from 0 to 255	1 byte
numeric(p,s)	Whole or fractional numbers from –10^38 to 10^38; p is the precision (number of digits), and s is the size (the number of decimal points)	5–17 bytes
decimal(p,s)	same as numeric	
float(n)	Whole or fractional numbers from –1.79E308 to 1.79E308	8 bytes
real	Whole or fractional numbers from –3.40E38 to3.40E38	4 bytes
char(n)	Characters (up to 8,000). n specifies the number of characters	1 byte/char
varchar(n)	Variable length characters (up to 8,000). n specifies the number of characters	1 byte/char stored
money	Currency values with accuracy to four decimal places	8 bytes
smallmoney	Currency values with accuracy to four decimal places	4 bytes
datetime	Date and time Date format: 01-JAN-1753 – 31-DEC-9999 Time format: Number of milliseconds since midnight of a given date	8 bytes
smalldatetime	Date and time Date format: 01-JAN-1753 – 31-DEC-9999 Time format: Number of minutes since midnight of given date	4 bytes
binary(n)	Binary representation (up to 8000 bytes)	n+4 bytes
varbinary(n)	Variable binary representation (up to 8000 bytes) number of bytes actually stored +4	
text and image	Text: character data up to 2 GB Image: binary data up to 2 GB	number of bytes stored
bit	boolean values (0 or 1)	1 bit
datetime	Date and time Date format: 01-JAN-1753 – 31-DEC-9999 Time format: Number of milliseconds since midnight of a given date	8 bytes

COMPLETING THE FUNCTIONAL REQUIREMENTS AND MASTER SCHEDULE, AND VALIDATING THE PHYSICAL DESIGN

In Chapters 4 and 5, you started the functional requirements with the vision, the conceptual design, and the logical design. In this chapter, in the main part of the functional requirements, you describe the candidate components with the package classes as a separate section. Add an appendix to the functional requirements for the physical database design and for the user interface prototypes.

Next, you update the master schedule with tasks in 40-hour increments. Development leads perform the top-level estimating of the project.

6

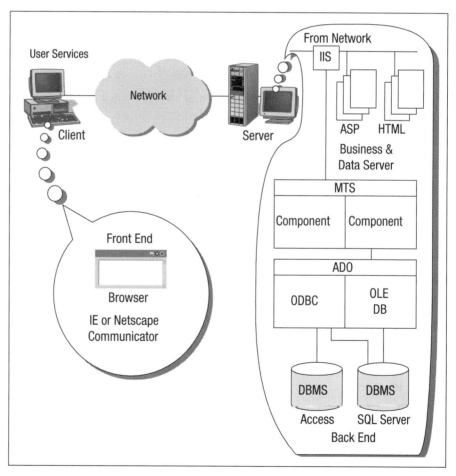

Figure 6.7   Gantt chart showing phases.

Development team members do the task-level estimating, since they are the ones who will perform the tasks. (Microsoft recommends a bottom-up approach in developing the schedule, which means letting the workers who do the job estimate the work that they do.) Each task has a measurable starting point and ending point. The ending point results in a deliverable, either a document or a section of code. Each task also has a single owner. When estimating time for a task, remember to include additional buffer time for any issues that may arise during the task. Some developers include 10 to 20 percent additional time to account for uncertainty. As first shown in Figure 4.5, Figure 6.7 shows a starting Gantt chart that includes the developing phase and the stabilization phase at a high level. You will work with the details of this schedule in Hands-On Project 6.14.

Periodically throughout the physical design process, schedule physical design reviews to allow your peers—other software engineers and system designers—to validate your physical design. These design reviews ensure that nothing is missing from the physical design. After the review, revise your physical design to incorporate comments from your peers. Two or more design reviews are normal in the software development process.

When all of the tasks are accomplished in the planning phase, this phase ends in a Project Plan Approved milestone, which signals the start of the developing phase.

CHAPTER SUMMARY

This chapter shows how to map the conceptual and logical design into a physical design. The physical design provides a layout of the application's structure and illustrates how to deploy the pieces of the application structure. It provides a framework for the development team to use when coding the application. The conceptual, logical, and physical designs are a work in process and are not considered complete after the planning phase. In fact, nothing is ever complete in software development because software always changes. For example, while coding the system, the development team may find errors in the design and in the requirements. They need to make the necessary changes in a systematic fashion and plan for changes. The goal of the planning phase is to limit the amount of change that occurs in the developing phase. A good plan limits the number of changes and helps reduce development time.

REVIEW QUESTIONS

1. A three-dimensional box represents a _____ in a UML deployment diagram.
    a. node
    b. connection
    c. note
    d. none of the above

2. A node is a(n) _____ device.
    a. NIC
    b. cabling
    c. non-networked
    d. networked

3. A _____ represents a connection in a UML deployment diagram.
    a. triangle
    b. three-dimensional box
    c. line
    d. none of the above

4. The _____ diagram shows the application and hardware components needed for the system.
    a. component
    b. class
    c. deployment
    d. none of the above

5. _____ contain one or more classes from the logical design and instructions on how to package them.
    a. Nodes
    b. Components
    c. Objects
    d. none of the above

6. Visual Modeler contains a deployment diagram to illustrate the application and hardware components needed in a system.
    a. True
    b. False

7. Visual Modeler does not contain component diagrams to illustrate how classes are packaged.

    a. True

    b. False

8. MTS uses _____ ActiveX components.

    a. in-process

    b. out-of-process

    c. between-processes

    d. none of the above

9. _____ is a personal database management system used for small databases of less than 1 GB.

    a. Microsoft SQL Server

    b. Microsoft Access

    c. Microsoft FoxPro

    d. none of the above

10. _____ is a client/server database management system used for small and large databases that handle mission-critical information.

    a. Microsoft SQL Server

    b. Microsoft FoxPro

    c. Microsoft Access

    d. none of the above

11. In Microsoft Access, the data type used for storing combinations of text and numbers with a size up to 255 characters is _____.

    a. memo

    b. date/time

    c. text

    d. number

12. In Microsoft Access, the data type used for storing numeric data, except for money, is _____.

    a. text

    b. date/time

    c. number

    d. memo

13. In Microsoft Access, the data type used for storing money is _____.

    a. currency

    b. memo

    c. text

    d. number

14. In Microsoft Access, the data type used for storing dates and times is _____.

    a. text

    b. date/time

    c. memo

    d. number

15. In Microsoft Access, the data type used for storing lengthy text, such as notes and descriptions, is _____.

    a. text

    b. number

    c. date/time

    d. memo

16. In Microsoft SQL Server, the data type used for storing combinations of text and numbers with a size of up to 255 characters is _____.

    a. int

    b. money

    c. varchar(n)

    d. numeric(p,s)

17. In Microsoft SQL Server, the data type used for storing numeric data, except for money, is _____.

    a. varchar(n)

    b. numeric(p,s)

    c. int

    d. money

18. In Microsoft SQL Server, the data type used for storing money is _____.

    a. varchar(n)

    b. numeric(p,s)

    c. money

    d. int

19. In Microsoft SQL Server, the data type used for storing dates and times is
_____.

   a. numeric(*p,s*)

   b. varchar(*n*)

   c. money

   d. int

20. In Microsoft SQL Server, the data type used for storing lengthy text, such
as notes and descriptions, is _____.

   a. numeric(*p,s*)

   b. date/time

   c. int

   d. varchar(*n*)

HANDS-ON PROJECTS

Project 6.1
Explain the differences between using storyboards and using Visual Studio to
prototype user interfaces.

Project 6.2
Using storyboarding, prototype the course management user interfaces
for CTIS.

Project 6.3
Using storyboarding, prototype the student management user interfaces
for CTIS.

Project 6.4
Using storyboarding, prototype the assignment management user interfaces
for CTIS.

Project 6.5
Choose and assign classes to components in Visual Modeler, using the logical
design of the course management process in Chapter 5. Save the model in the
Chapter_06 folder.

Project 6.6
Choose and assign classes to components in Visual Modeler, using the logical
design of the student management process in Chapter 5. Save the model in the
Chapter_06 folder.

Project 6.7

Choose and assign classes to components in Visual Modeler, using the logical design of the grades management process in Chapter 5. Save the model in the Chapter_06 folder.

Project 6.8

Choose and assign classes to components in Visual Modeler, using the logical design of the assignment management process in Chapter 5. Save the model in the Chapter_06 folder.

Project 6.9

Using Microsoft Access data types, assign the appropriate data types for the following fields:

a. Price

b. Cost

c. Start Date

d. Address

e. City

f. State

g. Zip

h. Quantity

i. Total Cost

j. Fax Number

k. Subject field of a memo or email

l. Credit Card as a Yes/No field

m. Cash as a Yes/No field

Project 6.10

Using Microsoft SQL Server data types, assign the appropriate data types for the following fields:

a. Price

b. Cost

c. Start Date

d. Address

e. City

f. State

g. Zip

h. Quantity

i. Total Cost

j. Fax Number

k. Subject field of a memo or email

l. Credit Card as a Yes/No field

m. Cash as a Yes/No field

Project 6.11

Create a physical database design for the course management process, using the logical design in Chapter 5, for:

a. Microsoft Access

b. Microsoft SQL Server

Project 6.12

Create a physical database design for the student management process, using the logical design in Chapter 5, for:

a. Microsoft Access

b. Microsoft SQL Server

Project 6.13

Create a physical database design for the assignment management process, using the logical design in Chapter 5, for:

a. Microsoft Access

b. Microsoft SQL Server

Project 6.14

Using the Gantt chart in Figure 6.7, change the schedule to reflect 40-hour tasks in the developing phase for each subsystem for which you created a physical design.

THE MSF DEVELOPING PHASE AND SOFTWARE CONFIGURATION MANAGEMENT

AFTER READING THIS CHAPTER AND COMPLETING THE EXERCISES, YOU WILL BE ABLE TO:

➤ Define the developing phase process

➤ Define software configuration management

➤ Use Visual SourceSafe to manage source files

➤ Define the team roles in the developing phase

When the planning phase is complete, the developing phase starts. The development team starts creating code from the functional specification and the conceptual, logical, and physical design. The project team usually begins the coding phase by translating the outline of the components from Visual Modeler into Visual Basic and coding the subroutines and functions. After you code the components, change the code in Visual Basic and reverse-engineer the code into Visual Modeler. Because the development team does not update the code and change the model during the coding phase, reverse-engineering is the only way to keep the model and the code up to date. The project team considers each document and model in the planning phase as a work in progress that needs to be updated throughout the developing phase.

As you begin coding the application, control each version of the code and documentation, using a configuration management tool, such as Microsoft's Visual SourceSafe. Visual SourceSafe lets you maintain multiple versions of the code files, including a record of all changes made to that file.

Software configuration management is a critical piece of a team-based project. It ensures that only one person can make changes to source code files at any one time, and prevents files from being accidentally replaced by another person's version. Most companies consider configuration management the most costly part of any project, yet it prevents a variety of problems.

As a new programmer, you need to develop good programming management habits such as keeping your code under source code control. This chapter investigates the use of configuration management with Visual SourceSafe, and introduces the developing phase of a software development project.

CHAPTER OVERVIEW

In the last few chapters, you learned how to plan an information system project. In this chapter, you can use your programming skills and focus on the developing phase and software configuration management. You will have the opportunity to work with different Visual Basic technologies, using both Visual Basic and Visual Interdev to create user interfaces and software components. You will use Microsoft Access and Microsoft SQL Server to create the database you designed in the physical design. You will also use Web technologies such as HTML and DHTML to create interactive Web applications. Before you can play with the Visual Basic technologies, however, you need to understand the importance of Microsoft Visual SourceSafe for managing your source files.

DEVELOPING PHASE

During this phase, the development team creates the code from the conceptual, logical, and physical design of the system. The developing phase culminates in the Scope Complete/First Use milestone. When the developing phase ends, the development team performs an assessment to ensure that:

➤ All features are built to meet the specifications. Your team is responsible for making sure that all features agreed upon during the planning phase are coded as documented in the requirements.

➤ Developers can use and evaluate the product for the first time. Your team is responsible for making sure that the code compiles and runs for testers, developers, and users.

➤ Customers can use the product for the first time.

➤ Infrastructure is deployed for test purposes. Usually, your development team works in an environment that is set up for creating code. Your testers work in a separate environment that matches a user's typical configuration.

➤ A plan of deployment is in place. After the system is tested and verified, your team needs to create a deployment plan that describes how and where the system is going to run and who is going to support it.

The Scope Complete/First Use milestone consists of the following tasks:

➤ **User interface development** Design and create the user interface with the help of the user, other developers, user education, and usability specialists. Completing this task leads to a visual design freeze interim milestone.

➤ **User, business, and data services development** Design and create the objects and components for each service layer.

➤ **Database development** Design and create the database schema and stored procedures. Completing this task leads to a Database freeze interim milestone.

➤ **Content development** Design and create the data or HTML content required for the product to function properly.

➤ **Usability testing** Provide a product the testers can work with to assess its usability and suggest improvements to make the product easier to use.

➤ **Testing and fixing bugs** Provide a product the testers can work with to find and report bugs to development. Development then fixes the bugs.

➤ **Infrastructure deployment** Distribute any software, hardware, and communications technology needed to meet the Scope Complete/First Use milestone.

7

As they complete these tasks, the development team creates several internal releases for testers to use to check against the requirements. The functional specification freezes when the development team releases a stable product to testing.

To accomplish these tasks, follow the steps below:

1. Set up software configuration management.
2. Create the database schema in SQL Server and Access.
3. Create necessary stored procedures.
4. Create the business objects from the business and data services layers.
5. Create the user interfaces.
6. Validate that code meets the functional specifications.
7. Test code to ensure that it meets functional specifications.
8. Fix bugs in the code.
9. Release the first functional product.

TEAM ROLES

In the last section, you investigated the process involved in developing a product. During this process, you are a member of a project team. Table 7.1 illustrates the team roles and responsibilities for the developing phase.

Table 7.1 Team roles and responsibilities for the developing phase.

Team Roles	Responsibilities
Product management	Works with customers and their expectations, pricing, and packaging
Program management	Tracks the project, including schedule and budgets, to resolve risks and other issues
Development	Creates code for product features and tests units of the code
User education	Builds elements that will support end users (e.g., training and product handbooks)
Testing	Tests product and reports bugs, and makes sure the product is stable at each milestone
Logistics management	Operates and supports the product and sets up the infrastructure

SOFTWARE CONFIGURATION MANAGEMENT

Before you can start coding, you need to set up the software configuration management tool for your project. Software configuration management allows a team of developers to manage multiple versions of products under development. Version control provides the following:

➤ **Team coordination** Allows only one person at a time to modify a file. This guarantees that only one person can make changes, so another team member does not accidentally overwrite your changes.

➤ **Version tracking** Keeps track of new and old versions of source code and other files to use for finding bugs and for other tracking purposes. It also allows programmers to remove revised source code and restore the previous version, if the new changes do not work out.

➤ **Reusable or object-oriented code** Allows programmers to create components that can be used across multiple projects

Microsoft Visual SourceSafe (VSS) is Microsoft's configuration management tool to track and maintain source code. Figure 7.1 illustrates how to use Visual SourceSafe with teams.

Microsoft supplies Microsoft Visual SourceSafe on the Visual Studio CD. It supports a variety of configurations, including single-tier and client/server options. If you are working with this book in a team environment, install Visual SourceSafe in client/server mode, which places the Visual SourceSafe database on the server. For more information on installing Visual SourceSafe on the server, see the MSDN Library for Visual SourceSafe online documentation.

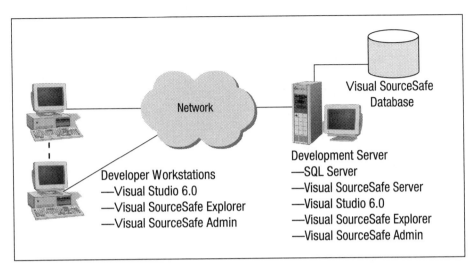

Figure 7.1   The development environment.

On a network, developers use workstations running either Windows 95/98 or Windows NT. These developer workstations contain Visual SourceSafe Explorer and Visual SourceSafe Admin. The development server contains Visual SourceSafe Server, Explorer, and Admin. The server is where the VSS database resides in a team environment. Developers need access to source code through a centralized server.

Before your team can use the VSS database, a VSS administrator must set up the database for your project. The administrator uses the VSS Administrator tool to do this, either on the workstation or on the server. This includes creating a project and user accounts for that project.

If this is a brand new project, the developer will add new files to a project using VSS Explorer. VSS Explorer saves these new files on the VSS server. While doing this, the developer works in a directory reserved for storing all project files. Developers manage their working environment in an orderly manner using folders to store their work files.

When a developer needs access to a specific piece of code, the developer uses VSS Explorer to check out the code. Checking out the code copies the code from the database and stores it on the developer workstation with read and write permissions in the working folder. Because developers perform all their work on the workstation, a read-only copy of all the code resides in a working folder on the workstation. To make sure that the code on the workstation is up to date, the copy from the database overwrites the file on the workstation. The server stores the most current code files in the VSS database. The developer changes and compiles the code on the workstation to make sure it works. Then the developer checks the code back into the database. VSS saves the changed code in the database as a different version and makes the working file read-only.

If someone else tries to use the same code after the developer has checked out the code, he or she receives an error message. This is important because in team-based projects, the project manager assigns you and other team members tasks. These tasks could overlap with someone else's, and you could be accessing the same code to make changes. Only one person can update a code file at a time; this ensures that all changes are saved, including your changes and your team members' changes.

As a developer, you expect the source files for your project to be stored in the VSS database. If your project team needs to create a new environment, such as for testers, then the administrator uses the code from the VSS database to create the new environment. This guarantees that source code files are stored in one place.

Microsoft Visual SourceSafe

Microsoft Visual SourceSafe lets you track versions of files without regard to file type, such as source code, graphics, word-processing documents, spreadsheets, PowerPoint slides, HTML files, sound files, and video files. VSS manages projects by saving them to a VSS database. VSS lets you administer VSS from an Admin account where you can create projects, user accounts for projects, and a new database; assign user rights to projects; and perform other administrator duties. You use the Visual SourceSafe Administrator application to administer VSS.

Use VSS from a user account that allows you to:

➤ **Check out** Gain exclusive access to a file to make changes.

➤ **Check in** Commit changes to files to a VSS database.

➤ **Add files** Add new files not in VSS to the project.

➤ **Undo check out** Cancel a checked-out file.

➤ **Create a new project** Create a new VSS project in the database.

➤ **Administer Web projects** Manage and deploy Web sites from within VSS.

You use the Visual SourceSafe Explorer application to use a VSS project. Now that you have reviewed some of the features of VSS, you need to understand how VSS works, which is illustrated in Figure 7.2.

The VSS Administrator environment shows the users and the users' rights, and whether they are logged in. The VSS Administrator environment menus are listed below:

➤ **Users** Add users, delete users, edit users, and change the password of the Admin.

➤ **Tools** Assign rights by project and by user, or copy other users' rights.

➤ **Archive** Back up and restore projects.

```
2. Check out
```

Figure 7.2   The Visual SourceSafe Administrator environment.

 When you first install VSS, the Admin account has no password. You need to use the Change Password feature to supply a password, so that no one with unauthorized access can use VSS Administrator.

To change the password of the Admin account:

1. Click the Start button on the taskbar. Point to Programs | Microsoft Visual Studio 6.0 | Microsoft Visual SourceSafe, and then click Visual SourceSafe 6.0 Admin. The location of Microsoft Visual SourceSafe on the Start menu may vary, depending upon where it was installed on your system.

2. Select Admin from the user list if necessary.

3. Click Change Password on the Users menu. Press the Tab key to move the cursor to the New Password textbox. Type "CTIS" and press the Tab key. Retype CTIS in the Verify Password textbox. Then click OK.

4. When you see the message "The user's password has been successfully changed," click the OK button.

Store the Admin user's password to CTIS in a safe place. After you change the Admin password, the next step is to create a user account.

To create a new user:

1. Click Add User from the Users menu.

2. In the User name text box, type "CTIS". Press the Tab key.

3. In the Password text box, type "CTIS". Press the Enter key.

4. The CTIS user appears in the user list.

To delete a user, select the user in the list and click Delete User in the Users menu. To edit a user (change the username only), select the user in the list and click Edit User in the Users menu.

After you create the users, create the project, using Visual SourceSafe Explorer. Figure 7.3 shows the Visual SourceSafe Explorer environment.

The Visual SourceSafe environment consists of the following panes:

➤ **Projects pane** Lists the different projects registered with Visual SourceSafe.

➤ **Contents pane** Lists the files for each project and the details about the files.

➤ **Details pane** Lists the current actions against the VSS database, such as when files are checked out and checked back in.

7

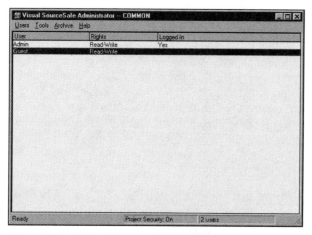

Figure 7.3 Visual SourceSafe Explorer environment.

Now create a project in VSS Explorer.

To create a project and set up the working folder in VSS Explorer:

1. Click the Start button on the taskbar. Point to Programs | Microsoft Visual
   Studio 6.0 | Microsoft Visual SourceSafe, and then click Microsoft Visual
   SourceSafe 6.0. The location of Microsoft Visual SourceSafe on the Start menu
   may vary, depending upon where it was installed on your system.

2. If necessary, log in as username CTIS and password CTIS, and then click
   OK.

3. Click Create Project on the File menu.

4. In the project textbox, type "CTIS" and press Enter.

5. Select the CTIS project in the Projects pane.

6. Click Set Working Folder on the File menu to set up a development
   environment for you to work in, on your development workstation.

7. In the Name textbox, type "c:\XYZ\CTIS" where XYZ are your initials,
   and click the Create Folder button. This creates a folder called XYZ\CTIS.
   Store all files in the CTIS project in this folder when working with VSS.

8. Click the OK button.

Under the CTIS project, you should create the following subprojects:

➤ **documents** Store documentation for the project, such as the requirements.

➤ **user_svc_src** Store source code for the project for user services.

➤ **business_svc_src** Store source code for the components for business and
   data services.

➤ **db_schema** Store the scripts to create the tables and columns for the database.

➤ **db_stored_proc** Store the scripts to create the stored procedures for the database.

These subprojects let you manage your project by the different application services. You will create the subprojects as an exercise at the end of this chapter.

After you create the CTIS project, press ALT +TAB to switch to VSS Administrator to assign rights to the project for the user account you created earlier. The rights in VSS are the following:

➤ **Read** Read the projects and files in the projects.

➤ **Check In/Check Out** Check in and check out files in VSS.

➤ **Add/Rename/Delete** Add new files and projects, rename files and projects, and delete files and projects.

➤ **Destroy** Destroy a project permanently from the database; the administrator should be the only one removing projects from the database.

Make sure that the only users who have access to the project are those who have a right to know. Any other users should have their rights revoked. For instance, in CTIS, the guest account has full access to the CTIS project by default. You should delete this user or give the user read-only rights to the projects. By default, VSS disables project security.

To enable project security and give the guest account read-only access:

1. Click Options on the Tools menu.
2. Select the Project Security tab.
3. Click the Enable Project Security check box.
4. Click the OK button.
5. Click Rights By Project on the Tools menu.
6. Select the root ($/) project.
7. Select the guest user in the right column.
8. Remove the checkmarks from all rights except read. Setting the root project rights affects all children's projects in the hierarchy below it. If you only wanted to affect a particular project's rights, then you would select the project and change the rights for that project only.
9. Click the Close button.
10. Exit VSS Administrator.

Once you have set project rights, you need to add files into VSS using VSS Explorer.

To add files to VSS using VSS Explorer:

1. Select the CTIS project from the Projects pane.
2. Click Add Files on the File menu.
3. Using the Folders view, select the Chapter_07 folder from your Student Disk.
4. Select course.mdl.
5. Click the Add button.
6. At the Add File with course.mdl dialog box, click OK. VSS adds the course.mdl file to the CTIS project.
7. At the Add File dialog box, click the Close command button.

On a daily basis, make sure your files are up to date. The best way to do this is to use the "get the latest version" function of VSS of all files in a project, at the start of your day.

To get the latest version of all files for a project, using VSS Explorer:

1. Select the CTIS project in the Projects pane.
2. Click Get Latest Version from the SourceSafe menu.
3. In the Get CTIS dialog box, select Recursive. This opens all files in all subprojects under the CTIS project as read-only. Then click OK.
4. Verify in Windows Explorer that the file course.mdl exists under the c:\XYZ\CTIS folder.

Now you are ready to begin work. The two processes you will do often are checking files in and checking files out from the project.

To make changes to a file and view its history in VSS:

Checking out a file

1. Select the CTIS project in the Projects pane.
2. Select the course.mdl file in the Contents pane.
3. Click Check Out in the SourceSafe menu.
4. Click OK in the Check Out dialog box. The file is copied to the c:\XYZ\CTIS folder with read and write privileges. A red checkmark appears next to the file, along with the name of the user.
5. Open the file using Visual Modeler. At this point, you can make changes to the file and save them to the c:\XYZ\CTIS folder. Change a parameter and save the model. Exit Visual Modeler.

Checking in the file

1. In VSS Explorer, select the course.mdl file in the Contents pane.

2. In the SourceSafe menu click Check In.

3. In the Comments field, comment on the changes you made to the file. Click OK in the Check in dialog box. VSS commits changes to the file and supplies a revision history for you. VSS also makes the file in the working folder read-only.

Viewing file history

1. After you check in the file, you can view its history. Select the course.mdl file.

2. Click Show History from the Tools menu and then click OK in the History Options dialog box. You see two versions of the file.

3. Select version 2 and click the Details button. You see the comment you made to this file.

4. Click the Close button twice.

5. Exit VSS Explorer.

You now have the necessary tools to work with VSS. Be sure to make daily backup copies of the database. This prevents you from losing more than a day's work.

CHAPTER SUMMARY

In this chapter, you investigated the developing phase process and software configuration management. Before you can code, you need to set up the VSS environment. Source code control is an absolute must for every project because otherwise, you risk losing the entire project.

REVIEW QUESTIONS

1. When the _____ phase is complete, the _____ phase starts.
   a. planning, developing
   b. developing, planning
   c. envisioning, developing
   d. none of the above

2. _____ manages source code in software development projects.
   a. Visual Basic
   b. Visual J++
   c. Visual SourceSafe
   d. none of the above

3. The developing phase culminates in the _____ milestone.
   a. Scope Complete/First Use
   b. Vision Approved
   c. Project Plan Approved
   d. none of the above

4. The _____ interim milestone allows no other changes to the user interface.
   a. Database Freeze
   b. Visual Design Freeze
   c. Functional Specification
   d. Internal Release

5. The _____ interim milestone freezes the database design to allow for component creation.
   a. Database Freeze
   b. Internal Release
   c. Functional Specification
   d. Visual Design Freeze

6. _____ works with customers and their expectations during the developing phase.
   a. Product Management
   b. User Education
   c. Development
   d. Program Management

7. _____ tracks the project during the developing phase.
   a. Program Management
   b. User Education
   c. Product Management
   d. Development

8. _____ creates code for product features during the developing phase.
   a. Program Management
   b. Development
   c. User Education
   d. Product Management

9. _____ builds elements that will support end users during the developing phase.

    a. User Education

    b. Development

    c. Program Management

    d. Product Management

10. _____ performs tests and reports bugs to make sure the product is stable at each milestone during the developing phase.

    a. User Education

    b. Logistics Management

    c. Program Management

    d. Testing

7

11. _____ operates and supports the product during the developing phase.

    a. Testing

    b. Program Management

    c. Logistics Management

    d. User Education

12. _____ is the ability of a team of developers to manage multiple versions of products under development.

    a. Software configuration management

    b. Software development

    c. Software management

    d. none of the above

13. _____ allows you to gain exclusive access to a file to make changes.

    a. Check out

    b. Check in

    c. Add file

    d. none of the above

14. _____ allows you to commit changes to files to the VSS database.

    a. Check out

    b. Add file

    c. Check in

    d. none of the above

15. _____ allows you to add new files not in VSS to the project.

    a. Check out

    b. Check in

    c. Add files

    d. none of the above

16. _____ allows you to cancel a check out of a file.

    a. Check in

    b. Check out

    c. Undo check out

    d. Add new files

17. _____ allows you to create a new VSS project in the database.

    a. Check out

    b. Undo check out

    c. Check in

    d. Create a new project

18. The _____ menu lets you add users, delete users, edit users, and change the password of users.

    a. Archive

    b. Users

    c. Tools

    d. none of the above

19. The _____ menu lets you assign rights by project and by user or copy other users' rights.

    a. Archive

    b. Tools

    c. Users

    d. none of the above

20. The _____ menu allows you to back up and restore projects.

    a. Tools

    b. Users

    c. Archive

    d. none of the above

HANDS-ON PROJECTS

Project 7.1

Discuss the interim milestones necessary in the developing phase.

Project 7.2

Discuss the tasks and steps involved in the developing phase.

Project 7.3

Discuss the team roles and responsibilities for the developing phase.

Project 7.4

Discuss the values of configuration management.

Project 7.5

Create the following subprojects under the CTIS project.

a. documents

b. user_svc_src

c. business_svc_src

d. db_schema

e. db_stored_proc

Project 7.6

Move the course.mdl file from CTIS to the documents subproject.

a. Open the VSS Explorer.

b. Select course.mdl in the Projects pane.

c. Press the Del key to permanently remove the file from VSS.

d. Select the Documents subproject.

e. Click Add Files on the File menu.

f. Select course.mdl from the Chapter_07 folder.

g. Click the Add button, and then click OK on the Add Folder dialog box.

h. Click the Close button.

i. Exit VSS Explorer.

Project 7.7

Create a new user account, using VSS Administrator.

   a. Open VSS Administrator and log in.

   b. Click Add User in the Users menu.

   c. In the User name text box, type "CTIS1". Press the Tab key.

   d. In the Password text box, type "CTIS". Press the Enter key. The CTIS user appears in the user list.

   e. Exit VSS Administrator.

Project 7.8

Compare and contrast the features of VSS Explorer and VSS Administrator.

Project 7.9

Discuss the key benefits of using VSS.

CHAPTER EIGHT

IMPLEMENTING DATA SERVICES WITH SQL SERVER

AFTER READING THIS CHAPTER AND COMPLETING THE EXERCISES, YOU WILL BE ABLE TO:

➤ Create database objects, such as tables, views, stored procedures, and database diagrams, using the SQL Data Definition Language (DDL)

➤ Insert new data, delete old data, and modify existing data, using the SQL Data Manipulation Language (DML)

➤ Create simple queries using the **SELECT** statement

➤ Create complex queries using joins

➤ Use built-in functions and stored procedures to manipulate data

➤ Create stored procedures using Transact-SQL in SQL Server

If you followed the instructions in the previous chapter, you completed setting up VSS and are ready to begin programming.

During the developing phase, you need to design and create the database schema and stored procedures to complete the database development task. Usually, this task is completed by a database administrator, not a programmer. You create queries and stored procedures after the database administrator creates the database schema.

Before you do this, however, you must understand how to interact with the database, using the structured query language (SQL). Once you master SQL, then you can learn how to create stored procedures and create the database schema.

You must install SQL Server for Windows 98/NT Workstation or Windows NT 4.0 before you can complete this chapter. See the software installation instructions for help. You must also restore the CTIS database before you can complete this chapter. Refer to Appendix B for instructions on creating an SQL Server database and restoring CTIS. You should also review the database schema in Appendix C to complete the Hands-On Projects in this chapter.

CHAPTER OVERVIEW

In the last chapter, you learned about the tasks for developing an information system and setting up Visual SourceSafe. You are ready to learn how to create queries using SQL, stored procedures, and the database schema in SQL Server. This chapter uses the Data View window in Microsoft Visual Basic to interact with SQL Server. Because SQL Server is a complex product, you will only learn the basics for developing information systems. Learning how to administer SQL Server is beyond the scope of this book.

VISUAL BASIC VISUAL DATABASE TOOLS

Microsoft's Visual Database tools help you create and modify database schemas such as tables, views, stored procedures, and queries. The Visual Database tools provide two designers:

➤ Query Designer uses visual design techniques to create SQL statements to query and update databases.

➤ Database Designer uses visual design techniques to create, modify, delete, and define database objects for databases that you are connected to.

Setting Up The Visual Database Tools Environment

Visual Basic provides Visual Database tools to assist in working with databases. First, you initiate a database environment connection.

To create a data link to SQL Server:

1. Click the Start button on the Taskbar. Point to Programs, Microsoft Visual Studio 6.0, and then click Microsoft Visual Basic 6.0. The location of Microsoft Visual Basic on the Start menu may vary, depending on where it was installed on your system.

2. Click the Cancel button on the New Project window.

3. Select Data View Window from the View menu. Figure 8.1 shows the Data View window.

   There are two options on the Data View window. The first option sets up data links to a database for the Visual Basic environment. The second option allows you to view data environments, enabling you to maintain data links in your projects.

4. Right-click the Data Links folder. Select Add a Data Link from the menu. Figure 8.2 shows the different OLE DB providers loaded on your system.

5. Select the Microsoft OLE DB provider for SQL Server.

6. Click the Next button. Figure 8.3 shows the Data Link Properties window Connection tab.

Figure 8.1   Data View window.

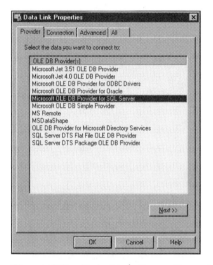

Figure 8.2   Data Link Properties window Provider tab.

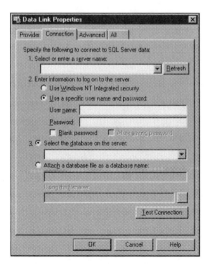

Figure 8.3   Data Link Properties window Connection tab.

7. Enter the following information:

➤ Select or enter your server name, such as "CRT_SERVER"

➤ Enter information to log on to the server

➤ Choose Windows NT Integrated Security, an option that allows your SQL Server database to use the operating system logon security mechanism for authentication, instead of the built-in security in SQL Server

➤ Select the database on the server, such as "CTIS"

 If you don't know your server name, right-click Network Neighborhood on your desktop, and then click Properties on the shortcut menu. Click the Identification tab. The Computer name is the name of your server.

8. Click the OK button.

9. Change the Data Link name to CTIS and press Return.

10. Click the + sign next to the CTIS data link to show the database objects.

11. Click the + sign next to Tables to show all tables in the database. Figure 8.4 shows the results of these actions in the Data View window.

QUERY DESIGNER

After you make a connection to the database using a data link, you can use Query Designer to run queries against the database. Query Designer provides a graphical environment to execute queries. Figure 8.5 shows the Query Designer environment.

The Query Designer environment contains several panes:

➤ The Diagram pane displays the input sources, such as tables or views, that you are querying.

Figure 8.4 Data View window with expanded tables.

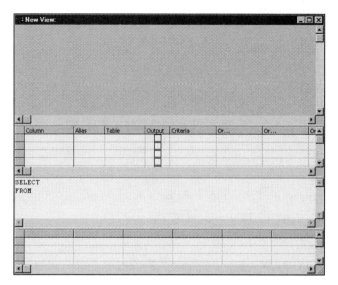

Figure 8.5   Query Designer environment.

➤ The Grid pane displays the query options, such as which columns to display, which rows to filter, how to group rows, and other options.

➤ The SQL pane displays the SQL statement for your query.

➤ The Results pane displays the results of your query.

Structured Query Language (SQL)

SQL, often pronounced "ess cue ell" or "sequel," consists of commands that allow you to manipulate databases. SQL has syntax or rules you must follow to interact with databases. The **SELECT** statement allows you to look at data in one or more tables. A **SELECT** statement returns a result set, which is rows that are the results of a query.

SELECT *Statement*

The syntax of the **SELECT** statement is:

```
SELECT column-list
FROM    table-name
[WHERE condition]
[GROUP BY column-list]
[HAVING condition]
[ORDER BY column-name [DESC]]
```

The items in brackets are optional in a **SELECT** statement, and the order of the items in the **SELECT** statement is important.

The simplest form of the **SELECT** statement is used to retrieve every column and every row of a single table, as in the example below:

```
SELECT *
FROM    STUDENTS;
```

 This **SELECT s**tatement is seldom used in "real world" applications, unless you are writing SQL to test a system or administer a database.

The * for the column list is the syntax for selecting all columns. The query will return all columns and rows from the STUDENTS table.

To run a query:

1. From the Data View window, right-click the Views folder and select New View.

2. Move the Data View window from the Query Designer view.

3. Maximize the New View child window.

4. Type in the SQL pane:

```
SELECT  *
FROM    STUDENTS;
```

5. Right-click the Diagram pane and select Hide pane.

6. Right-click the Grid pane and select Hide pane.

7. Click Run from the Query menu. Figure 8.6 shows the results of the query.

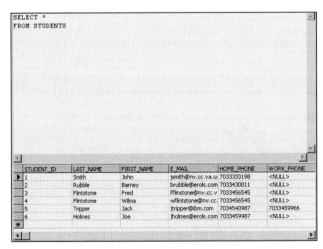

Figure 8.6   Results of a simple SELECT.

You can select the following information:

➤ All columns and all rows in a table

```
SELECT  *
FROM    STUDENTS;
```

➤ Only certain columns in a table

```
SELECT  LAST_NAME, FIRST_NAME
FROM    STUDENTS;
```

This **SELECT** statement displays all rows with only the LAST_NAME and FIRST_NAME columns from the STUDENTS table.

➤ Unique values within a column

```
SELECT  DISTINCT
LAST_NAME
FROM    STUDENTS;
```

DISTINCT prevents duplicates on column name from being displayed.

SELECT *Statement's* WHERE *Clause*

You can add a **WHERE** clause to a **SELECT** statement to define conditions that must be met before a row displays the results. You must follow certain rules when using a **WHERE** clause. The **WHERE** clause must consist of a column or expression with a comparison operator and a value. A condition clause returns either **TRUE** or **FALSE**. If the condition returns **TRUE**, then the row belongs to the result set. You define the condition clause as shown in Table 8.1.

NULL columns are columns that are empty or that have missing information.

When determining the syntax of values, remember:

➤ Characters are quoted with single quotes.

➤ SQL's string values are case-sensitive, so 'John' and 'JOHN' are different values.

➤ Dates are quoted, such as '12/31/99'.

➤ Numbers are not quoted, such as 10.

Table 8.1 Parts of the **WHERE** clause.

Column Or Comparison Value	Description	Expression	Operator
LAST_NAME	=	'Holmes'	Exact match, equal to
POINTS_EARNED	>	50	Greater than
POINTS_EARNED	<	50	Less than
GRADE_DATE	<=	'10/30/98'	Less than or equal to
GRADE_DATE	>=	'10/30/98'	Greater than or equal to
LAST_NAME	<>	'Holmes'	Not equal to
MAX_POINTS * (WEIGHT/100)	=	20	Equal to
CLASS_NUMBER	IN	('CP 108', 'IST 208')	Equal to any member in the list
WORK_PHONE	IS	NULL	Is empty; has missing or no existing data
WORK_PHONE	IS NOT	NULL	Contains data; is not empty
CLASS_NUMBER	LIKE	'IST%', '%208'	A percent sign can match zero or more characters before or after the indicated value. The first example will match all classes that have IST in the beginning of the string. It might match values such as IST 208, IST 220, and others. The second value contains 208 at the end of the string. It might match values such as IST 208, ESR 208, and others
CLASS_NUMBER	LIKE	'IST 20_'	The underscore matches exactly one character. It might match values such as IST 208 and others

 SQL evaluates the **WHERE** clause one row at a time. When the **WHERE** clause results in a true value, SQL includes the row in the results set.

The following queries show the usage of a **WHERE** clause:

➤ greater than

```
SELECT    *
FROM      GRADES
WHERE     POINTS_EARNED > 50;
```

This greater than query displays all rows with grades greater than 50.

➤ equal to

```
SELECT      *
FROM        GRADES
WHERE       POINTS_EARNED = 90;
```

This equal to query displays all rows with grades equal to 90.

➤ **IN**

```
SELECT      *
FROM        GRADES
WHERE       POINTS_EARNED IN (90,95);
```

This **IN** query displays all rows with grades equal to 90 or 95.

➤ The **IN** query could be rewritten:

```
SELECT      *
FROM        GRADES
WHERE       POINTS_EARNED = 90
OR  POINTS_EARNED = 95;
```

In a **WHERE** clause, you can include multiple conditions in the **SELECT** query. To include multiple conditions, you must use a logical operator between conditions. You might use multiple conditions if the results you want pass several rules to be included in the result set. Table 8.2 lists the logical operators with examples of how to use them.

SELECT Statement's ORDER BY Clause

When you are using the **SELECT** query without an **ORDER BY** clause, SQL could sort the rows in any order. You can only guarantee the order of records by using the **ORDER BY** clause.

The **ORDER BY** clause sorts rows in a table by any column or groups of columns, in either ascending or descending order.

For example:

```
SELECT    LAST_NAME,FIRST_NAME
FROM      STUDENTS
WHERE     LAST_NAME = 'Flintstone'
ORDER BY LAST_NAME, FIRST_NAME;
```

Table 8.2 Logical operators.

Operator	Function	Example
NOT	If condition returns TRUE, the NOT condition returns FALSE. If condition returns FALSE, the NOT condition returns TRUE.	SELECT * FROM STUDENTS WHERE WORK_PHONE IS NOT NULL;
AND	If both conditions are TRUE, returns TRUE. Otherwise, returns FALSE.	SELECT * FROM STUDENTS WHERE LAST_NAME = 'Smith' AND FIRST_NAME = 'John'; Returns all rows where the FIRST_NAME is John and LAST_NAME is Smith.
OR	If either condition is TRUE, returns TRUE. Otherwise, if both are FALSE, then returns FALSE.	SELECT * FROM STUDENTS WHERE LAST_NAME = 'Smith' OR FIRST_NAME = 'John'; Returns any row where the LAST_NAME is Smith or the FIRST_NAME is John.

This query sorts the records by LAST_NAME and FIRST_NAME.

If you use the **DESC** keyword in the **ORDER BY** clause, then SQL will sort the records in **DESC** order. For example:

```
SELECT    LAST_NAME,FIRST_NAME
FROM      STUDENTS
WHERE     LAST_NAME = 'Flintstone'
ORDER BY LAST_NAME DESC, FIRST_NAME DESC;
```

This query sorts records in reverse order by LAST_NAME and FIRST_NAME.

Using Functions In **SELECT** Statements

Functions operate on data to alter the data's appearance. There are two types of functions: scalar and aggregate.

Scalar functions operate on the data one row at a time. Examples of scalar functions are listed in Table 8.3.

You can use the SQL books online to find other scalar functions to use in your queries.

Table 8.3 Examples of scalar functions.

Function	Description	Example
ROUND (numeric_expression, length[, function])	Returns the first argument (numeric expression) to the number of decimal places in the second argument (length). If the length is negative, then rounding takes place to the left of the decimal.	SELECT ROUND (125.225,2), rounded ROUND(125.225,-1) RESULTS: 125.23120
ISNULL (check_expression, replacement_value)	Returns the replacement_value if the check_expression is null. Useful in changing a NULL column into a value that can be used in calculations.	SELECT ISNULL (WORK_PHONE,0) FROM STUDENTS; RESULTS: Returns 0 for WORK_PHONE column that contain a NULL value for each row
string1 + string2 (Concatenation)	Returns string1 concatenated to string2	SELECT LAST_NAME+', '+FIRST_NAME FROM STUDENTS; Returns Last_Name, First_Name for each row
UPPER(string1)	Returns string1 in all uppercase. Useful in WHERE clauses to find strings that might be in mixed case.	SELECT UPPER (LAST_NAME) FROM STUDENTS; RESULTS: Returns LAST_NAME in all caps for each row
LEN(string1)	Returns the length of the character string, string1	SELECT LEN (LAST_NAME) FROM STUDENTS; RESULTS: Returns length of LAST_NAME for each row
DATEADD (datepart,number,	Returns the addition of the number to the date, depending upon what part of the date to add (datepart) datepart year yy, yyyy quarter qq, q month mm, m dayofyear dy, y day dd, d week wk, ww hour hh minute mi, n second ss, s milliseconds ms	SELECT DATEADD (day, 21, date) GRADE_DATE) FROM GRADES; abbreviations RESULTS: Adds 21 days to the GRADE_DATE of every row returned

(continued)

Table 8.3   Examples of scalar functions *(continued)*.

Function	Description	Example
DATEDIFF(datepart, startdate, enddate)	Returns the number of specified units of time between two dates	SELECT DATEDIFF (week, '8/26/98', '12/19/98') RESULTS: Returns the number of weeks between 8/26/98 and 12/19/98, which is 16
GETDATE	Gets the current date and time	SELECT GETDATE() RESULTS: 1/19/99 8:00:00 AM
CAST(expression as datatype)	Converts an expression to a datatype	SELECT CAST ('12/01/98' AS DATETIME) RESULTS: Converts the string '12/01/98' to a DATETIME datatype
CONVERT (data_type[(length)], expression [, style])	Same as CAST	SELECT CONVERT (varchar,get date(),1) Style 1 is mm/dd/yy, and Style 101 is mm/dd/yyyy. Refer to SQL online documentation for other formats.

When using functions in your queries, notice that the column returns with no name. You can use an alias to give an explicit name to an expression or to a column, as in the example below:
SELECT CAST('12/1/98' AS DATETIME) AS NEWDATE
RESULTS: It supplies an alias **NEWDATE** for the column name for the above example.

Aggregate functions allow you to perform math on a group of rows in a query. They return a single row with the result of the aggregate function. The most common aggregate functions are listed in Table 8.4.

SELECT *Statement's* GROUP BY *Clause*

Use the **GROUP BY** clause to return a single row of summary information for each group of rows selected from a table. Group functions, unlike scalar functions, return results based on groups of rows, rather than on single rows. In a query, you must list all columns or expressions from the **GROUP BY** clause in the column list along with the grouping (i.e., aggregate function).

For example, you may want to know the students' average for each category. The **SELECT** query is:

```
SELECT CATEGORY_ID, AVG(POINTS_EARNED)
FROM        GRADES
GROUP BY    CATEGORY_ID;
```

Table 8.4   Examples of aggregate functions.

Function	Description	Example
AVG (column_name)	Averages the values in a column	SELECT AVG(POINTS_EARNED) FROM GRADES; RESULTS: Returns the average of all grades in the GRADES table
COUNT (column_name)	Counts the values in a column	SELECT COUNT(*) FROM STUDENTS; RESULTS: Returns the number of rows in the STUDENTS table
MAX (column_name) FROM	Finds the largest value in a column GRADES;	SELECT MAX(POINTS_EARNED) RESULTS: Returns the MAX grade from the GRADES table
MIN (column_name)	Finds the smallest value in a column	SELECT MIN(POINTS_EARNED) FROM GRADES; RESULTS: Returns the MIN grade from the GRADES table
SUM (column_name)	Totals the column RESULTS:	SELECT SUM(POINTS_EARNED) FROM GRADES; Returns the total sum of all grades from the GRADES table

Notice that **CATEGORY_ID** is the column being grouped in the previous query. This query returns the average for each **CATEGORY_ID**. For example, the query might return the following:

```
CATEGORY_ID    AVG(POINTS_EARNED)
          1    95
          2    80
          3    75
```

For example, you might want to know how many grades are in each category. The **SELECT** query is:

```
SELECT CATEGORY_ID, COUNT(*)
FROM     GRADES
GROUP BY  CATEGORY_ID;
```

This query returns the number of grades in each category, as in the following example:

```
CATEGORY_ID   COUNT(*)
        1     1
        2     1
        3     4
```

Group functions operate on groups of rows, while scalar functions work on each row. Group functions supply summary information.

SELECT *Statement's* HAVING *Clause*

The **WHERE** clause filters on a row-by row-basis. The **HAVING** clause filters on a group-by-group basis. It works in conjunction with the **GROUP BY** clause.

For example, you might want to know how many grades are in each category that has more than one grade. The **SELECT** query is:

```
SELECT CATEGORY_ID, COUNT(*)
FROM    GRADES
GROUP BY       CATEGORY_ID
HAVING COUNT(*) > 1;
```

This query returns the number of grades in each category that has more than one grade.

Joins

Relational databases may store data needed for a query in more than one table. For example, the STUDENT_SCHEDULE table consists of a foreign key that matches the primary key in the STUDENTS table. Joins give you the ability to combine the tables. You can display data from two tables by adding a condition in the **WHERE** clause, whereby the foreign key in one table is equal to the primary key in another table.

For example, if you need to know what the schedule is for each class, use the following query:

```
SELECT *
FROM   CLASSES AS CLS,CLASS_SCHEDULE AS CS
WHERE  CLS.CLASS_ID = CS.CLASS_SCHEDULE_ID;
```

In the results of this SQL statement, CS.★, CLS.CLASS_NAME replaces ★.

An alias lets you rename a column. You should use aliases, such as CLASSES AS CLS or GRADES GRD, to make your SQL read better.

The **FROM** clause must contain all tables from which you need data. The **WHERE** clause must contain the JOIN conditions matching the primary key of one table to the foreign key of the other table. If you don't want to show certain columns, then you can select only the columns you want in the column list of the **SELECT** clause. Make sure that you specify which table the column is located in.

You can also join three or more tables together. For example, you might need to know for which classes students are registered. The SELECT query is:

```
SELECT S.LAST_NAME, S.FIRST_NAME, CLS.CLASS_NAME
FROM    STUDENTS S, STUDENT_SCHEDULES SS, CLASS_SCHEDULE CS, CLASSES CLS
WHERE   S.STUDENT_ID = SS.STUDENT_ID
AND     SS.CLASS_SCHEDULE_ID = CS.CLASS_SCHEDULE_ID
AND     CS.CLASS_ID = CLS.CLASS_ID;
```

Note that you needed three JOIN conditions to join four tables together properly.

Remember that in JOIN conditions, you must join each table on the basis of the foreign key and primary key relationship.

DATABASE DESIGNER

After you establish a connection to the database via a data link, you can use Database Designer to create tables in the database. Database Designer provides a graphical environment for creating database objects. Figure 8.7 shows the Database Designer table creation environment.

The Database Designer table creation environment contains several columns:

➤ **Column Name** Name of a column

➤ **Datatype** Different datatypes supported by SQL Server

➤ **Length** Size of the datatype

➤ **Precision** Number of digits in a number

➤ **Scale** Number of digits to the right of the decimal

➤ **Allows Nulls** Allows a column to have a NULL value

➤ **Default Value** Columns, when created, can default to a certain value

➤ **Identity** Whether or not the column is a primary key, which is required to be a one-up counter

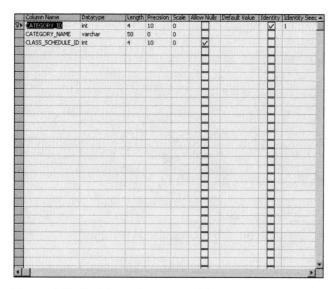

Figure 8.7 Database Designer table creation environment.

➤ **Identity Seed** Value to use as the start for the counter

➤ **Identity Increment** Counter value to increment by

Database Designer lets you create tables and columns graphically, using SQL Data Definition Language (DDL). Behind the scenes, SQL is creating the table and its columns, using the following syntax:

```
CREATE TABLE tablename
{
    column_name datatype      constraints
};
```

To create the instructor's table, you would use the following SQL statement:

```
CREATE TABLE INSTRUCTORS
{
    INSTRUCTOR_ID    INT           NOT NULL    IDENTITY    PRIMARY KEY,
    LAST_NAME        VARCHAR(35)   NOT NULL,
    ...
    WEB_ADDRESS      VARCHAR(200)
};
```

To delete a table from the database, you would use the DROP SQL command:

```
DROP TABLE INSTRUCTORS;
```

To modify a column in a table, you can drop the table and re-create it.

Creating A Table

You can create tables in Database Designer to implement the physical database design from Chapter 6.

To create the INSTRUCTORS table from Chapter 6:

1. Make sure that the Data View window is open and that there is a link to the CTIS SQL Server database.

2. Right-click the Tables folder, and then click New Table on the shortcut menu.

3. In the Choose Name dialog box, enter "INSTRUCTORS".

4. Enter the data as shown in Figure 8.8.

5. Right-click the INSTRUCTOR_ID row and select Set Primary Key.

6. Click the Close button on the Choose Name dialog box.

7. Click Yes in the Visual Basic dialog box to save the table.

Modifying An Existing Table

Because you created the INSTRUCTORS table, you must now add the INSTRUCTOR_ID to the CLASS_SCHEDULE table. Currently, the CLASS_SCHEDULE table does not show which instructor is teaching each class.

Column Name	Datatype	Length	Precision	Scale	Allow Nulls	Default Value	Identity	Identity Seed
INSTRUCTOR_ID	int	4	10	0			✓	1
LAST_NAME	varchar	35	0	0				
FIRST_NAME	varchar	35	0	0				
PHONE_NUMBER	varchar	10	0	0				
E_MAIL	varchar	200	0	0	✓			
WEB_ADDRESS	varchar	200	0	0	✓			

Figure 8.8 INSTRUCTORS table data entry.

To modify the CLASS_SCHEDULE table:

1. Make sure the Data View window is open and there is a link to the CTIS SQL Server database.

2. Right-click the CLASS_SCHEDULE table.

3. Select Design from the menu.

4. Add INSTRUCTOR_ID, as shown in Figure 8.9.

5. Click the Close button.

6. Click Yes in the Visual Basic dialog box.

 In a database that contains live data, do not delete columns in tables or tables from the database in a production environment. Use a development environment to do your database development first. Any changes to the database structure, after a system is in place, require a database administrator to write a database conversion program to update a production database.

Deleting A Column In A Table Or A Table In The Database

Once you add a table and modify columns in that table, you can delete the column or table if necessary. While in Design view, you can remove a column by selecting the column and pressing the Delete key. To remove a table from a database, select the table in the Data View window and press the Delete key. Be careful when deleting columns and tables; they may be in use by the application.

Column Name	Datatype	Length	Precision	Scale	Allow Nulls	Default Value	Identity	Identity Seed
CLASS_SCHEDULE_ID	int	4	10	0			✓	1
SECTION	varchar	10	0	0	✓			
YEAR	varchar	4	0	0	✓			
TERM	varchar	6	0	0	✓			
CLASS_ID	int	4	10	0	✓			
INSTRUCTOR_ID	int	4	10	0	✓			

Figure 8.9 Adding INSTRUCTOR_ID to CLASS_SCHEDULE table.

Relating Tables

In the previous sections, you added an INSTRUCTORS table and modified the CLASS_SCHEDULE table to include the INSTRUCTOR_ID. Now you need to create a relationship using the Database Diagrams folder.

To add a relationship to the RELATIONSHIP diagram:

1. Click the + sign next to the Database Diagram folder to expand the folder in the Data View window.
2. Right-click the RELATIONSHIP diagram, and then select New Table on the shortcut menu.
3. Select Open.
4. Move the INSTRUCTORS table next to the CLASS_SCHEDULE table.
5. Scroll the CLASS_SCHEDULE until you see INSTRUCTOR_ID.
6. In the INSTRUCTORS table, right-click INSTRUCTOR_ID.
7. Select Set Primary Key. A little key appears to the left of INSTRUCTOR_ID.
8. Select INSTRUCTOR_ID from the INSTRUCTORS table.
9. Drag INSTRUCTOR_ID from the INSTRUCTORS table and drop it on INSTRUCTOR_ID in the CLASS_SCHEDULE table.
10. The Create Relationship dialog box appears, as shown in Figure 8.10.
11. Click the OK button.
12. Close the diagram.
13. Click Yes in the Visual Basic dialog box.
14. Click Yes in the Save dialog box.

Figure 8.10   Create Relationship dialog box.

Entering Data Into Tables

Once you have defined the database schema, you can enter test data into the database.

To enter test data into the INSTRUCTORS table:

1. Right-click the INSTRUCTORS table in the Data View window.

2. Select Open from the menu.

3. Enter the following data:

```
LAST_NAME  Morneau
FIRST_NAME Keith
PHONE_NUMBER       7033232197
E_MAIL     nvmornk@nv.cc.va.us
WEB_ADDRESS        http://www.nv.cc.va.us/home/kmorneau
```

4. Close the Run Table window.

Database Designer lets you enter data graphically, using SQL DML. Behind the scenes, SQL is inserting records into the table and its columns, using the following syntax:

```
INSERT
INTO INSTRUCTORS (LAST_NAME,FIRST_NAME,PHONE_NUMBER,E_MAIL,WEB_ADDRESS)
VALUES ('Morneau','Keith','7033232197','nvmornk@nv.cc.va.us','http://
www.nv.cc.va.us/home.kmorneau');
```

Modifying And Deleting Existing Data

You added a relationship between INSTRUCTORS and CLASS_SCHEDULE on INSTRUCTOR_ID. Now, you need to update that relationship.

To update data in the CLASS_SCHEDULE table:

1. Right-click CLASS_SCHEDULE in the Data View window.

2. Select Open from the shortcut menu.

3. Change the INSTRUCTOR_ID column to a 1 for all rows in the table. This assigns Keith Morneau as the instructor for the two classes.

4. Close the Run Table window.

Database Designer lets you modify and delete data graphically, using SQL DML. Behind the scenes, SQL is updating records in a table, using the following syntax:

```
UPDATE INSTRUCTORS
SET    INSTRUCTOR_ID = 1;
[WHERE condition]
```

You can add the **WHERE** clause to the end of the query to update one or more rows, depending upon whether the row meets the condition. Since you want to update all rows, this query does not need a **WHERE** clause.

You can also delete a row by highlighting the row and pressing the Delete key. Behind the scenes, SQL uses the following syntax to delete a row:

```
DELETE FROM table-name
WHERE condition;
```

Views

A view is like a stored query that allows you to take a snapshot of your data from one or more tables. Some developers think you do not need views. Others think they are important. Consult with your team to decide whether to use views in your application. Views are very handy if you want some users to have access to only certain pieces of data. You will degrade performance of your queries if you use views in your application. Views require several more steps in running your queries in SQL Server.

To find out for which classes students are registered, use the following **SELECT** query:

```
SELECT S.LAST_NAME,S.FIRST_NAME,CLS.CLASS_NAME
FROM    STUDENTS S,STUDENT_SCHEDULES SS,CLASS_SCHEDULE CS,CLASSES CLS
WHERE   S.STUDENT_ID = SS.STUDENT_ID
AND     SS.CLASS_SCHEDULE_ID = CS.CLASS_SCHEDULE_ID
AND     CS.CLASS_ID = CLS.CLASS_ID;
```

Instead of entering this query often, you could create a view.

To create a view:

1. From the Data View window, right-click Views.
2. Select New View from the shortcut menu.
3. Enter the above query in the SQL pane.
4. Select Run from the Query menu. Fix any errors.
5. Remove the semicolon.
6. Close the New View window.
7. Click Yes in the Visual Basic dialog box.
8. Change the name of the view to STUDENT_REGISTRATIONS.

Now you can use the STUDENT_REGISTRATIONS view in your queries like any other table. For example, you can type SELECT * FROM STUDENT_REGISTRATIONS, and it will run the query you typed in to create the view in the first place.

8

Stored Procedures

SQL is a nonprocedural language and works with sets of data. SQL Server uses a set of procedural extensions to SQL called Transact-SQL. Transact-SQL is a programming language that allows you to write logic and save this logic in a stored procedure. This section provides only an overview of Transact-SQL. You should already know how to program in a procedural language, such as Visual Basic, to understand the syntax of Transact-SQL and how to use it in SQL Server.

Transact-SQL provides procedural capabilities such as:

➤ Assignment statements

➤ If/Else Logic

➤ Case logic

➤ Loops

➤ Error handling

➤ Transaction handling

Transact-SQL allows you to create compiled programs that run in the SQL Server environment. This improves system performance because it prevents SQL statements from being parsed, compiled, and run. SQL Server runs stored procedures as compiled programs and therefore they exhibit a faster execution time than their SQL counterparts. Also, running a stored procedure on the server reduces network performance because the code is run on the server and results are returned to the client.

You can use **SELECT**, **INSERT**, **UPDATE**, and **DELETE SQL** statements in Transact-SQL. SQL is a set-processing language. Instead of a row, it works on a set of data.

Variables

In Transact-SQL, you can store values in variables. Variables store results for calculations or processing of data within a program. As the program executes, the values stored in the variables can change.

There are two types of variables in Transact-SQL:

➤ **Local variables** Variables you declare as local variables are only seen by the procedure declaring them. The syntax for local variable declaration in SQL Server is:

```
DECLARE @v_varname datatype, @v_varname1 datatype
```

The datatype is any valid SQL Server internal datatype. These are the same datatypes you used in Chapter 6. One variable naming convention used in stored procedures is using v_ as a prefix to variables, g_ as a prefix to global variables, and p_ as a prefix to arguments or parameters. Microsoft does not recommend a particular naming convention in SQL Server.

➤ **Global variables** Variables you declare as global are seen by all connections to the database and by all stored procedures. The syntax for a global variable declaration in SQL Server is:

```
DECLARE @@g_varname datatype
```

Examples of variable declarations are:

```
DECLARE @v_age int
DECLARE @v_date datetime, num_of_months int
DECLARE @v_lastname varchar(35), @v_firstname varchar(35)
```

Assigning Values To Variables
Once you have defined the variables you are going to use, you can assign values to those variables. The syntax for assigning a value to a variable is:

```
SELECT @v_varname = 0
```

The following are examples of assignment statements:

```
SELECT @v_age = 13
SELECT @v_counter = @v_counter + 1
SELECT @v_lastname = 'Morneau'
```

Flow Control
Now you know how to declare variables and assign values to variables. You must also understand the syntax of the flow control statements in Transact-SQL. Table 8.5 defines the different flow control statements supported in Transact-SQL.

Error Handling
The next step in Transact-SQL is to learn how to return errors to the client. The statement used to return errors is **RAISERROR**. The syntax of **RAISERROR** is:

```
RAISERROR({msg_id | msg_str}, severity, state[, argument1[, argument2]])
[WITH LOG]
```

The msg_id is the error number. The msg_str is the error description. After you raise an error, the global variable @@ERROR, set by SQL Server when an error occurs, passes the value as the msg_id. An error message of severity 14 or lower is an informational message. An error message of severity 15 is a warning message. An error message of severity 16 or higher is an error.

Table 8.5   Flow control.

Construct	Description	Example
BEGIN..END	Defines a block of statements. Usually used with IF, ELSE, or WHILE	IF @v_age < 20 BEGIN SELECT @v_message = 'You are young' SELECT @v_type = 'Youth' END

IF..ELSE	Defines a conditional statement that executes code after the THEN IF TRUE, or optionally executes code after the ELSE IF FALSE	IF @v_age < 20
		BEGIN
		SELECT @v_message =
		        'You are young'
		SELECT @v_type = 'Youth'
		
		END
		ELSE
		BEGIN
		SELECT @v_message =
		        'You are old'
		SELECT @v_type = 'Adult'
		END

GOTO label	Unconditionally branches to the line following the label	GOTO Goodbye ... Goodbye: SELECT @v_message = 'Goodbye'
RETURN (n)	Exits unconditionally with a return code of n	RETURN (0) or RETURN(1) Returns 0 for successful operation and 1 for unsuccessful operation

WHILE	The looping construct that executes a block of statements until the WHILE condition is false	SELECT @v_counter = 0
		WHILE @v_counter <> 20
		BEGIN
		    PRINT @v_counter
		    SELECT @v_counter =
		@v_counter + 1
		END

... BREAK	Exits the innermost WHILE loop unconditionally	SELECT @v_counter = 0
		WHILE @v_counter <> 20
		BEGIN
		    PRINT @v_counter
		    SELECT @v_counter =
		@v_counter + 1
		    IF @v_counter = 10
		    BEGIN
		        BREAK
		    END
		END

(continued)

Table 8.5   Flow control *(continued)*.

Construct	Description	Example
CASE	Replaces multiple IF..THEN..ELSE IF..THEN..ELSE with a simpler representation	CASE WHEN @v_age <= 20 THEN SELECT @v_type = 'Youth' WHEN @v_age >=20 and @v_age <=50 SELECT @type = 'Middle Age' ELSE SELECT @type = 'Old Age' END

Severity errors of 19 or higher must use the **WITH LOG** statement. Windows NT logs these messages in the Windows NT event log. The Windows NT event log logs only severe errors (errors that cause an application or service to crash) that occur in the Windows NT environment.

Operators
Transact-SQL supplies the standard arithmetic operators, as listed in Table 8.6.

Using Stored Procedures And Transaction Processing
You have enough information at this point to learn the syntax of a stored procedure:

```
CREATE PROCEDURE proc_name
@p_argument1 datatype,
@p_argument2 datatype
AS
...
RETURN (0)
```

This syntax allows you to declare a name for your stored procedure, declare arguments, provide the processing, and return successfully from the procedure. A common type of stored procedure you will be using is included below.

Table 8.6   Arithmetic operators

Symbol	Operation
+	Additon
-	Subtraction
x	Multiplication
/	Divion
%	Module, which returns the remainder of a division operation

You can use — as a comment delimiter in Transact-SQL.

```
-- This procedure inserts a row into the category table
CREATE PROCEDURE proc_insert_category
@p_category varchar(50)
AS
INSERT INTO CATEGORIES (CATEGORY_NAME)
VALUES (@p_category)
RETURN (0)
```

The above stored procedure example accepts one argument, @p_category, and inserts this category into the CATEGORIES table. For this example, this code is fine. When the **INSERT** statement is run, SQL Server explicitly commits, or makes the changes permanent in the database, on statement completion. If you had to perform multiple inserts, then explicitly committing each statement would not be efficient. Instead, use a transaction. A transaction is a group of statements that are either committed at once or are all rolled back (uncommitted). For example, let's say you want to add a class to the schedule. You notice that this information is in two tables, CLASSES and CLASS_SCHEDULE. You need two **INSERT** statements to enter this data into the tables. Let's say the power goes out after processing the first row in the CLASSES table. This creates a data consistency problem because the schedule data was never entered into the CLASS_SCHEDULE table. To prevent this from happening, create a transaction for both **INSERT** statements. Now if something unexpected happens after you process the first row, the entire transaction is canceled. Use the following syntax to create a transaction:

```
BEGIN TRAN [name]
       INSERT...
       INSERT...
-- Commit the current transaction
COMMIT TRAN [name]
or
-- Cancel the current transaction
ROLLBACK TRAN [name]
```

You need to modify the above stored procedure to handle transactions properly. The new stored procedure is:

```
-- This procedure inserts a row into the category table
CREATE PROCEDURE proc_insert_category
@p_category varchar(50)
AS
BEGIN TRAN
```

```
INSERT INTO CATEGORIES (CATEGORY_NAME)
VALUES (@p_category)
IF (@@ERROR <> 0) Goto OnError
COMMIT TRAN
RETURN (0)
OnError:
ROLLBACK TRAN
RETURN (1)
```

After the **INSERT** statement, check to see if the insert was successful. If it wasn't, roll back the transaction. Otherwise, commit it. A global variable **@@ERROR** returns a 0 if successful. It returns nonzero for an error. A return status of 0 is successful. A return status of 1 is unsuccessful.

You can do one last thing with your stored procedure. You can include some business rules against the data before you insert the data. This is extra protection against invalid data in the database.

The revised stored procedure is the following:

```
-- This procedure inserts a row into the category table
CREATE PROCEDURE proc_insert_category
@p_category varchar(50)
AS
BEGIN TRAN
If @p_category IS NULL Goto CatError
INSERT INTO CATEGORIES (CATEGORY_NAME)
VALUES (@p_category)
IF (@@ERROR <> 0) Goto OnError
COMMIT TRAN
RETURN (0)
OnError:
ROLLBACK TRAN
RETURN (1)
CatError:
RAISERROR('Category information cannot be blank!',16,-1)
Return (1)
```

Although SQL Server has built-in error handling, it is difficult to read and understand the messages. You should therefore catch errors and return readable messages, as above, in your stored procedures. You should map the SQL Server error messages to user-defined error messages within the database (e.g., create a table in the database just for error handling, and define error numbers and descriptions for common errors). This makes maintenance easy.

Next, you need to learn how to create, modify, and delete stored procedures in Database Designer.

To create a stored procedure in Database Designer:

1. Run Visual Basic and show the Data View window (if not already running).

2. Right-click the Stored Procedures folder.

3. Select New Stored Procedure to see the Stored Procedure editor.

4. Enter the stored procedure above.

5. Click the Save to Database icon on the toolbar If you receive a message asking whether to overwrite the item, click Yes.

6. Debug any errors.

This saves the stored procedure to the database.

To modify a stored procedure, right-click the procedure in the Data View window, and select Design from the shortcut menu. The Stored Procedure editor changes CREATE PROCEDURE to ALTER PROCEDURE. To delete a stored procedure, click the stored procedure and press the Delete key.

To run a stored procedure and verify the results of the stored procedure:

1. In the Data View window, right-click Views.

2. Select New View from the shortcut menu.

3. Right-click the Diagram pane and select Hide Pane.

4. Right-click the Grid pane and select Hide Pane.

5. Type EXEC proc_insert_category "Lab" in the SQL pane.

6. Select Run from the Query menu.

7. When you see a message indicating how many rows were affected by the query, click OK.

8. Type "SELECT * FROM CATEGORIES;" in the SQL pane.

9. Select Run from the Query menu.

10. Verify that the Lab row is in the table.

Cursors

Cursors are groups of rows returned from a query that allow you to scroll the group one row at a time. Cursors help you do row-by-row processing in the database. Complete the following steps to use a cursor:

1. DECLARE a cursor.

2. OPEN the cursor.

3. PROCESS the cursor by FETCHING from it until there are no more rows to fetch. A global variable @@FETCH_STATUS is set to zero when the pointer is at the end of a cursor.

4. CLOSE the cursor.

5. DEALLOCATE the cursor.

First, declare a cursor using the syntax below:

```
DECLARE cur_cursor_name CURSOR FOR
select-query
```

After you declare a cursor, open it. The following syntax opens a cursor:

```
OPEN cur_cursor_name
```

Next, process the cursor, using a WHILE loop. The syntax for processing a cursor is:

```
FETCH NEXT FROM cur_cursor_name INTO @var-list
WHILE (@@FETCH_STATUS = 0)  -- Keep fetching until no more rows
@@FETCH_STATUS <> 0 in cursor
BEGIN
      ...
      FETCH NEXT FROM cur_cursor_name INTO @var-list
END
```

The **FETCH** statement returns the next row in the cursor. The **@@FETCH_STATUS** variable allows you to determine whether you are at the end of the cursor. After the cursor has been processed, you must close the cursor and return the cursor resources to the database (deallocate), using the following syntax:

```
CLOSE cur_cursor_name
DEALLOCATE cur_cursor_name
```

Following is an example of a stored procedure that uses a cursor. Using a cursor, you can build a stored procedure that searches the database for grades that meet certain criteria. The initial search criteria are:

➤ Grades earned in August of 1998

➤ Points earned are greater than 80

```
CREATE PROCEDURE proc_find_grades
AS
DECLARE @v_GRADE_DATE DATETIME
DECLARE @v_POINTS_EARNED SMALLINT
DECLARE cur_find_grades CURSOR FOR
SELECT GRADE_DATE,POINTS_EARNED from GRADES
OPEN cur_find_grades
```

```
FETCH NEXT FROM cur_find_grades INTO @v_GRADE_DATE, @v_POINTS_EARNED
WHILE (@@FETCH_STATUS = 0)
BEGIN
      IF ((@v_GRADE_DATE >= CAST('08/1/98' AS DATETIME) AND
(@v_GRADE_DATE <= CAST('08/31/98' AS DATETIME))) AND
(@v_POINTS_EARNED > 80))
      SELECT @v_GRADE_DATE AS GRADE_DATE,
@v_POINTS_EARNED AS POINTS_EARNED
      FETCH NEXT FROM cur_find_grades INTO @v_GRADE_DATE,
@v_POINTS_EARNED
END
CLOSE cur_find_grades
DEALLOCATE cur_find_grades
RETURN (0)
```

The SELECT clause in the IF statement returns a result set with the results of the stored procedure.

CHAPTER SUMMARY

This chapter presented the basics of using Database Designer and Query Designer in Visual Basic in an SQL Server environment. As a programmer, you are responsible for creating queries using SQL and for creating stored procedures using Transact-SQL. A database administrator creates, updates, and deletes tables and relationships. This chapter showed how to use Database Designer to create basic tables and relationships. Usually, in a team environment, you consult with a database administrator concerning these tasks. You can find additional information about SQL and Transact-SQL in SQL Server online books.

REVIEW QUESTIONS

1. Microsoft Visual Database tools consists of:
   a. Query Designer and Database Designer
   b. Designer Database and Designer Queries
   c. Query Database and Database Query
   d. none of the above

2. Which tool uses visual design techniques to create and run SQL statements?
   a. Designer Database
   b. Query Designer
   c. Database Designer
   d. none of the above

3. Which tool uses visual design techniques to create database objects, such as tables, views, and stored procedures?

    a. Designer Database

    b. Query Designer

    c. Database Designer

    d. none of the above

4. _____ consist(s) of commands that allow you to manipulate databases.

    a. Variables

    b. SLL

    c. Visual Basic

    d. SQL

5. A(n) _____ statement allows you to view data in one or more tables.

    a. **DELETE**

    b. **INSERT**

    c. **UPDATE**

    d. **SELECT**

6. Which clause in a **SELECT** statement allows you to filter rows in one or more tables?

    a. **SELECT**

    b. **ORDER BY**

    c. **WHERE**

    d. **GROUP BY**

7. Which clause in a **SELECT** statement allows you to sort rows in one or more tables?

    a. **WHERE**

    b. **SELECT**

    c. **ORDER BY**

    d. **HAVING**

8. Which clause in a **SELECT** statement allows you to filter by groups of rows?

    a. **ORDER BY**

    b. **WHERE**

    c. **SELECT**

    d. **HAVING**

9. Which clause in a **SELECT** statement allows you to select the columns you want to view in a result set?

    a. **ORDER BY**

    b. **SELECT**

    c. **WHERE**

    d. **GROUP BY**

10. The wildcard character in SQL that allows you to view all columns in a table is _____.

    a. !

    b. ★

    c. ^

    d. &

11. Is "John" the same as "JOHN" in SQL?

    a. Yes

    b. No

12. What are the valid logical operators in SQL? Choose all that apply.

    a. XOR

    b. OR

    c. NOT

    d. AND

13. What function allows you to round numbers?

    a. ROUND

    b. ISNULL

    c. +

    d. none of the above

14. _____ is to each row as _____ is to groups of rows.

    a. Yes, No

    b. Scalar, aggregate

    c. Aggregate, scalar

    d. Scalar, scalar

15. Which of the following are valid aggregate functions? Choose all that apply.

    a. ISNULL

    b. COUNT

    c. CAST

    d. AVG

16. _____ is a special result set that allows you to scroll the set one row at a time.

    a. SELECT

    b. INSERT

    c. CURSOR

    d. none of the above

17. To retrieve the next row of a cursor, the statement used is _____:

    a. **NEXT**

    b. **CURSOR**

    c. **OPEN**

    d. **FETCH**

18. To close a cursor properly, the statement used is _____.

    a. **CURSOR**

    b. **FETCH**

    c. **CLOSE**

    d. **OPEN**

19. Which of the following SQL statements belong to DML? Choose all that apply.

    a. **CREATE**

    b. **SELECT**

    c. **INSERT**

    d. **UPDATE**

20. Which of the following SQL statements belong to DDL? Choose all that apply.

    a. **CREATE**

    b. **INSERT**

    c. **UPDATE**

    d. **SELECT**

HANDS-ON PROJECTS

Project 8.1

Using Query Designer, create and run the following queries.

   a. Write a query that shows all categories. Show only the category name in the result set. Sort in ascending order by category.

   b. Write a query that shows only the students' names and home phone numbers.

   c. Write a query that shows only the students' names and email addresses.

   d. Write a query that shows all students with the last name of Smith.

   e. Write a query that shows anyone with either the first name of John or the last name of Flintstone.

   f. Write a query that shows the instructors' names and what they are teaching in the fall of 1998.

   g. Write a query that shows what classes a student has registered for. Show only the student's name and the class names.

   h. Write a query that shows all students registered for CP 108. Show only the student names, the class number, and the class name.

   i. Write a query that shows a student with a failing grade in the fall of 1998. Show the student name, the class name, the category, and the grade.

   j. Write a query that shows how many failing grades each student has in the fall of 1998. Show only the student name and the number of failing grades.

   k. Write a query that finds the average grade by each category. Show the student name, the class name, the category, and the average.

   l. Modify the query in item k to only show average grades above a 90 percent.

   m. Write a query that counts the number of grades in each category. Show the class name, the category name, and the number of grades.

Project 8.2

Using Query Designer, create and run the following views.

   a. Modify the STUDENT_RESERVATION view and add term, year, and section to the view.

   b. Create a new view that shows the term, year, class number, class name, section, and instructor teaching the class.

   c. Create a new view that shows the categories for each class and the grade distribution.

   d. Create a new view that shows the term, year, instructor, class name, section, and students registered.

e. Create a new view that shows the student contact information.

f. Create a new view that shows the instructor contact information.

Project 8.3

Using Database Designer, enter more test data for all the tables in the CTIS database. Make sure that all the data is properly related in the tables. (*Note:* This helps you understand the underlying database structure.)

a. CATEGORIES

b. CLASS_SCHEDULE

c. CLASSES

d. GRADE_DISTRIBUTIONS

e. GRADES

f. INSTRUCTORS

g. STUDENT_SCHEDULES

h. STUDENTS

8

Project 8.4

Using Database Designer, create the tables and the relationships you generated from the Assignment Management subsystem from your physical design.

a. Create the tables using Table Designer.

b. Create the relationships using the Database Diagram.

c. Create test data for these tables.

Project 8.5

Using the Stored Procedure editor, create the following stored procedures, using the techniques learned in this chapter.

a. Create a proc_update_category that passes the category_id and the category_name to the procedure, and updates the category in the table.

b. Create a proc_delete_category that passes the p_category_id to the procedure, and deletes the category from the table.

c. Create the insert, update, and delete stored procedures for the following tables:

i) STUDENTS

ii) INSTRUCTORS

iii) GRADES

iv) CLASSES

v) CLASS_SCHEDULE

vi) STUDENT_SCHEDULES

vii) GRADE_DISTRIBUTIONS

viii) ASSIGNMENTS

Project 8.6

Using the Stored Procedure editor, create the following stored procedure, using cursors.

a. For each student, drop the lowest quiz grade for a particular class requested. (*Hint*: Create two records in the result set using the SELECT @before_average AS BEFORE_AVERAGE, @after_average AS AFTER_AVERAGE statement.) Create additional test data to verify that your procedure works properly.

Project 8.7

Challenge Problem: Using all the techniques you learned in this chapter, solve the following problem.

For each class, determine the students' final grades. Calculate the final grade, finding the average grade of each category for each student for each class, multiplied by the weight of each category, divided by 100. Next, sum all weighted grades to get the average for the class. You can use temporary tables if necessary.

CHAPTER NINE

CREATING COMPONENTS FROM BUSINESS SERVICES AND DATA SERVICES USING VISUAL BASIC 6.0

AFTER READING THIS CHAPTER AND COMPLETING THE EXERCISES, YOU WILL BE ABLE TO:

➤ Define Component Object Model (COM)

➤ Define Distributed Component Object Model (DCOM)

➤ Define middleware

➤ Describe the differences between in-process servers (ActiveX DLL), out-of-process servers (ActiveX EXE), and ActiveX controls

➤ Create ActiveX DLL components in Visual Modeler

➤ Generate components from Visual Modeler to Visual Basic

➤ Code component methods in Visual Basic

➤ Code a test client to verify component functionality

➤ Reverse-engineer Visual Basic code into Visual Modeler

➤ Use Microsoft Transaction Server (MTS) to create transaction-oriented components

➤ Use Microsoft Transaction Server Explorer to install components in MTS

➤ Use Microsoft Message Queue Server (MSMQ) to create asynchronous applications

After you've implemented the physical design, the development team freezes the database schema. This allows them to develop components from the business services and data services of your model.

As you begin coding components, use the Visual Modeler Code Generation Wizard to generate a code skeleton for you to start with. In this chapter, you will learn to create ActiveX DLL components, using Microsoft Transaction Server and Microsoft Message Queue Server.

 You need to have Visual Studio 6.0 completely installed to use this chapter effectively. If you are using Windows 95/98, skip the Microsoft Message Queue Server section of this chapter. Windows 95/98 does not currently support this technology.

CHAPTER OVERVIEW

In the last chapter, you learned how to write SQL statements, create database schemas, and create Stored Procedures in SQL Server. You've already created part of the data services in the database.

You can now create the next part of the system—the components—which are created from the business and data services of the logical design. Recall that *components* are self-contained precompiled software units (code) that can be reused in one or more applications. Components provide specific functionality to an application, and contain one or more objects.

The level of difficulty in this chapter is intermediate to advanced. You should not attempt this chapter until you have a firm introductory knowledge of Visual Basic.

In this chapter, you will create ActiveX components (in-process servers). You will create them both as standalone components and in the context of Microsoft Transaction Server. You will also learn how to administer MTS. You use Microsoft Message Queue Server to create MTS ActiveX components. Recall the importance of configuration management from Chapter 7. You will use Visual SourceSafe throughout this chapter.

MIDDLEWARE

Software components created using ActiveX technology fall into a broad category of software called middleware. Middleware allows clients and servers to communicate with each other over a network (see Figure 9.1). Middleware ties the client software and server software together. The only service it provides is delivering data between a client and a server. Middleware hides the details and complexities of the operating system and the network software.

You will investigate several kinds of middleware software, such as object-specific middleware (for example, COM, DCOM, and ActiveX), database-specific middleware (such as ODBC, OLE DB, and ADO), and transaction and queueing middleware (such as MTS and MSMQ).

Component Object Model (COM) And Distributed Component Object Model (DCOM)

COM is Microsoft's standard for object interaction and supplies the plumbing (a standard approach for an object to supply its services to another object and access services of another object) so that objects can communicate with each other. You can create COM objects in any language such as Visual Basic, Visual J++, and Visual C++. DCOM is Microsoft's standard that enhances COM so that objects located on a single machine or across machines on the network can

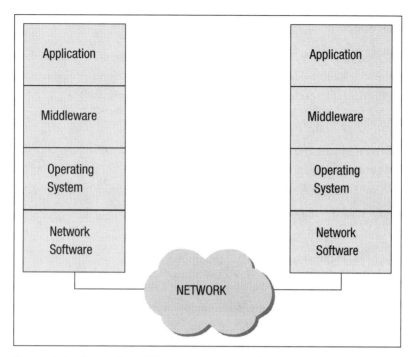

Figure 9.1   Role of middleware in a networked environment

9

interact or communicate with each other. COM only handles interaction of objects on a single machine. Figure 9.2 illustrates COM/DCOM technologies.

Several technologies that use COM/DCOM are:

➤ **Compound document management**   Object linking and embedding (OLE) supplies the technology to embed objects. It provides a copy of the object to embed or link, and another copy in its own file that serves as a shortcut from the object to other objects or applications. For example, Microsoft Office supplies OLE capability in each of its applications. You can link or embed an Excel spreadsheet in a Word document. When you need

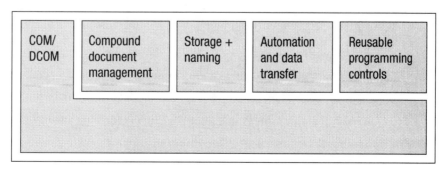

Figure 9.2   COM/DCOM technologies.

to change the spreadsheet, you double-click the Excel object. If the object is embedded (i.e., a copy of the Excel object is part of Word), then the Excel application opens in Word and allows you to change the object. In this case, Word is called a container object because Word contains the Excel object. If the object is linked (i.e., a copy of the Excel object is stored in its own file), Excel opens the spreadsheet in the Excel window. After you change the spreadsheet, the updated object appears in Word.

➤ **Storage and naming** A dynamic-link library (dll), an executable (exe), or a control (ocx) are different ways COM/DCOM objects are stored. Windows uses a class identifier (CLSID) to uniquely identify each component stored. The Windows registry stores the CLSIDs and the name of the component (PROGID), which is the name of the project with a period and the name of the class. If you need to find your component in the Registry, search for PROGID first, determine the CLSID, and use the CLSID to find all instances of the component in the Registry.

Do not change the Windows Registry unless absolutely necessary. All configuration information, including hardware and software, is stored in the Registry. Making a mistake in the Registry could render your computer unusable.

➤ **Automation and data transfer** Windows supports two types of automation. The first is an in-process server (ActiveX DLL), which allows your component to run in the same address space as your application. The second is an out-of-process server (ActiveX EXE), which allows your component to run in its own address space, separate from the application that called it.

➤ **Reusable, programmable controls** ActiveX controls are special COM objects that are created as mini-GUI applications that run in the context of an application and are reusable. Examples of controls are text boxes, labels, and command buttons. You can reuse these controls in any application.

Figure 9.3 shows the interaction between DCOM objects on a network.

This chapter explains how to create ActiveX DLLs, using Microsoft Visual Basic 6.0. You need to accomplish several tasks to create ActiveX DLL components:

1. Set up Visual Basic to interact with Visual Modeler.

2. Map logical classes into components in Visual Modeler, if necessary.

3. Prepare the components for code generation.

4. Generate the components in Visual Basic.

5. Use Visual Basic to code the components.

6. Compile and test the components.

7. Prepare and compile components into ActiveX DLLs.

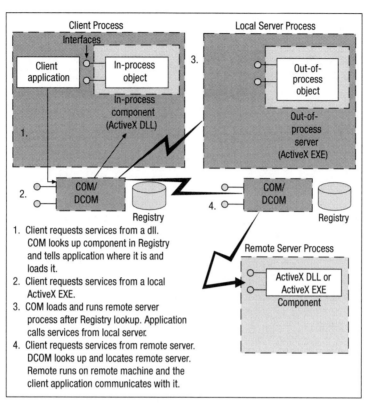

Figure 9.3   DCOM object interaction.

In this chapter, you will generate a component from the CLASSES table you used in Chapter 8.

Introduction To The Visual Basic 6.0 Environment

Before you begin setting up Visual Basic, investigate the Visual Basic environment. The Visual Basic Integrated Development environment provides a graphical way of designing Visual Basic applications. From a single environment, you can manage your files in a project, code your program, and run your program to see the results immediately. Figure 9.4 shows the Visual Basic 6.0 environment.

Visual Basic contains the following windows:

➤ **Toolbox** By default, the toolbox stores all the available controls. You can add controls to the toolbox, if necessary.

➤ **Form Designer** The Form Designer is where you create Visual Basic forms in your projects.

➤ **Code Editor window** The Code Editor window is an ASCII text editor that allows you to enter code.

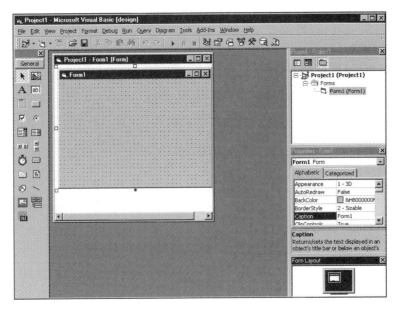

Figure 9.4 Visual Basic 6.0 environment.

➤ **Form Layout window** The Form Layout window allows you to position the forms on your screen.

➤ **Properties window** The Properties windows allows you to view and update control and object properties used in Visual Basic.

➤ **Project Explorer** The Project Explorer window allows you to manage all the files you use in your Visual Basic application.

Setting Up Visual Basic To Interact With Microsoft Visual Modeler

Visual Basic lets third-party vendors include *add-ins*, mini programs that enhance the functionality of the Visual Basic environment. Microsoft supplies an add-in to Visual Basic for Visual Modeler. You need to install this add-in before Visual Modeler can interact with Visual Basic.

To install the Visual Modeler add-in:

1. Click the Start button on the taskbar. Point to Programs, Microsoft Visual Studio 6.0, and then click Microsoft Visual Basic 6.0. The location of Microsoft Visual Basic 6.0 on the Start menu may vary, depending upon where it was installed on your system.

2. Click Cancel in the New Project dialog box.

3. Click Add-Ins, and then Add-In Manager on the menu bar to load Add-In Manager.

4. Scroll down the list box and click Visual Component Manager 6.0.

5. In the Load Behavior frame, click Loaded/Unloaded and Load on Startup, if necessary. You need to select both options to allow Visual Basic to load these add-ins on startup.

6. Repeat Steps 3-5 for Visual Modeler Add-In and Visual Modeler Menus Add-In.

7. Click OK to close Add-In Manager.

8. Click Exit in the File menu.

Now, when you load Visual Basic, the Visual Modeler add-in loads.

Using Microsoft Visual Modeler To Generate An ActiveX DLL In Visual Basic 6.0

After you have set up Visual Basic to work with Visual Modeler, your next step is to map logical classes into components and configure those components to generate code correctly.

To map logical classes into components and generate Visual Basic code:

1. Load Visual SourceSafe Explorer and log on as CTIS with a password of CTIS.

2. Add class.mdl from the Chapter_09 folder of the CD to the Documents project under project CTIS.

3. Select the CTIS folder, then click SourceSafe, Get Latest Version. Make sure that the Recursive and Build Tree options are checked, and that the Make Writable option is not checked.

4. If you need to set the working folder, click the CTIS project in the Browse window, click Set Working Folder on the File menu, then type "c:\work\ctis" in the Name text box and click OK.

5. Check out class.mdl. Make sure to change the path in the To: box to "c:\work\ctis\documents".

6. Load Visual Modeler and open c:\work\CTIS\documents\class.mdl.

7. In the Browser window, right-click the Component View folder.

8. Point to New, and then click Component.

9. Change the name of the component to "<<DLL>> comCourse". The <<DLL>> stereotype tells Visual Modeler you are creating an ActiveX DLL.

10. Right-click <<DLL>> comCourse and click Open Specification.

11. Click the Realizes tab.

12. Click clsClass, press the Ctrl key, and click clsClassData.

13. Right-click the selected files and click Assign. This assigns both logical classes to the comCourse component.

14. Click the General tab.

15. Select Visual Basic as the language.

16. Click OK to close the Component Specification dialog box.

17. Click Save on the File menu to save the model.

18. Right-click comCourse and click Generate Code.

19. When the Code Generation Wizard appears, click Next.

20. In the Select Classes dialog box, click Next.

21. In the Preview Classes dialog box, click Next.

22. In the General Options dialog box, make sure Include Comments is selected. Remove all the other selections.

23. Click Next.

24. In the Finish dialog box, click Finish. Visual Modeler creates the skeleton Visual Basic ActiveX DLL for you automatically.

25. In the Delete Classes dialog box, click Form1 to remove it from the project.

26. Click OK.

27. In the Summary dialog box, click Close. You now have a skeleton of a Visual Basic DLL in Visual Basic.

28. In Visual Basic, click Save Project on the File menu. (Note: Make sure to save the files under the c:\work\CTIS\business_svc_src\comCourse folder. Click the New Folder button to create a new folder called comCourse.)

29. Click No on Add Project To SourceSafe.

30. Using SourceSafe Explorer, create the comCourse project under business_svc_src.

31. Add the Visual Basic files to the project.

32. Close Visual SourceSafe Explorer.

33. Click Exit on the File menu to exit Visual Basic.

Using ActiveX Data Objects (ADO) And OLE DB To Communicate With The Database

Before you can begin coding, you need to understand the theory behind the classes. Figure 9.5 shows the class diagram for course information.

First, examine the function of clsClassData. This class's responsibility is to interact with the database because it's created under the data services of the

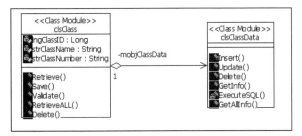

Figure 9.5 Class diagram for course information.

application model. You can tell that this class needs to have insert, update, and delete functions because you need to be able to insert, update, and delete data in the database. The function of the **GetInfo** method is to get a single row from the CLASSES table; the function of the **GetAllInfo** method is to get all rows from the CLASSES table. ExecuteSP function must communicate with the database and pass a function call to a stored procedure in the database.

Next, consider how you will write code to interact with the database. Use ADO because it supplies an object model that allows you to interact with the database. Figure 9.6 illustrates how an application connects to a database.

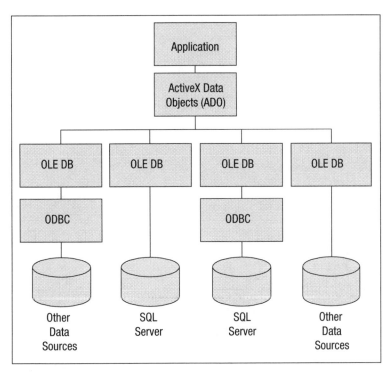

Figure 9.6 How an application connects to a database.

An application accesses a database using a built-in component called ActiveX Data Objects (ADO). ADO communicates through a data provider's OLE DB driver to the actual database or any other types of data sources, either directly or through an ODBC driver. Database manufacturers supply their own OLE DB driver to communicate to their database management system. Microsoft supplies a component interface to each of the providers' OLE DB drivers. Figure 9.7 shows the UML class diagram of ADO.

The following list describes each ADO object:

➤ **Connection** Using the connection object, you can access the data in a database such as SQL Server. The connection object allows you to connect to the database, send queries and receive results from the database, and disconnect from the database. Also, the connection object supplies a transaction interface. Table 9.1 describes the useful properties and methods of the connection object. Additional properties and methods can be found in the online documentation for Visual Basic.

➤ **Command** Using the command object, you can send and retrieve results of queries and stored procedures, instead of using the Execute method of the connection object. Table 9.2 describes the methods and properties of the command object.

➤ **Parameters collection and parameter object** A parameters collection holds one or more parameter objects, which are the arguments passed in a stored procedure or SQL statement. A *collection* is a special data type in Visual Basic that is a dynamic list of items. The collection grows and shrinks

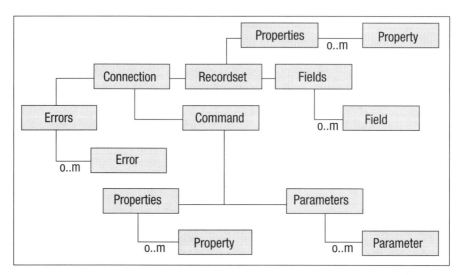

Figure 9.7 UML class diagram of ADO.

Table 9.1   Useful properties and methods of the connection object.

Property/Method	Name	Description
Method	Open	Opens a new connection to the database
Method	Close	Closes a connection to the database
Method	Execute	Runs an SQL query or stored procedure
Method	BeginTrans	Starts a new transaction
Method	CommitTrans	Commits a transaction successfully
Method	RollbackTrans	Cancels a transaction
Property	Attributes	Determines where to begin a new transaction when an old one ends
Property	CommandTimeout	Number of seconds to wait before terminating a command with an error
Property	ConnectionString	Information needed to create a connection to the database such as driver name, database name, username, and password
Property	CursorLocation	Location of cursor (e.g., adUseClient on the client or adUseServer on the Server)
Property	DefaultDatabase	Sets or returns the default database to use for a connection
Property	Provider	Sets or returns the provider of the OLE DB driver
Property	State	Returns whether the connection is open (adStateOpen) or closed (adStateClosed)
Property	Version	Returns the version of ADO

as necessary, depending on the number of items in the collection. Tables 9.3 and 9.4 describe the methods and properties of the parameters collection and the parameter object. A parameter object is a single instance of a parameter, while a parameters collection contains many parameter objects.

➤ **Recordset** Using the recordset object, you can send a query to the database and return a cursor. Recall that a *cursor* allows row-by-row processing of an SQL result set. A *recordset* holds rows of data that contain columns or fields. Table 9.5 describes the useful methods and attributes of the recordset object. Additional properties and methods can be found in the online documentation.

➤ **Fields collection and field object** A fields collection allows you to access the column or field data of the current record of the recordset. Tables 9.6 and 9.7 describe the useful methods and properties of the fields collection and field object. Refer to the Visual Basic online documentation for additional methods and properties.

Table 9.2 Useful properties and methods of the command object.

Property/ Method	Name	Description
Method	CreateParameter	Creates a parameter object in the parameters collection. The parameter object supplies argument information for a stored procedure
Method	Execute	Runs the SQL statement or stored procedure specified in the CommandText property
Property	ActiveConnection	Sets the connection to use with this command object. Must be set to send and retrieve SQL statements or stored procedures to the database
Property	CommandText	The text of the SQL statement or stored procedure name to execute
Property	CommandTimeout	The number of seconds to wait when executing a command before an error is returned
Property	CommandType	Type of query Examples: **AdCmdUnknown** 0 Unknown type of query **AdCmdText** 1 SQL statement **AdCmdTable** 2 Name of the table **AdCmdStoredProc** 4 Stored procedure or query, which is stored in the data source
Property	Name	Allows a name to be assigned to the command object
Property	State	Returns whether the command is open (adStateOpen) or closed (adStateClosed)

Table 9.3 Useful properties and methods of the parameters collection.

Property/ Method	Name	Description
Method	Append	Adds a parameter object to the collection
Method	Delete	Removes a parameter from the collection
Method	Refresh	Updates the collection with changes to the parameters
Property	Count	Returns the number of parameter objects in the collection
Property	Item	Returns the contents of a parameter object in the collection

Table 9.4   Useful properties and methods of the parameter object.

Property/Method	Name	Description
Property	Attributes	Type of data that the parameter accepts
Property	Direction	Determines whether the parameter object is for input, output, or both
Property	Name	Name of the parameter
Property	NumericScale	Number of decimal places in a numeric parameter
Property	Precision	Number of digits in a numeric parameter
Property	Size	Maximum size in bytes of the parameter
Property	Type	Data type of the parameter. Examples: **adInteger**, **adVarChar**, **adNumeric**. Refer to the Visual Basic online documentation for more data types
Property	Value	Value assigned to a parameter

Table 9.5   Useful properties and methods of the recordset object.

Property/Method	Name	Description
Method	AddNew	Creates a new record in a recordset
Method	CancelBatch	Cancels a pending batch update of the recordset
Method	CancelUpdate	Cancels an update to the recordset
Method	Clone	Creates a duplicate of current recordset
Method	Close	Closes an open recordset
Method	Delete	Deletes the current row in a recordset
Method	MoveFirst	Moves the recordset pointer to the first record in the recordset
Method	MoveNext	Moves to the next record in the recordset
Method	MovePrevious	Moves to the previous record in the recordset
Method	MoveLast	Moves to the last record in the recordset
Method	NextRecordSet	Moves to the next recordset in the query
Method	Open	Opens a new cursor on a recordset
Method	Requery	Updates the current recordset by rerunning the query
Method	Update	Saves any changes made to the current record
Method	UpdateBatch	Writes all pending batch updates
Property	ActiveConnection	The connection object that a recordset belongs to

9

(continued)

Table 9.5 Useful properties and methods of the recordset object *(continued)*.

Property/Method	Name	Description
Property	BOF	True, if the recordset pointer is at the beginning of the recordset
Property	CursorLocation	Location of cursor on the client (adUseClient) or on the server (adUseSever)
Property	CursorType	The type of cursor used in the recordset
Property	EOF	True, if the recordset pointer is at the end of the recordset
Property	RecordCount	Number of records in the recordset
Property	State	Returns whether the recordset is open or closed

Table 9.6 Useful properties and methods of the fields collection.

Property/Method	Name	Description
Method	Refresh	Updates the collection to include changes in the fields collection
Property	Count	Number of fields in the collection
Method	Item	Returns the contents of a field or column

Table 9.7 Useful properties and methods of the field object.

Property/Method	Name	Description
Method	AppendChunk	Appends data to a large text or binary field such as a memo field or a graphic
Method	GetChunk	Gets data from a large text or binary field
Property	Name	Name of the field
Property	NumericScale	Number of decimal places in a numeric field
Property	OriginalValue	Value of the field before any changes were made
Property	Precision	Number of digits in a numeric field
Property	Type	Data type of the field
Property	Value	The value assigned to the field

➤ **Errors collection and error object** You will use the errors collection and error object to determine the errors that occurred in the ADO operation. Tables 9.8 and 9.9 define the useful methods and properties of the errors collection and error object.

Table 9.8   Useful properties and methods of the errors collection.

Property/ Method	Name	Description
Method	Clear	Clears the errors collection of all error objects
Method	Item	Returns an error object
Property	Count	Returns the number of error objects in the collection

Table 9.9   Useful properties and methods of the error object.

Property/ Method	Name	Description
Property	Description	Error message
Property	Number	Error number

➤ **Properties collection and property object** The properties collection and property object provide a provider-defined characteristic of an ADO object. Basically, providers of OLE DB drivers can add their own properties to the ADO object model. Details about these objects can be found in the online documentation. You will not use these objects in your programming for this chapter.

Coding The **clsClassData** *Class*

One way to understand how to use the ADO objects is to code the **clsClassData** class. Visual Basic uses a class module to allow you to code UML classes.

To code the **clsClassData** class's **ExecuteSP** procedure:

1. Click the Start menu. Point to Programs, Microsoft Visual Studio 6.0, and then click Microsoft Visual Basic 6.0.

2. Click the Existing tab in the New Project dialog box. Locate c:\work\ CTIS\business_svc_src\comCourse in the Look in list box.

3. Click the comCourse project and then click Open.

4. Log on to Visual SourceSafe.

5. In Project Explorer, double-click Class Modules to open it, if necessary. Right-click clsClassData, and then click Check out to check out the file from SourceSafe.

6. Double-click clsClassData to open the Code window, if necessary.

7. Maximize the Code window.

8. Create a subroutine called ExecuteSP, then enter the following code. To do so, copy the code from the code09-01.txt file on your CD and paste it in the Code window. Be sure to delete any sample code in the Visual Basic window first.

9

```
Private Sub ExecuteSP(qrySP as ADODB.Command)
Dim strConn As String
Dim mvarConn As New ADODB.Connection
On Error GoTo RecordFailure
   strConn = "File Name=" & App.Path & "\ctis.udl"
   mvarConn.Open strConn
   Set qrySP.ActiveConnection = mvarConn
   qrySP.Execute
   mvarConn.Close
   Exit Sub
RecordFailure:
   mvarConn.Close
   Err.Raise Err.Number, "ExecuteSQL", Err.Description
End Sub
```

9. Click Save clsClassData.cls in the File menu.

To copy code into the Code window, navigate to the Chapter_09 folder on the CD. Double-click the appropriate text file to open it in Notepad. On the Edit menu, click Select All. Then press Ctrl+C to copy all the text. Close Notepad and click in the Code window. Then press Ctrl+V to paste the text in the Code window.

Review the above code to understand its syntax. The function of the ExecuteSP subroutine is to open a connection with the database, execute the stored procedure passed into the subroutine, and close the connection to the database. Also, you code the subroutine to handle all run-time errors.

When working with MTS, you need to open a database connection, do some work, and immediately close the database connection. This frees connection resources so other users can access them. If you leave a database connection open throughout the life of the application, it holds onto those resources. If many users connecting to the database did this, you could run out of resources on the server. This also affects the performance of your system.

The first two lines of code declare a variable for the connection string and a variable for the connection object. The next line of code enables the Visual Basic subroutine to catch all run-time errors.

Syntax
On Error Goto label

Syntax Dissection

➤ When a run-time error occurs in a routine, Visual Basic branches to the line with the label in it.

Syntax Code Example

```
On Error GoTo RecordFailure
   strConn = "File Name=" & App.Path & "\ctis.udl"
   mvarConn.Open strConn
   Set qrySP.ActiveConnection = mvarConn
   qrySP.Execute
   mvarConn.Close
   Exit Sub
RecordFailure:
   mvarConn.Close
Err.Raise Err.Number, "ExecuteSQL", Err.Description
```

Syntax Code Dissection

➤ The first line enables the routine to catch run-time errors and branch to the RecordFailure error handler when a run-time error occurs.

➤ Visual Basic monitors the lines between the On Error and RecordFailure label for a run-time error, and will branch to RecordFailure if a run-time error occurs.

➤ RecordFailure is the beginning of the error routine that runs when a run-time error occurs. The first line of the error handler closes the database connection, and the second line raises a run-time error to be caught by the calling program. Err is a global Visual Basic object that handles Visual Basic run-time errors. The Err object has two properties: Number, the run-time error number; and Description, the run-time error description.

The first line of code after the On Error statement is strConn = "File Name=" & App.Path & "\ctis.udl", which sets up a connection string for an OLE DB driver. This example uses a Universal Data Link (UDL) to set up the connection string for a connection object. UDLs let you save connection information to a file, so you can change the connection information without having to recompile your code. You save the information separately from the application, to allow you to change connection information on the fly.

To create a UDL file:

1. On the Windows Desktop, right-click a blank area, point to New, and then click Microsoft Data Link. Microsoft Data Link is a special utility that allows you to store connection information to your data sources in a file.

2. Change the name to "ctis.udl".

3. Double-click the ctis data link to launch the Data Link properties. Notice that this looks very similar to creating a data link using the Data View window.

4. Click the Provider tab and select Microsoft OLE DB Provider for SQL Server.

5. Click the Next button.

6. If you are running Windows NT Server, enter the following information:
   Select or enter Server name: <name of your server>
   Enter information to log on to server: Use Windows NT integrated security
   Select database on server: CTIS

   If you are running Windows 95/98 or Windows NT Workstation, enter the following information:
   Select or enter your Server name: <name of your server>
   Enter information to log on to server: Use a specific name and password. Use sa for the username with no password (check the No Password checkbox)
   Select database on server: CTIS

   If you do not know your Server name, right-click the Network Neighborhood icon on the Windows Desktop and then click Properties on the shortcut menu. Click the Identification tab. The Computer name is your Server name.

7. Click the OK button.

8. Copy the data link to the c:\work\CTIS\business_svc_src\comCourse folder.

9. Using Visual SourceSafe Explorer, add ctis.udl into SourceSafe in CTIS\business_svc_src\comCourse project.

The App.Path part of the string allows your application to read the correct ctis.udl file from the proper directory. App.path says to use the path where the application resides.

The following explains the next few lines of code:

Syntax Code Example

```
mvarConn.Open strConn
Set qrySP.ActiveConnection = mvarConn
qrySP.Execute
mvarConn.Close
Exit Sub
```

Syntax Code Dissection

➤ The first line passes the connection information to the Open method of the connection object, to open a connection to the database.

➤ The ActiveConnection property of the Command object needs to be set to the connection object.

➤ The stored procedure passed into the subroutine executes.

➤ The connection object closes the connection to the database.

➤ The label for the error handler is after the next line of code, which requires an Exit Sub to make sure the subroutine ends without running the error handler.

This subroutine passes a command object that contains the information for a stored procedure in the database. If a run-time error occurs, the RecordFailure error handler catches the run-time error. This is important because you do not want your application to crash in the middle of processing a subroutine. Error handlers supply a mechanism for you to handle errors that occur in your code and prevent unwanted application crashes. They also release resources that are open and no longer required.

Code the **clsClassData** class to insert, update, and delete data from the CLASSES table in the database.

To code the **clsClassData** class to insert, update, and delete data:

1. Add the following code in the Code window of **clsClassData**. To do so, copy the code from the code09-02.txt file on the CD and paste it in the Code window.

9

```
'##ModelId=368A244E0185
Public Function Insert(strClassNumber As String, strClassName As _
 String) As String
Dim qrySP As New ADODB.Command
On Error GoTo ProcError
  qrySP.CommandText = "proc_insert_class"
  qrySP.CommandType = adCmdStoredProc
  qrySP.Parameters.Append qrySP.CreateParameter(, adVarChar, _
   adParamInput, 7, strClassNumber)
  qrySP.Parameters.Append qrySP.CreateParameter(, adVarChar, _
   adParamInput, 50, strClassName)
  Call ExecuteSP(qrySP)
  Insert = ""
  Exit Function
ProcError:
  Insert = Str(Err.Number) & vbCr & Err.Description
End Function


'##ModelId=368A24A90045
Public Function Update(lngClassID As Long, strNumber As String, _
 strNewClass As String) As String
Dim qrySP As New ADODB.Command
  On Error GoTo ProcError
    qrySP.CommandText = "proc_update_class"
    qrySP.CommandType = adCmdStoredProc
    qrySP.Parameters.Append qrySP.CreateParameter(, adInteger, _
     adParamInput, 4, lngClassID)
```

```
        qrySP.Parameters.Append qrySP.CreateParameter(, adVarChar, _
          adParamInput, 7, strNumber)
        qrySP.Parameters.Append qrySP.CreateParameter(, adVarChar, _
          adParamInput, 50, strNewClass)
        Call ExecuteSP(qrySP)
        Update = ""
        Exit Function
    ProcError:
        Update = Str(Err.Number) & vbCr & Err.Description
    End Function


    '##ModelId=368A252500BC
    Public Function Delete(lngClassID As Long) As String
    Dim qrySP As New ADODB.Command
      On Error GoTo ProcError
        qrySP.CommandText = "proc_delete_class"
        qrySP.CommandType = adCmdStoredProc
        qrySP.Parameters.Append qrySP.CreateParameter(, adInteger, _
          adParamInput, 4, lngClassID)
        Call ExecuteSP(qrySP)
        Delete = ""
        Exit Function
    ProcError:
        Delete = Str(Err.Number) & vbCr & Err.Description
    End Function
```

2. Right-click clsClassData in Project Explorer and click Save clsClassData.cls to save the changes.

The following example explains how to insert data in the database using ADO:

Syntax Code Example

```
'##ModelId=368A244E0185
Public Function Insert(strClassNumber As String, strClassName As _
  String) As String
Dim qrySP As New ADODB.Command
On Error GoTo ProcError
  qrySP.CommandText = "proc_insert_class"
  qrySP.CommandType = adCmdStoredProc
  qrySP.Parameters.Append qrySP.CreateParameter(, adVarChar, _
    adParamInput, 7, strClassNumber)
  qrySP.Parameters.Append qrySP.CreateParameter(, adVarChar, _
    adParamInput, 50, strClassName)
  Call ExecuteSP(qrySP)
  Insert = ""
  Exit Function
ProcError:
  Insert = Str(Err.Number) & vbCr & Err.Description
                        End Function
```

Syntax Code Dissection

➤ The Insert function takes the arguments, and **Class Number** and **Class Name**, and returns a string, an error message.

➤ A Command object is declared as qrySP.

➤ **CommandText** property is set to "proc_insert_class".

➤ **CommandType** property is set to adCmdStoredProc, which is a stored procedure.

 Verify your **proc_insert_class** stored procedure using the Data View window to make sure it matches the stored procedure call in this example. Otherwise, you need to update this code or the stored procedure to match the number of arguments between the stored procedure and the command object.

➤ The **proc_insert_class** stored procedure passes in two arguments, the class number and the class name. This requires two parameter objects to be appended to the parameters collection. To append a parameter object into the collection, use the following:

```
qrySP.Parameters.Append CreateParameter (, adVarChar_
    adParamInput, 7,strClassNumber)
```

The first argument is the name of the parameter. The second argument is the data type. The third argument is the type of parameter (input, output, or both). The fourth argument is the size of the data in bytes. The fifth argument is the actual data.

➤ The next line of code calls the ExecuteSP subroutine discussed previously.

The update and delete functions are similar to those of the previous example, except that the arguments are passed to the functions. In the update function, you need to pass the primary key class ID, the class number, and the class name to properly update the data in the CLASSES table. If the class number or the class name changes, you have no reference to the old data to update; therefore, you need to pass the class ID. The delete function passes in the class ID only. You need to be completely sure you delete the correct record in the CLASSES table.

The ExecuteSQL, GetInfo, and GetAllInfo functions work by passing in SQL statements and returning an ADO Recordset object. The GetInfo function passes a class ID and returns only a single row from the CLASSES table. Use this to update an existing record in the CLASSES table. The GetAllInfo function returns all rows from the CLASSES table. Use this when you need a user to select a CLASS from a list of CLASSES.

To code the ExecuteSQL, GetInfo, and GetAllInfo functions:

1. Add the following code in the Code window of clsClassData. To do so, copy the code from the code09-03.txt file on your data disk and paste it in the Code window.

```
'##ModelId=368A256A022E
Public Function GetInfo(lngClassID As Long) As ADODB.Recordset
Dim qrySP As New ADODB.Command
On Error GoTo ProcError
  qrySP.CommandText = "select * from CLASSES where CLASS_ID =" & _
   Str(lngClassID)
  qrySP.CommandType = adCmdText
  Set GetInfo = ExecuteSQL(qrySP)
  Exit Function
ProcError:
  Set GetInfo = Nothing
End Function


'##ModelId=368A256A022F
Private Function ExecuteSQL(qrySP As ADODB.Command) As _
 ADODB.Recordset
Dim strConn As String
Dim recSQL As New ADODB.Recordset
Dim mvarConn As New ADODB.Connection
On Error GoTo RecordFailure
  strConn = "File Name=" & App.Path & "\ctis.udl"
  mvarConn.Open strConn
  Set qrySP.ActiveConnection = mvarConn
  Set recSQL = qrySP.Execute
  Set ExecuteSQL = recSQL
  Exit Function
RecordFailure:
  Err.Raise Err.Number, "ExecuteSQL", Err.Description
End Function


'##ModelId=368BAA7403E5
Public Function GetAllInfo() As ADODB.Recordset
Dim qrySP As New ADODB.Command
On Error GoTo ProcError
  qrySP.CommandText = "select * from CLASSES"
  qrySP.CommandType = adCmdText
  Set GetAllInfo = ExecuteSQL(qrySP)
  Exit Function
ProcError:
  Set GetAllInfo = Nothing
End Function
```

2. Right-click clsClassData in Project Explorer, then click Save clsClassData.cls to save the changes.

Writing The Test Client To Test clsClassData

You have successfully coded the clsClassData class. Your next job is to test this code to make sure it works properly. The easiest way to do this is to change the project from an ActiveX DLL to a standard EXE and code a MAIN subroutine to test each function of the clsClassData class. Why? When you compile an ActiveX DLL, Visual Basic creates a comCourse.DLL file, which is not easy to debug. Instead, you can change the project to a standard EXE, write a test client, and verify that the functions work. Once the testing is complete, change the project back to an ActiveX DLL and compile.

To code the MAIN subroutine:

1. Right-click the comCourse project in the Project Explorer, and click Check Out to check out the project. This allows you to make temporary changes to the project.

2. Click comCourse properties in the Project menu.

3. Change the Project Type to Standard EXE.

4. Click OK to close the Project Properties dialog box.

5. Click OK on the Visual Basic message.

6. Click Add Module in the Project menu.

7. Click Open in the Add Module dialog box.

8. Type the following in the Module's Code window:

```
Private Sub Main()
    Dim objClassData As New clsClassData
    Dim strResult As String
    Dim recSQL As New ADODB.Recordset
    strResult = objClassData.Insert("CP 101", "Intro")
    If strResult <> "" Then
        MsgBox strResult
    End If
    Set objClassData = Nothing
End Sub
```

9. Click References in the Project menu. You need to add references to the ADO components so that you can use them in your program.

10. Click Microsoft ActiveX Data Objects 2.0 Library and Microsoft ActiveX Data Objects Recordset 2.0 Library. This enables you to use the ADO object library in your code. Otherwise, you will get errors when you compile your code.

11. Click OK.

12. Click Run on the toolbar.

13. Using the Data View window, verify that the new record is in the CLASSES table.

14. Right-click module1 in Project Explorer, and then click Remove module1.

15. Click No in response to Save file.

You will check all other functions in an exercise at the end of this chapter.

Transaction Processing (TP)

In the last section, you started creating an ActiveX DLL by coding the **clsClassData** class. This creates an object to directly interact with the database. If changes occur to the database connectivity, this object changes and does not affect other pieces of code. This object hides the details of the database connectivity from other objects and user interfaces. The next object you will create is a business service object that interacts with the data service object and the user service objects. This object is clsClass and ensures that the requests from a user service object transfer the data service object to the database. It guarantees that changes made to the database are permanent and correct. One way to protect your application from failures is to use transaction processing.

Transaction processing is the ability of various components to work in unison with each other. A *transaction* is a unit of work that you define. It can be a series of insert, update, and delete statements that you treat as a unit in a database. You worked with this type of transaction in Transact-SQL in Chapter 8. It can also be different components that do various jobs that are also treated as a unit. A transaction consists of several properties whose initial letters form the acronym ACID:

➤ **Atomicity** Atomicity is the breaking down of work into units that you define. All of the actions in the transaction succeed or fail as a unit.

➤ **Consistency** Consistency allows a system to be in a correct stable state at the end of the transaction or when the transaction aborts. It returns the system to its initial state.

➤ **Isolation** An isolated transaction cannot be affected by other transactions that execute concurrently. A transaction is isolated from other simultaneous transactions. This means that a transaction will not see partial results of another transaction while it is running.

➤ **Durability** After the transaction successfully completes, a durable transaction is permanent and survives any type of failure, including power failures.

All transaction-processing systems must adhere to the above properties of a transaction. You will use a transaction-processing system called Microsoft Transaction Server (MTS) to handle transactions with your components.

Review the following example of a transaction: You have an order component that needs to update the billing database and the inventory database when an order is taken from the user. After your user completes an order, the order component adds information to the inventory database first, to show that an item has sold, and then it adds information to the billing database so you can bill your customer for the work the user wants you to accomplish. After processing the inventory information, the power fails. Without a transaction, the billing information never makes it to the billing database. This leaves your system in an incomplete state and may mean that your customer doesn't receive a bill. With a transaction, your application will remove the inventory information and leave your system in the state it was in before the customer order. Now your system can rerun your transaction from the beginning to make sure the data updates properly in both databases.

Microsoft Transaction Server (MTS)

MTS is Microsoft's transaction-processing system. You will code your clsClass class using MTS and create an MTS component using an ActiveX DLL. Before you can code an MTS component, you need to understand how MTS works. Figure 9.8 illustrates how MTS works with ActiveX DLL components.

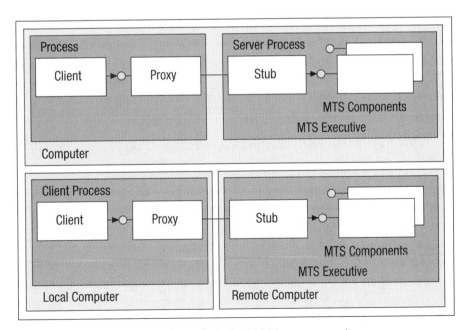

Figure 9.8 How MTS works with ActiveX DLL components.

MTS components are special ActiveX DLL components. They are different from a typical ActiveX DLL because they run inside the MTS run-time environment (MTS executive). MTS components are either local or remote. You can put MTS components on any machine on your network. As the names imply, a local component runs in the MTS executive locally, and a remote component runs in the MTS executive remotely. MTS determines where components are and runs the component on the machine that hosts it. When a client process calls an MTS component, it calls a proxy that determines where the component resides. It communicates with the stub component (a component that contains the interfaces but no code) that launches the actual MTS component, whether is it local or remote.

Before you write an ActiveX DLL that enables an MTS component to run in the MTS run-time environment, consider the requirements of MTS components:

➤ Must be implemented as an in-process server (ActiveX DLL). Other types of components cannot run in the MTS run-time environment.

➤ Must be registered with the MTS environment using MTS Explorer.

➤ Must be apartment-threaded, which means that the component can run in one or more threads.

➤ Must not create or terminate threads. The MTS environment takes care of those details.

➤ Must not programmatically alter its security. The MTS environment takes care of those details.

➤ Must be maintained as stateless components—they should not maintain local data between client calls. This means that an MTS component does its unit of work and terminates. You should not keep the component active while the client needs it. The client calls and creates the component when needed. Microsoft recommends that you stay away from stateful components, which maintain local data between client calls. Stateless components scale up easily compared to stateful components. This allows MTS to pool resources and allocate them to clients only when necessary.

All MTS components require an MTS context, an object that allows your component to run in the MTS environment. MTS uses a second object to track the transaction of the component. The following lines of code set up a context for a component:

Syntax Code Example

```
Dim objContext as ObjectContext
Set objContext = GetObjectContext()
```

Syntax Code Dissection

➤ objContext is a variable for the MTS context object.

➤ The next line creates the object context for the current object.

After you set up a context for your component, make sure to commit or roll back a transaction if your code is successful or unsuccessful, respectively.

Syntax Code Example
```
objContext.setComplete
```

Syntax Code Dissection

➤ This code commits an MTS transaction. All transactions inside a main MTS transaction cast a vote. If all transactions complete successfully, then all transactions are made permanent.

Syntax Code Example
```
objContext.setAbort
```

Syntax Code Dissection

➤ This code rolls back an MTS transaction. All transactions in a main MTS transaction cast a vote. If one of the transactions fails (setAbort), then all transactions are aborted.

You need to update the **clsClass** class in Visual Basic. This object represents the business service object. The clsClass class contains the class ID, class name, and class number properties. These properties temporarily store the class information from the user service. The **clsClass** class contains the **Retrieve**, **RetrieveALL, Save, Validate**, and **Delete** methods. Retrieve passes in the class ID and returns a single row from the CLASSES table. RetrieveALL returns all rows from the CLASSES table. The Save function either inserts or updates class information in the database via the clsClassData class. The Delete function removes a class from the CLASSES table via the clsClassData class.

To code the **clsClass** class and compile the ActiveX DLL component:

1. Right-click the clsClass class from Project Explorer and click Check Out.

2. Double-click clsClass from Project Explorer. In the Properties window, change the Instancing property to S-Multi-use.

3. Add the clsClass code in the clsClass Code window with the following. To do so, copy the code from the code09-04.txt file on your data disk and paste it in the Code window.

```
Option Base 0
Option Explicit

'##ModelId=368A27560181
Private lngClassID As Long

'##ModelId=368A2775018F
Private strClassName As String
```

```vb
'##ModelId=368AB90D0248
Private strClassNumber As String

'##ModelId=368A2CD20388
Private mobjClassData As New clsClassData

'##ModelId=368A27940310
Public Function Retrieve(lngID As Long) As ADODB.Recordset
Dim recSQL As New ADODB.Recordset
Dim objContext As ObjectContext
lngClassID = lngID
On Error GoTo TransactionError
    Set objContext = GetObjectContext()
    Set recSQL = mobjClassData.GetInfo(lngID)
    If recSQL Is Nothing Then
      Err.Raise -1, "No records returned"
    End If
    Set Retrieve = recSQL
    If Not objContext Is Nothing Then
      objContext.SetComplete
    End If
  Exit Function
TransactionError:
    If Not objContext Is Nothing Then
      objContext.SetAbort
    End If
    Set Retrieve = Nothing
End Function

'##ModelId=368A28A602D8
Public Function RetrieveALL() As ADODB.Recordset
Dim objContext As ObjectContext
Dim recSQL As New ADODB.Recordset
On Error GoTo TransactionError
    Set objContext = GetObjectContext()
    Set recSQL = mobjClassData.GetAllInfo()
    If recSQL Is Nothing Then
      Err.Raise -1, "No records returned"
    End If
    Set RetrieveALL = recSQL
    If Not objContext Is Nothing Then
      objContext.SetComplete
    End If
  Exit Function
TransactionError:
    Set RetrieveALL = Nothing
    If Not objContext Is Nothing Then
```

```
        objContext.SetAbort
      End If
End Function


'##ModelId=368A27D500BB
Public Function Save(ByVal lngID As Long, ByVal strNumber As _
  String, ByVal strName As String) As String
Dim objObjectContext As ObjectContext
Dim strResult As String
lngClassID = lngID
strClassName = strName
strClassNumber = strNumber
On Error GoTo ValidateError
  strResult = Validate()
    If strResult <> "" Then
      Err.Raise -1, "Validate",strResult
    End If
On Error GoTo TransactionError
  Set objObjectContext = GetObjectContext()
  If lngClassID = 0 Then
    strResult = mobjClassData.Insert(strClassNumber, strClassName)
    If strResult <> "" Then
      Err.Raise Err.Number
    End If

    If Not objObjectContext Is Nothing Then
      objObjectContext.SetComplete
    End If

  Else
    strResult = mobjClassData.Update(lngClassID, strClassNumber, _
    strClassName)

    If strResult <> "" Then
      Err.Raise Err.Number
    End If

    If Not objObjectContext Is Nothing Then
      objObjectContext.SetComplete
    End If
    Else
    strResult = mobjClassData.Update(lngClassID, strClassNumber, _
    strClassName)

    If strResult <> "" Then
      Err.Raise Err.Number
    End If
```

9

```
        If Not objObjectContext Is Nothing Then
          objObjectContext.SetComplete
        End If


    End If
    Save = ""
    Exit Function
ValidateError:
    Save = strResult
    Exit Function
TransactionError:

    If Not objObjectContext Is Nothing Then
     objObjectContext.SetAbort
    End If


    Save = "Transaction Failed!"
End Function


'##ModelId=368A28190091
Public Function Validate() As String
  If strClassName = "" Then
     Validate = "Must enter a class name!"
  End If
End Function


'##ModelId=368AB90E033A
Public Function Delete(lngClassID As Long) As String
Dim objObjectContext As ObjectContext
Dim strResult As String

On Error GoTo TransactionError
    Set objObjectContext = GetObjectContext()

    strResult = mobjClassData.Delete(lngClassID)

    If strResult <> "" Then
      Err.Raise Err.Number
    End If

    If Not objObjectContext Is Nothing Then
      objObjectContext.SetComplete
    End If

    Delete = ""
    Exit Function

TransactionError:
```

```
If Not objObjectContext Is Nothing Then
 objObjectContext.SetAbort
End If

Delete = "Transaction failed!"
End Function
```

4. Click comCourse properties in the Project menu.

5. Select ActiveX DLL in Project Type.

6. Select Apartment Threaded in the Threading Model.

7. Click the Make tab.

8. In Version number, click Auto Increment to increment the revision number each time the project compiles.

9. Click OK.

10. Click References in the Project menu.

11. Select Microsoft Transaction Server Type Library and then click OK.

12. Click Make comCourse.dll in the File menu to compile your project into an ActiveX DLL.

13. Check in all files to commit changes to Visual SourceSafe.

14. Click Exit in the File menu to exit Visual Basic.

You have successfully compiled an ActiveX DLL. Remember that you should test all your classes in your project before you create a component.

Once you create the ActiveX DLL, you must add the component to the MTS environment, using MTS Explorer.

MTS Explorer

MTS Explorer is responsible for installing and configuring components for use with the MTS environment. Figure 9.9 shows the MTS Explorer environment.

The Explorer hierarchy describes how MTS Explorer organizes components:

➤ **Computers** Computers show where the components are installed.

➤ **Packages** MTS uses packages to organize components.

➤ **Components** ActiveX DLL components are stored here.

➤ **Roles** Roles determine how users use the components and configure the security of a component.

➤ **Interfaces** Components contain interfaces so that users can interact with the component. The interface is the contract between the component and its user.

➤ **Methods** Methods are functions that can be used with the component.

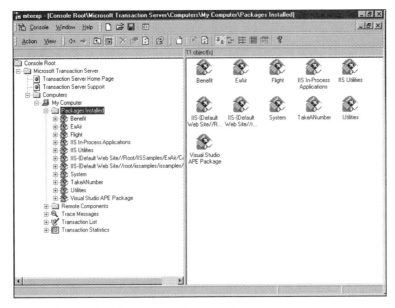

Figure 9.9 MTS Explorer environment.

The left pane of MTS Explorer shows the hierarchy, and the right pane displays the contents of the selected item in the left pane.

To install the comCourse component in MTS:

1. Expand the Computers and My Computers folders.
2. Right-click Packages Installed in My Computer, and then point to New and click Package.
3. Click Create An Empty Package.
4. Enter CTIS for the name of the package.
5. Click Next.
6. Click Interactive User in Set Package Identity, if not already selected.
7. Click Finish.
8. In the CTIS package, right-click Components, point to New, and then click Component.
9. In the Component Wizard, click Install new components.
10. Click Add Files in the Install Components dialog box.
11. Select c:\work\CTIS\business_svc_src\comCourse\comCourse.dll and then click Open.
12. Click Finish.
13. Right-click comCourse.clsClass and then click Properties.
14. Click the Transaction tab.

15. Click Requires A Transaction.
16. Click OK.

Code A Test Client To Test The comCourse Component

After you have set up the comCourse component in MTS, you need to test the component to make sure that you can connect to the component.

To test the comCourse component:

1. Click the Start menu.
2. Point to Programs, Microsoft Visual Studio 6.0, and then click Microsoft Visual Basic 6.0.
3. In the New Project window, select Standard EXE and then click Open.
4. Click Project1 Properties in the Project menu.
5. In Startup Object, select Sub Main.
6. Click OK.
7. Click Add Module in the Project menu.
8. Click Module in New Module, and then click Open.
9. Type the following code in the Module's Code window:

```
Private Sub Main()
Dim objClass As Object
Dim strResult As String
Set objClass = CreateObject("comCourse.clsClass")
strResult = objClass.Save(0, "IT 100", "Intro")
End Sub
```

In the previous sections, you declared the variable of the object you are using, such as:

```
Dim objClass as New comCourse.clsClass
```

This is called early binding. Visual Basic resolves objects during compile time with early binding. It also requires that you create a reference to this object in the Visual Basic environment. In this example, you are using the CreateObject function to create an object. This is called late binding. Visual Basic resolves objects during run-time with late binding. Early binding is always more efficient than late binding because Visual Basic resolves the object before it runs, not while it is running. A late binding object requires more overhead because it is resolved during run-time. Unfortunately, MTS only recognizes objects in the MTS environment using late binding, not early binding.

10. Click the Run button on the toolbar.

11. Verify the results of the code using the Data View window.

12. Click the Run button again. An error message appears. Click OK.

13. In MTS Explorer, you can view the transaction statistics of the previous operations. Double-click Transaction Statistics in the left pane. View the results.

Testing the other interfaces to the comCourse component is left as an exercise at the end of the chapter. You have successfully created a comCourse component, installed it in MTS, and written a test client to test the comCourse interfaces.

Reverse-Engineer The comCourse Component Into Visual Modeler

You have made changes to the classes in Visual Basic that affect the logical model in Visual Modeler. You need to make sure that you keep the model up to date with the Visual Basic ActiveX DLL. You can do this by reengineering the Visual Basic code into Visual Modeler.

To reverse engineer a Visual Basic comCourse component:

1. Using VSS Explorer, check out class.mdl.

2. Open comCourse.vbp in Visual Basic.

3. Click the Add Ins menu, and then point to Visual Modeler and click Reverse Engineering Wizard.

4. Click OK.

5. Click Next on the Welcome screen.

6. Click Next to accept the default on the Selection of Project Items dialog box.

7. Click Next to accept the defaults on the Assignment of Project Items dialog box.

8. Click Finish.

9. Click Close on Summary.

10. From the File menu, click Save in Visual Modeler.

11. From the File menu, click Exit in Visual Modeler.

12. In Related Documents in Project Explorer in Visual Basic, right-click class.mdl and then click Check in on the shortcut menu.

13. From the File menu, click Exit in Visual Basic.

14. Click No in the Visual Basic dialog box.

Introduction To Message Queuing

In the last section, you investigated how to create ActiveX DLL components in MTS. This section introduces the concept of message queuing. A *queue* is a special data structure that processes items in a first in, first out fashion. A grocery line is an example of a queue. The first person in line checks out first, and the last person checks out last.

Applications that run on different machines have different ways to communicate:

➤ Send a request and expect an immediate response. For example, an HTTP request is sent from a Web browser to a Web server. The Web server immediately responds with a Web page to the browser.

➤ Send a request and expect a response in a fixed period of time. For example, you write a check at a grocery store and expect a response after the grocery store sends the check to the bank. The bank then responds with the funds for the written check.

➤ Send a request and do not expect a response.

The first type of communication is similar to what you coded in the last section. You called a function from the clsClass object, and you expected an immediate response. This is called *synchronous communication*. The second and third application types do not expect an immediate response. This is called *asynchronous communication*. In asynchronous communication, the client process and the server process do not need to be running at the same time. To perform asynchronous communication, you need a message queue to queue requests between the client process and server process. When the server process is down, the client process continues to work and passes requests to a queue. When the server process comes online, it processes all queued requests. For example, voice mail queues messages for later retrieval. When you are ready to review your messages, you listen to each message and save or discard messages as you prefer.

In CTIS, you could use message queuing in various situations, such as a student or instructor requesting access to your CTIS application, or an instructor posting grades.

Message queuing is a mechanism you can use in software development to implement asynchronous communication. Microsoft Message Queue Server (MSMQ) is Microsoft's implementation of message queuing and asynchronous communication.

Microsoft Message Queue Server (MSMQ)

MSMQ is Microsoft's message-queuing solution that allows developers to create message-based scalable solutions. Figure 9.10 shows how MSMQ works.

On the server, a server application works directly with queues to receive and process requests from the clients. A queue manager is responsible for queue management. Two types of clients are available in MSMQ:

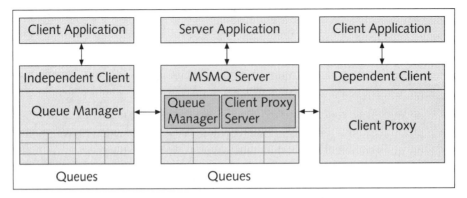

Figure 9.10 How MSMQ works.

➤ **Independent clients** If a client machine is configured as an independent client, the server process can be down without affecting your client application. An independent client sets up temporary queues on the client machine if none exist on the network. When the server process is up and running, then the messages in the client queues are forwarded to the server for processing. A local queue manager on the client processes queue requests to local queues and forwards requests to the server.

➤ **Dependent clients** If a client machine is configured as a dependent client, the server must be up and running at all times. A client proxy on the client forwards all queue requests to the proxy server, which interacts with the queue manager on the server.

MSMQ server allows you to log all queue activity in a Journal queue. You can then monitor messages in queues. If a message times out in a queue, MSMQ places it in the Dead Letter queue.

Interact with MSMQ using the MSMQ application programming interface (API). The MSMQ API consists of MSMQQueueInfo, an object that creates, opens, and deletes queues; MSMQQueue, an object that opens, closes, and receives messages; and MSMQMessage, an object that sends and creates the message being queued.

Tables 9.10 through 9.12 show the properties and methods of each MSMQ object.

MSMQ Explorer

MSMQ Explorer is responsible for creating, administering, and viewing sites, connected networks, computers, and queues on your MSMQ server. Figure 9.11 shows the MSMQ Explorer environment.

The Explorer hierarchy describes how MSMQ Explorer organizes queues:

➤ **Sites** A site is a name of a network that contains computers.

➤ **Computers** Computers are machines that host queues.

Table 9.10   Useful properties and methods of MSMQQueueInfo.

Property/Method	Name	Description
Method	Create	Creates a new queue
Method	Delete	Deletes a queue
Method	Open	Opens an existing queue
Property	Label	Shows the name given to a queue
Property	PathName	Shows the path of the queue, such as computer_name\queue_name

Table 9.11   Useful properties and methods of MSMQQueue.

Property/Method	Name	Description
Method	Open	Opens a queue
Method	Close	Closes an open queue
Method	Receive	Removes and returns a message off the top of the queue

9

Table 9.12   Useful properties and methods of MSMQMessage.

Property/Method	Name	Description
Method	Send	Places a message in the queue
Property	Label	Shows the name of the message
Property	Body	Shows the body of the message
Property	DestinationQueue	Shows what the queue uses to send the message
Property	ResponseQueueInfo	Shows what the queue uses to place response messages

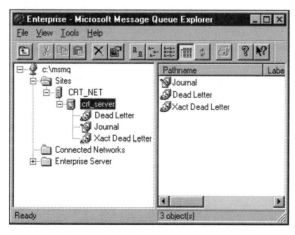

Figure 9.11   MSMQ Explorer environment.

➤ **Queues**   Queues store messages that you can send and retrieve.

➤ **Connected Networks**   These are other networks that supply queues.

➤ **Enterprise Server**   This is the server that manages MSMQ.

The left pane of Explorer displays the MSMQ hierarchy, and the right pane shows the contents of the selected part of the hierarchy.

When using MSMQ, you create, configure, and delete queues. You also purge messages from queues.

To create a queue using MSMQ Explorer:

1. Click the Start menu.
2. Point to Programs, Windows NT 4.0 Option Pack, Microsoft Message Queue, and then click Explorer to start MSMQ Explorer.
3. Expand Sites, your Site, and your Computer to view queues stored on the server.
4. Right-click your Computer, point to New, and click Queue.
5. Enter CTIS for the name of the queue. Also, select Transactional to allow the queue to be a part of a transaction.
6. Click OK.
7. Create another queue called dummy.

To delete a queue using MSMQ Explorer:

1. Right-click the dummy queue, and then click Delete.
2. Click Yes.

Refer to MSMQ Explorer online documentation to learn other tasks you can accomplish with MSMQ Explorer.

Since you coded the comCourse component already, you need to learn how to code the comCourse component with MSMQ by adding three new functions—SaveMSMQ, DeleteMSMQ, and GetFromQueueMSMQ—to clsClassData, for clsClass. You also need to add a module for user-defined data types. Create two user-defined data types to facilitate sending a message to the queue. The udtClass contains:

➤ strMode As String * 1: This allows the message to be "I" for insert, "U" for update, and "D" for delete.

➤ lngClassID As Long

➤ strClassNumber As String * 7

➤ strClassName As String * 50

➤ intErrorNumber As Integer: This allows you to send an error number back as a response if necessary.

➤ intErrorMessage As String ★ 100: This allows you to send an error description back as a response.

To make sending messages to a queue as simple as possible, convert the above data type to a string on the transmitting end and convert it back to a user data type on the receiving end. The function Lset allows you to do this automatically.

The clsClass class works with the client and sends a message to the CTIS queue. The clsClassData class works with the server to process messages off the queue. In message queuing, create not only a client process, but also a server process to work with MSMQ. In the previous section, you let MTS and ADO handle the processing to the database.

To add MSMQ functions to comCourse:

1. Click the Start menu.
2. Point to Programs, Microsoft Visual Studio 6.0, and then click Microsoft Visual Basic 6.0.
3. In the New Project dialog box, click the Existing tab and locate c:\work\CTIS\business_svc_src\comCourse\comCourse.vbp.
4. Click Open.
5. Log on to Visual SourceSafe.
6. Check out all files in Project Explorer.
7. Click Add Module in the Project menu. Click Open. Click the new module in Project Explorer.
8. In the Properties window, change the name of the module to modMessage.
9. Type the following code in modMessage's Code window:

```
Public Type udtClass
  strMode As String * 1
  lngClassID As Long
  strClassNumber As String * 7
  strClassName As String * 50
  intErrorNumber As Integer
  intErrorMessage As String * 100
End Type

Public Type udtString
  strMessage As String * 164
End Type
```

10. Double-click clsClass in Project Explorer to open the Code window.

11. Add the following functions to clsClass. To do so, copy the code from the code09-05.txt file on your data disk and paste it in the Code window.

```
Public Function SaveMSMQ(ByVal qname As String, ByVal lngID As Long, _
 ByVal strNumber As String, ByVal strName As String) As String
Dim objObjectContext As ObjectContext

Dim msgClass As udtClass
Dim msgString As udtString
Dim QueueInfo As New MSMQ.MSMQQueueInfo
Dim Msg As New MSMQ.MSMQMessage
Dim queue As MSMQ.MSMQQueue
Dim strResult As String

lngClassID = lngID
strClassName = strName
strClassNumber = strNumber

With msgClass
  .lngClassID = lngClassID
  .strClassNumber = strClassNumber
  .strClassName = strClassName
  .strMode = "I"
  .intErrorNumber = 0
  .intErrorMessage = ""
End With

On Error GoTo ValidateError
  strResult = Validate
  If strResult <> "" Then
    Err.Raise -1, "Validate", strResult
  End If

On Error GoTo TransactionError
 Set objObjectContext = GetObjectContext()

 QueueInfo.PathName = qname
 Set queue = QueueInfo.Open(MQ_SEND_ACCESS, MQ_DENY_NONE)

  If lngClassID = 0 Then

    msgClass.strMode = "I"
    LSet msgString = msgClass
    Msg.Label = "comCourse.clsClass"
    Msg.Body = msgString.strMessage
```

```
        If (objObjectContext.IsInTransaction) Then
          Msg.Send queue, MQ_MTS_TRANSACTION
        Else
          Msg.Send queue, MQ_SINGLE_MESSAGE
        End If

        queue.Close

  If Not objObjectContext Is Nothing Then
        objObjectContext.SetComplete
        End If

    Else

      msgClass.strMode = "U"
      LSet msgString = msgClasse
      Msg.Label = "comCourse.clsCourse"
      Msg.Body = msgString.strMessage

      If objObjectContext.IsInTransaction Then
        Msg.Send queue, MQ_MTS_TRANSACTION
      Else
        Msg.Send queue, MQ_SINGLE_MESSAGE
      End If

      queue.Close

      If Not objObjectContext Is Nothing Then
        objObjectContext.SetComplete
      End If

    End If
    Set queue = Nothing
    Set Msg = Nothing
    Set QueueInfo = Nothing
    SaveMSMQ = ""
    Exit Function
ValidateError:
    SaveMSMQ = "Validation failed!"
    Exit Function
TransactionError:

    If Not objObjectContext Is Nothing Then
     objObjectContext.SetAbort
    End If
```

9

```
    Set queue = Nothing
    Set Msg = Nothing
    Set QueueInfo = Nothing
    SaveMSMQ = "Transaction failed!"


End Function

Public Function DeleteMSMQ(qname As String, lngClassID As Long) As_
  String
Dim objObjectContext As ObjectContext

Dim msgClass As udtClass
Dim msgString As udtString
Dim QueueInfo As New MSMQ.MSMQQueueInfo
Dim Msg As New MSMQ.MSMQMessage
Dim queue As MSMQ.MSMQQueue

With msgClass
  .lngClassID = lngClassID
  .strClassNumber = strClassNumber
  .strClassName = strClassName
  .strMode = "D"
  .intErrorNumber = 0
  .intErrorMessage = ""
End With

On Error GoTo TransactionError
    Set objObjectContext = GetObjectContext()

    QueueInfo.PathName = qname
    Set queue = QueueInfo.Open(MQ_SEND_ACCESS, MQ_DENY_NONE)

    msgClass.strMode = "D"
    LSet msgString = msgClass
    Msg.Label = "comCourse.clsClass"
    Msg.Body = msgString.strMessage

    If objObjectContext.IsInTransaction Then
      Msg.Send queue, MQ_MTS_TRANSACTION
    Else
      Msg.Send queue, MQ_SINGLE_MESSAGE
    End If

    queue.Close

    If Not objObjectContext Is Nothing Then
      objObjectContext.SetComplete
    End If
```

```
            DeleteMSMQ = ""

    TransactionError:

        If Not objObjectContext Is Nothing Then
         objObjectContext.SetAbort
        End If

        DeleteMSMQ = "Transaction failed!"
    End Function
```

12. Double-click clsClassData to open the Code window.

13. Add the following function to clsClassData. To do so, copy the code from
    the code09-06.txt file on your data disk and paste it in the Code window.

```
Public Function GetFromQueueMSMQ(qname As String) As String
Dim objObjectContext As ObjectContext
Dim strResult As String
Dim msgClass As udtClass
Dim msgString As udtString
Dim QueueInfo As New MSMQ.MSMQQueueInfo
Dim Msg As MSMQ.MSMQMessage
Dim queue As MSMQ.MSMQQueue


On Error GoTo TransactionError
    Set objObjectContext = GetObjectContext()

    QueueInfo.PathName = qname
    Set queue = QueueInfo.Open(MQ_RECEIVE_ACCESS, MQ_DENY_NONE)

    Set Msg = queue.Receive(Transaction:=MQ_MTS_TRANSACTION, _
     ReceiveTimeout:=10)


    queue.Close

    msgString.strMessage = Msg.Body
    LSet msgClass = msgString
    strResult = ""
    Select Case Msg.Label
    Case "comCourse.clsClass"

      Select Case msgClass.strMode
      Case "I"
        strResult = Insert(msgClass.strClassNumber,_
          msgClass.strClassName)
      Case "U"
```

9

```
                    strResult = Update(msgClass.lngClassID,_
                       msgClass.strClassNumber, msgClass.strClassName)
                  Case "D"
                    strResult = Delete(msgClass.lngClassID)
                  End Select

            End Select

            If Not objObjectContext Is Nothing Then
               objObjectContext.SetComplete
            End If

            GetFromQueueMSMQ = strResult

      TransactionError:

            If Not objObjectContext Is Nothing Then
             objObjectContext.SetAbort
            End If

            GetFromQueueMSMQ = "Transaction failed!"
      End Function
```

14. Click clsClassData in Project Explorer.

15. In the Properties window, check to make sure the Instancing property is set to 5 - Multi-use.

16. Click References in the Project menu.

17. Click Microsoft Message Queue Object Library and then click OK.

18. Click Save Project in the File menu.

19. Click Save in the Save As dialog box.

20. Click OK in Add Files to SourceSafe.

21. On the File menu, click Make comCourse.dll to compile the ActiveX DLL. Click OK.

22. Click Yes in the Make Project dialog box to replace the existing comCourse.dll.

23. Check in all files in Visual SourceSafe.

24. Click Exit in the File menu.

25. Delete the old comCourse component in MTS Explorer. (Delete both classes listed in MTS Explorer.)

26. Create the new comCourse component in MTS Explorer.

Your next step is to create a test client and A test server to verify the functionality of your new functions.

To create a test client and test server:

1. Start Visual Basic and create a New STANDARD EXE Project.

2. Right-click Form1 in Project Explorer, and then click Remove Form1. On the Project menu, click Project1 Properties. Then change the Startup Object to Sub Main, if necessary.

3. Add a module to the Project.

4. In the Code window, type the following code. When you're finished, replace "crt_server" with the name of your server.

```
Public Sub Main()
   Dim objClass As Object
   Dim strResult As String
   Set objClass = CreateObject("comCourse.clsClass")
   strResult = objClass.SaveMSMQ("crt_server\CTIS", 0, "CP 107",_
   "C/S Arch")
   'Set objClass = CreateObject("comCourse.clsClassData")
   'strResult = objClass.GetFromQueueMSMQ("crt_server\CTIS")
   Set objClass = Nothing
End Sub
```

5. Click Run on the toolbar.

   Your test client placed a message on the queue.

6. Open the CTIS queue in MSMQ Explorer to view your message. You might have to refresh the queue to see the message.

7. Comment the third and fourth lines of code and remove the comments from the next two lines of code. This sets up the test server.

8. Click Run on the toolbar.

   Your test server removes a message from the queue and adds a row to the CLASSES table.

9. Verify the entry of the new row in the CLASSES table, using the Data View window.

10. Click Exit in the File menu in Visual Basic.

You have successfully added MSMQ functionality to your comCourse component. MSMQ allows you to create message-passing distributed applications using Visual Basic.

CHAPTER SUMMARY

In this chapter, you surveyed the different middleware technologies from Microsoft. The underlying technology that ties all the technologies together is COM/DCOM. You need COM/DCOM components to create ActiveX DLL components. Visual Basic allows you to create ActiveX components using MTS and MSMQ. You use the ADO object model to interact with tables and stored procedures in databases. Microsoft also supplies Data Access Objects (DAO) and Remote Data Objects (RDO) to interact with databases. Refer to the Visual Basic online documentation to review these technologies. Using these technologies is similar to using ADO. Microsoft recommends you use ADO whenever possible in accessing databases. You use MTS to create transaction-oriented components, and it gives you the power to access multiple databases under one transaction. You use MSMQ to create asynchronous applications that require the client to be disconnected from the network. MSMQ allows you to create multiple servers that can process from the same queue if the load is too much for one process to handle. You could easily configure and scale your application with MSMQ. This is very useful for a mobile sales force, for example, who need to move their client computers from place to place without network connectivity.

REVIEW QUESTIONS

1. _____ are self-contained precompiled software units (code) that can be reused in one or more applications.

   a. Objects

   b. Components

   c. Classes

   d. none of the above

2. _____ is a broad category of software needed to allow clients and a server to communicate with each other over a network.

   a. Middleware

   b. MSMQ

   c. MTS

   d. none of the above

3. _____ is Microsoft's standard for object interaction that supplies the plumbing needed for objects to communicate with each other.

   a. COM

   b. MTS

   c. Middleware

   d. none of the above

4. You can create components in the following languages. Choose all that apply.

   a. Visual InterDev

   b. Visual C++

   c. Visual J++

   d. Visual Basic

5. Windows uses a(n) _____ to uniquely identify each component stored in the registry.

   a. CLS

   b. ID

   c. CLSID

   d. none of the above

6. An in-process server is also known as:

   a. ActiveX EXE

   b. Standard EXE

   c. ActiveX DLL

   d. add-ins

7. An out-of-process server is also known as:

   a. ActiveX EXE

   b. Standard EXE

   c. add-ins

   d. ActiveX DLL

8. These mini-applications enhance the functionality of the Visual Basic environment:

   a. Standard EXE

   b. ActiveX EXE

   c. ActiveX DLL

   d. add-ins

9. You can use _____ to communicate with a database.

   a. add-ins

   b. Standard EXE

   c. ADO

   d. ActiveX DLL

10. This ADO object is responsible for connecting to, querying, and disconnecting from a database:

    a. command

    b. properties

    c. parameter

    d. connection

11. This ADO object is responsible for sending and receiving SQL queries and stored procedures.

    a. parameter

    b. connection

    c. properties

    d. command

12. _____ let you save connection information to a file.

    a. Universal Data Links

    b. ActiveX Data Objects

    c. Data Access Objects

    d. none of the above

13. A(n) _____ is a unit of work that you define.

    a. object

    b. class

    c. transaction

    d. none of the above

14. _____ is the breaking down of work into units that you define, where all units of the transaction succeed or fail.

    a. Durability

    b. Isolation

    c. Atomicity

    d. Consistency

15. A transaction that cannot be affected by other transactions that execute concurrently has:

   a. durability

   b. atomicity

   c. consistency

   d. isolation

16. _____ allows a system to be in a correct state at the end of the transaction.

   a. Durability

   b. Atomicity

   c. Isolation

   d. Consistency

17. A transaction that is permanent and that survives any type of failure, including power failures, has:

   a. durability

   b. consistency

   c. isolation

   d. atomicity

18. _____ is Microsoft's transaction-processing system.

   a. ADO

   b. MTS

   c. MSMQ

   d. none of the above

19. Visual Basic resolves objects during compile time with _____ binding.

   a. intermediate

   b. late

   c. early

   d. none of the above

20. Visual Basic resolves objects at run time with _____ binding.

   a. early

   b. intermediate

   c. late

   d. none of the above

9

21. _____ is Microsoft's asynchronous messaging solution.

    a. MSMQ

    b. MTS

    c. ADO

    d. none of the above

HANDS-ON PROJECTS

Project 9.1

In a written document, define the steps necessary to create an ActiveX DLL component.

Project 9.2

In a written document, define the steps necessary to create an MTS component.

Project 9.3

In a written document, define the steps necessary to create an MTS component with MSMQ.

Project 9.4

You created a comCourse component in this chapter. Write a test client and test server to test each function in the comCourse objects.

Project 9.5

Using the techniques in this chapter, create the following classes and components in Visual Modeler. Generate the following components in Visual Basic:

    a. comCourse including **Class** and **ClassSchedule** classes

    b. comGrade including **Grade**, **GradeDistribution**, and **Category** classes

    c. comUser including **Student**, **Instructor**, and **StudentSchedule** classes

    d. comAssignment

Project 9.6

Using the techniques in this chapter, create the following MTS components and fix the stored procedures if necessary. Do not forget to install the components in MTS. Reverse-engineer the components from Visual Basic into Visual Modeler to keep the models up to date.

    a. comCourse

    b. comGrade

    c. comUser

    d. comAssignment

Project 9.7

Using the techniques in this chapter, write a test client for each of the components.

Project 9.8

Using the techniques in this chapter, add the appropriate functions to each of the following components to allow them to use MSMQ. Code the messages to be sent to the queue only. Do not forget to reinstall the components in MTS.

    a. comCourse

    b. comGrade

    c. comAssignment

Project 9.9

Create a comCTISReceiveQueue component that expands the GetFromQueueMSMQ from comCourse to include all components in Hands-On Project 9.8. Remove the GetFromQueueMSMQ from the comCourse component and add the functionality to the comCTISReceiveQueue component. Do not forget to register the component in MTS.

9

Project 9.10

Using the techniques in this chapter, create test clients to test the MSMQ functionality of Project 9.7.

Project 9.11

Using the techniques in this chapter, create a test server to test the new functionality in Project 9.8.

CHAPTER TEN

CREATING "TRADITIONAL" USER INTERFACES AND USER SERVICES WITH VISUAL BASIC 6.0

AFTER READING THIS CHAPTER AND COMPLETING THE EXCERCISES, YOU WILL BE ABLE TO:

➤ Create an SDI and MDI interface in Visual Basic

➤ Create user services

➤ Use business objects in your user interface

➤ Define user interface guidelines

➤ Use both keyboard and mouse interactions with your user interface

➤ Create menus and different controls in your interface

➤ Apply user-assistance techniques to make it easy to use the interface

➤ Create a simple data report

The Application model contains three services: user, business, and data. In Chapter 8, you investigated how to create data services in SQL Server using SQL and stored procedures. In Chapter 9, you created business services in Visual Basic as ActiveX DLLs using MSMQ and MTS. This chapter explains how to create user services in Visual Basic.

One step in the development process is to create user interfaces and user services, both of which run on the client and the server. Users interact with the system on the client. To the users, the system is the user interface; therefore, you need to make sure the user interface works for the system. As explained in Chapter 2, you can provide one of two kinds of user interfaces. The first one is a single-document interface (SDI), in which the application consists of a single primary window and supplemental secondary windows. The desktop and task bar manage the primary and secondary windows. The second type of interface is a multiple-document interface (MDI), in which the application consists of a single parent window with supplemental child windows or documents. MDI applications can present different views of the same or related data.

Each type of interface uses business objects to interact with the database. Remember that user services interact with business services, which interact with data services. You will use the business objects created in Chapter 9 in this chapter.

As you are creating the user services, use the designs you created in Chapters 4 through 6 in Visual Modeler and the drawings of screen shots to guide you in this chapter.

CHAPTER OVERVIEW

In Chapters 8 and 9, you created database schemas, stored procedures, data services, and business services. You worked with the business and data services of the Application model. In this chapter, you will create a user interface for the business objects you created in the last chapter. You will also use basic user interface guidelines while creating the application.

In the Chapter_10 folder on your CD, you'll find a component called comUser in the comUser folder. Compile the component and register it in MTS before completing this chapter. Also, you need to load and run the stored procedures, using the Data View window. Refer to Chapters 8 and 9 if you need assistance in compiling components and stored procedures. Finally, on your CD, change the properties of the CTIS.udl file to point to your server. See the Tip below for instructions.

To change the properties of CTIS.udl, right-click the Network Neighborhood icon on your desktop and then click Properties. Click the Identification tab. The Computer Name is the name of your server. Click OK. Double-click the CTIS.udl file in any component subfolder. Change the Server Name to the name of your server. If you are using Windows 95/98, click Use Specific User Name and Password, type "sa" for the username, and then click the No Password checkbox to check it. Click OK.

In this chapter, you will use the conceptual, logical, and physical designs you created in Chapters 4 through 6 to guide you in creating the user interfaces. These include the Visual Modeler models and screen prototypes you created. You will create an SDI and MDI user interface from the system administrator's perspective. The system administrator is responsible for adding instructors and students to the CTIS system.

USER INTERFACE GUIDELINES

In Chapter 5, you learned how to design a user interface. Now you can create those user interfaces you designed. An effective user interface is critical to the user's overall perception of the application. You need to consider several things when creating user interfaces:

➤ **Layout** and **organization** Allow the information to flow either horizontally or vertically. The most important information is always located in the upper-left corner of the screen. The ordering of the information is important and needs to be logical.

 When working in teams, determine the user interface standards that all team members will use in creating the interfaces. These keep the look and feel the same among all forms in your application.

➤ **Font** You can use 8, 10, or 12 points for the font size. You can use one or two types of sans serif fonts in the interface. Never use italics or underlining because they make the text hard to read.

➤ **Colors** Although color is appealing, it can also be distracting. You should use a light gray for the background and black for the text. Avoid using a dark background with a light foreground because it makes the text appear blurry to the user. Because color is a very subjective property in a user interface, keep the colors neutral.

➤ **Graphics** Like color, graphics can be distracting. Use icons in your interfaces if they convey meaning to the user, but do not overuse graphics, because they may distract users from their task, which is to fill in the data on the screen.

➤ **Controls** You can group related controls together with white space or a frame. Table 10.1 illustrates different common controls used in the user interface.

➤ **Access keys** In the caption property of a control, you can use the & symbol before the character you want to use as an access key. For example, in the caption property of a label, &Name underlines the N, which means you can press ALT + N on the keyboard to access the item next to the label on the form. Access keys let users work with both the keyboard and the mouse to interact with a program.

➤ **Controlling focus** The **tabindex** property of each control allows you to determine in which order the control receives focus when the user presses the Tab key. Not all controls have a tabindex property.

Table 10.1 Common controls used in user interfaces.

Control	Description	Naming Convention (three-character prefix)
Label	Used to display information only. Usually used with a text box to explain the information that needs to be entered in the text box	lbl
Text box	Used to enter data into the form	txt
Command button	Used to execute a command	cmd
List box	Used to display a list of items	lst
Combo box	Used to display a single selection from a list of items	cmb
Check boxes	Used to select one or more choices from a fixed list of items	chk
Option buttons	Used to select one and only one choice from a list of choices. Usually used with a frame	opt
Frame	Used to group related controls together on a form	fra

USING VISUAL BASIC FORMS TO CREATE THE USER INTERFACE

The form object in Visual Basic allows you to create user interfaces. You can place controls on the user interface and write code in the Code window of a form as you do for class modules. You can use *events*, which are actions by the user or by other objects, to communicate with your form and other objects. You use event procedures to write code to handle events. Controls can raise events or you can write code to send events to your form and cause your form to do certain actions. Table 10.2 illustrates the events of a Visual Basic form.

Table 10.2 Events in a Visual Basic form (important events only).

Code	Event Raised	Description
load frmName	Form_Load	Loads the form into memory.
frmName.show	Form_Activate	When the form becomes the active form, the Form_Activate event is raised.
Unload frmName	Form_QueryUnload Form_Unload	When a form unloads, the QueryUnload event is raised first, then the Unload event is raised. QueryUnload is useful in asking if the user wants to exit, and it gives the user the ability to cancel this action.

PREVIEWING THE SINGLE-DOCUMENT INTERFACE (SDI) APPLICATION

In the last sections, you investigated how to create user interfaces. You can put your new knowledge to work by investigating the functionality of the instructor and student application before you code it. You will create, update, and delete a user in the application.

To run the User application:

1. In the Chapter_10 folder of your CD, double-click User.exe, using Windows Explorer.

2. Click New.

3. Enter the following data for a student:

   Last Name: Rivers

   First Name: John

   Home Phone: 7033333232

   Work Phone: 7033234444

   EMail: jrivers@erols.com

4. Click Save to save the record to the database.

5. Click Yes to save the record.

6. Click John Rivers and then click Update.

7. Change the Work Phone to 7033233322.

8. Click Save to update the record.

9. Click Yes to save it. The record is updated.

10. Click John Rivers and then click Delete.

11. Click Yes to delete the record.

12. Click Exit in the File menu.

13. Click Yes to exit.

You are using all the code you created in Chapters 8 and 9. The user interface uses the business objects, and the business objects call the stored procedures in SQL Server. You do not see the interface between the business objects and the database. This allows you to change the components without affecting the interface of the SDI application. The key to database-driven applications is to be able to view records, and to insert, update, and delete data from tables. There are many techniques you can use to interact with databases. This chapter illustrates one way of accessing data.

10

Creating An SDI User Interface

Keeping the user interface guidelines in mind, you will create a single-document interface in Visual Basic. Before you can code the user interfaces, you need to understand how to use the IIF function and the ADO recordset object you examined in Chapter 9. You will investigate message box usage later in the chapter.

Code Example

```
' Declare a recordset object
  Private rsStudents as new ADODB.Recordset
  . . .
  Set objStudent = CreateObject("comUser.clsStudent")
  . . .
' Retrieve all records from the STUDENTS table
  Set rsStudents = objStudent.RetrieveALL()
  If Not rsStudents.EOF Then
  'Loop through the recordset and add items to a list box
    rsStudents.MoveFirst
    Do While Not rsStudents.EOF
      lstUsers.AddItem Str(rsStudents("STUDENT_ID")) & vbTab & _
rsStudents("LAST_NAME") & " " & rsStudents("FIRST_NAME") &
      vbTab & "S"
    rsStudents.MoveNext
  Loop
End If
```

Code Dissection

➤ You need to declare a variable of type recordset **(ADODB.Recordset)**. Recall from Chapter 9 that the recordset object is a cursor that allows you to process the recordset a row at a time.

➤ The rsStudents("column_name") syntax allows you to access the data in the column of the recordset from the **Fields** collection.

➤ You need to create a reference to the **clsStudent** class from the comUser component.

➤ You need to retrieve a recordset that contains all rows from the STUDENTS table (objStudent.RetrieveALL( )).

➤ Recall from Chapter 9 that the **EOF** property tells you whether you are at the end of the recordset. If it is the end, then **EOF** is true.

➤ The first **IF** statement makes sure that rows were returned from the function. If not, skip processing.

➤ The **WHILE** loop allows you to process the recordset one row at a time. The **MoveFirst** method moves the recordset pointer to the first record in the recordset. The **MoveNext** method moves the recordset pointer to the next record in the recordset.

➤ The **AddItem** method allows you to add an Item to the list box in different columns.

Syntax

```
IIF(expr,truepart,falsepart)
```

Dissection

➤ The **IIF** function is a shorthand version of an **IF** statement that returns a value.

➤ The **expr** argument allows you to specify an expression.

➤ If the **expr** is true, the IIF function returns the truepart.

➤ If the **expr** is false, the IIF function returns the falsepart.

Code Example

```
IIF(rsStudents("LAST_NAME") IS NULL, "", rsStudents("LAST_NAME"))
```

Code Dissection

➤ When the recordset returns a result, some of the columns in the **Fields** collection can be NULL. Visual Basic does not treat NULLs very easily.

➤ You must check to see whether the column returned is NULL. If it is, then return "". Otherwise, return the column.

10

You decide to code the process of inserting, updating, and deleting students and instructors in the database. You also need to create a user interface that will insert, update, and delete students and/or instructors. This interface will display the list of students and instructors currently in the database and also create them. Specify "I" as instructor and "S" as student in the list box. To keep the interface simple, use the same interface for instructors and students.

To show the students and instructors currently in the database:

1. Click the Start menu. Point to Programs, Visual Studio 6.0, and then click Microsoft Visual Basic 6.0.

2. In the New Project dialog box, click Standard EXE and then click Open.

3. Click Project1 in Project Explorer.

4. Change the name of the project to User in the Properties window.

5. Click Form1 in Project Explorer.

6. Change the name of the form to frmSelection in the Properties window.

7. Click Save Project in the File menu.

8. Create a directory called C:\work\CTIS\user_svc_src\sdi and change to that directory. Click Save.

9. Click Save in the Save Project As dialog box.

10. Click Yes in the Add this project to SourceSafe dialog box.

11. Log on to SourceSafe as CTIS with password CTIS. Click OK.

12. Expand the project tree $/CTIS/user_svc_src/.

13. Type "SDI" in the Project text box. Click Create. Make sure to create the project in the user_svc_src directory.

14. Click Yes when asked if you would like to create a project.

15. Click OK to add files to SourceSafe.

16. Check out all files in Project Explorer.

17. Create the following user interface (Figure 10.1). The steps below provide detailed instructions.

You need to name the controls lstUsers, cmdNew, cmdUpdate, cmdDelete, mnuFile, and mnuHelp.

To create menu controls:

1. Use the menu editor to create a hyphen and **Exit** command in the File menu. Name the **Exit** command **mnuFileExit.**

2. Use the menu editor to create a hyphen and the **About CTIS** command in the Help menu. Name the **About CTIS** command **mnuHelpAbout**.

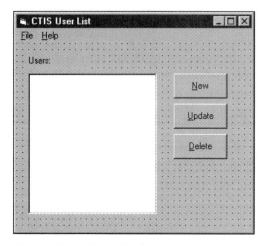

Figure 10.1 User List form.

3. Double-click the form's background to display the Code window.

4. Enter the following code. To do so, copy the code from the code10-01.txt file on your data disk and paste it in the code window.

To copy code into the Code window, navigate to the Chapter_10 folder on your Student Data Disk. Double-click the appropriate text file to open it in Notepad. On the Edit menu, click Select All. Then press Ctrl+C to copy all the text. Close Notepad and click in the Code window. Then press Ctrl+V to paste the text in the Code window.

```
Public objStudent As Object
Public objInstructor As Object
Private lngChoice As Long
Private strChoice As String

Private rsStudents As New ADODB.Recordset
Private rsInstructors As New ADODB.Recordset

Private strResult As String

Private Sub cmdDelete_Click()

  Dim intAnswer As Integer
  intAnswer =_
    MsgBox("Are you sure you want to Delete this record?",_
    vbExclamation + vbYesNo, "Delete")
  If intAnswer = vbYes Then

  If strChoice = "S" Then
    strResult = objStudent.Delete(lngChoice)
  Else
    strResult = objInstructor.Delete(lngChoice)
  End If

  If strResult <> "" Then
    intAnswer = MsgBox(strResult, vbCritical + vbOKOnly, "Delete")
  End If
  Call RefreshForm
  End If
End Sub

Private Sub cmdNew_Click()
  Load frmUser
  frmUser.optInstructor.Enabled = True
```

10

```
          frmUser.optStudent.Enabled = True
          frmUser.optStudent.Value = True
          frmUser.lngID = 0
          frmUser.txtFirstName = ""
          frmUser.txtLastName = ""
          frmUser.txtEMail = ""
          frmUser.txtURL = ""
          frmUser.txtHomePhone = ""
          frmUser.txtWorkPhone = ""
          frmUser.Show vbModal
      End Sub

      Private Sub cmdUpdate_Click()
        Load frmUser
        If strChoice = "S" Then
          frmUser.optStudent.Value = True
          frmUser.optInstructor.Enabled = False
          frmUser.lngID = IIf(IsNull(rsStudents("STUDENT_ID")), "", _
            rsStudents("STUDENT_ID"))
          frmUser.txtFirstName = IIf(IsNull(rsStudents("FIRST_NAME")), _
            "", rsStudents("FIRST_NAME"))
          frmUser.txtLastName = IIf(IsNull(rsStudents("LAST_NAME")), "", _
            rsStudents("LAST_NAME"))
          frmUser.txtEMail = IIf(IsNull(rsStudents("E_MAIL")), "", _
            rsStudents("E_MAIL"))
          frmUser.txtURL.Enabled = False
          frmUser.txtHomePhone.Enabled = True
          frmUser.txtHomePhone = IIf(IsNull(rsStudents("HOME_PHONE")), _
            "", rsStudents("HOME_PHONE"))
          frmUser.txtWorkPhone = IIf(IsNull(rsStudents("WORK_PHONE")),_
            "", rsStudents("WORK_PHONE"))
        Else
          frmUser.optInstructor.Value = True
          frmUser.optStudent.Enabled = False
          frmUser.lngID = IIf(IsNull(rsInstructors("INSTRUCTOR_ID")), "",_
            rsInstructors("INSTRUCTOR_ID"))
          frmUser.txtFirstName = IIf(IsNull(rsInstructors("FIRST_NAME")),_
            "", rsInstructors("FIRST_NAME"))
          frmUser.txtLastName = IIf(IsNull(rsInstructors("LAST_NAME")),_
            "", rsInstructors("LAST_NAME"))
          frmUser.txtEMail = IIf(IsNull(rsInstructors("E_MAIL")), "",_
            rsInstructors("E_MAIL"))
          frmUser.txtURL = IIf(IsNull(rsInstructors("URL")), "",_
            rsInstructors("URL"))
          frmUser.txtHomePhone.Enabled = False
          frmUser.txtURL.Enabled = True
          frmUser.txtWorkPhone = IIf(IsNull(rsInstructors("PHONE _
            NUMBER")), "", rsInstructors("PHONE_NUMBER"))
```

```
      End If
      frmUser.Show vbModal
    End Sub

    Private Sub Form_Load()
      Set objStudent = CreateObject("comUser.clsStudent")
      Set objInstructor = CreateObject("comUser.clsInstructor")

      Call RefreshForm
    End Sub

    Public Sub RefreshForm()
      cmdUpdate.Enabled = False
      cmdDelete.Enabled = False
      cmdNew.Enabled = True

      lstUsers.Clear


      Set rsStudents = objStudent.RetrieveALL()
      Set rsInstructors = objInstructor.RetrieveALL()

      If Not rsStudents.EOF Then

      rsStudents.MoveFirst
      Do While Not rsStudents.EOF
        lstUsers.AddItem Str(rsStudents("STUDENT_ID")) & vbTab & _
          rsStudents("LAST_NAME") & " " & rsStudents("FIRST_NAME") & _
          vbTab & "S"
        rsStudents.MoveNext
      Loop

      End If

      If Not rsInstructors.EOF Then

      rsInstructors.MoveFirst
      Do While Not rsInstructors.EOF
        lstUsers.AddItem Str(rsInstructors("INSTRUCTOR_ID")) & vbTab & _
          rsInstructors("LAST_NAME") & " " & rsInstructors("FIRST_NAME") & _
          vbTab & "I"
        rsInstructors.MoveNext
      Loop

      End If
```

10

```
            End Sub

            Private Sub Form_QueryUnload(Cancel As Integer,_
              UnloadMode As Integer)
              Dim intAnswer As Integer
              intAnswer = MsgBox("Are you sure you want to exit?",_
                vbExclamation + vbYesNo, "Exit")
              If intAnswer = vbNo Then
                Cancel = 1
              End If
            End Sub

            Private Sub Form_Unload(Cancel As Integer)
              Set objStudent = Nothing
              Set objInstructor = Nothing
            End Sub

            Private Sub lstUsers_Click()
              Dim intFirst As Integer
              Dim intSecond As Integer

              cmdUpdate.Enabled = True
              cmdDelete.Enabled = True
              cmdNew.Enabled = True

              intFirst = InStr(lstUsers.List(lstUsers.ListIndex), vbTab)
              intSecond = InStr(intFirst, lstUsers.List(lstUsers.ListIndex),_
                vbTab)
              lngChoice = Val(Left(lstUsers.List(lstUsers.ListIndex), intFirst))
              strChoice = Trim(Right(lstUsers.List(lstUsers.ListIndex),_
                intSecond - 2))

              If InStr(strChoice, "S") > 0 Then
                  strChoice = "S"
              Else
                  strChoice = "I"
              End If

              If strChoice = "S" Then
                rsStudents.MoveFirst
                Do While Not rsStudents.EOF
                    If rsStudents("STUDENT_ID") = lngChoice Then
                      Exit Sub
                    End If
```

```
            rsStudents.MoveNext
        Loop
     Else
        rsInstructors.MoveFirst
        Do While Not rsInstructors.EOF
           If rsInstructors("INSTRUCTOR_ID") = lngChoice Then
              Exit Do
           End If
           rsInstructors.MoveNext
        Loop
     End If
  End Sub


  Private Sub mnuExit_Click()
     Unload Me
  End Sub
```

5. Add a new form to the project and change the name to frmUser. Then check out frmUser.

6. Create the user interface illustrated in Figure 10.2. The steps below provide detailed instructions.

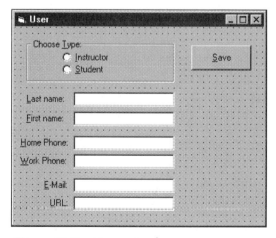

Use fraUserChoice, optStudent, optInstructor, txtLastName, txtFirstName, txtWorkPhone, txtHomePhone, txtEMail, and txtURL for the control names. Use cmdSave for the name of the command button. Replace **txt** with **lbl** for the label names on the form.

Figure 10.2   User entry form.

To enter the control names:

1. Double-click the frmUser's background to display the Code window.

2. Enter the following code. To do so, copy the code from code10-02.txt on the Data folder on the CD and paste it in the Code window.

```
Public lngID As Long
Private Sub cmdSave_Click()
  Dim strResult As String
  Dim intAnswer As Integer
On Error Goto SaveError
  intAnswer = MsgBox("Are you sure you want to Save this record?",_
    vbExclamation + vbYesNo, "Save")
  If intAnswer = vbYes Then
  If optInstructor.Value = True Then
    strResult = frmSelection.objInstructor.Save(lngID,_
      IIf(txtLastName.Text = "", "", txtLastName.Text),_
      IIf(txtFirstName.Text = "", "", txtFirstName.Text),_
      IIf(txtWorkPhone.Text = "", "", txtWorkPhone.Text),_
      IIf(txtEMail.Text = "", "", txtEMail.Text), IIf(txtURL.Text =_
"","", txtURL.Text))
  Else
    strResult = frmSelection.objStudent.Save(lngID,_
      IIf(txtLastName.Text = "", "", txtLastName.Text),_
      IIf(txtFirstName.Text = "", "", txtFirstName.Text),_
      IIf(txtEMail.Text = "", "", txtEMail.Text), IIf(txtHomePhone.Text =_
"", "", txtHomePhone.Text), IIf(txtWorkPhone.Text = "", "",_
      txtWorkPhone.Text))
  End If

  If strResult <> "" Then
    intAnswer = MsgBox(strResult, vbCritical + vbOKCancelOnly,_
      "Save")
  Else
    frmSelection.RefreshForm
    Unload frmUser
  End If
  End If
SaveError:
End Sub

Private Sub optInstructor_Click()
   txtURL.Enabled = True
   txtHomePhone = ""
   txtHomePhone.Enabled = False
End Sub
```

```
Private Sub optStudent_Click()
  txtURL = ""
  txtURL.Enabled = False
  txtHomePhone.Enabled = True

End Sub
```

3. Click User Properties on the Project menu.

4. Change the Startup Object to frmSelection, if necessary, and then click OK.

5. Click References on the Project menu.

6. Click Microsoft ActiveX Data Objects 1.5 Library and Microsoft ActiveX Data Objects Recordset 1.5 Library. (The version number will reflect the current version of your software.)

7. Click OK.

8. Click Run on the toolbar.

9. Verify that the functions work as expected.

10. Click Save Project on the File menu.

11. Check in all files.

12. Click Exit on the File menu.

Creating An MDI User Interface

In the last few sections, you investigated how to create an SDI application. For practice, you can now use the same forms and turn the SDI application into an MDI application. (You generally create MDI forms from scratch.)
Before you begin, open the User application and save all the files in a different directory so that you can create the MDI application.

 In the real world, you create MDI applications from scratch. In this section, you will reuse the SDI forms to make it easier for you to create the MDI application.

To convert an SDI application to an MDI application:

1. Click the Start menu. Point to Programs, Microsoft Visual Studio 6.0, and click Microsoft Visual Basic 6.0.

2. Click the Existing tab.

3. Change the current directory to c:\work\CTIS\user_svc_src\sdi and click User.

4. Click Open.

5. Log on to Visual SourceSafe as CTIS with the password CTIS.

6. In Project Explorer, click the User project.

7. Click Save Project As in the File menu.

8. Create a directory in user_svc_src called MDI. Change to that directory.

9. Change the project name to userMDI.

10. Click Save.

11. In the SourceSafe dialog box, click OK.

12. Click No in the Add Project to SourceSafe dialog box.

13. Save frmSelection and frmUser to the MDI directory, using the Save As option.

14. Use Windows Explorer to verify that you moved all files to MDI.

15. In the Properties window, change the name of the project to UserMDI.

16. Click Add Project to SourceSafe in the Tools and SourceSafe menus.

Now you can add the files to SourceSafe. You can also convert two forms so that they appear in the context of the parent window, and add a border to the child windows to distinguish them from the parent window.

To add the files to SourceSafe:

1. Log on to SourceSafe.

2. Create an MDI project in $/CTIS/user_svc_src. Change the default name from userMDI to MDI, if necessary

3. Click OK when the project is created.

4. Click OK in the Add Files to SourceSafe dialog box.

5. Check out all files from SourceSafe.

6. All MDI applications have a parent form. Click Add MDI Form in the Project menu.

7. Click Open in the Add MDI Form dialog box.

8. In the Properties window, change the name of the MDI Form to frmMDIUser.

9. Change the caption of the MDI Form to Users.

10. Click Save frmMDIUser on the File menu.

11. Click Save in the Save File As dialog box.

12. Click OK in the Add Files to SourceSafe dialog box.

13. Check out frmMDIUser.

14. You need to change frmSelection and frmUser to child forms. Double-click frmSelection.

15. Change the MDIChild property to True in the Properties window to make the form a child form. Child forms appear in the context of the MDI form.

16. Change the BorderStyle to 1 – Fixed Single.

17. Double-click frmUser.

18. In the Properties window, change the MDIChild property to True to make the form a child form. Child forms appear in the context of the MDI form.

19. Change the BorderStyle to 1 – Fixed Single.

20. Click Save Project on the File menu.

21. Click UserMDI properties on the Project menu.

22. Change the StartUp Object to frmMDIUser.

23. Click OK.

Now you can remove and add menus so that they appear on the parent window and not on the child windows.

To remove and add menus:

1. Remove the menus from the frmSelection form.

2. On the frmMDIUser form, add the following menus:

File – mnuFile	Edit – mnuEdit	Window – mnuWindow,	Help
New – mnuFileNew	Cut – mnuEditCut	Check the	———
Close – mnuFileClose	Copy – mnuEditCopy	Window List option	About
———	Paste – mnuEditPaste		CTIS
Exit – mnuFileExit			

3. Double-click the frmMDIUser form's background to display the Code window.

4. Enter the following code. To do so, copy the code from the code10-03.txt file on your data disk and paste it in the code window.

```
Private Sub MDIForm_Load()
  Load frmSelection
  frmSelection.Show
  frmMDIUser.mnuEdit.Enabled = False
End Sub

Private Sub mnuEdit_Click()
  If TypeOf Screen.ActiveControl Is TextBox Then
    If Screen.ActiveControl.SelText = "" Then
```

```
            mnuEditCopy.Enabled = False
            mnuEditCut.Enabled = False
        Else
            mnuEditCopy.Enabled = True
            mnuEditCut.Enabled = True
        End If
    End If


    If Clipboard.GetText = "" Then
        mnuEditPaste.Enabled = False
    Else
        mnuEditPaste.Enabled = True
    End If
End Sub
Private Sub mnuEditCopy_Click()
    Clipboard.Clear
    If TypeOf Screen.ActiveControl Is TextBox Then
        Clipboard.SetText Screen.ActiveControl.SelText
    ElseIf TypeOf Screen.ActiveControl Is ComboBox Then
        Clipboard.SetText Screen.ActiveControl.Text
    ElseIf TypeOf Screen.ActiveControl Is PictureBox _
            Then
        Clipboard.SetData Screen.ActiveControl.Picture
    ElseIf TypeOf Screen.ActiveControl Is ListBox Then
        Clipboard.SetText Screen.ActiveControl.Text
    Else
        ' No action makes sense for the other controls.
    End If
End Sub

Private Sub mnuEditCut_Click()
    ' First do the same as a copy.
    mnuEditCopy_Click
    ' Now clear contents of active control.
    If TypeOf Screen.ActiveControl Is TextBox Then
        Screen.ActiveControl.SelText = ""
    ElseIf TypeOf Screen.ActiveControl Is ComboBox Then
        Screen.ActiveControl.Text = ""
    ElseIf TypeOf Screen.ActiveControl Is PictureBox _
            Then
        Screen.ActiveControl.Picture = LoadPicture()
    ElseIf TypeOf Screen.ActiveControl Is ListBox Then
        Screen.ActiveControl.RemoveItem _
            Screen.ActiveControl.ListIndex
    Else
        ' No action makes sense for the other controls.
```

```
        End If
    End Sub

    Private Sub mnuEditPaste_Click()
        If TypeOf Screen.ActiveControl Is TextBox Then
            Screen.ActiveControl.SelText = Clipboard.GetText()
        ElseIf TypeOf Screen.ActiveControl Is ComboBox Then
            Screen.ActiveControl.Text = Clipboard.GetText()
        ElseIf TypeOf Screen.ActiveControl Is PictureBox _
                Then
            Screen.ActiveControl.Picture = _
                Clipboard.GetData()
        ElseIf TypeOf Screen.ActiveControl Is ListBox Then
            Screen.ActiveControl.AddItem Clipboard.GetText()
        Else
            ' No action makes sense for the other controls.
        End If
    End Sub

    Private Sub mnuFileClose_Click()
      Unload ActiveForm
    End Sub

    Private Sub mnuFileExit_Click()
      Unload frmMDIUser
    End Sub

    Private Sub MDIForm_QueryUnload(Cancel As Integer, UnloadMode As_
      Integer)
      Dim intAnswer As Integer
      intAnswer = MsgBox("Are you sure you want to exit?", _
        vbExclamation + vbYesNo, "Exit")
      If intAnswer = vbNo Then
        Cancel = 1
      End If
    End Sub

    Private Sub mnuFileNew_Click()
    Load frmSelection
    frmSelection.Show
    End Sub
```

5. Remove vbModal from the Show methods section of the frmSelection Code window.

6. In the frmSelection Code window, change the MsgBox function in the Query_Unload event from Exit to Close.

7. Click Save Project on the File menu.

8. Click Start on the toolbar.

9. Verify that the MDI application works like the SDI application.

You coded this MDI application to work very much like the SDI application. The big difference is that the MDI form acts as a container to the child forms. This gives you the ability to create menus that work with different child windows. For example, the Edit menu contains Cut, Copy, and Paste functions. These functions work between different child windows. Currently, you support only the frmSelection form and the frmUser form in the MDI application. The advantage of the MDI application is that the MDI form can handle more than one child form at a time. You will allow the frmUser form to open multiple windows from the frmSelection window. This gives you flexibility to work with different views of the frmUser form.

To allow your MDI application to support multiple frmUsers:

1. Double-click the **frmSelection** form to display the Code window.

2. Review the following code and make any necessary changes.

```
Private Sub cmdNew_Click()
  Dim frmUser1 As New frmUser
  'Load frmUser
  frmUser1.Left = 0
  frmUser1.Top = 0
  frmUser1.optInstructor.Enabled = True
  frmUser1.optStudent.Enabled = True
  frmUser1.optStudent.Value = True
  frmUser1.lngID = 0
  frmUser1.txtFirstName = ""
  frmUser1.txtLastName = ""
  frmUser1.txtEMail = ""
  frmUser1.txtURL = ""
  frmUser1.txtHomePhone = ""
  frmUser1.txtWorkPhone = ""
  frmUser1.Show
End Sub

Private Sub cmdUpdate_Click()
  Dim frmUser1 As New frmUser
  'Load frmUser
  frmUser1.Left = 0
  frmUser1.Top = 0
  If strChoice = "S" Then
    frmUser1.optStudent.Value = True
    frmUser1.optInstructor.Enabled = False
    frmUser1.lngID = IIf(IsNull(rsStudents("STUDENT_ID")), "",_
```

```
                  rsStudents("STUDENT_ID"))
            frmUser1.txtFirstName = IIf(IsNull(rsStudents("FIRST_NAME")),_
              "", rsStudents("FIRST_NAME"))
            frmUser1.txtLastName = IIf(IsNull(rsStudents("LAST_NAME")), "",_
              rsStudents("LAST_NAME"))
            frmUser1.txtEMail = IIf(IsNull(rsStudents("E_MAIL")), "",_
              rsStudents("E_MAIL"))
            frmUser1.txtURL.Enabled = False
            frmUser1.txtHomePhone.Enabled = True
            frmUser1.txtHomePhone = IIf(IsNull(rsStudents("HOME_PHONE")),_
              "", rsStudents("HOME_PHONE"))_
            frmUser1.txtWorkPhone = IIf(IsNull(rsStudents("WORK_PHONE")),_
              "", rsStudents("WORK_PHONE"))_
        Else
            frmUser1.optInstructor.Value = True
            frmUser1.optStudent.Enabled = False
            frmUser1.lngID = IIf(IsNull(rsInstructors("INSTRUCTOR_ID")),_
              "", rsInstructors("INSTRUCTOR_ID"))
            frmUser1.txtFirstName = IIf(IsNull(rsInstructors("FIRST_NAME")),_
              "", rsInstructors("FIRST_NAME"))
            frmUser1.txtLastName = IIf(IsNull(rsInstructors("LAST_NAME")),_
              "", rsInstructors("LAST_NAME"))
            frmUser1.txtEMail = IIf(IsNull(rsInstructors("E_MAIL")), "",_
              rsInstructors("E_MAIL"))
            frmUser1.txtURL = IIf(IsNull(rsInstructors("URL")), "",_
              rsInstructors("URL"))
            frmUser1.txtHomePhone.Enabled = False
            frmUser1.txtURL.Enabled = True
            frmUser1.txtWorkPhone = IIf(IsNull(rsInstructors_
              ("PHONE_NUMBER")), "", rsInstructors("PHONE_NUMBER"))
        End If
        frmUser1.Show
    End Sub
```

10

3. Click Save Project in the File menu.

4. Click Start on the toolbar.

5. Click New on the frmSelection form.

6. Click Window and then click CTIS User List.

7. Click New to display a second frmUser form. (You can also click the Update button to display a second form.)

8. Close all the windows.

9. Click Exit on the File menu.

The key to the above code is the following:

```
Dim frmUser1 as New frmUser
. . .
frmUser1.Show
```

The **Dim** statement creates a new frmUser form and frmUser1.Show displays the form for you. This allows you to create several instances of frmUser in the MDI application.

You can use the MDI or SDI application type when creating user interfaces for your projects. User interface standards dictate which type of application you use in your projects.

USER ASSISTANCE

To make your application accessible and inviting to your users, provide plenty of user assistance. *User assistance* provides help in working with your application, and can make it easy to use. There are several ways you can supply user assistance:

➤ **Help files**: Your application is not complete without a Help system. Chapter 12 illustrates how to create a Help system in Visual Studio.

➤ **ToolTips** When your mouse points to an object in your application, a rectangular object appears with text that describes the item. For example, when you place your mouse over a tool in a toolbar, you see the name of the tool. To provide user assistance, you can type text in any control that has a **ToolTipText** property.

➤ **Toolbars** Toolbars are special panels that supply shortcuts to the most commonly used commands in your application. Toolbars appear under the menu bar.

➤ **Status bar** At the bottom of the form, a status bar displays information about the current state of an application or about what is currently being viewed. For example, if you are about to click the New command in the File menu, the status bar displays Creating A New User List.

➤ **Message boxes** Message boxes are secondary windows that display information about the current situation of the application. An example of a message box is shown in Figure 10.3.

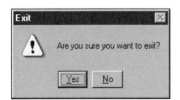

Figure 10.3 An example of a message box.

Use an icon in the message box to indicate the type of message you're displaying. The message should be appropriate to the current situation and clearly written. Poorly written messages cause user frustration and increased support costs. The command buttons in a message box can be different constants, such as **vbInformation + vbOKOnly** (displays the information icon and the OK button), **vbCritical + vbRetryCancel** (displays the critical icon and two buttons, Retry and Cancel), **or vbExclamation + vbYesNo** (displays the exclamation icon and two buttons, Yes and No). There are several different types of messages:

➤ **Information** Information message boxes supply information about the results of a command and provide no user choices. The constants used in information message boxes are vbInformation and vbOkOnly.

➤ **Warning** Warning message boxes alert the user to a condition that requires a decision that will cause a permanent change. Warning messages are usually in the form of a question such as "Are you sure you want to exit?" The constants used in warning message boxes are vbExclamation and vbYesNo. In Windows 3.1, you use the vbQuestion icon. In Windows 95, the standard is to use the vbExclamation instead of vbQuestion.

➤ **Critical** Critical message boxes alert the user to a serious situation that requires the user's intervention before the application can continue. An example of a critical message is "a:\ is not accessible. The device is not ready." The constants used in critical messages are vbCritical and vbRetryCancel.

The most common way to implement message boxes is by using the MSGBOX function.

Syntax

```
iretcode = MsgBox(prompt[, buttons] [, title])
```

Dissection

➤ The **iretcode** is the constant that the MsgBox returns, depending upon the user's choice. The MsgBox will return vbYes for Yes, vbNo for No, vbRetry for Retry, vbCancel for Cancel, or vbOK for OK.

➤ The **prompt** is the actual message being displayed.

➤ The **buttons** variable specifies which icon and buttons to display.

➤ The **title** is the name of the message box that appears in the title bar of a form.

Examples of the buttons argument are:

➤ *vbInformation + vbOKOnly* Displays the information icon and the OK button

➤ *vbCritical + vbRetryCancel* Displays the critical icon and the Retry and Cancel buttons

10

➤ **vbExclamation + vbYesNo** Displays the exclamation icon and the Yes and No buttons

Refer to online help for explanations of all the button options.

Syntax
```
intAnswer = MsgBox("Are you sure you want to exit?", vbExclamation +
vbYesNo, "Exit")
```

Dissection

➤ The above code displays the message box in Figure 10.3.

Creating ToolTips, Toolbars, And Status Bars

In the last section, you saw the different ways to supply user assistance in your application. Now you can create ToolTips, a toolbar, and a status bar in your MDI application.

To create ToolTips, a toolbar, and a status bar:

1. Click Components on the Project menu.

2. Select Microsoft Windows Common Controls 6.0, and then click OK to add a toolbar and a status bar to the toolbox.

3. Add the toolbar to the MDI form.

4. Add the status bar to the MDI form.

5. Add an image list to the MDI form.

6. Right-click the image list and then click Properties.

7. Select 16 x 16 and then click the Images tab.

8. Click Insert Picture.

9. Change to the c:\Program Files\Microsoft Visual Studio\Common\Graphics\Bitmaps\Tlbr_W95 folder.

10. Click New.bmp and then click Open.

11. Type New in the Key text box.

12. Click Insert Picture.

13. Click Cut.bmp and then click Open.

14. Type Cut in the Key text box.

15. Click Insert Picture.

16. Click Copy.bmp and then click Open.

17. Type Copy in the Key text box.

18. Click Insert Picture.

19. Click Paste.bmp and then click Open.

20. Type Paste in the Key text box.

21. Click OK to close the Property Pages.

22. Right-click the Toolbar control and then click Properties.

23. Select ImageList1 from the Image List combo box and then click OK.

Now you're ready to set up the buttons.

To set up the buttons:

1. Click the Buttons tab.

2. Click Insert Button.

3. Type "New" in the Key text box.

4. Type "1" in the Image text box.

5. Type "New" in the ToolTipText text box.

6. Click Insert Button.

7. Type "Cut" in the Key text box.

8. Type "2" in the Image text box.

9. Type "Cut" in the ToolTipText.

10. Click Insert Button.

11. Type "Copy" in the Key text box.

12. Type "3" in the Image text box.

13. Type "Copy" in the ToolTipText text box.

14. Click Insert Button.

15. Type "Paste" in the Key text box.

16. Type "4" in the Image text box.

17. Type "Paste" in the ToolTipText text box.

18. Click OK.

19. Type the following code in frmMDIUser to enable the toolbar:

```
Private Sub Toolbar1_ButtonClick(ByVal Button As MSComctlLib.Button)
   Select Case Button.Key
      Case "New"
        Call mnuFileNew_Click
      Case "Cut"
        Call mnuEdit_Click
        Call mnuEditCut_Click
      Case "Copy"
```

10

```
        Call mnuEdit_Click
        Call mnuEditCopy_Click
    Case "Paste"
Call mnuEdit_Click
Call mnuEditPaste_Click
End Select
End Sub
```

20. Click Save Project in the File menu.

21. Right-click the status bar and then click Properties.

22. Click the Panels tab and type "5000" in the Minimum Width text box.

23. Click OK.

24. In the Code window of frmSelection, type the following code to display text in the status bar:

```
Private Sub Form_Activate()
    frmMDIUser.StatusBar1.Panels(1).Text = "CTIS User List"
End Sub
```

25. In the Code window of frmUser, type the following code to display text in the status bar:

```
Private Sub Form_Activate()
    frmMDIUser.StatusBar1.Panels(1).Text = "Insert or update a _
        student or an instructor."
End Sub
```

26. Click Start on the toolbar.

27. Verify the functioning of the toolbar, ToolTips, and status bar.

28. Click Save Project on the File menu.

Simple Reports

You have successfully created a toolbar and status bar, and used ToolTips with your toolbar. You can add more ToolTips by setting the **ToolTipText** property of controls that support ToolTips. To complete the user interface, you need to add reports to it. A *report* gives the user a printed representation of the data in your tables. To create a data report in Visual Basic, complete the following tasks:

➤ Create a data environment in Visual Basic. A *data environment* provides an interactive design environment to create run-time access to your data.

➤ After you set up the data environment, create a connection to the database.

➤ After you set up a data connection, set up an SQL query to use when creating the report.

➤ Create a data report in Visual Basic in the form you want and add the appropriate code to run the report at run time.

To create a data environment:

1. Click Add Data Environment on the Project menu.

2. In the Properties window, change the name of the data environment to envCTIS.

3. Change the name of the connection to conCTIS.

4. Right-click conCTIS and then click Properties.

5. Click Microsoft OLE DB Provider for SQL Server.

6. Click Next.

7. Enter your server name.

8. Click Use Windows NT Integrated Security.

9. Select CTIS for the database.

10. Click OK.

11. Right-click conCTIS and then click Add Command.

12. Change the name of the command to rsStudents.

13. Right-click rsStudents and then click Properties.

14. Click SQL Statement and type SELECT STUDENT_ID, LAST_NAME, FIRST_NAME FROM STUDENTS in the SQL text box.

15. Click OK.

16. Save the Project, add the files to SourceSafe, and check out the environment.

Before you can create a report, you need to understand the data report environment. Figure 10.4 shows the data report environment.

➤ **Report header** This section displays the information at the top of the report only.

➤ **Page header** Like the header in a Word document, the information in a page header is displayed at the top of each page of the report.

➤ **Group header/footer** This section displays the repeating section of the report, where the data is grouped according to certain criteria. For example, if you display a summary report, you could display subtotals based on certain criteria and display the grand total at the end of the report. You can add functions to a report, such as average, min, max, sum, and others, using the **FunctionType** property of a function control. You can use this control in most sections.

10

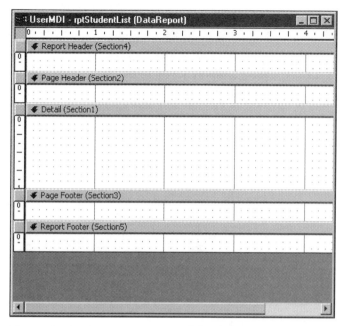

Figure 10.4   A report consists of the following sections.

➤ **Detail** This section displays the repeating part of the report where the information is shown.

➤ **Page footer** Like the footer in a Word document, the information in the footer is displayed at the bottom of each page of the report.

➤ **Report footer** This section displays information at the end of the report.

To create a data report:

1. Click Add Data Report on the Project menu.

2. Change the name of the report to rptStudentList.

3. Change the following properties:
   Data Source: envCTIS
   Data Member: rsStudents

4. Right-click the report and then click Retrieve Structure to retrieve the structure of the query from the database.

5. Click Yes.

6. Right-click the Page Header section, point to Insert Control, and then click Label.

7. Change the caption of the label to Student_ID.

8. In the Page Header section, insert two labels, one with the caption of Last Name and another with the caption of First Name. Align them in columns as shown in Figure 10.5.

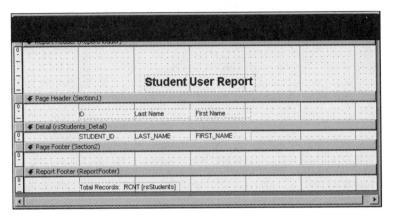

Figure 10.5   Student User Report format.

9. Right-click the Detail section, click Insert Control, and then click TextBox.

10. Change the **Data Member** property to rsStudents, and change the **Data Field** property to STUDENT_ID.

11. Insert two text boxes, one with Data Field set to LAST_NAME and one with Data Field set to FIRST_NAME. Set the **Data Member** property in both text boxes to rsStudents.

12. Right-click the Page Header section and then click Insert Control and Current Date (Long Format).

13. Right-click the Page Header section and then click Insert Control and Current Page Number.

    See Figure 10.5 for the complete report format.

14. Right-click the Report Footer section and then click Insert Control and Function to add a function to the report.

15. Change the FunctionType to 4 – RptFuncRCnt.

16. Add a label with the caption Total Records: before the function.

17. Click Save Project on the File menu.

18. Click Save on the Save File As dialog box.

19. Click OK in the Add Files to SourceSafe dialog box.

20. Check out the report.

To add a Reports menu and Student Listing command:

1. Use the menu editor to add a Reports (mnuReports) menu before the Window menu of the MDI form. Add a Student Listing (mnuReportsStudent) command in the Reports menu.

10

2. Add the following code to the MDI form Code window to display the report from the menu:

```
Private Sub mnuReportStudent_Click()
  rptStudentList.Show vbModal
End Sub
```

3. Click Start on the toolbar.

4. Click Student Listing in the Reports menu.

You can export the report to a file or print the report from the Report window.

5. Close the Report window.

6. Close all windows.

7. Click Exit in the File menu.

8. Click Yes to exit.

9. Click Save Project in the File menu in Visual Basic.

10. Check in all files.

11. Click Exit in the File menu.

CHAPTER SUMMARY

This chapter surveyed two different ways to create user interfaces and user services: SDI and MDI applications. A basic application consists of forms, reports, menus, toolbars, ToolTips, and status bars. The user interface is what the user views as the application, even if the application exists on many machines. Because the user interface is critical to the success of a system, you must make sure that the user interface is consistent and that the user assistance is helpful. The best way to do this is to include the user in the user interface design and creation. You can hold periodic meetings to make sure that the user approves of the user interface.

REVIEW QUESTIONS

1. On a form, the information needs to flow either _____ or _____. Choose all that apply.
   a. diagonally
   b. vertically
   c. horizontally
   d. none of the above

2. Never use _____ or underlining, because it makes the text hard to read.

   a. bold

   b. unusual fonts

   c. italics

   d. none of the above

3. _____ attract your eye before any other element on the screen.

   a. Numeric characters

   b. Alphabetic characters

   c. Graphics

   d. Lines

4. Use a _____ control to display information only.

   a. text box

   b. list box

   c. label

   d. command button

5. Use a _____ control to enter data on the form.

   a. text box

   b. command button

   c. label

   d. list box

6. Use a _____ control to display a list of items.

   a. text box

   b. command button

   c. label

   d. list box

7. Use a(n) _____ before a character to indicate an access key.

   a. *

   b. ^

   c. &

   d. %

8. The _____ property allows you to determine the order in which the control receives focus.

   a. tabindex

   b. caption

   c. index

   d. control

9. The load form command raises the _____ event.

   a. Form_Activate

   b. Form_Load

   c. Form_Unload

   d. Form_QueryUnload

10. The unload form command raises the _____ event.

    a. Form_Load

    b. Form_QueryUnload

    c. Form_Unload

    d. Form_Activate

11. Which property in a recordset object tells you whether you are at the end of the recordset?

    a. BOF

    b. EOF

    c. MoveFirst

    d. none of the above

12. The _____ function is a shorthand version of an IF statement that returns a value.

    a. IF

    b. IIF

    c. WHILE

    d. none of the above

13. _____ are special panels that supply shortcuts to most commonly used commands in your application.

    a. Toolbars

    b. ToolTips

    c. Status bars

    d. none of the above

14. _____ are special secondary windows that display information about the current situation in the application.

    a. Toolbars

    b. ToolTips

    c. Status bars

    d. Message boxes

15. _____ messages alert the user to a condition that requires a decision that will cause a permanent change.

    a. Warning

    b. Critical

    c. Information

    d. none of the above

16. _____ messages alert the user to a serious condition that requires user intervention before the application can continue.

    a. Warning

    b. Critical

    c. Information

    d. none of the above

10

17. _____ messages supply information about the results of a command and provide no user choices.

    a. Warning

    b. Critical

    c. Information

    d. none of the above

HANDS-ON PROJECTS

Project 10.1

Using the techniques covered in this chapter and the user interface designs in Chapter 5, create an SDI user interface for the STUDENT_SCHEDULES form.

Project 10.2

Using the techniques covered in this chapter and the user interface designs in Chapter 5, create an MDI user interface for the following forms (including toolbar, status bar, message boxes, and ToolTips):

    a. CATEGORIES

    b. CLASSES

    c. CLASS_SCHEDULE

    d. GRADE_DISTRIBUTION

    e. GRADES

Project 10.3

Create the following report for the form in Hands-On Project 10.1:
STUDENT_SCHEDULES

Project 10.4

Create the following reports for the forms in Hands-On Project 10.2:

    a. CATEGORIES

    b. CLASSES

    c. CLASS_SCHEDULE

    d. GRADE_DISTRIBUTION

    e. STUDENT GRADE REPORT BY CLASS

    f. STUDENT TRANSCRIPT

    g. GRADES REPORT BY STUDENT

    h. GRADES REPORT BY CLASS AND BY STUDENT

Project 10.5

For the MDI application in this chapter, create the following reports:

    a. INSTRUCTOR LISTING

    b. STUDENT INFORMATION (all student fields)

    c. INSTRUCTOR INFORMATION (all instructor fields)

Project 10.6

For the MDI application in this chapter, add appropriate message boxes for the
frmUser form. (Hint: Add warning messages before you close the form. Add
information messages in SDI and MDI applications to tell users whether the
insert, update, or delete operation was a success or failure.)

CREATING WEB USER INTERFACES AND USER SERVICES USING VISUAL INTERDEV 6.0

AFTER READING THIS CHAPTER AND COMPLETING THE EXCERCISES, YOU WILL BE ABLE TO:

➤ Describe the World Wide Web and its architecture

➤ Define HTML and DHTML

➤ Define and create scripts using VBScript and JavaScript

➤ Define and create Active Server Pages

➤ Create an interactive Web site with Visual Interdev 6.0

Developing software applications in a client/server environment provides you with many options. You have been creating a software application using the three-services architecture consisting of user services, business services, and data services. In user services, you can create a user interface by using an SDI or an MDI, or by creating a Web-based interface. By separating the business services and data services from the user services, you create a mechanism that allows you to create a user interface that best satisfies the user requirements.

In Chapter 8, you created data services using stored procedures in SQL Server. In Chapter 9, you created business service and data service objects in Visual Basic, using MTS and ActiveX DLLs. Chapters 10 and 11 present you with two different ways to create a user interface for your system. Chapter 10 demonstrated the traditional approach of using an SDI or MDI. Chapter 11 presents the alternative of using the Web. One reason to use the Web is to centralize your work. Because the application resides on the server, you can easily develop and maintain the application in one central location. Another reason to use the Web is that it allows you to reach people throughout the world, if necessary. Most importantly, the total cost of ownership for a Web application is less than that of traditional applications, because the two components you need—the browser and the Web server—are free in most operating systems. The deployment costs of a Web application are also less than those of traditional applications. Users can access the application online, saving developers the added cost of media, such as compact discs, for distributing the application. The Web, therefore, presents an efficient, cost-effective alternative for developing applications. In this chapter, you will tour Web technologies and create a sample Web site for CTIS.

CHAPTER OVERVIEW

In the last chapter, you created traditional user interfaces in Visual Basic 6.0, using SDI and MDI techniques. In this chapter, you will create user interfaces, using Web technologies in Visual Interdev 6.0. This chapter assumes some knowledge and skill with Web technologies, presents an overview of the technologies, and explains how to create interactive Web sites with Visual Interdev. This chapter is not an exhaustive introduction to Web technologies, but a basic overview of the topic. For more information on Web technologies, see complete texts devoted to this.

INTRODUCTION TO THE WORLD WIDE WEB

Since the introduction of the World Wide Web in the early 1990s, the Web has evolved from a static-document environment, where Web pages contained unchanging information, to a dynamic environment where Web pages change each time a user visits. Tim Berners-Lee is known as the founder of the World Wide Web. Before you can use the Web to create your user interfaces, you need to review its basic technologies.

World Wide Web Architecture

The Web evolved out of client/server architecture, which uses server-based applications to communicate with local or remote clients. The Web consists of a Web browser and a Web server. The Web browser is a graphical application that runs on the client, requests Web resources (such as HTML pages, images and icons, and Web applications), and interprets those resources as an electronic page. The Web server is a service that runs on the server and supplies Web resources to the browser. Figure 11.1 illustrates the Web architecture.

A Web browser, such as Microsoft Internet Explorer, runs on a Web client. Microsoft Internet Information Server (IIS), a Web server application, runs on a server. The user requests Web resources by entering a Uniform Resource Locator (URL) request in the Web browser. Figure 11.2 shows the components of a URL.

The first part of the URL is the application-level protocol you are using for your request—in this case, the Hypertext Transport Protocol (HTTP). The second part of the URL is the name of the Web server where the Web resource resides, such as www.nv.cc.va.us. The third part of the URL is the path showing where the Web resource folder resides, such as /home/kmorneau. The last part of the URL specifies the Web resource you are requesting, such as default.htm.

After the browser sets up a connection with the server and transmits the request to the server, the server responds with the Web resource. Examples of Web resources are:

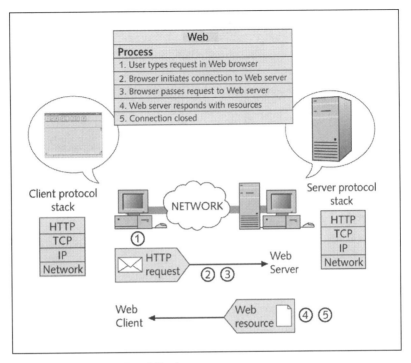

Figure 11.1   WWW architecture.

11

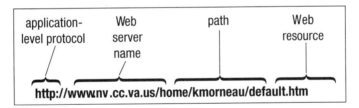

Figure 11.2   URL request.

➤ **Hypertext Markup Language (HTML) documents** Are like word-processing documents that supply different tags that tell a browser how to display the page

➤ **HTML forms** Are like Visual Basic forms; you place controls on an HTML document to create an automated form

➤ **Graphics** Such as graphical interchange format (GIF) and Joint Photographic Experts Group format (JPG) images

➤ **Java applets** A special Java technology created by Sun Microsystems that runs in a Web browser

➤ **ActiveX controls** An ActiveX component created by Microsoft that usually supplies an interface such as a label, text box, and list box

➤ **Active Server Pages (ASP)** A type of Web page consisting of scripts running on the server that allows you to interact with electronic HTML forms and databases, using Visual Basic technologies

 To learn more about creating HTML documents, refer to *http:// www.ncsa.uiuc.edu/General/Internet/ WWW/HTMLPrimer.html.*

 To learn more about creating HTML forms, refer to *http:// www.cc.ukans.edu/~acs/docs/other/forms-intro.shtml.*

Dynamic HTML (DHTML)

The previous section briefly reviewed traditional HTML documents and forms. Dynamic HTML is the next generation standard that allows for customizable and dynamic Web pages. HTML is the standard that allows you to create Web pages, while DHTML is the standard that allows you to manipulate the HTML on a Web page. The basis of DHTML is the Document Object Model (DOM), a standard created by Microsoft. This hierarchical object model allows you to reference and manipulate any object in your HTML document (e.g., tables, forms, graphics, styles, and other HTML tags). Internet Explorer 4.0, for example, uses DOM in its browser. DOM allows you to write scripts that manipulate any part of the HTML document's tags dynamically. You will use DOM later in this chapter in Visual Interdev.

 DHTML is such an important standard in Web pages that it can only be completely discussed in a book-length text. For more information about DHTML, refer to the MSDN library.

Client Scripting

While HTML and DHTML let you create and manipulate Web documents, scripting lets you create executable code in your Web pages. You can use two different scripting languages to write scripts in your HTML documents: VBScript and JavaScript. VBScript is a scripting language created by Microsoft and is a subset of Visual Basic. JavaScript is a scripting language created by Netscape Communications Corporation. Internet Explorer supports both scripting languages. As described in this section, scripts download to, and execute on, the client. You will be using different scripts later in this chapter. First, you need to understand how to read scripts.

VBScript

VBScript uses the basic syntax of Visual Basic (see Chapters 9 and 10) and is not case-sensitive. The following is an example of an HTML document with VBScript.

Code Example

```
<HTML>
<HEAD>
<SCRIPT LANGUAGE=VBScript>
<!-
dim var1
function display()
var1 = 10
msgbox("The contents of var1 is: " & var1)
end function
//- ->
</SCRIPT>
</HEAD>
<BODY>
<input type=button name=cmdDisplay value=display
onclick="display()">
</BODY>
</HTML>
```

Code Dissection

➤ The tag <SCRIPT LANGUAGE=VBScript>...</SCRIPT> tells your browser that what follows is a VBScript.

➤ You usually include a script in the header section of the HTML document.

➤ <!- -... //- -> is a comment in HTML, and it prevents browsers that cannot read scripts from displaying the script on the page.

➤ DIM var1 declares a variable in VBScript. Unlike Visual Basic, VBScript only contains variables of type variant.

➤ The function...end function syntax is similar to Visual Basic.

➤ You can use the **Msgbox** statement as in Visual Basic. You can also use the Msgbox function as described in Chapter 10.

To learn more about creating scripts using VBScript, refer to *http://msdn.microsoft.com/scripting/default.htm*

JavaScript, Or JScript

JavaScript, also called JScript, runs in Netscape and Internet Explorer browsers and is case-sensitive. While VBScript is a subset of Visual Basic, JavaScript is a C and C++ sibling. The following code is an example of an HTML document using JavaScript.

Code Example

```
<HTML>
<HEAD>
<SCRIPT LANGUAGE=JavaScript>
<!-
var var1
function display()
{
var1 = 10;
alert("The contents of var1 is: " & var1)
}
 //- ->
</SCRIPT>
</HEAD>
<BODY>
<input type=button name=cmdDisplay value=display
onclick="display()">
</BODY>
</HTML>
```

Code Dissection

➤ The tag <SCRIPT LANGUAGE=javascript>...</SCRIPT> tells your browser that what follows is a JavaScript.

➤ You usually include a script in the header section of the HTML document.

➤ <!— ... //—> is a comment in HTML and prevents browsers that cannot read scripts from displaying the script on the page.

➤ var var1; declares a variable in JavaScript. The ; ends a statement in JavaScript.

➤ The function {} statement is different from VBScript.

To learn more about creating and using JScript, refer to *http://msdn.microsoft.com/scripting/default.htm*

Server Scripting

While you can write scripts on the client using VBScript and JavaScript, you can also use them to write scripts on the server. Active Server Pages (ASP) is a server-side scripting environment that allows you to create powerful, rich, and dynamic Web server applications using IIS. In ASP, you can use HTML pages and forms, VBScript or JavaScript, and ActiveX components. You can create these pages by writing the script with Visual Interdev as your development platform. ASP files have the extension .asp.

Because ASP scripts run on the server, many types of browsers support them. If you are trying to create a Web application supported by many types of browsers, then ASP is the logical choice. Server-side scripts also take advantage of the server's processing power.

With client-side scripting, on the other hand, you have to research the features each browser supports to make sure your scripts are compatible with all kinds of browsers, including Microsoft Internet Explorer, Netscape Communicator, and other, older browsers that may not support scripting. You will be using ASP pages in the Visual Interdev environment to create a Web application for CTIS, using Visual Interdev, later in this chapter.

The following HTML code shows the difference between client-side scripts and server-side scripts.

11

Code Example
```
<HTML>
<HEAD>
<SCRIPT LANGUAGE="VBScript" RUNAT="Server">
  Server side script that runs on the server
</SCRIPT>
<SCRIPT LANGUAGE="VBScript">
  Client side script that runs on the client
</SCRIPT>
</HEAD>
<BODY>
<% Server side VBScript that runs on the server %>
</BODY>
</HTML>
```

Code Dissection

➤ The line <SCRIPT LANGUAGE="VBScript" RUNAT="SERVER"> ...</SCRIPT> tells the IIS server that this script runs on the server before transmitting it to the client.

➤ The line <SCRIPT LANGUAGE="VBScript">…</SCRIPT> tells the IIS server that this script should be transmitted to the client and, then tells the browser to run this script on the client.

➤ The <% … %> tag combination tells the IIS server to run the scripting logic on the server and pass the results to the client.

INTRODUCTION TO WEB APPLICATION DEVELOPMENT

In the previous sections, you surveyed important Web technology concepts. The second part of this chapter shows you how to create a sample CTIS Web application using Visual Interdev. When you create Web applications, you can use two Microsoft software packages: FrontPage and Visual Interdev. Although these two tools work together to create Web applications, each serves a different purpose. Use FrontPage to create the visual interface of the Web application. Use Visual Interdev to create the code that makes Web pages dynamic and interactive. Web page designers use FrontPage to create professional-looking Web sites. Web application developers use Visual Interdev to create dynamic and interactive Web applications. Before you use Visual Interdev to create Web applications, you should understand how a Web application works in an IIS environment. Figure 11.3 explains the components of a Web application in IIS and the ASP object model.

When any user accesses a Web application on the server supplying the URL, IIS creates an application object and initializes any server variables in the server environment. When a user accesses a Web page in the application, IIS creates a session object that tracks the user's session with the application. Each user in a Web application has his or her own session object. The application object stores

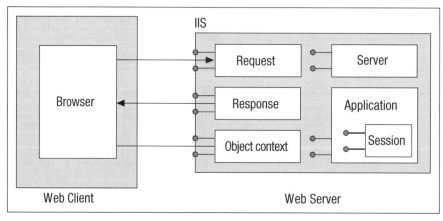

Figure 11.3 Components of a Web application.

in a Web application any settings that are the same between sessions. The server object exposes properties and methods you can use on the server, such as creating your own objects.

After the application and server objects initialize, a Web application consisting of HTML forms displays in the browser. The user completes the form and submits it to the server. The request object handles all the data on the form for the server to use. As the server begins to respond to the request, the response object creates a response to the browser. The ObjectContext object allows you to create MTS transactions in Web pages.

The next sections describe each server component in detail, and provide examples of using the components.

Application Object

The application object initializes server variables used throughout the life of a Web application, and supplies the necessary interface to create Web applications. Table 11.1 describes the properties and methods of the application object.

Session Object

The session object initializes a user's session inside a Web application, and provides a mechanism for creating server variables and launching common events in a user's session. Table 11.2 describes the properties and methods of the session object.

Server Object

The server object provides an interface to the server's environment, and supplies the necessary interface to create user-defined objects in an ASP page. Table 11.3 describes the properties and methods of the server object.

Table 11.1   Useful properties and methods of the application object.

Property/Method	Name	Description
Property	Contents	Contains all the items added through scripts
Property	staticObjects	Contains all the items added through the <OBJECT> tag
Method	lock	Prevents any other client from modifying Web application properties
Method	unlock	Allows other clients to modify Web application properties
Event	onstart	Fires when an application first starts
Event	onend	Fires when an application exits

Table 11.2 Useful properties and methods of the session object.

Property/Method	Name	Description
Property	Contents	Contains all the items added through scripts
Property	staticObjects	Contains all the items added through the <OBJECT> tag
Property	timeout	Sets the timeout property for the session state in the application in minutes
Method	Abandon	Ends a session
Event	onstart	Fires when a new client accesses a Web application
Event	onend	Fires when a client ends the session

Table 11.3 Useful properties and methods of the server object.

Property/Method	Name	Description
Property	scripttimeout	The length of time a script can run before timing out
Method	CreateObject	Creates an instance of an ActiveX object
Method	mappath	Converts a virtual path to a physical path

Request Object

The request object supplies the information about the user's request to your Web application (Web site). Table 11.4 lists the different properties and methods of the request object.

Table 11.4 Useful properties and methods of the request object.

Property/Method	Name	Description
Property	TotalBytes	The size of the request in bytes
Property	ClientCertificate	Special security object that contains your electronic signature, and values sent from the browser. Used in implementing security in ASP
Property	Cookies	Packets of user information that are stored as files on the client machine. The cookies collection stores the contents of a cookie that is passed by the browser
Property	Form	Values of the form elements sent by the browser
Property	QueryString	Values of the variables in an HTTP query string

(continued)

Table 11.4 Useful properties and methods of the request object *(continued)*.

Property/Method	Name	Description
Property	ServerVariables	Values of the environment and HTTP variables
Method	BinaryRead	A way to retrieve data sent to the server as part of the user's POST request

Response Object

The response object supplies an interface for coding an HTML document response to the request sent by the user to the Web application. Table 11.5 describes the different properties and methods of the response object.

ObjectContext Object

The ObjectContext object allows you to interface with MTS so that ASP pages become transactions. You studied transactions with MTS in Chapter 9. Refer to Chapter 9 for information on using the ObjectContext object with transactions.

Table 11.5 Useful properties and methods of the response object.

Property/Method	Name	Description
Property	Cookies	Contents of the cookie collection you want to send to the browser
Property	buffer	Indicates whether to buffer the contents of the response until complete
Property	status	Status of the HTTP request returned by the server
Method	appendtolog	Adds text to a Web server log
Method	binarywrite	Sends text to the browser without any text conversions, which means that the object will not add HTML tags to the data before sending
Method	clear	Removes any buffered output
Method	end	Stops processing the page and returns results to the browser
Method	flush	Sends buffered output immediately
Method	redirect	Redirects a browser to a different URL
Method	write	Writes text and/or variables to the current page as a string

11

INTRODUCTION TO VISUAL INTERDEV 6.0

You will use the objects described above in the ASP object model in the Visual Interdev environment. In this section, you will tour the Visual Interdev 6.0 environment. When you create database-driven Web applications in Visual Interdev, you work with the following four components:

➤ **Web browser** A browser, such as Internet Explorer, to test the functionality of the Web application

➤ **Visual Interdev client** The application development environment used to create the Web application

➤ **Web server** A server, such as Internet Information Server, to host the Web application that Visual Interdev communicates with when creating files

➤ **Database server** A database server, such as SQL Server, to store the data that your Web application interacts with

Visual Interdev uses two modes when managing projects. *Local mode* provides the development area while you are coding the Web application. You should use this mode whenever possible. *Master mode* provides the area where users work with your Web application. Do not allow your users to use the Web application from the same location in which you are developing it.

Visual Interdev Environment

The Visual Interdev environment looks and feels similar to the Visual Basic environment you investigated in Chapter 10. Figure 11.4 illustrates the Visual Interdev 6.0 environment.

The Visual Interdev environment consists of the following windows:

➤ **Toolbox** Includes objects you can use in the Visual Interdev environment. The toolbox consists of several sections of tools. The HTML section lists standard HTML forms tags such as textbox, label, and listbox. The Server Objects section lists standard ASP objects on the server such as ADO Recordset and ADO command. You investigated ADO in Chapter 9. The Design Time Controls (DTC) section provides an automated scripting environment for creating electronic forms. The ActiveX Controls section lists visual controls that allow you to enhance the functionality of your Web form using ActiveX technology. Using ActiveX controls in your Web forms means you must use Internet Explorer as your Web browser. If you use Netscape Communicator, you need a special plug-in to view ActiveX controls on your Web forms.

The toolbox also consists of three different tabs. The HTML tab allows you to view a hierarchical tree of all HTML tags used in your Web pages. The Toolbox tab allows you to view the objects you can use in your Web pages.

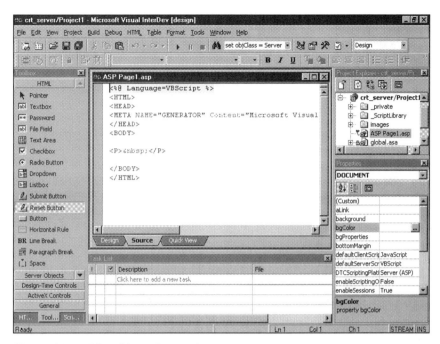

Figure 11.4 Visual Interdev environment.

The Scripting Outline tab provides you with a hierarchical view of all your objects in your Web page, and also allows you to enter, update, or delete event procedures that support the objects.

➤ **Web page** Shows the Web page under development in three views. Design view provides a WYSIWYG look at the Web page. Source view shows the HTML and scripts used in the Web page. Quick View shows the page rendered in a browser (only for HTML pages). You can develop an HTML page, a traditional HTML document (.htm or .html extension); an ASP page, an HTML document with server scripts (.asp extension); a style page, a special type of page that allows you to create a common look and feel in your Web application (.css extension); or a site diagram, a diagram that allows you to manage the Web application graphically.

➤ **Properties window** Allows you to change properties of objects in the Web application.

➤ **Project Explorer** Manages all the files in a Web application.

➤ **Task List** Allows you to keep track of your Web project tasks.

In Chapters 4 through 6, you created the conceptual, logical, and physical design of the Login process in CTIS. In the Chapter_11 folder of the CD, compile the comLogin component in Visual Basic and install the component in MTS before you complete the next section.

Depending on your software configuration, you may receive an error message regarding your references when you compile the component. Change the references to reflect your system and recompile. Also, when compiling, you should overwrite the comLogin.dll file.

Refer to Chapter 9 for details on how to compile components in Visual Basic and how to install components in MTS. You will need to add a user_ID column to the Instructors table and the Students table. Add user_IDs to the existing students and instructors in the tables. Refer to Chapter 8, "Modifying An Existing Table," for details on how to add columns to an existing table and change data in tables. After you add the columns to the existing tables, you will need to add a student record with user_ID of STUDENT1 and an instructor record with user_ID of INSTRUCTOR1.

SETTING UP SQL SERVER TO AUTHENTICATE STUDENTS AND INSTRUCTORS IN YOUR WEB APPLICATION

In the last sections, you reviewed the technologies involved in creating Web applications. You are now ready to start coding a Web interface for CTIS. Use SQL Server to authenticate users in the CTIS Web application because CTIS users will use Windows or other operating systems and different Web browsers. If you use SQL Server to authenticate users from the server, you can be sure that you are compatible with all operating systems and browsers. Throughout this book, you used Windows NT integrated security when connecting to SQL Server. This chapter changes the security philosophy so that you now log in to SQL Server with a specific username and password. This allows you to restrict access to sensitive information, such as grades. You will use SQL Server *roles*, groups of users who have certain rights and privileges in the database, to restrict this access. You will create two roles, one for students and one for instructors. The student role will allow access to student-related information only. The instructor role will allow access to all student and other information in the database. When you create a user in SQL Server, you assign the user to a student role or an instructor role, as appropriate.

To enter a user into the CTIS database in SQL Server:

1. Click the Start menu. Point to Programs, then Microsoft SQL Server 7.0, and then click Enterprise Manager to start SQL Server Administration.

2. Expand the SQL Server Group, your Windows NT Server, and Security items.

3. Right-click logins, and then click New login.

4. Enter the following information:

   Name: STUDENT1

5. Select SQL Server authentication.

6. Change the Database to CTIS.

7. Click OK.

8. When you see a message about gaining access to default database, click Yes. You will set the permissions in the next set of steps.

You added a user called STUDENT1 to the SQL Server database. The next step is to create a role called STUDENT and add STUDENT1 to the role.

To create a user role called STUDENT and add STUDENT1 to the role:

1. Expand the DATABASES and CTIS folders.

2. Right-click Roles, and then click New Database Role.

3. Enter "STUDENT" in the Name text box, and then click OK.

4. Add a new role called "Instructor".

5. Double-click Roles.

6. Double-click the Instructor role, and then click Permissions.

7. Select Select, Insert, Update, and Delete for tables CATEGORIES, CLASSES, CLASS_SCHEDULE, GRADES, GRADE_DISTRIBUTIONS, INSTRUCTORS, STUDENTS, and STUDENT_SCHEDULES.

8. Select EXEC permissions for all **proc_ stored** procedures.

   This allows an instructor to select from the tables and insert, update, and delete from the tables. This will also allow an instructor to run all stored procedures.

9. Click OK to update the role. Click OK in the Database Role Properties dialog box.

10. Double-click the Student role, and then click Permissions.

11. Select Select, Insert, Update, and Delete for tables STUDENTS, and STUDENT_SCHEDULES.

12. Select EXEC permissions for all **proc stored** procedures.

13. Click Apply to update the role.

14. Select Select for tables CATEGORIES, CLASSES, CLASS_SCHEDULE, GRADES, GRADE_DISTRIBUTIONS, and INSTRUCTORS.

    This allows a student to only view these tables and not change them.

11

15. Click OK. and then click OK again in the Database Role Properties dialog box.

16. Right-click Users, and then click New Database User.

17. Select STUDENT1 as the login name.

18. Select Student in the Database role membership.

19. Click OK.

20. Click the Close button to close SQL Server Enterprise Manager.

21. Click Yes to save console settings, if necessary.

Using the techniques above, add an INSTRUCTOR1 user and add the instructor to the INSTRUCTOR role. Then you're ready to use SQL Server to authenticate students and instructors.

CREATING A WEB APPLICATION WITH VISUAL INTERDEV

This section shows you how to create a Web application in Visual Interdev. Note that this section is an overview on how to create Web applications and is not a comprehensive guide to creating Web applications. The basic steps for creating a Web project are listed below:

1. Generate a Visual Interdev Web project.

2. Create a site diagram to manage the Web resources in your Web project. This step is optional but suggested, especially for large sites.

3. Create the content of the Web resources from the site diagram.

4. Run and test the Web project.

Creating The Web Project

The first step in Visual Interdev is to create a Web project, which specifies settings for the Web application, such as the location of the files.

To create a Web project in Visual Interdev:

1. Click the Start menu. Point to Programs, then Microsoft Visual Studio 6.0, and then click Microsoft Visual Interdev 6.0.

2. In the New Project dialog box, enter the following information:
   Name: CTIS
   Location: c:\Work\CTIS\user_svc_src\web\CTIS

3. Click the New Web project icon in the dialog box.

4. Click Open.

5. On the Web Project Wizard—Step 1 of 4 page, select Local Mode and then click Next. Also, specify the server you want to use.

6. Click Next on the Web Project Wizard—Step 2 of 4 page.

7. Click Next on the Web Project Wizard—Step 3 of 4 page.

8. Select Modern Contrast Theme, and then click Finish on the Web Project Wizard—Step 4 of 4 page.

9. Click the Project menu, and then click Add to Source Control in the Source Control menu.

10. In the Initial Solution Add dialog box, click the Solution button.

11. Log in to Visual SourceSafe as username CTIS, and enter "CTIS" as the password. Click OK.

12. Create a project called Web in user_svc_src in CTIS.

13. Select Web, and then click OK.

14. Click OK in the Add to Source Control dialog box.

15. Enter "$/CTIS\user_svc_src\web" in the text box for the project name.

    If you receive an error about a missing user in Visual SourceSafe, add the user in Visual SourceSafe Admin and retry adding the project to Visual SourceSafe.

16. Click OK when you see a message stating that the project was added successfully to SourceSafe.

Creating A Site Diagram In Visual Interdev

After you create the Web project, you need to create a site diagram to manage the Web site. A site diagram gives you a graphical, hierarchical representation of the files in the Web site. You will create a hierarchical representation of the CTIS Web application. When a user visits CTIS, a home page appears with several options. One option is to log in to CTIS. You investigated how the login process works in Chapters 4 through 6. You will create the login pages based on the conceptual, logical, and physical designs. The next page will be a Login HTML page that requests the username and password of the user. When the user submits the form, then the Login ASP page verifies the username and password of the user. If the user is a student, then the student access HTML page is displayed. If the user is an instructor, then the instructor access HTML page is displayed. This page contains a link to Course Management, which you will code in this section by inserting, updating, and deleting classes based on the conceptual, logical, and physical designs created in Chapters 4 through 6.

To add a site diagram to the CTIS Web project:

1. Click Project in the menu bar, point to Add Web Item, and then click Site Diagram.

2. Change the name of the site diagram to CTIS.wdm.

3. Click Open.

4. In the Site Designer dialog box, click OK.

5. Click the Home Page icon. Right-click in the home page, and then click New HTML Page.

6. Change the name of the page to Login. This creates a page called Login.htm.

7. Right-click the Login page, and then click New ASP Page on the shortcut menu.

8. Change the name of the page to Login.

9. Right-click the Login ASP page, and then click New HTML Page on the shortcut menu.

10. Change the name of the page to Instructor. This will display the different selections an instructor can make.

11. Right-click the Login ASP page, and then click New HTML Page on the shortcut menu.

12. Change the name of the page to Student. This will display the different selections a student can make.

13. Right-click the Instructor page, and then click New ASP Page on the shortcut menu.

14. Change the name of the page to Courses. This page displays the different course offerings, using a table.

15. Right-click the Courses ASP page, and then click New ASP Page on the shortcut menu.

16. Change the name of the page to CoursesView. This page displays the options of inserting, updating, and deleting class data.

17. Click Save CTIS.wdm on the File menu. This will update the Web site to contain blank files for the site diagram you created.

Creating The Login HTML Page

After you create the site diagram, which created empty pages for you, you need to fill those pages with information. In this section, you will add information to the Login.htm page, which is a form that allows you to log in to the Web application. The OK button on the Login form calls the Login.asp page, which verifies the existence of a user in the SQL Server database. The Login.htm HTML document is the electronic form that allows the user to enter login information. The Login.asp page is a script that uses the information from the login form to verify the existence of the user in the SQL Server database.

Refer to the Login process prototype in Chapter 6 to understand the contents of the Login form.

To create the Login.htm page:

1. On the site diagram, double-click the first Login page (Login.htm) to open it. Make sure you click outside the name box.
2. In the toolbox, click the HTML tab, which shows all the common HTML tags available for creating forms.
3. Next to the Server Objects tab, click the down arrow to expose the Label HTML tag.
4. Drag the label onto the Login.htm page.
5. Type "Username".
6. Drag the textbox HTML tag onto the Login.htm page.
7. Change the following properties in the Properties window:
   ID: txtUserName
   NAME: txtUserName
8. Press Shift+Enter next to the text box.
9. Drag the Label HTML tag onto the Login.htm page.
10. Type "Password".
11. Drag the Password HTML tag onto the Login.htm page.
12. Change the following properties in the Properties window:
    ID: **txtPassword**
    NAME: **txtPassword**
13. Press the Enter key next to the Password text box.
14. Drag the Submit button HTML tag onto the Login.htm page.
15. Change the following properties in the Properties window:
    ID: **cmdOK**
    NAME: **cmdOK**
    VALUE: **OK**
16. Drag the Reset button HTML tag onto the Login.htm page.

11

17. Change the following properties in the Properties window:
ID: **cmdCancel**
NAME: **cmdCancel**
VALUE: **Cancel**

18. Drag to select the entire contents of the page.

19. Click the Center button on the Formatting toolbar.

20. Position the cursor before the Username label, and then press the Enter key.

21. Click the new line above the Username label.

22. In the Paragraph Format drop-down box, change the Paragraph Format from Normal to Heading 1.

23. Type "CTIS Login Form".

24. Click the Source tab in the Login.htm window. This displays the HTML tags for the operations you completed above.

25. After the <H1>...</H1> tag, type "<FORM id=frmLogin name=frmLogin action="login.asp" method=post>". This tells the browser that you are working with an HTML form. When you click OK to submit the form, the login.asp server script file runs.

26. Before the </BODY> tag, type "</FORM>" to end the form.

27. Between the <TITLE> and </TITLE> HTML tags, type "CTIS Login Form". This title is displayed in the title bar of the browser when the form runs.

28. Click Save Login.htm in the File menu.

You have finished creating the Login form. Now you need to create the Login Active Server Page to handle the submission of the username and password on the Login HTML page.

Creating The Login Active Server Page
You will create an ASP page to handle the submission of the username and password on the Login HTML page.

To create the Login ASP page:

1. Double-click CTIS.wdm in Project Explorer.

2. Double-click the second Login page (ASP). After the first line, enter "<% Response. Buffer = True %>".

 To copy code into the Code window, navigate to the Chapter_11 folder on the CD. Double-click the appropriate text file to open it in Notepad. On the Edit menu, click Select All. Then press Ctrl+C to copy all the text. Close Notepad and click where you want to insert the code. Then press Ctrl+V to paste the text.

3. Enter the following information between the <BODY>...</BODY> tags. To do so, copy the code from the code11-01.txt file on the CD and paste it between the tags.

```
<% DIM objLogin
    set objLogin = CreateObject("comLogin.clsLogin")
    ON ERROR Resume Next
    Call objLogin.VerifyUser(Request.Form("txtUsername"), _
      Request.Form("txtPassword"))
    If objLogin.UserType = "" Then
      Response.Write _
        "<CENTER><H1><P>Login Failed! <BR> Try Again!</H1></P>"
      Response.Write _
        "<P><A HREF=login.htm>Login Again</A></P></CENTER>"
    Else
      If Ucase(objLogin.UserType) = "INSTRUCTOR" Then
        Application.Lock
        Session("UserType") = "Instructor"
        Session("Username") = Request.Form("txtUserName")
        Session("Password") = Request.Form("txtPassword")
        Application.Unlock
        Response.Redirect "instructor.htm"
      Else
        Application.Lock
        Session("UserType") = "Student"
        Session("Username") = Request.Form("txtUserName")
        Session("Password") = Request.Form("txtPassword")
        Application.Unlock
        Response.Redirect "student.htm"
      End If
    End If
    Response.End
%>
```

4. Click Save Login.asp in the File menu.

You have entered the Login.asp script. You need to understand how this script works before you can run the Login process.

Code Example

```
1    <%@ Language=VBScript %>
2    <HTML>
3    <HEAD>
4    <META NAME="GENERATOR" Content="Microsoft Visual Studio 6.0">
5    <LINK REL="stylesheet" TYPE="text/css" _
        HREF="_Themes/mdcont/THEME.CSS" VI6.0THEME="Modern Contrast">
```

```
6    <LINK REL="stylesheet" TYPE="text/css" _
        HREF="_Themes/mdcont/GRAPH0.CSS" VI6.0THEME="Modern Contrast">
7    <LINK REL="stylesheet" TYPE="text/css" _
        HREF="_Themes/mdcont/COLOR0.CSS" VI6.0THEME="Modern Contrast">
8    <LINK REL="stylesheet" TYPE="text/css" _
        HREF="_Themes/mdcont/CUSTOM.CSS" VI6.0THEME="Modern Contrast">
     </HEAD>
9    <BODY>
10   <% DIM objLogin
11   Set objLogin = CreateObject("comLogin.clsLogin")
12   ON ERROR Resume Next
13   Call objLogin.VerifyUser(Request.Form("txtUsername"), _
        Request.Form("txtPassword"))
14   If objLogin.UserType = "" Then
15   Response.Write _
        "<CENTER><H1><P>Login Failed! <BR> Try Again!</H1></P>"
16   Response.Redirect "login.htm"
17   Response.Write _
        "<P><A HREF=login.htm>Login Again</A></P></CENTER>"
18   Else
19   If Ucase(objLogin.UserType) = "INSTRUCTOR" Then
20   Application.Lock
21   Session("UserType") = "Instructor"
22   Session("Username") = Request.Form("txtUserName")
23   Session("Password") = Request.Form("txtPassword")
24   Application.Unlock
25   Response.Redirect "instructor.htm"
     Else
26   Application.lock
27   Session("UserType") = "Student"
28   Session("Username") = Request.Form("txtUserName")
29   Session("Password") = Request.Form("txtPassword")
30   Application.Unlock
31   Response.Redirect "student.htm"
32   End If
33   End If
34   Response.End
35   %>
36   </BODY>
37   </HTML>
```

Code Dissection

➤ The ASP page's job is to generate a response page the browser displays, or to redirect the browser to a different page.

➤ The first line of code defines the scripting language.

➤ Recall that all HTML documents start with the <HTML> tag and end with the </HTML> tag.

➤ The header portion of an HTML document defines the cascading style sheets to be used with this page. A *style sheet* is a special file that defines the appearance of HTML elements on a page. A *theme* is a group of style sheets that defines the color, layout, backgrounds, and other visual elements in HTML.

➤ The CreateObject statement creates an object for the comLogin ActiveX DLL.

➤ The On Error Resume Next statement ignores any run-time errors in the code.

➤ The next line (13) verifies the existence of a user in the database, and returns whether the user is a student or an instructor.

➤ The request object stores information about the user entered on the Login form. The Request.Form method allows you to access the elements from the form.

➤ The If clause checks to see if the username and password entered are valid. If they are not valid, it displays an error and asks the user to log in again.

➤ Otherwise, if the user is an instructor, it will store the UserType, Username, and Password as Session variables, and redirect the page to the instructor start page.

➤ Otherwise, if the user is a student, it will store the UserType, Username, and Password as Session variables, and redirect the page to the student start page. These variables can be used on other pages to log in to the database.

➤ As you recall, Application.Lock prevents other users from changing variables. Application.Unlock allows users to change variables.

➤ Response.End terminates the page and sends it back to the browser.

Creating The Instructor Page

The last two sections illustrated how to add login functionality to your Web site using SQL Server. The Login.asp page will redirect you to the instructor.htm page if the user is an instructor. The instructor.htm page displays the different subsystems in CTIS. These subsystems will be links to their appropriate pages. You will code the Course subsystem so that it allows you to view, insert, update, and delete courses.

To create the instructor.htm page:

1. Double-click the CTIS.wdm file in Project Explorer to open the site diagram.

2. Double-click the Instructor page in the site diagram to open the Instructor.htm file.

3. Click the Center button on the Formatting toolbar.

4. Change the Paragraph Format from Normal to Heading 1.

5. Type "Instructor Options" and press Enter.

6. In the Source Tab, remove the <H1>...</H1> tags on the line after Instructor Options.

7. Click the Center button on the Formatting toolbar.

8. Change the Paragraph Format from Heading 1 to Menu List.

9. Type "Course Management" and press Shift+Enter.

10. Type "Class List" and press Shift+Enter.

11. Type "Class Schedules" and press Shift+Enter.

12. Type "Grades Management" and press Shift+Enter.

13. Type "Student Management" and press Shift+Enter.

14. Type "Assignment Management".

15. Highlight the Class List and click Link in the HTML menu.

16. In the URL text box, type "Courses.asp", and delete http://.

17. Click OK.

Updating The comCourse Component To Add Login Security

Now that you have created the login functionality, which logs a user in to the Web application, you are ready to begin coding the Course Management subsystem, specifically the Class List. In this chapter, you added a layer of security to the CTIS application. You created a login form that authenticates users before allowing them into the system. Now you need to add a security option to the comCourse component to allow your code to authenticate users when they are saving or deleting data. Currently, you use the Windows NT built-in authentication to validate users. You decide to add a login process to SQL Server instead of the Windows NT authentication, because users could be using browsers other than Internet Explorer. Windows NT authentication works with Internet Explorer only.

To add a layer of security to the comCourse component:

1. Click the Start menu. Point to Programs, then Microsoft Visual Studio 6.0, and then click Microsoft Visual Basic 6.0.

2. Click the Existing tab and change the directory to c:\work\CTIS\ business_svc_src\comCourse.

3. Click the comCourse project.

4. Click Open.

5. Log in to Visual SourceSafe, if necessary.

6. Check out modMessage in the Modules folder, and clsClass and clsClassData in the Class Module folder.

7. Add strUsername and strPassword to modMessage. To do so, copy the code from the code11-02.txt file on the CD and paste it in modMessage, replacing the current code.

```
Public Type udtClass
  strMode As String * 1
  lngClassID As Long
  strClassNumber As String * 7
  strClassName As String * 50
  strUsername As String * 35
  strPassword As String * 35
  intErrorNumber As Integer
  intErrorMessage As String * 100
End Type

Public Type udtString
  strMessage As String * 254
End Type
```

11

8. Add strUsername and strPassword to clsClass. To do so, copy the code from the code11-03.txt file on the CD and paste it in clsClass, replacing the original code.

```
Option Base 0
Option Explicit

'##ModelId=368A27560181
Private lngClassID As_ Long

'##ModelId=368A2775018F
Private strClassName As_ String

'##ModelId=368AB90D0248
Private strClassNumber As String

'##ModelId=368A2CD20388
Private mobjClassData As New clsClassData

Public Function SaveMSMQ(ByVal qname As String, ByVal lngID As_
Long, ByVal strNumber As String, ByVal strName As String, ByVal_
strUsername As String, ByVal strPassword As String) As String
```

```
Dim objObjectContext As ObjectContext
Dim strResult As String
Dim msgClass As udtClass
Dim msgString As udtString
Dim QueueInfo As New MSMQ.MSMQQueueInfo
Dim Msg As New MSMQ.MSMQMessage
Dim queue As MSMQ.MSMQQueue

lngClassID = lngID
strClassName = strName
strClassNumber = strNumber

With msgClass
  .lngClassID = lngClassID
  .strClassNumber = strClassNumber
  .strClassName = strClassName
  .strMode = "I"
  .strUsername = strUsername
  .strPassword = strPassword
  .intErrorNumber = 0
  .intErrorMessage = ""
End With

On Error GoTo ValidateError
  strResult = Validate()
On Error GoTo TransactionError
  Set objObjectContext = GetObjectContext()
  QueueInfo.PathName = qname
  Set queue = QueueInfo.Open(MQ_SEND_ACCESS, MQ_DENY_NONE)
  If lngClassID = 0 Then
    msgClass.strMode = "I"
    LSet msgString = msgClass
    Msg.Label = "comCourse.clsClass"
    Msg.Body = msgString.strMessage
    If (objObjectContext.IsInTransaction) Then
      Msg.Send queue, MQ_MTS_TRANSACTION
    Else
      Msg.Send queue, MQ_SINGLE_MESSAGE
    End If

    queue.Close

    If Not objObjectContext Is Nothing Then
      objObjectContext.SetComplete
    End If
  Else
```

```
    msgClass.strMode = "U"
    LSet msgString = msgClass
    Msg.Label = "comCourse.clsClass"
    Msg.Body = msgString.strMessage
    If objObjectContext.IsInTransaction Then
      Msg.Send queue, MQ_MTS_TRANSACTION
    Else
      Msg.Send queue, MQ_SINGLE_MESSAGE
    End If
    queue.Close

    If Not objObjectContext Is Nothing Then
      objObjectContext.SetComplete
    End If
  End If
  Set queue = Nothing
  Set Msg = Nothing
  Set QueueInfo = Nothing
  SaveMSMQ = ""
  Exit Function
ValidateError:
  SaveMSMQ = strResult
  Exit Function
TransactionError:
  If Not objObjectContext Is Nothing Then
   objObjectContext.SetAbort
  End If
  Set queue = Nothing
  Set Msg = Nothing
  Set QueueInfo = Nothing
  SaveMSMQ = "Transaction failed!"
End Function

Public Function DeleteMSMQ(qname As String, lngClassID As Long, _
  strUsername As String, strPassword As String) As String
Dim objObjectContext As ObjectContext

Dim msgClass As udtClass
Dim msgString As udtString
Dim QueueInfo As New MSMQ.MSMQQueueInfo
Dim Msg As New MSMQ.MSMQMessage
Dim queue As MSMQ.MSMQQueue

With msgClass
  .lngClassID = lngClassID
  .strClassNumber = ""
```

11

```
            .strClassName = ""
            .strMode = "D"
            .strUsername = strUsername
            .strPassword = strPassword
            .intErrorNumber = 0
            .intErrorMessage = ""
        End With

        On Error GoTo TransactionError
            Set objObjectContext = GetObjectContext()

            QueueInfo.PathName = qname
            Set queue = QueueInfo.Open(MQ_SEND_ACCESS, MQ_DENY_NONE)

            msgClass.strMode = "I"
            LSet msgString = msgClass
            Msg.Label = "comCourse.clsClass"
            Msg.Body = msgString.strMessage

            If objObjectContext.IsInTransaction Then
              Msg.Send queue, MQ_MTS_TRANSACTION
            Else
              Msg.Send queue, MQ_SINGLE_MESSAGE
            End If

            queue.Close

            If Not objObjectContext Is Nothing Then
              objObjectContext.SetComplete
            End If

            DeleteMSMQ = ""

            Exit Function

    TransactionError:

        If Not objObjectContext Is Nothing Then
          objObjectContext.SetAbort
        End If

        DeleteMSMQ = "Transaction failed!"
    End Function
```

```vb
'##ModelId=368A27940310
Public Function Retrieve(lngID As Long, strUsername As String, _
  strPassword As String) As ADODB.Recordset
Dim recSQL As New ADODB.Recordset
Dim objContext As ObjectContext
lngClassID = lngID
On Error GoTo TransactionError
    Set objContext = GetObjectContext()
    Set recSQL = mobjClassData.GetInfo(lngClassID, strUsername, _
      strPassword)
    If recSQL Is Nothing Then
      Err.Raise -1, "No records returned"
    End If
    Set Retrieve = recSQL
    If Not objContext Is Nothing Then
      objContext.SetComplete
    End If
  Exit Function
TransactionError:
    If Not objContext Is Nothing Then
      objContext.SetAbort
    End If
    Set Retrieve = Nothing
End Function

'##ModelId=368A28A602D8
Public Function RetrieveALL(strUsername As String, strPassword As _
  String) As ADODB.Recordset
Dim objContext As ObjectContext
Dim recSQL As New ADODB.Recordset
On Error GoTo TransactionError
    Set objContext = GetObjectContext()
    Set recSQL = mobjClassData.GetAllInfo(strUsername, strPassword)
    If recSQL Is Nothing Then
      Err.Raise -1, "No records returned"
    End If
    Set RetrieveALL = recSQL
    If Not objContext Is Nothing Then
      objContext.SetComplete
    End If
  Exit Function
TransactionError:
    Set RetrieveALL = Nothing
    If Not objContext Is Nothing Then
      objContext.SetAbort
    End If
End Function
```

11

```
'##ModelId=368A27D500BB
Public Function Save(ByVal lngID As Long, ByVal strNumber As _
  String, ByVal strName As String, ByVal strUsername As String, _
  strPassword As String) As String
Dim objObjectContext As ObjectContext
Dim strResult As String
lngClassID = lngID
strClassName = strName
strClassNumber = strNumber
On Error GoTo ValidateError
  strResult = Validate()
On Error GoTo TransactionError
  Set objObjectContext = GetObjectContext()
  If lngClassID = 0 Then
    strResult = mobjClassData.Insert(strClassNumber, strClassName, _
      strUsername, strPassword)
    If strResult <> "" Then
      Err.Raise Err.Number
    End If

    If Not objObjectContext Is Nothing Then
      objObjectContext.SetComplete
    End If

  Else
    strResult = mobjClassData.Update(lngClassID, strClassNumber, _
      strClassName, strUsername, strPassword)

    If strResult <> "" Then
      Err.Raise Err.Number
    End If

    If Not objObjectContext Is Nothing Then
      objObjectContext.SetComplete
    End If

  End If
  Save = ""
  Exit Function
ValidateError:
  Save = strResult
  Exit Function
TransactionError:

  If Not objObjectContext Is Nothing Then
   objObjectContext.SetAbort
  End If
```

```
      Save = "Transaction Failed!"
   End Function


   '##ModelId=368A28190091
   Public Function Validate() As String
     If strClassName = "" Then
        Validate = "Must enter a class name!"
     End If
   End Function



   '##ModelId=368AB90E033A
   Public Function Delete(lngClassID As Long, strUsername As String, _
     strPassword As String) As String
   Dim objObjectContext As ObjectContext
   Dim strResult As String


   On Error GoTo TransactionError
       Set objObjectContext = GetObjectContext()

       strResult = mobjClassData.Delete(lngClassID, strUsername, _
         strPassword)

       If strResult <> "" Then
         Err.Raise Err.Number
       End If

       If Not objObjectContext Is Nothing Then
         objObjectContext.SetComplete
       End If

       Delete = ""
       Exit Function

   TransactionError:

     If Not objObjectContext Is Nothing Then
      objObjectContext.SetAbort
     End If

     Delete = "Transaction failed!"
   End Function
```

11

9. Add strUsername and strPassword to clsClassData. To do so, copy the code from the code11-04.txt file on the CD and paste it in clsClassData, replacing the original code.

```
Option Base 0
Option Explicit


'##ModelId=368A244E0185
Public Function Insert(strClassNumber As String, strClassName As _
  String, strUsername As String, strPassword As String) As String
Dim qrySP As New ADODB.Command
On Error GoTo ProcError
  qrySP.CommandText = "proc_insert_class"
  qrySP.CommandType = adCmdStoredProc
  qrySP.Parameters.Append qrySP.CreateParameter(, adVarChar, _
    adParamInput, 7, strClassNumber)
  qrySP.Parameters.Append qrySP.CreateParameter(, adVarChar, _
    adParamInput, 50, strClassName)
  Call ExecuteSP(qrySP, strUsername, strPassword)
  Insert = ""
  Exit Function
ProcError:
  Insert = Str(Err.Number) & vbCr & Err.Description
End Function


'##ModelId=368A24A90045
Public Function Update(lngClassID As Long, strNumber As String, _
  strNewClass As String, strUsername As String, strPassword As _
  String) As String
Dim qrySP As New ADODB.Command
  On Error GoTo ProcError
    qrySP.CommandText = "proc_update_class"
    qrySP.CommandType = adCmdStoredProc
    qrySP.Parameters.Append qrySP.CreateParameter(, adInteger, _
      adParamInput, 4, lngClassID)
    qrySP.Parameters.Append qrySP.CreateParameter(, adVarChar, _
      adParamInput, 7, strNumber)
    qrySP.Parameters.Append qrySP.CreateParameter(, adVarChar, _
      adParamInput, 50, strNewClass)
    Call ExecuteSP(qrySP, strUsername, strPassword)
    Update = ""
    Exit Function
ProcError:
    Update = Str(Err.Number) & vbCr & Err.Description
End Function


'##ModelId=368A252500BC
Public Function Delete(lngClassID As Long, strUsername As String, _
  strPassword As String) As String
Dim qrySP As New ADODB.Command
  On Error GoTo ProcError
```

```
        qrySP.CommandText = "proc_delete_class"
        qrySP.CommandType = adCmdStoredProc
        qrySP.Parameters.Append qrySP.CreateParameter(, adInteger, _
            adParamInput, 4, lngClassID)
        Call ExecuteSP(qrySP, strUsername, strPassword)
        Delete = ""
        Exit Function
ProcError:
        Delete = Str(Err.Number) & vbCr & Err.Description
End Function


'##ModelId=368A256A022E
Public Function GetInfo(lngClassID As Long, strUsername As String, _
    strPassword As String) As ADODB.Recordset
Dim qrySP As New ADODB.Command
On Error GoTo ProcError
    qrySP.CommandText = "select * from CLASSES where CLASS_ID =" & _
        Str(lngClassID)
    qrySP.CommandType = adCmdText
    Set GetInfo = ExecuteSQL(qrySP, strUsername, strPassword)
    Exit Function
ProcError:
    Set GetInfo = Nothing
End Function


'##ModelId=368AB9070113
Private Sub ExecuteSP(qrySP As ADODB.Command, strUsername As _
    String, strPassword As String)
Dim strConn As String
Dim mvarConn As New ADODB.Connection
On Error GoTo RecordFailure
    strConn = "File Name=" & App.Path & "\ctis.udl"
    mvarConn.Open strConn, strUsername, strPassword
    Set qrySP.ActiveConnection = mvarConn
    qrySP.Execute
    mvarConn.Close
    Exit Sub
RecordFailure:
    mvarConn.Close
    Err.Raise Err.Number, "ExecuteSQL", Err.Description
End Sub


Private Function ExecuteSQL(qrySP As ADODB.Command, strUsername As _
    String, strPassword As String) As ADODB.Recordset
Dim strConn As String
Dim recSQL As New ADODB.Recordset
Dim mvarConn As New ADODB.Connection
```

11

```
On Error GoTo RecordFailure
  strConn = "File Name=" & App.Path & "\ctis.udl"
  mvarConn.Open strConn, strUsername, strPassword
  Set qrySP.ActiveConnection = mvarConn
  Set recSQL = qrySP.Execute
  Set ExecuteSQL = recSQL
  Exit Function
RecordFailure:
  Err.Raise Err.Number, "ExecuteSQL", Err.Description
End Function


'##ModelId=368BAA7403E5
Public Function GetAllInfo(strUsername As String, strPassword As _
  String) As ADODB.Recordset
Dim qrySP As New ADODB.Command
On Error GoTo ProcError
  qrySP.CommandText = "select * from CLASSES"
  qrySP.CommandType = adCmdText
  Set GetAllInfo = ExecuteSQL(qrySP, strUsername, strPassword)
  Exit Function
ProcError:
  Set GetAllInfo = Nothing
End Function


Public Function GetFromQueueMSMQ(qname As String, strUsername As _
  String, strPassword As String) As String
Dim objObjectContext As ObjectContext
Dim strResult As String
Dim msgClass As udtClass
Dim msgString As udtString
Dim QueueInfo As New MSMQ.MSMQQueueInfo
Dim Msg As MSMQ.MSMQMessage
Dim queue As MSMQ.MSMQQueue


On Error GoTo TransactionError
    Set objObjectContext = GetObjectContext()

    QueueInfo.PathName = qname
    Set queue = QueueInfo.Open(MQ_RECEIVE_ACCESS, MQ_DENY_NONE)

    Set Msg = queue.Receive(Transaction:=MQ_MTS_TRANSACTION, _
      ReceiveTimeout:=10)


    queue.Close
```

```
msgString.strMessage = Msg.Body
LSet msgClass = msgString
strResult = ""
Select Case Msg.Label
Case "comCourse.clsClass"

  Select Case msgClass.strMode
  Case "I"
    strResult = Insert(msgClass.strClassNumber, _
      msgClass.strClassName, msgClass.strUsername,
      msgClass.strPassword)
  Case "U"
    strResult = Update(msgClass.lngClassID, _
      msgClass.strClassNumber, msgClass.strClassName, _
      msgClass.strUsername, msgClass.strPassword)
  Case "D"
    strResult = Delete(msgClass.lngClassID, _
      msgClass.strUsername, msgClass.strPassword)
  End Select

End Select

If Not objObjectContext Is Nothing Then
  objObjectContext.SetComplete
End If

GetFromQueueMSMQ = strResult

TransactionError:

If Not objObjectContext Is Nothing Then
  objObjectContext.SetAbort
End If

GetFromQueueMSMQ = "Transaction failed!"
End Function
```

10. Save the project.
11. Remake the project into a comCourse.dll.
12. Check in all files.
13. Exit Visual Basic.

Creating The Courses.asp Page

In the last section, you updated the component to validate the username and password any time you want to access the database. Now you need to create a courses form to view all the available courses. This section uses design-time controls (DTC) that allow you to automatically generate scripts that connect and interact with a database. Some of the design-time controls in the toolbox include the following:

➤ **Recordset** Allows you to create a recordset on the page you are working on.

➤ **Label, Textbox, Listbox, Checkbox, Option Group,** and **Button** Allow you to bind these controls to a data source.

➤ **Grid** Allows you to view data in tabular form from the recordset on the page.

➤ **RecordsetNavBar** Allows you to view and use the standard navigation bar with recordsets, such as MoveFirst, MoveNext, MovePrevious, and MoveLast.

➤ **FormManager** Allows you to create a data-driven form. You can create event-driven forms with this DTC in Visual Interdev.

You are ready to create the Courses.asp Web page. This page lists the classes being offered, and also creates a link to the page that inserts, updates, and deletes classes in the CLASSES table.

To create the Courses.asp page:

1. Double-click the CTIS.wdm file in Project Explorer to open the site diagram.

2. Double-click the Courses page in the site diagram to display the page.

3. Click the Design tab.

4. Click Insert Table in the Table menu.

5. Change to 1 row and 2 columns. Change the border size to zero.

6. Click OK.

7. Change the Paragraph Format from Normal to Heading 2 in the Formatting toolbar.

8. Type "Course Directory" in the first column.

9. Click the Source tab, and then click between the second pair of <TD>...</TD> HTML tags.

10. Double-click Button in the Design-Time Control tab.

11. Click Yes to include the Scripting Object Model.

12. Click the Design tab.

13. Change the following properties for Button:
    Name: **cmdCoursesView**
    ID: cmd**CoursesView**
    Caption: **Courses View**

14. Double-click the Recordset DTC.

15. Click Add Data Connection on the Project menu.

16. If you see a message that says This File Has Been Modified Outside Of The Source Editor. Do You Want To Reload It? click Yes To All.

17. In the Select Data Source dialog box, type "CTIS" in the DSN Name text box, and then click New.

18. In the Create New Data Source dialog box, click SQL Server, and then click Next.

19. In the Create New Data Source dialog box, type "CTIS" as the name of the file you want to save this connection to.

20. Click Next.

21. Click Finish.

22. In the Create a New Data Source to SQL Server dialog box, click (local).

23. Click Next.

24. Select with SQL Server Authentication in the Authentication dialog box and remove the Login ID.

25. Type "sa" for the Login ID, with no password.

26. Click Next on the Authentication dialog box.

27. Select Change The Default Database To, click CTIS in the drop-down list, and then click Next.

28. Click Finish on the Localization dialog box.

29. Click OK on the ODBC for Microsoft SQL Server setup dialog box.

30. Click OK on the Select Data Source dialog box.

31. Click OK on the SQL Server Login dialog box.

32. In the Connection1 Properties dialog box, change the connection name to "conCTIS".

33. Click OK.

34. If you see a message that says global.asa Has Been Modified Outside Of Source Editor, click No.

35. When completed, a connection is set up in global.asa, and the connection appears in the Data View window. *Global.asa* is a special file in ASP that contains startup events for application and session objects. It also stores database connection information. Verify in the Data View window that this connection has been set up.

Now you're ready to set the properties of the recordset and complete the rest of the Courses.asp page.

11

To complete the Courses.asp page:

1. Right-click the Recordset DTC on the Courses.asp page, and then click Properties on the shortcut menu.

2. Change the name of the recordset to "rsCourses".

3. Click Close.

4. Change the following information on rsCourses Recordset:
   Connection: conCTIS
   Database Object: Tables
   Object Name: CLASSES

5. Click the Save button to save the Courses.asp page.

6. Place the cursor on the right side of the rsCourses Recordset and then press Enter.

7. Double-click the Grid DTC on the Design-Time Controls toolbox.

8. Right-click the Grid DTC, and then click Properties on the shortcut menu.

9. On the General tab, change the name of the grid to "grdCourses".

10. On the Data tab, click rsCourses in the Recordset drop-down list box.

11. Select all fields in the Available Fields list box.

12. Click OK.

13. Click the Save button to save the Courses.asp page.

14. Click the Source tab in Source Editor.

15. Click the Script Outline in the toolbox.

16. Expand Server Objects and Events.

17. Expand the cmdCoursesView object.

18. Double-click the event onClick to create a new event in Source Editor.

19. Enter "Response.Redirect("CoursesView.asp")".

20. Click the Save button on the toolbar.

Creating The CoursesView.asp Page

In the last section, you created a Courses page that displays the available courses. Now you can create a mechanism to insert, update, and delete courses from the database. The CoursesView button in the Courses.asp page links you to the CoursesView.asp page. This page is an event-driven form managed by the Form Manager DTC. This form contains several buttons and the text boxes for the data in the CLASSES table. The New, Update, and Delete buttons let you insert and update records in the CLASSES table.

The Save button allows you to do the actual inserting and updating. The Cancel button allows you to cancel the current operation. The Delete button removes the currently selected record on the form. To manage the buttons and the text boxes, the Form Manager DTC manages the events on the form. The form can be in three states: browse, new, and update. The browse state allows the text boxes to be read-only. The new state enables all text boxes for data entry, and clears out the contents of the text boxes. The update state enables the text boxes for the current record. To create a transition between states, an event must occur. Figure 11.5 illustrates the states of a form and the events that transform it into a new state.

You use a UML statechart diagram to illustrate the states, transitions, and events of a form. A rounded rectangle represents a state. A filled-in circle with an arrow pointing to a state indicates the initial state of a form, which is BROWSE in Figure 11.5. The lines between states illustrate a transition. The arrow on the end of a line signifies the next possible state for the form. The text on a line illustrates the event that fires for a form to change states. For instance, to go from the BROWSE state to the NEW state, a **cmdNew_onclick** event must fire. Each event causes a sequence of actions to occur during the transition between states.

To create the CoursesView.asp page:

1. Double-click CTIS.wdm in Project Explorer.

2. Double-click CoursesView.asp.

11

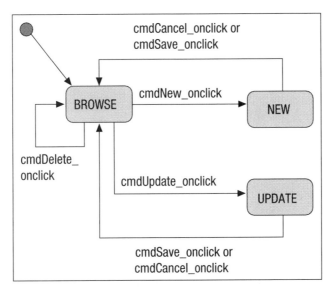

Figure 11.5   UML statechart diagram of a form.

3. If you see the Open File dialog box, click the Check Out command button.

4. In the Source Code Editor, click the Design tab.

5. In the Design-Time Controls toolbox, double-click the FormManager DTC. Click Yes to enable the Scripting Model.

6. Double-click the Recordset DTC. If you see the SQL Server Login, log in to SQL Server with the username "sa" and no password.

7. Right-click the Recordset DTC and then click Properties on the shortcut menu.

8. Change the name of the recordset to rsClasses, and then click Close.

9. Change the following recordset properties:
Connection: **conCTIS**
Database Object: **Tables**
Object Name: **Classes**

10. Click to the right of the recordset object and then press Enter.

Once you put a recordset object on the page, you need to create the main section of the page.

To create the CoursesView main section:

1. Click Insert Table on the Table menu.

2. Change to 1 row and 2 columns. Change the border size to zero.

3. Click OK.

4. Change the Paragraph Format from Normal to Heading 2 in the Formatting toolbar.

5. Type "Course View" in the first column.

6. Click the Source tab, and then click between the second pair of <TD>...</TD> HTML tags.

7. Double-click Button in the Design-Time Control toolbox.

8. Right-click Button1 and then click Properties on the shortcut menu.

9. Change the following properties:
Name: **cmdNew**
Caption: **New**

10. Click OK.

11. Click to the right of the cmdNew button.

12. Double-click Button in the Design-Time Control toolbox.

13. Right-click Button1 and then click Properties on the shortcut menu.

14. Change the following properties:
Name: **cmdUpdate**
Caption: **Update**

15. Click OK.

16. Click to the right of the cmdUpdate button.

17. Double-click Button in the Design-Time Control toolbox.

18. Right-click Button1 and click Properties on the shortcut menu.

19. Change the following properties:
Name: **cmdDelete**
Caption: **Delete**

20. Click OK.

21. Click to the right of the cmdDelete button.

22. Double-click Button in the Design-Time Control toolbox.

23. Right-click Button1, and then click Properties on the shortcut menu.

24. Change the following properties:
Name: **cmdSave**
Caption: **Save**

25. Click OK.

26. Click to the right of the cmdSave button.

27. Double-click Button in the Design-Time Control toolbox.

28. Right-click Button1, and then click Properties on the shortcut menu.

29. Change the following properties:
Name: **cmdCancel**
Caption: **Cancel**

30. Click OK.

31. Click to the right of the cmdCancel button.

32. Double-click Button in the Design-Time Control toolbox.

33. Right-click Button1, and then click Properties on the shortcut menu.

34. Change the following properties:
Name: **cmdCourseDirectory**
Caption: **Course Directory**

35. Click OK.

36. Click Save CoursesView.asp on the File menu.

37. Click above the </BODY> tag.

38. Double-click Label in the Design-Time Control toolbox.

11

39. Right-click Label1, and then click Properties on the shortcut menu.

40. Change the following properties:
Name: **lblCourseNumber**
Recordset: **rsClasses**
Field/Expression: **Course number**:

41. Click OK.

42. Click to the right of the label.

43. Double-click Textbox in the Design-Time Control toolbox.

44. Right-click Textbox1, and then click Properties on the shortcut menu.

45. Change the following properties:
Name: **txtCourseNumber**
Recordset: **rsClasses**
Field: **CLASS_NUMBER**

46. Click OK.

47. Click to the right of the text box.

48. Enter <BR> next to the Textbox DTC.

49. Double-click Label in the Design-Time Control toolbox.

50. Right-click Label1, and then click Properties on the shortcut menu.

51. Change the following properties:
Name: **lblCourseName**
Recordset: **rsClasses**
Field/Expression: **Course name**:

52. Click OK.

53. Click to the right of the label.

54. Double-click Textbox in the Design-Time Control toolbox.

55. Right-click Textbox1, and then click Properties on the shortcut menu.

56. Change the following properties:
Name: **txtCourseName**
Recordset: **rsClasses**
Field: **CLASS_NAME**

57. Click OK.

58. Click to the right of the text box.

59. Enter <BR> next to the Textbox DTC.

60. Double-click Textbox in the Design-Time Control toolbox.

61. Right-click Textbox1, and then click Properties on the shortcut menu.

62. Change the following properties:
    Name: **txtCourseID**
    Recordset: **rsClasse**s
    Field: **CLASS_ID**
    Visible: **uncheck**

63. Click OK.

64. Click to the right of the text box.

65. Enter <BR> next to the Textbox DTC.

66. Double-click RecordsetNavBar. This allows you to browse through records on your form.

67. Right-click RecordsetNavBar1, and then click Properties on the shortcut menu.

68. Change the following properties:
    Recordset: **rsClasses**
    Update on Move: **Checked**

69. Click OK to close the Properties dialog box.

70. Click Save CoursesView.asp on the File menu.

After you successfully create the ASP page, you can add the states of the form using FormManager1.

To add states to the form:

1. Right-click the FormManager1 object, and then click Properties on the shortcut menu.

2. Enter BROWSE in the New Mode text box, and then click the > button. This adds the BROWSE state to the Form Mode list box.

3. Enter NEW in the New Mode text box, and then click the > button.

4. Enter UPDATE in the New Mode text box, and then click the > button.

5. Click BROWSE in the Form Mode list box.

6. Enter the information from Table 11.6 in the Actions Performed By Mode grid.

7. Click NEW in the Form Mode list box.

8. Enter the information from Table 11.7 in the Actions Performed By Mode grid (Table 11.7).

9. Click UPDATE in the Form Mode list box.

10. Enter the information from Table 11.8 in the Actions Performed By Mode grid (Table 11.8).

11. Click the Action tab.

12. Enter the information from Table 11.9 in the Form Mode Transitions grid (Table 11.9).

Table 11.6 Actions Performed By Mode (BROWSE).

Object	Member	Value
cmdNew	disabled	false
cmdUpdate	disabled	false
cmdDelete	disabled	false
cmdCourseDirectory	disabled	false
cmdSave	disabled	true
cmdCancel	disabled	true
txtCourseName	disabled	true
txtCourseNumber	disabled	true

Table 11.7 Actions Performed By Mode (NEW).

Object	Member	Value
cmdNew	disabled	true
cmdUpdate	disabled	true
cmdDelete	disabled	true
cmdCourseDirectory	disabled	true
cmdSave	disabled	false
cmdCancel	disabled	false
txtCourseName	disabled	false
txtCourseNumber	disabled	false
txtCourseNumber	value	" "
txtCourseName	value	" "
txtCourseID	value	" "

Table 11.8 Actions Performed By Mode (UPDATE).

Object	Member	Value
cmdNew	disabled	true
cmdUpdate	disabled	true
cmdDelete	disabled	true
cmdCourseDirectory	disabled	true
cmdSave	disabled	false
cmdCancel	disabled	false
txtCourseName	disabled	false
txtCourseNumber	disabled	false

Table 11.9   Form Mode Transitions.

Current Mode	Object	Event	Next Mode
BROWSE	cmdNew	onClick	NEW
BROWSE	cmdUpdate	onClick	UPDATE
BROWSE	cmdDelete	onClick	BROWSE
NEW	cmdCancel	onClick	BROWSE
NEW	cmdSave	onClick	BROWSE
UPDATE	cmdCancel	onClick	BROWSE
UPDATE	cmdSave	onClick	BROWSE

13. Click the Close button to close the Properties window.

14. Click Save CoursesView.asp on the File menu.

After you set up the states in Form Manager, code the command button events in the ASP page.

To code the command button events:

1. Click the Script Outline tab in the toolbox.

2. Expand the Server Objects & Events folders.

3. Expand the cmdNew object.

4. Double-click the **onClick** event. Your cursor will be placed in the script part of the page.

5. Enter the following code. To do so, copy the code from the code11-05.txt file on the CD and paste it on the page, replacing the original code.

```
sub cmdNew_onclick()
  txtCourseID.value = 0
End Sub
sub cmdCourseDirectory_onclick()
  Response.Redirect "courses.asp"
End Sub

sub cmdCancel_onclick()
  rsClasses.requery
  rsClasses.MoveFirst
End Sub

Sub cmdSave_onclick()
  dim CourseID
  dim objClass
  dim strResult
  set objClass = CreateObject("comCourse.clsClass")
  if txtCourseID.value = "" Then
```

11

```
        CourseID = 0
      Else
        CourseID = clng(txtCourseID.value)
      End If
      strResult = _
  objClass.Save(CourseID,txtCourseNumber.value,txtCourseName.value, _
      Session("Username"),Session("Password"))
      if strResult <> "" Then
        Response.Write "<CENTER><H2>" & strResult & _
          "</CENTER></H2><BR>"
        Response.Write "<A HREF=CoursesView.asp>Course View</A><BR>"
        Response.End
      Else
        cmdCancel_onclick()
      End If
    End Sub

    sub cmdDelete_onclick()
      dim objClass
      dim strResult
      dim lngID
      set objClass = CreateObject("comCourse.clsClass")
      lngID = CLng(txtCourseID.value)
      strResult = _
        objClass.Delete(CLng(lngID),Session("Username"),Session("Password"))
      if strResult <> "" Then
        Response.Write "<CENTER><H2>" & strResult & _
          "</CENTER></H2><BR>"
        Response.Write "<A HREF=CoursesView.asp>Course View</A><BR>"
        Response.End
      Else
        cmdCancel_onclick
      End If
    End Sub
```

6. Click Save CoursesView.asp on the File menu.

7. Right-click Login.htm in Project Explorer, and then click Set As Start Page to set the login page as the start page.

8. Click the Start button on the toolbar to run the Web application. Use username "instructor1" and no password to log in to the Web application.

9. When you see a message asking if you want to enable ASP debugging, click Yes.

10. Verify the functionality of the Web application.

You have completed creating and testing the Web application using a combination of ASP, HTML, and DTCs.

CHAPTER SUMMARY

In this chapter, you investigated Internet and Web technologies that enable you to create dynamic Web applications. Visual Interdev gives you a development environment to create fully interactive Web sites. You reviewed HTML, JavaScript, VBScript, Design-Time Controls, and other technologies used to create Web applications. Creating Web applications is only one user interface method you can use. Creating user interfaces in Visual Basic is another way. By creating business objects in Chapter 9, you gave yourself the flexibility to create a Visual Basic application in Chapter 10, and a Web application in this chapter. You need to decide during the design process which method suits your project's needs. CTIS needs a Web application so that the entire student body and instructors can use CTIS with little or no configuration necessary on the client computers. You created the Visual Basic interfaces in Chapter 10 as an alternative to the Web. It is also useful to create system administrator functionality in a Visual Basic application rather than in a Visual Interdev application.

REVIEW QUESTIONS

Some of the questions below cover material you should be familiar with from your review of HTML documents.

1. Who is the founder of the World Wide Web?
    a. Tim Berners-Lee
    b. Tim Lee Jackson
    c. Tim Lee-Berners
    d. none of the above

2. When requesting a Web page with a URL, what application do you use?
    a. HTTP
    b. TCP/IP
    c. FTP
    d. none of the above

3. What does URL stand for?
    a. Uniform Resource Locator
    b. Universal Resource Link
    c. Universal Resource Location
    d. none of the above

4. Which of the following are examples of Web resources? Choose all that apply.

   a. Visual Basic Application

   b. HTML document

   c. Active Server Page

   d. Java Applet

5. <HTML> and </HTML> are called _____ in HTML.

   a. tags

   b. documents

   c. formats

   d. none of the above

6. Which tag or tags bold text?

   a. HR>

   b. B>...</B><

   c. <U>...</U>

   d. <I>...</I><

7. Which tag or tags underline text?

   a. <U>...</U><

   b. <HR>

   c. B>...</B>

   d. <I>...</I>

8. Which tag or tags italicize text?

   a. <HR>

   b. U>...</U><

   c. B>...</B>

   d. <I>...</I><

9. Which next-generation standard upgrades the current standard to allow for fully customizable and dynamic Web pages?

   a. ASP

   b. HTML

   c. DHTML

   d. none of the above

10. Which two scripting languages can you use in Internet Explorer?
    a. VBScript
    b. JavaScript
    c. ASP
    d. none of the above

11. Which Microsoft technology allows you to create server-side scripts?
    a. ASP
    b. JavaScript
    c. VBScript
    d. none of the above

12. Which ASP object supplies the information about the user's request to your Web site?
    a. request
    b. server
    c. application
    d. response

13. Which ASP object supplies the response to the request sent by the user via the Web application?
    a. response
    b. request
    c. application
    d. server

11

14. Which ASP object supplies the necessary interface for creating Web-based applications?
    a. request
    b. application
    c. server
    d. response

15. Which ASP object supplies the necessary interface for creating a session with your Web application?
    a. application
    b. request
    c. session
    d. response

HANDS-ON PROJECTS

Project 11.1

Explain the different modes in which Visual Interdev can manage projects.

Project 11.2

Explain the four components of Visual Interdev.

Project 11.3

In Chapter 10, you created an MDI application that entered instructor or student information. In this chapter, you added a user_ID to the INSTRUCTORS table and to the STUDENTS table.

a. Update the MDI application to support this new field.

b. Update the comUser component with this new field.

c. Be sure to delete the comUser component in MTS and install the new comUser component.

d. Change the appropriate stored procedures to accept a new field: user_id.

Project 11.4

In this chapter, you added user authentication with SQL Server. You changed the comCourse component to authenticate users based on username and password. Using the techniques in this chapter, update the following components to authenticate with SQL Server:

a. comCourse (schedule)

b. comGrade

c. comAssignment

Project 11.5

You need to complete the instructor section of the CTIS Web site. Add Web pages like the Courses page in this chapter for the following:

a. Course Management

   i) Course Schedules

b. Grades Management

   i) Category

   ii) Grade Distribution

   iii) Grade Assignment

c. Student Management

  i) Student Information (use comUser to enter, modify, and delete students)

  ii) Student Registration (allow instructors to register students for their classes using STUDENTS_SCHEDULE table)

d. Instructor Management

  i) Instructor Information (use comUser to enter, modify, and delete instructor information for the person logged into CTIS)

e. Assignment Management

  i) Assignment Information

Project 11.6

Complete the student section of the CTIS Web site. You need to add Web pages like the Courses page for the following:

a. The home page of CTIS currently contains nothing. Add the following to this page:

  i) Allow a student to request a login.

  ii) Allow a student to log in to CTIS.

b. Student Management

  i) Student Information

  ii) Student Registration

c. Grades Management

  i) Grades by Student (allow program to display grades only for the student logged in)

d. Assignment Management

  i) View Assignments

11

Project 11.7

Change Hands-On Projects 11.5 and 11.6 to use MSMQ. Refer to Chapter 9 for guidance.

Project 11.8

Challenge Problem: Your job is to design and create reports in Visual Interdev for CTIS. Using the Grid DTC or using ASP and tables, create the following reports:

a. Course Management

  i) Course Listing (all columns in CLASSES table)

   b. Grades Management

      i) Final Grade Report for a student by class

      ii) Grades for all students for a single assignment

      iii) Grades for a single student for all assignments

   c. Student Management

      i) Student Listing (all columns in STUDENTS table)

      ii) Student Information for a single student

   d. Assignment Management

      i) Assignment Listing (all columns from ASSIGNMENTS table)

CHAPTER TWELVE

INTRODUCTION TO ONLINE HELP AND APPLICATION LOCALIZATION

AFTER READING THIS CHAPTER AND COMPLETING THE EXCERCISES, YOU WILL BE ABLE TO:

➤ Understand the purpose of an online Help system

➤ Navigate Microsoft HTML Help Workshop

➤ Create an online Help system for CTIS

➤ Understand the purpose of localizing an application

➤ Describe the issues involved in application localization

During the developing phase, you complete the visual design, the database design, and the functional specifications. Chapter 8 ended with the database freeze interim milestone, which indicates that you've completed the database design. Chapters 9 through 11 resulted in the completed features, the visual design freeze, and the functional specification freeze interim milestones, which indicate that you've completed the visual design and functional specifications. You will meet the scope complete/first use milestone when the alpha version of the software is released and test cases are completed. Chapter 13 describes the process recommended by Microsoft for testing software and releasing interim code. This process extends from the developing phase through the stabilization phase to the release milestone.

As part of the developing and stabilization phases, the user education team designs and develops tools for learning and using the system, which includes user training, online Help systems, and user manuals. Documentation begins after the interim milestones in the developing phase. In this chapter, you will investigate online Help systems and create one using Microsoft HTML Help Workshop.

Often, during the developing phase, you learn whether your application will be sold internationally. If it will be, you need to localize the software and the documentation, which means you must translate them for another language and culture. In this chapter, you will also investigate the issues involved in application localization.

CHAPTER OVERVIEW

Chapters 8 through 11 explored how to take the conceptual, logical, and physical designs and use Visual Basic and Visual Interdev to create applications that fulfill the main objectives of the developing phase. As part of the developing phase, the user education team also creates the online Help to document the system. In this chapter, you will investigate two ways to make your software accessible to your users. One way is to implement online Help, and the other is to localize it for international users. Because CTIS is predominantly a Web application, and uses a variety of HTML documents, you will first learn how to create an HTML Help system using Microsoft HTML Help Workshop 1.21, Microsoft's latest standard for online Help.

 To use Microsoft HTML Help Workshop 1.21, you must visit Microsoft's Web site at www.microsoft.com. Go to the Downloads section, and, under Web Publishing Tools, choose HTML Help for Authoring. Click the Download Microsoft HTML Help 1.21 link to install this application on your system. Before you attempt to follow the instructions or complete the exercises for this chapter, you must install HTML Help Workshop 1.21 from Microsoft's Web site.

Another way to make your software accessible is to localize your system if your targeted audience is international. You will investigate techniques and issues involved in application localization later in this chapter.

HELP SYSTEMS

As part of system creation, you must include online Help to make your product easy to use, and to provide a place where your users can find information about your system. Because they can make your software easy to learn and use, online Help systems are critical to the overall success of a project. Microsoft provides the tools you need to create these Help systems (you must have Visual Studio installed to complete this section).

There are two ways to create online Help in Microsoft environments:

➤ **Microsoft Help Workshop** A set of tools and information for creating Help files in WinHelp format, primarily for Windows 95 and Windows NT 4.0. You can find the Help Workshop on the Visual Studio CD Disk 3 in the \common\tools\vb\hcw folder. (Use the setup.exe installation program to install the Workshop on your machine.) WinHelp Help systems created with the Help Workshop can run on any Windows 95 or NT 4.0 system, but cannot be used on the Web.

➤ **Microsoft HTML Workshop** A set of tools and information for creating Help files in HTML format, primarily for Windows 98 and Windows 2000, and for Help Web sites for different browsers. You can use either an ActiveX control or a Java applet to create a Web site that allows users to interact with your Help files. HTML Help is a new online Help standard based on the HTML format, and was designed by Microsoft to replace the WinHelp format.

 For more information on Microsoft HTML Help, refer to *http://msdn.microsoft.com/workshop/author/htmlhelp/default.asp.*

Previewing The CTIS Help System

As part of creating the CTIS system, you need to create the online Help that explains how to use the system. You can use the Online Help Viewer to preview the CTIS Help system you will create in this chapter.

 To complete this section and others, you must first install Microsoft HTML Help Workshop from Microsoft's Web site.

To preview the CTIS Help System:

1. On the CD in the Chapter_12 folder, double-click the **CTIS.chm** Help file to run the help system using the Microsoft Online Help Viewer. Figure 12.1 illustrates the CTIS HTML Help system. The Contents tab displays the different topics in the Help system. The Index tab shows the keywords you can select to search for related Help topics.

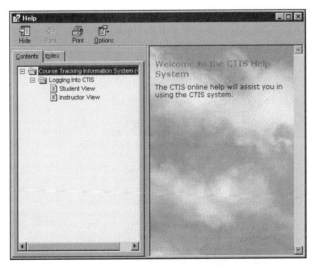

Figure 12.1   CTIS Help system.

2. If necessary, expand the Course Tracking Information System (CTIS) topic entry in the Contents tab. Click Logging into CTIS. The right pane displays the Help topic for logging into CTIS.

3. If necessary, expand the Logging into CTIS topic entry in the Contents tab. Click Student View. The right pane will display the Help topic describing the Student view in the CTIS application.

4. Click the Close button to exit the CTIS Help system.

Introduction To Microsoft HTML Help Workshop 1.21

Microsoft HTML Help Workshop consists of a set of tools for creating online Help using HTML. These tools allow you to create the components of HTML Help, including the topics containing feature descriptions and task instructions, the graphics illustrating the content, such as screen illustrations and icons, and navigational tools, such as the table of contents and index. Figure 12.2 shows the Microsoft HTML Help Workshop environment.

The HTML Help Workshop window includes the following tabs where you can set project-wide options, and create a table of contents and index.

➤ **Project** Tracks the Help file settings in your Help project, such as the names of the compiled Help files and the table of contents and index files. HTML Help Workshop updates this information automatically. Figure 12.2 shows the Project tab in HTML Help Workshop.

➤ **Contents** Where you create the table of contents for your Help system. Figure 12.3 shows the Contents tab in HTML Help Workshop.

➤ **Index** Lists keywords that you can select to display Help files associated with those keywords. Figure 12.4 shows HTML Help Workshop with the Index tab selected.

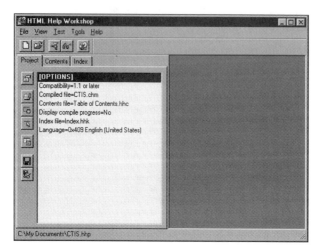

Figure 12.2 Microsoft HTML Help Workshop.

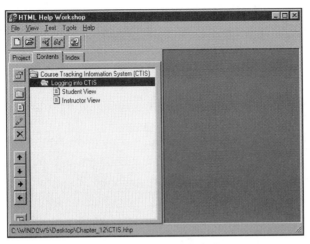

Figure 12.3 Microsoft HTML Help Workshop with Contents tab selected.

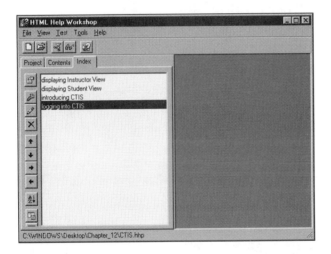

12

Figure 12.4 HTML Help Workshop with Index tab selected.

Table 12.1 describes the functions of the buttons in the Contents tab.

Table 12.1 Functions of the buttons in the Contents tab.

Button	Function
Properties	Sets properties for the table of contents
Insert a Heading	Displays a topic entry in the table of contents. Headings usually link to a Help file and act as main topics that contain subtopics
Insert a Page	Displays a topic entry in the table of contents and also link to a Help file, usually for a subtopic
Edit a Selection	Edits a topic entry

(continued)

Table 12.1 Functions of the buttons in the Contents tab *(continued)*.

Button	Function
Delete a Selection	Deletes a topic entry from the table of contents
Move Selection Up	Moves a selected entry up in the table of contents tree
Move a Selection Down	Moves a selected entry down in the table of contents tree
Move a Selection Right	Makes a main topic entry into a subtopic entry
Move a Selection Left	Makes a subtopic entry into a main topic entry
View HTML Source	Views the HTML source of the selected topic
Save File	Saves the HTML file you are currently viewing

Table 12.2 describes the functions of the buttons in the Index tab.

Creating The CTIS Online Help System

When creating an online Help system, organize your topics similar to other standard online Help systems in other applications, such as Microsoft Office 2000. You can use those online Help systems as a guide.

For CTIS, you will first create a Help project, which specifies settings such as names of files in the Help system, and then set up the Contents and Index tabs the user sees in the Help window. Next, you can create the table of contents to display in the Contents tab. The table of contents includes headings and subheadings that link to particular HTML Help files in your system. Then you can create an index to display in the Index tab. The index is a list of keywords that also link to particular HTML Help files. When users click a heading or a

Table 12.2 Functions of the buttons in the Index tab.

Button	Function
Properties	Sets properties for the index
Insert a Keyword	Inserts a keyword in the index
Edit a Selection	Edits a topic entry
Delete a Selection	Deletes a topic from the index
Move Selection Up	Moves a selection up in the list of keywords
Move a Selection Down	Moves a selection down in the list of keywords
Move a Selection Right	Makes a main topic entry into a subtopic entry
Move a Selection Left	Makes a subtopic entry into a main topic entry
Sort Keywords Alphabetically	Sorts the index alphabetically
View HTML Source	Views the HTML source of the selected topic
Save File	Saves the HTML file you are currently viewing

keyword in either tab, they see the Help topic in the HTML file you specified. Although many Help system authors start by creating Help topics in HTML Help files, this chapter explains how to set up the preliminary tools, and then concentrates on creating the Help topics.

Creating The Project And Setting Up The Workshop Environment

You can start developing online Help by creating a Help project and setting up the Contents and Index tabs in the HTML Help Workshop environment.

To create a Help project and set up the Contents and Index tabs:

1. Click the Start menu. Point to Programs, then to HTML Help Workshop, and then click HTML Help Workshop.

2. In the File menu, click New to create a new project.

3. Click Project, and then click OK to launch the Project Wizard.

4. On the New Project dialog box, click Next.

5. In the New Project – Destination dialog box, enter or select the destination of the Chapter_12 folder on your Student Disk. For example, enter a:\Chapter_12\CTIS. This creates a Help project in the CTIS subfolder of your Chapter_12 folder, and specifies that all the Help files should be stored there. Then click Next.

6. If you are prompted, click Yes in the HTML Help Workshop dialog box to replace the file.

7. Click Next in the New Project – Existing Files dialog box.

8. Click Finish in the New Project – Finish dialog box.

9. Click the Contents tab.

10. In the Table of Contents Not Specified dialog box, click OK to indicate that you want to create a table of contents for this Help project.

11. Click Save in the Save As dialog box.

12. Click the Index tab.

13. In the Index Not Specified dialog box, click OK to indicate that you want to create an index for this Help project.

14. Click Save in the Save As dialog box.

15. If a dialog box appears to ask you to overwrite the file, click Yes. You have just created and set up the CTIS Help project that contains two components of the CTIS Help system.

Introduction To The HTML Help Image Editor

Now you can begin to develop the graphics and the Help content. Most good Help systems include meaningful graphics, such as illustrations of the windows and toolbars in your system. Start by touring the HTML Help Image Editor and learning how to capture screens you can use in your Help system.

The HTML Help Image Editor contains tools for capturing screens and editing the graphics you want to use in your online Help. Figure 12.5 illustrates the HTML Help Image Editor environment.

The HTML Help Image Editor environment includes the following windows:

➤ **HTML Help Image Editor** Is the parent window that allows you to manipulate the child windows, and provides commands for image editing.

➤ **Browse** Lists the image files you can edit in the current working directory.

➤ **Image** Displays the image you captured or are ready to edit.

Capturing Screens To Use In Your Help System

One way to create graphics for your Help system is to capture screens you want to illustrate. For example, you can capture the Login screen in CTIS so you can display it in the login Help topic.

To capture screens in CTIS:

1. In HTML Help Workshop, click the HTML Help Image Editor option on the Tools menu.

2. Open Internet Explorer.

3. On the File menu of Internet Explorer, click Open.

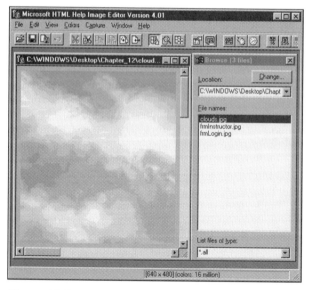

Figure 12.5 HTML Help Image Editor.

4. Enter "c:\Work\CTIS\user_svc_src\web\CTIS\CTIS_Local\Login.htm" in the Open text box, and then click OK.

5. In the HTML Help Image Editor, click the Using the Mouse option on the Capture menu to capture a screen by clicking your mouse.

6. Press the ALT+TAB keys until you see Internet Explorer.

7. Click inside the window displaying the Login form. The Image Editor captures this window and displays it in a window in the HTML Help Image Editor.

8. On the File menu, click Save As.

9. Change to the Chapter_12 folder on the CD, and then enter "frmLogin" as the name of the file.

10. In the Save As Type list, click the .jpg format. This is a common format used in HTML files.

11. Click Save. If prompted to overwrite the file, click Yes.

12. Click OK in the JPEG Compression Options dialog box.

13. On the File menu, click Exit.

14. Click No to All for any Unsaved Files to indicate you do not need to save any unsaved files.

You have created an image of the CTIS Login form by capturing the window displaying the form. Then you saved the image file as frmLogin.jpg, which you can insert in the appropriate HTML Help file.

12

Creating The HTML Help Content

When you create HTML Help content, you create an HTML file for each Help topic you want to include in your Help system. These are standard HTML files that can use the full range of HTML codes. For more information on HTML, see Chapter 11 and related Web sites. For CTIS, you can create an HTML file for a topic explaining how to log on to CTIS.

To create a Help file in HTML:

1. In HTML Help Workshop, click New on the File menu.

2. Click HTML File.

3. Type "Logging into CTIS" in the HTML Title dialog box, and then click OK.

4. HTML Help Workshop automatically generates the nonboldfaced code below. Enter the following code into the HTML document:

```
<!DOCTYPE HTML PUBLIC "-//IETF//DTD HTML//EN">
<HTML>
```

```
<HEAD>
<link REL="stylesheet" TYPE="text/css" HREF="coua.css">
<meta name="GENERATOR" content="Microsoft&reg; HTML Help Workshop
4.1">
<Title>Logging into CTIS</Title>
</HEAD>
<BODY>
<H2>CTIS Login Form</H2>
<P>This form allows you to log in to the CTIS system. When you _
enter your username and password, CTIS verifies you can use the _
system. </P>
<IMG SRC="frmLogin.jpg">
<P>
If you are a student, the Student view is displayed. If you are an
instructor, then the Instructor view is displayed.</P>
</BODY>
</HTML>
```

5. On the File menu, click Save file.

6. In the Save As dialog box, type Logging_into_CTIS.htm, and then click Save.

7. Click Yes if prompted to overwrite the existing file.

Creating The Table Of Contents

After you set up the project, you can create a table of contents in the Contents tab. You can add two main headings that link to main topics in the CTIS Help system: one for the introduction to CTIS, which links to the default topic, and one for logging in to CTIS, which links to the login instructions. The Logging into CTIS topic also includes subtopics explaining the Instructor and Student views; you can add subheadings to link to these topics.

To create a table of contents in the Contents tab:

1. Click the Contents tab.

2. Click the Insert a Heading button.

3. Type "Course Tracking Information System (CTIS)" in the Entry title text box. This text will appear as a main heading in the Contents tab.

4. Click the Add button.

5. Type "default.htm" in the File or URL text box. This links the heading to a particular HTML file, so that a user can click the heading to display the file you specify. In this case, it links to the default HTML file, which provides a brief overview of the Help system. The Online Help Viewer requires that a table of contents have at least one entry that links to a default.htm file.

6. Click OK. Default.htm appears in the list box.

7. Click OK in the Table of Contents entry dialog box. Now you're ready to add another entry to the table of contents.

8. Click the Insert a Heading button.

9. Click No in the Do you want to insert this entry at the beginning of the table of contents? dialog box. This option lets you insert an entry before or after the current entry. Selecting Yes inserts a new entry before the first entry, and selecting No inserts an entry after the first entry.

10. Type "Logging into CTIS" in the Entry title text box to create another table of contents entry.

11. Click the Add button.

12. Type "Logging_into_CTIS.htm" in the File or URL text box. This links the Logging into CTIS entry in the table of contents to the Logging_into_CTIS HTML file.

13. Click OK. Logging_into_CTIS.htm appears in the list box.

14. Click OK in the Table of Contents entry dialog box.

You've created two main headings in the Contents tab to link to main topics. Now you can create subheadings to link to related subtopics.

To add subheading entries to the table of contents:

1. Click Logging into CTIS.

2. Click the Move Selection Right button. This defines the Logging into CTIS heading as a subheading under Course Tracking Information System.

12

3. Click the Insert a Page button. HTML Help Workshop automatically considers a page to be a subtopic of the preceding topic.

4. Type "Student View" in the Entry title text box.

5. Click the Add button.

6. Type "Student_View.htm" in the File or URL text box.

7. Click OK. Student_View.htm appears in the list box.

8. Click OK in the Table of Contents entry dialog box.

9. Click the Insert a Page button.

10. Type "Instructor View" in the Entry title text box.

11. Click the Add button.

12. Type "Instructor_View.htm" in the File or URL text box.

13. Click OK. Instructor_View.htm appears in the list box.

14. Click OK in the Table of Contents entry dialog box. You have added two subheadings to the table of contents under the Logging Into CTIS heading.

15. Click Save Project on the File menu to save the project.

You have entered two main topic headings and two subtopic headings, and linked the topics to HTML pages containing Help topics.

Creating The Index

Next, you can create an index for your Help system. For CTIS, you can insert keywords and phrases to link to the topics that explain how to display the Instructor view and Student view, log on to CTIS, and read an introduction to the system.

To create an index for CTIS:

1. Click the Index tab.

2. Click the Insert a Keyword button to insert a keyword in the index.

3. Type "Displaying Instructor view" in the Keyword text box. This is the keyword text the user sees in the Index tab.

4. Click the Add button.

5. Type "Instructor_View.htm" in File or URL text box. This links the keyword to the Help topic in the Instructor_View.htm file.

6. Type "Instructor View" in the Title text box. This is the title for the HTML file you want to link to this entry.

7. Click OK. Instructor_View.htm appears in the list box.

8. Click OK in the Index Entry dialog box. You have added a keyword to the index for the Instructor View topic. Now you can add other keywords.

9. Click the Insert a Keyword button. If you are asked if you want to insert the entry at the beginning of the index, click No.

10. Type "Displaying Student view" in the Keyword text box.

11. Click the Add button.

12. Type "Student_View.htm" in the File or URL text box.

13. Type "Student View" in the Title text box.

14. Click OK. Student_View.htm appears in the list box.

15. Click OK in the Index Entry dialog box.

16. Click the Insert a Keyword button.

17. Type "Logging into CTIS" in the Keyword text box.

18. Click the Add button.

19. Type "Logging_into_CTIS.htm" in the File or URL text box.

20. Type "Logging into CTIS" in the Title text box.

21. Click OK. Logging_into_CTIS.htm appears in the list box. You have added three keywords to the index and linked them to the appropriate Help topics.

22. Click OK in the Index Entry dialog box.

23. Click the Insert a Keyword button.

24. Type "Introduction to CTIS" in the Keyword text box.

25. Click the Add button.

26. Type "default.htm" in the File or URL text box.

27. Type "Introduction to CTIS" in the Title text box.

28. Click OK. Default.htm appears in the list box.

29. Click OK in the Index Entry dialog box.

30. On the File menu, click Save Project.

You have set up two important tools for navigating your Help system: the Contents and Index tabs. Now that you've created the content of the Help topics, captured screens to use as illustrations, and set up the table of contents and index, you're ready to compile and run the Help system.

Compiling And Running The CTIS Help System

After you finish creating the HTML Help files, compile your online Help so you can include it with systems developed using Visual Basic or Visual Interdev. When you compile, HTML Help Workshop creates a Help system with topic pages, a table of contents, and an index. The compiled Help system is what you distribute to the users.

To compile and run the CTIS Help system:

1. On the File menu, click Compile.

2. In the Create a Compiled File dialog box, click Compile.

3. Click the View Compiled File button on the toolbar. If necessary, browse to the CTIS.chm file.

4. Click View in the View Compiled File dialog box.

5. Examine and test the CTIS Help system. For example, click the Logging into CTIS heading in the Contents tab to make sure it links to the appropriate topic.

6. Click the Close button to exit the Online Help Viewer.

You have created an online HTML Help system by creating Help topics in HTML files, adding graphics such as screen illustrations, setting up the Contents and Index tabs to help users find information, and then compiling the Help project.

Creating the online Help system is often managed by the user education team. This team is also responsible for localizing the software, if necessary. If your software is being developed for an international audience, you probably need to translate any text the user sees into another language and adapt your software to another culture.

INTRODUCTION TO APPLICATION LOCALIZATION

Once the design is set and your management decides to market your system internationally, the user education and development teams concentrate on making the software accessible to its targeted users. Besides designing the user interface, two ways to make your software accessible are creating accurate, easy-to-use online Help, and localizing the software if the audience is international. The goal of many software developers is to release software that has an international market. But a software product is only international if it adapts to the foreign market; ideally, everything in the user interface and documentation—everything the user sees and interacts with—should be translated into the language and culture of the system's users. *Application localization* is the process of adapting your software to a *locale*, which is the local conventions, culture, and language of your users. A language and a country define a locale. For example, English/U.S. and English/Canada are two different locales. Before you begin localizing your software, consider which language versions you want to provide. Then learn as much as you can about these locales and their users, or work with a localization expert who can provide this information. For example, you need to know how the users in a locale format time and date, abbreviate their currency, and separate decimal places. You may also need to know the units of measurement they use and the elements of a standard address and phone number.

To create international software, you must localize or translate all of the string resources in your application, such as the text that appears in your user interface. This includes menus, dialog boxes, messages, button names, ToolTips, and status bar text. You also need to adapt to locale-specific settings such as date/time, number, and currency in your system.

Consider the following when designing your user interfaces for an international market:

➤ **Messages** English text strings are normally shorter than their localized counterparts. Make sure to allow for growth of your text in your messages. For example, a button that says "Font" could be translated as "Serie di Caratteri" in Italian.

➤ **Menus and dialog boxes** Like messages, text strings in menus and dialog boxes will grow when the application is localized.

➤ **Icons and bitmaps** You use icons and bitmaps to depict certain commands or functions in an application. But an icon or bitmap that is standard in the U.S. is not necessarily standard in other locales. For example, an icon of an American mailbox with a red flag indicates new email to North American users, but may not to European or Asian users. A better symbol would be an envelope, which is universally understood. Avoid icons that contain text because the translated text may be longer than the English text. Also, make sure that icons and bitmaps are not culturally offensive. What is considered acceptable or lighthearted in the United States might be offensive in another culture. Use neutral graphics, and test them with users from different backgrounds and cultures.

➤ **Keyboard layouts** Make sure that the shortcut keys you use work in the locales that you are targeting. Locales can have different keyboard layouts. To test your shortcuts, you need to change Windows to the locale you are supporting.

Microsoft makes additional recommendations for localizing applications.

➤ Always use the system API to check for the names and locations of Windows standard directories, such as Programs, My Documents, and Control Panel, as these can differ on different language versions of the operating system. Otherwise, assuming a specific location name could cause your application to fail.

➤ Create a single world-wide executable file with language .dlls for each language. The best way to do this is to create a single executable that uses U.S. English resources that will run on any language system, but allow the application to be changed dynamically.

➤ Query for the default GUI font. System font metrics vary widely with different languages. Your application's interface may vary not simply on the translation of terms, but also on the default system font.

For more information on how to create localized applications, refer to the on-line documentation that comes with Visual Studio, and refer to related Web sites.

12

CHAPTER SUMMARY

Creating online Help and localizing software applications are two important issues in developing software applications. Well-designed Help is your user's guide to working with your application, and can make your user's experience with your software pleasant and productive. If you want to market your software internationally, you must localize your software application for a foreign audience. The best time to decide to localize your software is during the developing phase. However, the marketing team often decides to pursue international markets after the initial release of the software, which means the development team must change the application to support locales. The best approach may be to consider localization an issue for every application, and to incorporate the localization tips during the design phase, when you're creating the user interface. For more information, refer to the online documentation that comes with Visual Studio (MDSN Library).

REVIEW QUESTIONS

1. Which team is responsible for creating the online Help system?

    a. testing

    b. user education

    c. development

    d. logistics management

2. Which Microsoft Help application assists you in creating a Help system on a Web site?

    a. Microsoft Visual Interdev

    b. Microsoft HTML Help Workshop

    c. Microsoft Visual Basic

    d. Microsoft Help Workshop

3. Which tab in Microsoft HTML Help Workshop allows you to create a list of main topics and subtopics of the Help System?

    a. New

    b. Contents

    c. Index

    d. Image Editor

4. Which tab in Microsoft HTML Help Workshop allows you to create a list of keywords related to the Help System?

    a. Project

    b. New

    c. Index

    d. Contents

5. International software is marketable to:

    a. Europe

    b. Asia

    c. the United States

    d. the world

6. _____ is the process you use to adapt your software to the conventions, culture, and language of your users.

    a. Application software

    b. Application Help

    c. Application localization

    d. none of the above

7. A _____ comprises your user's environment, including local conventions, culture, and language spoken.

    a. locale

    b. section

    c. state

    d. Help project

8. A locale is defined by a _____ and a country.

    a. state

    b. location

    c. language

    d. none of the above

9. You must localize all the _____ resources in your application.

    a. data

    b. currency

    c. string

    d. none of the above

10. English text strings are usually _____ their localized counterparts.

    a. more complicated than

    b. shorter than

    c. as long as

    d. longer than

12

HANDS-ON PROJECTS

Project 12.1
Compare and contrast the WinHelp system versus the HTML Help system.

Project 12.2
Research how to use Microsoft HTML Help on your Web site.

Project 12.3
The Student view Help topic is incomplete. Using the techniques in this chapter, create an HTML file for the Student view.

Project 12.4

Create online Help for the Student Management subsystem in the CTIS Help system. Include the following features:

a. Contents

b. Index

c. HTML files using graphics

Project 12.5

Create online Help for the Assignment Management subsystem in the CTIS Help system. Include the following features:

a. Contents

b. Index

c. HTML files using graphics

Project 12.6

Create online Help for the Grades Management subsystem in the CTIS Help system. Include the following features:

a. Contents

b. Index

c. HTML files using graphics

Project 12.7

Create online Help for the Course Management subsystem in the CTIS Help system. Include the following features:

a. Contents

b. Index

c. HTML files using graphics

Project 12.8

Add the CTIS Help system to Visual SourceSafe.

COMPLETING THE DEVELOPING PHASE AND INTRODUCING THE STABILIZATION PHASE

AFTER READING THIS CHAPTER AND COMPLETING THE EXCERCISES, YOU WILL BE ABLE TO:

➤ Understand the testing process in the Microsoft Solutions Framework (MSF)

➤ Understand the roles of the different team members in the stabilization phase

➤ Define a bug

➤ Describe what goes into a bug report

➤ Describe how releases are managed

➤ Describe how applications are deployed

Chapters 4 through 11 focused on the tasks of the development team in the software development process. The development team designs and creates the system for the user. During and after development, the user education team designs and creates online documentation, as described in Chapter 12, and trains the users on the system. Finally, the testing team and the logistics management team perform their roles before releasing the system. The testing team verifies that the system works as described in the functional requirements and use case scenarios. The logistics management team deploys the technology infrastructure needed to test the system. This team also supports the entire infrastructure, and deploys or distributes the application when released.

CHAPTER OVERVIEW

This chapter focuses on the testing process that takes place during the developing and stabilization phases. The developing phase ends when the testing team completes the initial testing of all requirements and features. The stabilization phase starts with the first beta release of the software. A beta release of an application is the first external delivery of the software to the users. The stabilization phase involves the users, testers, developers, and logistics management team working together to deploy a working system. While the users, testers, and developers are involved in the testing process, logistics management is working to create installation packages to install the application for the user. The stabilization phase ends when the final release is deployed, or distributed to users.

AN INTRODUCTION TO THE STABILIZING PHASE

The testing and logistics management teams guide the software project through the stabilization phase. The goal of the stabilization phase is to continuously test the system until the number of bugs decreases and the product stabilizes, making it ready for release. During the stabilization phase, the testing team tests product usability and reports bugs to the development team. The testing team is responsible for two types of testing: coverage and usability. *Coverage testing* means that they test every feature and requirement in the functional requirements specification. *Usability testing* means that they test the software under different scenarios. These scenarios originate from use case scenarios and user involvement. The use case scenarios guide you in determining the way the user works with the system. From these scenarios, testers create test procedures to document how to test a certain scenario. The user becomes involved in the testing process during the beta release. The beta testing process involves the users and testers using the software in real-world situations and documenting bugs as they occur. The stabilization phase ends in the release milestone, when the development team releases the final version of the software to the logistics team. They, in turn, use the final version to create the setup program to deploy the system.

Team Roles

During the stabilization phase, each team member has a specific responsibility to the project. Table 13.1 illustrates the team roles and responsibilities during the stabilization phase.

Setting Up The Testing Environment

Before testing can begin, the logistics management team must create and set up the technology infrastructure, including the hardware and software components

Table 13.1   Team roles and responsibilities during the stabilization phase.

Team Role	Responsibility
Product management	Coordinates the beta test sites with the users, communicates project status, and markets the product to potential customers
Program management	Manages the beta testing process, tracks the schedule, and reports project status
Development	Fixes bugs and releases versions of the product
User education	Creates user documentation, including manuals and Help systems, and trains users
Testing	Creates test plans and test procedures, runs the tests, and reports bugs to development
Logistics management	Sets up the testing infrastructure and support system, and deploys the product

needed to test the system using its targeted platforms. For example, in the CTIS system, students and instructors use Windows 98 and Pentium computers at the college to do their work. Therefore, logistics management sets up a testing lab with Pentium computers running Windows 98. The CTIS system itself needs Pentium-class computers running Windows NT, so the lab contains Pentium computers running Windows NT to host the system. As a member of the logistics management team, your job is to test the system in an environment similar to the user's. Do not use the development environment to test the system, because it doesn't emulate the user's environment. After logistics management sets up the testing environment, the testing process can begin.

13

AN INTRODUCTION TO THE TESTING PROCESS

The testing process is the part of the software development life cycle that validates the software against the requirements as defined in the planning phase. The testing team tests every feature of the software, such as menus, dialog boxes, and data entry and validation, in an attempt to find errors in the system. Testing a system is an iterative process, meaning that one round of tests results in a list of errors, which development resolves, and another round of tests begins. The testing team is independent of the development team so that they can maintain their objectivity, making sure the product meets the original specifications. An independent team helps to ensure that you deliver a quality product.

As a member of the testing team, you must accomplish the following tasks during the testing process:

➤ **Create a test plan**   Create a test plan that describes testing strategies for each feature in the functional specification and use cases, such as manually entering data and selecting menus and menu options, or using automation tools to assist in the testing process. Define with development how to track and report bugs and manage software releases. Determine the technology infrastructure needed to test the system. For example, the test plan for the CTIS system outlines how to test its features, including the login process. Testers will enter known usernames in the database for students and instructors, and then enter unknown usernames to make sure that only the appropriate people can access CTIS.

➤ **Create a test specification** After product management approves the test plan, create a test specification for each requirement that includes the initial list of use cases and a plan on how to test the requirement. For example, one requirement in CTIS is that students and instructors have access to separate parts of the system. Supply a specification to test for valid and invalid students and instructors, and to verify that the functionality meets the requirement.

➤ **Create the test cases** Once product management approves the test specification, create test cases for each requirement. Test cases are step-by-step instructions for testing a requirement. Use the functional requirements to develop test cases. Consult case scenarios, such as those you created in Chapter 4, to assist you in creating the test cases. Figure 13.1 shows an example of a test case of the authentication use case for a student login, created in Chapter 4.

You know that someone can log on to CTIS as either a student or an instructor. This test case illustrates the login process for a student. It tests for unsuccessful and successful logins. The first column of the test case indicates whether the step passes or fails. The second column shows the actual step, and the last column shows the response to the step when carried out successfully.

➤ **Run the test cases** During the development process, the development team releases a new version of code that contains several features. This is called an internal release. Your job is to map the features to the requirements and to run the test cases associated with the release. You work through the test case with the software. If the test case passes, meaning that the software works as described in the test case, you approve the requirement. If the test case fails, you create a bug report, also called a change request (CR) or problem report (PR). Bug reports are discussed in more detail in "Reporting Bugs in Releases" later in this chapter. You pass the bug reports to development so they can fix the code accordingly.

➤ **Regression testing** After the development team fixes a bug in the software, they release another version of the software. Your job is to rerun the test cases to make sure that changes did not affect other parts of the system.

Types Of Tests

In the previsous sections, you examined how to set up the testing environment and the testing process. You will now review the types of tests used in the testing process: coverage and usability. The goal of coverage testing is to test every feature against every requirement of the product during the developing phase. Examples of coverage testing are unit tests performed by the developer; functional tests or feature tests that ensure that features are present and working; check-in tests to make sure that changes do not affect other code; and regression tests, which are a suite of automated tests that makes sure the code is stable.

The goal of usability testing is to test against the use case scenarios during the stabilization phase. Examples of usability testing are configuration tests that ensure that the product runs on the targeted hardware platform; compatibility tests to find bugs in the way the program works with other programs; stress tests to find bugs under severe operating conditions; performance tests to document the speed of the application; documentation and Help file tests to check the functionality of each link in the Help files; and alpha and beta tests, in which users work with preliminary versions of the application. Alpha and beta tests can take months to complete, depending upon the number of issues and bug reports that arise from the testing process.

Managing Releases In A Software Development Project

During the testing process, the testing team accepts releases from the development team. Software releases are given special version numbers, which are used to track the release during testing. The version number has a special format: <major>.<minor>.<revision>. An example of a version number is

13

Authentication Test Case – Student Login		
Pass/Fail	Step	Response
_____1.	Start CTIS	Login screen appears
_____2.	Log on to CTIS as a student, with username aaa and no password	An error page appears
_____3.	Click link to log on again	The login screen appears
_____4.	Log on to CTIS as a student, with username student1 and no password	The Student menu page appears

Figure 13.1 Test case of the login process for a student.

1.1.50. The first 1 signifies the release of a project that contains new and significantly enhanced features, and the second 1 signifies a minor release in a project. For example, after the golden release, you might have to supply patches or small bug fixes. To track these releases, increment the <minor> version number by one, to 1.2.50, for example. The 50 signifies the number of internal releases to fix bugs reported during a project. The way these numbers are incremented is determined company by company.

A typical software development project includes the following interim releases:

➤ **Internal releases** The development team delivers several internal releases to the testing team for acceptance. The testing team runs the test cases created for the requirements in the internal releases.

➤ **Alpha** An alpha is a release of the software that meets all the features and requirements of the project. The testing team continues to run test cases with the alpha releases. When they complete all the test cases, they validate the alpha release, reaching the scope complete/first use milestone of the developing phase. This signals the end of the developing phase.

➤ **Betas** The stabilization phase starts with the delivery of the first beta version of the software. As defined earlier, a beta is a release deployed to external beta test sites for user testing.

➤ **Release candidates** The development team releases a beta version of the software that is a *release candidate*, a software release close to the final version. The testing team verifies and tests the release candidate for any outstanding problems. A version number distinguishes the different releases of the software.

➤ **Golden release** The golden release is the final release of the product that will be deployed to the user by logistics management and is expressed as Version 1.0.

Reporting Bugs In Releases

As the development team releases software versions, and as testers accept releases after testing, the testing team reports bugs in the software to the development team. A *bug* is a controversial issue in the software that may or may not be a defect that represents a noncompliance with the requirements.

Examples of bugs that are defects:

➤ **Crashes** A test case causes the software to *crash*, which means that the software application stops running.

➤ **Requirement noncompliance** A test case causes a noncompliance with a requirement. A requirement states one thing while the software does another.

Examples of bugs that are not defects:

➤ **Enhancements** Suggestions by users or testers that would enhance the functionality of the system.

➤ **User issues** Suggestions by users that reflect their personal preferences for working with the application.

➤ **Design issues** Observations by users that a feature does not function as they expected it to, because of design decisions made during the design process. At this point in the software development process, design flaws cannot be fixed, and these changes are normally postponed until the next release.

When testers find a bug, they report it in a database, such as Microsoft Access, or on a manual form. This bug report contains information about the test case that revealed the bug, a description of the bug, the sequence of events that resulted in the bug, and the severity and priority of the bug. The severity levels are as follows:

➤ **Severity 1 — system crash** The system crashes, hangs, or stops working and requires either a warm or cold start to recover from the problem.

➤ **Severity 2 — major problem** The software has a serious problem either because of general protection faults, which may not always cause the system to crash, or because it does not operate as defined in the requirements, which does not cause the system to crash, but could cause loss of data or work.

➤ **Severity 3 — minor problem** The software has a defect in function that reflects a minor discrepancy between the documentation and the actual operation.

➤ **Severity 4 — trivial problem** The software has a cosmetic problem such as a misspelling in an error message. Severity 4 bugs also include enhancements or suggestions.

After identifying the severity of a bug, testers also assign a priority for fixing the bug. The priority levels are as follows:

➤ **Priority 1 — highest priority** The bug can be reproduced by following a simple sequence of events and must be fixed before the software can be released. The fix is obvious.

➤ **Priority 2 — high priority** The bug can be reproduced by following a complex sequence of events and should be fixed before the software is released. The fix is obvious.

13

➤ **Priority 3 — medium priority** The bug can only be reproduced intermittently, following a complex sequence of events, and does not need to be fixed before the software is released. A fix is not obvious.

➤ **Priority 4 — low priority** The bug is very difficult to reproduce, occurs only intermittently, and does not need to be fixed before the software is released. A fix is not obvious.

A team of developers and testers meets and discusses bug reports. The development manager prioritizes the bug reports and assigns them to developers to fix. When the bugs are resolved, the bug report is given a state. The bug report states are as follows:

➤ **As fixed** The developer fixes the bugs, tests the resolution, checks in the new code, assigns the fix to a release, and reassigns the bug to the tester.

➤ **As duplicated** The bug is a duplicate of another bug, which is resolved.

➤ **As postponed** The bug will be fixed in another release.

➤ **By design** The bug is intentional and agrees with the requirements.

➤ **Can't reproduce** The bug cannot be verified, meaning it cannot be reproduced.

➤ **Won't fix** The bug will not be fixed at all. This is an issue beyond the development team's control.

When the tester verifies that the bug has been fixed, the tester closes the bug report for the problem being tested.

DEPLOYING THE SYSTEM

During the stabilization phase, the logistics management team deploys the beta software versions to the users after the testing team accepts the releases. Depending on the type of application you create, logistics management creates installation packages for the released code. The types of applications are:

➤ **Single-tier** The application exists on a single machine and normally is a "traditional" application such as Microsoft Office. The logistics team needs to create a single installation package.

➤ **Two-tier** The application is split across two machines. Therefore, the logistics team needs to create two installation packages—one for the client and one for the server.

➤ **Three-tier** The application is split across three machines. Therefore, the logistics team needs to create three installation packages, one for each machine.

➤ **N-tier** The application is split across a number of machines, so the logistics team needs to create an installation package for each one.

For each application type, this book considers a system to consist of three services—user, business, and data. This means that the logistics management team needs to consider how to deploy the database, the business components, and the user interface.

You can use the following techniques to deploy an application:

➤ **Database deployment** When deploying a system, the database administrator uses a set of SQL scripts to create the database, tables, and stored procedures used when developing the software. If you are deploying an upgrade to a current system, you need to create an upgrade program that migrates the old database schema into the new database schema, and migrates the old data into the new database schema. This can be a difficult and time-consuming task.

➤ **Component deployment** When deploying components, you can use MTS Explorer to create new components, export packages from an existing computer, and import packages into a new computer. You can also create an automated setup program through Visual Basic to install components automatically.

 Refer to the Microsoft Transaction Server Help files in MTS Explorer to learn how to deploy MTS packages.

13

➤ **"Traditional" application deployment** When deploying a traditional Visual Basic application, such as a client/server application, you can use the Package and Deployment Wizard to create the setup program to deploy the application from a CD, file server, or Web server.

➤ **Web application deployment** When using Visual Interdev, you can deploy your Web applications onto the Web server of your choice directly through the Visual Interdev environment. If you create a Web project in Visual SourceSafe, you can deploy Web applications directly from Visual SourceSafe.

 Refer to the MSDN Library to learn how to use the Package and Deployment Wizard to create a setup program, and how to deploy Web applications using Visual Interdev and Visual SourceSafe.

When you are deploying a system, you need to make sure that you are deploying to the appropriate environment. You should create an environment for various teams to use: development during software development, testing during beta testing, and production during the final release. Do not deploy a system into the development environment, because the code changes continuously, making the environment unstable for formal testing.

Consider the example of CTIS deployment. CTIS is a hybrid system that consists of "traditional" applications, a Web application, and MTS components, but is mainly a Web application that uses MTS components. You can also use "traditional" applications to administer CTIS. Chapter 10 reviewed a system administrator application that created user accounts. To deploy the MTS components, use MTS Explorer and export the CTIS package. This creates a directory with all the components and the information needed to import these components into another server, if necessary. To deploy the CTIS Web application, you can use either Visual Interdev or Visual SourceSafe. If you need to deploy the "traditional" application from Chapter 10, then use the Visual Studio Package and Deployment Wizard. In summary, your deployment plan for CTIS would be to deploy the components with MTS Explorer, import the components into another server, if necessary, and deploy the CTIS Web application using Visual SourceSafe.

CHAPTER SUMMARY

This chapter completes the software development process using Microsoft Solutions Framework (MSF), by finishing the developing and stabilization phases. The testing and logistics management teams manage the end of the developing phase and the complete stabilization phase of MSF. The testing team makes sure the product is stable and reliable enough for delivery to the customer. Although it may take months of testing and retesting, a detailed and well-documented testing process ensures a quality product at the release milestone. After testing is complete, the logistics management team creates the installation packages, deploys the application to the user, and trains team members to staff the Help desk to support the application. Other team members review the bug reports to identify design changes and enhancements, and to prepare for the next release.

Throughout this book, you have investigated how MSF fits into the software development life cycle. You examined different hardware, software, and communications technologies you can use to deliver your products, and different Microsoft software technologies that you can use to create products. You learned how to design a system using the three services—user, business, and data—and the conceptual, logical, and physical design models. You also used UML to document your system graphically by hand and with Visual Modeler. You surveyed techniques for creating databases, components, and user interfaces.

You saw how online Help and localization integrate into the software development process. You also reviewed how to test and deploy software in a project. Overall, software development is a complicated, ever-changing process with high standards for success. As you complete each project, you learn fundamental lessons about how to improve the process. If you apply these lessons and adapt to changing requirements and designs, your software development projects will be successful ones.

REVIEW QUESTIONS

1. Which teams drive the stabilization phase? Choose all that apply.
    a. logistics management
    b. user education
    c. testing
    d. development

2. The stabilization phase ends in which milestone?
    a. release
    b. vision/scope approved
    c. scope complete/first use
    d. project plan approved

3. Which team is responsible for setting up the environment for testing in MSF?
    a. testing
    b. logistics management
    c. user education
    d. development

13

4. _____ are step-by-step instructions on how to test a requirement.
    a. Test specifications
    b. Regression tests
    c. Test plans
    d. Test cases

5. Releasing code to the testing team that contains some features, but not all of them, is called a(n) _____ release.
    a. golden
    b. alpha
    c. internal
    d. beta

6. _____ testing means testing every feature against every requirement of the product.

   a. Coverage

   b. Regression

   c. Usage

   d. Beta

7. _____ testing means testing against the use case scenarios.

   a. Usage

   b. Coverage

   c. Regression

   d. Beta

8. When the stabilization phase begins, a(n) _____ release is delivered to users for testing.

   a. alpha

   b. internal

   c. beta

   d. golden

9. A _____ is a controversial issue in software that may or may not be a defect.

   a. crash

   b. bug

   c. flaw

   d. none of the above

Hands-On Projects

Project 13.1

Compare and contrast the different types of tests in the testing process.

Project 13.2

Explain what a bug is. Give examples of bugs. Explain the bug reporting process.

Project 13.3
Explain the job of a tester.

Project 13.4
Explain the job of a member of the logistics management team.

Project 13.5
Create and run test cases for the following CTIS subsystems, using the techniques described in this chapter.

a. Student Management

b. Instructor Management

c. Assignment Management

d. Grades Management

e. Course Management

Project 13.6
Investigate how to use the Package and Deployment Wizard with the SDI application in Chapter 10. Create a step-by-step procedure to create a setup program from a folder.

Project 13.7
Investigate how to deploy a Web application (Chapter 11) using Visual Interdev. Create a step-by-step procedure to deploy the Web application to a Web server.

13

Project 13.8
Investigate how to deploy a Web application using Visual SourceSafe. Create a step-by-step procedure to deploy the Web application to a Web server.

Project 13.9
Investigate how to deploy MTS components using MTS Explorer. Create a step-by-step procedure to deploy the MTS components onto another server.

PREPARE FOR MICROSOFT CERTIFIED SOLUTIONS DEVELOPER MCSD EXAM 70-100

BOOK AND EXAM EXPERIENCE LEVEL

The goal of this book is to prepare you for the MCSD Exam 70-100 by teaching you how to design and create client/server applications. The MCSD certification prepares you to use Microsoft solutions to solve business problems as part of the software development process, and introduces you to related technologies.

This book is designed for someone who already has the following skills:

➤ Knowledge of computer systems fundamentals, including hardware and software

➤ Introductory knowledge of Visual Basic and the ability to create Visual Basic applications

➤ Introductory knowledge of database concepts and how to create simple databases

➤ User knowledge of Windows 95

➤ User knowledge of Microsoft Office

➤ User knowledge of Internet browsing and HTML

➤ User knowledge of email

In its Exam Preparation Guide, Microsoft also recommends that you have at least two years experience in the following areas:

➤ Analyzing customer needs and creating requirement specification documents for client/server solutions

➤ Creating process models, data models, components, and user interfaces

➤ Designing, developing, and implementing a client/server solution using Microsoft Windows and the Web

➤ Working with Microsoft Office and Microsoft Back Office

➤ Integrating new systems and applications into legacy environments

This book will help you gain the experience you need to successfully pass this exam and use Microsoft technologies in designing and creating solutions for customers. Use this book to practice Microsoft's suggested skills.

Exam Matrix

Table A.1 Mapping Exam 70-100 to the contents of *Architectures Exam Prep.*

Skills Measured By Exam 70-100	Chapter Cross-References
Analyzing Business Requirements	4
Analyze the scope of a project. Considerations include:	
Existing applications	
Anticipated changes in environment	
Expected lifetime of solution	
Time, cost, budget, and benefit trade-offs	
Analyze the extent of a business requirement	4
Establish type of problem, such as messaging problem or communication problem	
Establish business requirements	
Minimize total cost of ownership (TCO)	
Increase return on investment (ROI) of solution	
Analyze current platform and infrastructure	
Incorporate planned platform and infrastructure	
Incorporate planned platform and infrastructure into solution	
Analyze impact of technology migration	
Plan physical requirements, such as infrastructure	
Establish application environment, such as hardware platform, support, and operating system	
Identify organizational constraints, such as financial situation, company politics, technical acceptance level, and training needs	
Establish schedule for implementation of solution	
Identify audience	
Analyze security requirements	4
Identify roles of administration, groups, guests, and clients	
Identify impact on existing environment	
Establish fault tolerance	
Plan for maintainability	
Plan distribution of security context	
Plan for auditing	
Identify level of security needed	
Analyze existing mechanisms for security policies	

(continued)

Table A.1   Mapping Exam 70-100 to the contents of *Architectures Exam Prep* *(continued)*.

Skills Measured By Exam 70-100	Chapter Cross-References
Analyze performance requirements	4
Considerations include:	
Transactions per time slice	
Bandwidth	
Capacity	
Interoperability with existing standards	
Peak versus average requirements	
Response-time expectations	
Existing response-time characteristics	
Barriers to performance	
Analyze maintainability requirements	4
Considerations include:	
Breadth of application distribution	
Method of distribution	
Maintenance expectations	
Location and knowledge level of maintenance staff	
Impact of third-party maintenance agreements	
Analyze extensibility requirements. Solution must be able to handle the growth of functionality	4
Analyze availability requirements	4
Considerations include:	
Hours of operation	
Level of availability	
Geographic scope	
Impact of downtime	
Analyze human factors requirements.	4
Considerations include:	
Target users	
Localization	
Accessibility	
Roaming users	
Help	
Training requirements	
Physical environment constraints	
Special needs	

(continued)

Table A.1   Mapping Exam 70-100 to the contents of *Architectures Exam Prep* (continued).

Skills Measured By Exam 70-100	Chapter Cross-References
Analyze the requirements for integrating a solution with existing applications. Considerations include:	4
Legacy applications	
Format and location of existing data	
Connectivity to existing applications	
Data conversion	
Data enhancement requirements	
Analyze existing methodologies and limitations of a business	4
Considerations include:	
Legal issues	
Current business practices	
Organization structure	
Process engineering	
Budget	
Implementation and training methodologies	
Quality control requirements	
Customer's needs	
Analyze scalability requirements.	4
Considerations include:	
Growth of audience	
Growth of organization	
Growth of data	
Cycle of use	

Defining The Technical Architecture For A Solution	Chapter Cross-Reference
Given a business scenario, identify which solution type is appropriate. Solution types are single-tier, two-tier, and n-tier	2, 3, 5
Identify which technologies are appropriate for the implementation of a given business solution	2, 3, 5
Considerations include:	
Technology standards such as EDI, Internet, OSI, COMTI, and POSIX	
Proprietary technologies	
Technology environment of the company, both current and planned	
Selection of development tools	
Type of solution, such as enterprise, distributed, centralized, or collaborative	

(continued)

Table A.1   Mapping Exam 70-100 to the contents of *Architectures Exam Prep* *(continued)*.

Defining The Technical Architecture For A Solution	Chapter Cross-Reference
Choose a data-storage architecture Considerations include:	4, 5, 6
Volume	
Number of transactions per time increment	
Number of connections or sessions	
Scope of business requirements	
Extensibility requirements	
Reporting requirements	
Number of users	
Type of database	
Test the feasibility of a proposed technical architecture	13
Demonstrate that business requirements are met	
Demonstrate that use case scenarios are met	
Demonstrate that existing technology constraints are met	
Assess impact of shortfalls in meeting requirements	
Develop appropriate deployment strategy	13

Developing The Conceptual And Logical Design For An Application	Chapter Cross Reference
Construct a conceptual design based on a variety of scenarios that include context, workflow process, task sequence, and physical environment models. Types of applications include:	4, 5
SDI, MDI, console, and dialog desktop applications	
Two-tier, client/server, and Web applications	
N-tier applications	
Collaborative applications	
Given a conceptual design, apply the principles of modular design to derive the components and services of the logical design	5
Incorporate business rules into object design	5, 6
Assess the potential impact of the logical design on performance, maintainability, extensibility, scalability, availability, and security	5, 6

Developing Data Models	Chapter Cross Reference
Group data into entities by applying normalization rules	5
Specify the relationships between entities	5
Choose the foreign key that will enforce a relationship between entities and will ensure referential integrity	5

(continued)

Table A.1 Mapping Exam 70-100 to the contents of *Architectures Exam Prep* (continued).

Developing Data Models	Chapter Cross Reference
Identify the business rules that relate to data integrity	5
Incorporate business rules and constraints into the data model	5
Identify appropriate level of denormalization	5
Develop a database that uses general database development standards and guidelines	5, 6, 8

Designing A User Interface And User Services	Chapter Cross Reference
Given a solution, identify the navigation for the user interface	10, 11
Identify input validation procedures that should be integrated into the user interface	10, 11
Evaluate methods of providing online user assistance, such as status bars, ToolTips, and Help files	10, 11, 12
Construct a prototype user interface based on business requirements, user interface guidelines, and the organization's standards	10, 11
Establish appropriate and consistent use of menu-based controls	
Establish appropriate shortcut keys (accelerated keys)	
Establish appropriate type of output	10, 11

Deriving The Physical Design	Chapter Cross Reference
Assess the potential impact of the physical design on performance, maintainability, extensibility, scalability, availability, and security	6
Evaluate whether access to a database should be encapsulated in an object	9
Design the properties, methods, and events of components	9

AN INTRODUCTION TO SQL SERVER ADMINISTRATION

SQL Server is a database managed by an administrator who is responsible for designing and creating databases and tables, backing up, restoring, and monitoring the database, and performing other database-related tasks. As a software developer, you usually interact with your database administrator to take care of these common administration tasks. However, to use this book effectively, you must be able to perform database tasks on your own. This appendix shows you how to create, restore, and back up an SQL Server database.

APPENDIX OVERVIEW

Throughout this book, you use SQL Server as your database management system. To use this book effectively, you must learn a few SQL Server administration tasks. Before working on the procedures and exercises in this book, you must create and restore a database. To protect your data, you must also back up your database on a regular basis.

INTRODUCTION TO SQL SERVER ENTERPRISE MANAGER

SQL Server Enterprise Manager is a graphical tool that allows you to configure, manage, and maintain SQL Server databases. You will use SQL Server Enterprise Manager to manage SQL Server and its databases. Figure B.1 illustrates the SQL Server Enterprise Manager environment.

SQL Server Enterprise Manager is an administrative console tool that runs in *Microsoft's Management Console (MMC)*, an application that manages the hardware, software, and network components of different Windows operating systems. It provides a common interface to run all administrative tools, integrates administrative tools, configures the tools on different components, and saves configurations for use on other computers. The left pane in Enterprise Manager is the MMC Console tree, which provides a hierarchical view of the components in the SQL Server environment. Right-click an item in the Console tree to see a shortcut menu of related commands. The right pane is the Details window, which provides detailed information on the selected item in the Console tree.

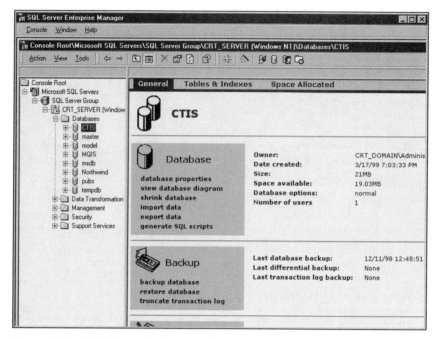

Figure B.1 SQL Server Enterprise Manager environment.

Creating A Database

Now that you're familiar with SQL Server Enterprise Manager, you can use it to create a database in SQL Server for CTIS.

 If you created the CTIS database when you installed SQL Server, then do not create it again. You can skip the following steps.

To create the CTIS database in SQL Server, if necessary:

1. Click the Start menu. Point to Programs, then to Microsoft SQL Server 7.0, and then click Enterprise Manager.
2. Expand the Microsoft SQL Servers folder in the MMC Console tree, if necessary.
3. Expand the SQL Server Group folder.
4. Expand your server folder. (If you do not know your server name, right-click Network Neighborhood on the Windows desktop. In the Identification tab, your server name is the Computer Name.)
5. Expand the Database folder.
6. If the CTIS database is not listed under Databases, right-click Databases, and then click New Database on the shortcut menu.

7. In the Name text box, type "CTIS", and then click OK to create the CTIS database.CTIS is the database you use in this book to assist you in creating the CTIS system.

8. Open the Databases folder, if necessary, to verify that the CTIS database exists.

Restoring A Database

You have successfully created the CTIS database in SQL Server. Your next task is to restore the current database from the CD to use throughout this book. You need to restore the CTIS database from the CD to complete the procedures beginning in Chapter 8.

To restore the CTIS database:

1. From the Appendix_B folder on the CD, use Windows Explorer to copy the CTIS.zip file to the c:\mssql7\backup folder.

2. Double-click CTIS.zip to unzip it and extract all the files to the c:\mssq l7\backup folder. You need a copy of WinZip or other compatible software to unzip the file.

3. In Enterprise Manager, expand the Databases folder, if necessary.

4. Right-click CTIS in the MMC Console tree. Point to All Tasks and click Restore Database. The Restore Database dialog box appears. Use this dialog box to choose the backup file from which you will restore.

5. In the Restore option group, click From Device.

6. In the Parameters section, click Select Devices.

7. In the Restore From section, click Add.

8. In the Filename text box, type "c:\mssql7\backup\CTIS.dmp".

9. Click OK to close the Choose Restore Definition dialog box.

10. Click OK in the Choose Restore Devices dialog box.

11. Click the Options tab, and then click the Force Restore Over Existing Database checkbox (to check it) to overwrite the current database with the backup.

12. If necessary, change the text in the Move to physical file name column to the following:
c:\mssql7\data\CTIS.mdf

c:\mssql7\data\CTIS_log.ldf

13. Click the General tab.

14. If necessary, change the text in the Restore as Database text box to "CTIS".

15. Click OK to restore the database.

16. In the Restore Of Database 'CTIS' Completed Successfully dialog box, click OK.

17. Expand the CTIS database and click Tables.

18. Verify that eight new tables of type user were restored.

Backing Up A Database

To protect yourself from lost data, get in the habit of periodically backing up your database. It is good practice to back up after each chapter.

To back up the CTIS database in SQL Server:

1. Right-click CTIS in the MMC Console tree. Point to All Tasks and click Backup Database. The SQL Server Backup dialog box appears.

2. If necessary, change the database name to "CTIS".

3. In the Destination section, select the first item, c:\MSSQL7\backup\ CTIS.dmp, in the list box, and then click the Remove button to delete the old backup file.

4. In the Destination section, click Add to add the file to which you want to back up.

5. In the Choose Backup Destination dialog box, type "c:\mssql7\backup\ CTIS_031599.dmp (where *031599* is the date of the current backup)" in the File text box.

6. Click OK.

7. In the Overwrite section, select Overwrite existing media to create a clean backup of the entire database.

8. Click OK in the SQL Server Backup dialog box to back up the database, and then click OK at the confirmation dialog box.

9. On the Console menu, click Exit to exit SQL Server Enterprise Manager.

10. Verify that a file CTIS_031599.dmp (where *031599* is the current date) exists in the c:\MSSQL7\backup folder.

This appendix demonstrates common database tasks in SQL Server that you need to understand to complete this book. Refer to the SQL Server online documentation to learn about other database management tasks in SQL Server, such as setting up SQL Server security for new users and roles.

APPENDIX C

DATABASE TABLES

APPENDIX C OVERVIEW

This appendix surveys the different tables in CTIS and their layouts. You will use this appendix to help you write queries in Chapter 8.

CATEGORIES TABLE

Figure C.1 shows the table layout of the CATEGORIES table. This table tracks the different categories in an instructor's grading policy. QUIZZES is an example of a category.

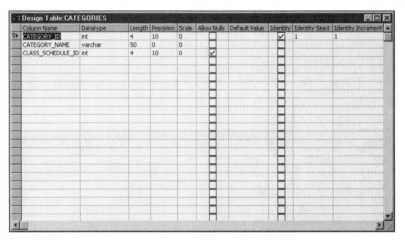

Figure C.1   CATEGORIES table layout.

CLASS_SCHEDULE Table

Figure C.2 shows the table layout of the CLASS_SCHEDULE table. The CLASS_SCHEDULE table tracks the different times each class is offered.

Design Table:CLASS_SCHEDULE

Column Name	Datatype	Length	Precision	Scale	Allow Nulls	Default Value	Identity	Identity Seed	Identity Increment
CLASS_SCHEDULE_ID	int	4	10	0			✓	1	1
SECTION	varchar	10	0	0	✓				
YEAR	varchar	4	0	0	✓				
TERM	varchar	6	0	0	✓				
CLASS_ID	int	4	10	0	✓				
INSTRUCTOR_ID	int	4	10	0	✓				

Figure C.2   CLASS_SCHEDULE table layout.

CLASSES Table

Figure C.3 shows the table layout of the CLASSES table. CLASSES tracks the class numbers and names for all classes offered.

Design Table:CLASSES

Column Name	Datatype	Length	Precision	Scale	Allow Nulls	Default Value	Identity	Identity Seed	Identity Increment
CLASS_ID	int	4	10	0			✓	1	1
CLASS_NUMBER	varchar	7	0	0					
CLASS_NAME	varchar	50	0	0					

Figure C.3   CLASSES table layout.

GRADE_DISTRIBUTIONS TABLE

Figure C.4 shows the table layout of the GRADE_DISTRIBUTIONS table. This table defines the instructor's grading policy for a class.

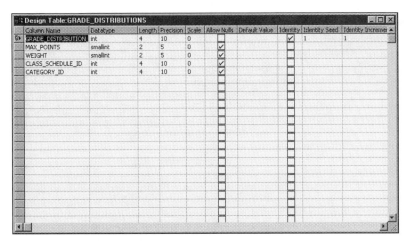

Figure C.4   GRADE_DISTRIBUTIONS table layout.

GRADES TABLE

Figure C.5 shows the table layout of the GRADES table. The GRADES table allows the instructor to track the different grades for each category for a student.

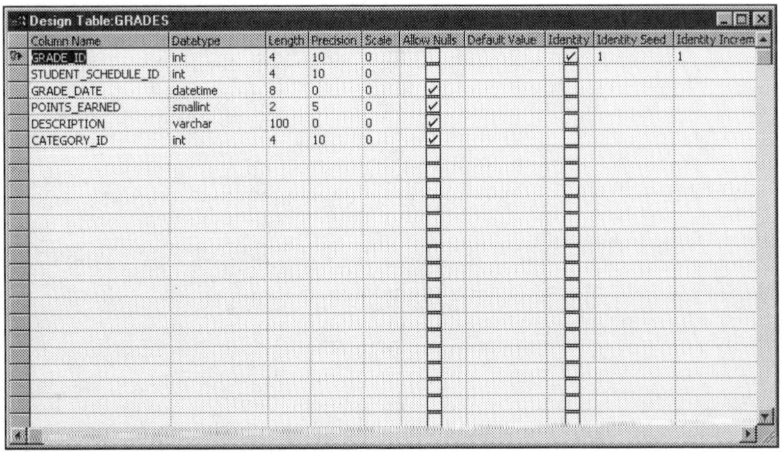

Figure C.5   GRADES table layout.

INSTRUCTORS TABLE

Figure C.6 shows the table layout of the INSTRUCTORS table. This table lists the instructors and their personal information.

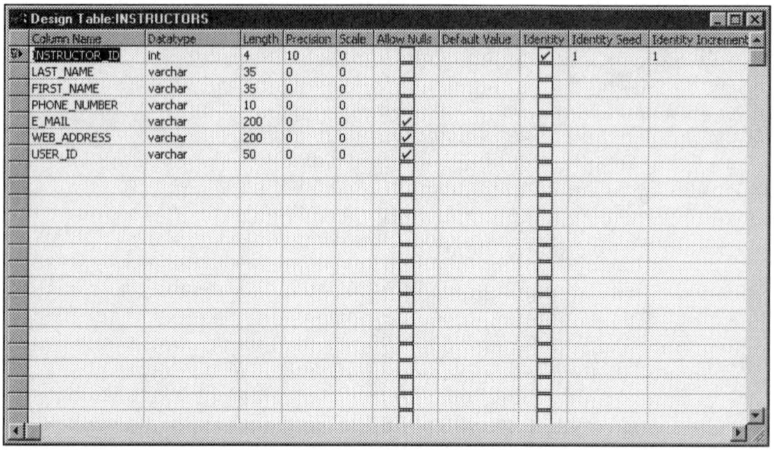

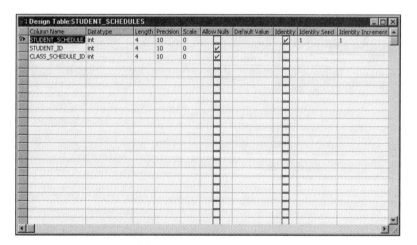

Figure C.6 INSTRUCTORS table layout.

STUDENT_SCHEDULES TABLE

Figure C.7 shows the table layout of the STUDENT_SCHEDULES table. This table supplies information about the classes the students are taking.

Figure C.7 STUDENT_SCHEDULES table layout.

STUDENTS TABLE

Figure C.8 shows the table layout of the STUDENTS table. The STUDENTS table lists the students and their personal information.

Column Name	Datatype	Length	Precision	Scale	Allow Nulls	Default Value	Identity	Identity Seed	Identity Increment
STUDENT_ID	int	4	10	0			✓	1	1
LAST_NAME	varchar	35	0	0					
FIRST_NAME	varchar	35	0	0					
E_MAIL	varchar	200	0	0	✓				
HOME_PHONE	varchar	10	0	0	✓				
WORK_PHONE	varchar	10	0	0	✓				
USER_ID	varchar	50	0	0	✓				

Figure C.8   STUDENTS table layout.

MCSD REQUIREMENTS

MCSD Requirements*

Core

Choose 1 from the desktop applications development group	
Exam 70-016	Designing and Implementing Desktop Applications with Microsoft Visual C++ 6.0
Exam 70-176	Designing and Implementing Desktop Applications with Microsoft Visual Basic 6.0
Choose 1 from the distributed applications development group	
Exam 70-015	Designing and Implementing Distributed Applications with Microsoft Visual C++ 6.0
Exam 70-175	Designing and Implementing Distributed Applications with Microsoft Visual Basic 6.0
This solution architecture exam is required	
Exam 70-100	Analyzing Requirements and Defining Solution Architectures

Elective

Choose 1 from this group	
Exam 70-015	Designing and Implementing Distributed Applications with Microsoft Visual C++ 6.0
Exam 70-016	Designing and Implementing Desktop Applications with Microsoft Visual C++ 6.0
Exam 70-029	Designing and Implementing Databases with Microsoft SQL Server 7.0
Exam 70-024	Developing Applications with C++ Using the Microsoft Foundation Class Library
Exam 70-025	Implementing OLE in Microsoft Foundation Class Applications
Exam 70-055	Designing and Implementing Web Sites with Microsoft FrontPage 98
Exam 70-057	Designing and Implementing Commerce Solutions with Microsoft Site Server 3.0, Commerce Edition
Exam 70-165	Developing Applications with Microsoft Visual Basic 5.0
	OR
Exam 70-175	Designing and Implementing Distributed Applications with Microsoft Visual Basic 6.0
	OR
Exam 70-176	Designing and Implementing Desktop Applications with Microsoft Visual Basic 6.0
Exam 70-069	Application Development with Microsoft Access for Windows 95 and the Microsoft Access Developer's Toolkit
Exam 70-091	Designing and Implementing Solutions with Microsoft Office 2000 and Microsoft Visual Basic for Applications
Exam 70-152	Designing and Implementing Web Solutions with Microsoft Visual InterDev 6.0

* This is not a complete listing—you can still be tested on some earlier versions of these products. However, we have tried to include the most recent versions so that you may test on these versions and thus be certified longer. We have not included any tests that are scheduled to be retired.

The MCSD program is being expanded to include FoxPro and Visual J++. However, these tests are not yet available and no test numbers have been assigned.

Core exams that can also be used as elective exams can be counted only once toward certification. The same test cannot be used as both a core and elective exam.

GLOSSARY

access modifiers
Modifiers that provide a special service by returning the contents of an attribute and assigning a value to the attribute.

activity diagram
A UML diagram that captures an operation as a set of actions.

aggregation
Making one class a part of another class.

application
A program separate from the operating system that users run to complete common tasks.

application localization
The process of adapting software to a locale.

application standards
These standards show how an application looks, feels, and interacts with a user.

asynchronous communication
Communication in which the client process and the server process do not need to be running at the same time.

auditing
The ability of a system to write security events to a file to track what users do in the system.

back end
The part of the application that runs on the server.

behavior
Defines all actions of an object.

browser
Allows you to see and access text and graphics on the Internet.

bug
A controversial issue in the software that may or may not be a defect and that represents noncompliance with the requirements.

business rules
Informal or formal rules or procedures for running a business.

business service
Part of an application that supplies business rules that transform data into information. Usually interacts with the user service.

class diagram
A UML diagram that captures the static structure of the objects and the relationships between objects.

clients
Specialized computers that request resources from the server through a network.

collaboration diagram
A UML diagram that captures the structure of objects, links, and interactions. It is similar to a sequence diagram.

collection
A special data type in Visual Basic that defines a dynamic list of items.

411

column attribute
A basic category; part of a table in a database that includes the attributes of a field.

communication services
Allow different systems to communicate with each other.

component
A self-contained precompiled software unit (code) that can be reused in one or more applications.

component diagram
A UML diagram that captures the physical representation of the objects in an application.

components
Contain one or more classes from the logical design and instructions to the development team on how to package them.

conceptual design perspective
During the planning phase of the process model, a perspective that developers use to fully understand the user's needs and to produce a set of models to illustrate this understanding.

constraint
A business rule that restricts the column or the table.

control
A user interface object.

cooperative multitasking
A method of multitasking in which applications yield control to other applications.

coverage testing
Testing every feature and every requirement in the functional requirements specification.

cursor
A group of rows returned from a query that allows you to scroll the group one row at a time, and do row-by-row processing of the database.

data
Raw facts that have no meaning on their own.

data communication
Electronic communication that transfers information in binary form between two computer devices.

data environment
An interactive design environment to create run-time access to data.

data service
Service that provides the mechanism for manipulating data.

database
An organized collection of data.

database service
A mechanism to store and retrieve information, such as accounting and financial data.

deployment diagram
A UML diagram that captures the deployment of objects on different hardware.

design-time controls
Part of the Visual Interdev environment that allows for automatic script generation that connects and interacts with a database.

device driver
Software that interacts with the hardware and network access protocol.

early binding
When an application resolves a variable at compile time.

email service
Allows you to exchange electronic mail.

encapsulation
The process of packaging attributes and services that are hidden from the external world.

entity
A person, place, object, event, or idea for which you want to store and process information.

events
Actions by the user or by objects to communicate with a form or other objects.

field
A basic category; part of a table in a database.

file service
Allows anyone with access to a server to store and retrieve files.

foreign key
The column that joins two or more tables together.

front end
The part of the application that runs on the client.

full-duplex
A dialog in which data is transmitted and received at the same time.

functional specification
A document that defines a product or service, created in the planning phase of the MSF Process model.

Gantt chart
A simple schedule that shows the phases, activities, and tasks of a project in calendar form.

half-duplex
A two-way communication in which data is transmitted and received alternately (not at the same time).

handshaking
Process in which once the computers are connected and data is transmitted, the receiving computer decides to accept or reject the data.

hub
A special network device that connects clients, servers, and printers. It manages communication between devices on the network.

hybrids
Special networks that are client/server networks and also peer networks.

information
Output from the computer that has meaning to the user; data processed by the information system into a useful form.

information hiding
Hiding the internal implementation of an object from the user.

infrastructure
The underlying hardware, software, and communications technology in an organization.

interactive approach
An approach to developing software in which multiple versions are released to create a new product from a current one.

interface
The definition of how an object will be exposed to the external world.

interface standards
Part of the application architecture model that consists of agreements on how information systems interact with each other.

internal release
During the development process, the development team releases to the testing organization a new version of code that contains several features.

Internet
Also known as the world's largest WAN. It connects individuals and businesses inexpensively on a WAN.

Internet service
Lets you transfer files and other information via the Internet.

intranet
Private Internets with security to protect a corporation's assets.

keyboard shortcuts
A way to use the computer without a mouse. Most consist of function keys, the Alt key, the Ctrl key, and the Shift key, in combinations with letters and with each other.

LAN (local area network)
Links computers that are geographically close together and shares the information of many users.

late binding
When an application resolves a variable at run time.

local mode
Development area used while coding Web applications.

locale
The conventions, culture, and language of a group of users.

logging
The ability of a system to write events to a log file to track errors in software.

logical design perspective
Represents the developers' view of the system during the planning phase of the process model and after the conceptual design.

master mode
Area in which users work with a Web application.

messaging
When a client computer sends a request message to a server and the server responds with a response message.

middleware
Type of technology that allows clients and servers to communicate with each other over a network. ActiveX is an example of middleware technology.

milestone
A significant event in the development process.

module
A group of services and data that includes objects, services, attributes, and interfaces.

multithreading
An application composed of one or more processes.

network
A group of two or more computers and other devices linked together to share resources.

network access protocol
A protocol that allows networked computers to communicate using NICs.

network management service
A mechanism for managing network resources from a central location.

node
Another name for a networked device.

normalize
To eliminate redundant information and other problems with database design from the logical data model. The process of splitting data up into multiple tables to remove redundant pieces of information.

null
A value in a column that contains nothing.

object
A discrete entity with state and behavior properties.

object diagram
A UML diagram that captures objects and their relationships, showing the interaction between the real objects in the system.

operating system
A program that coordinates the interaction between the computer and the application programs it is running.

operation
Another name for a behavior triggered by an external stimulus.

packages
A term that UML uses for the subsystems and parts that result from the breakdown of a system.

peers
Computers that provide both presentation management and service functions.

physical design perspective
Represents the developers' perspective when creating plans after the logical design. These plans include information about the physical environmental constraints.

Plug and Play
A design standard that allows Windows to automatically detect and install device drivers for any new devices.

preemptive multitasking
A process allowing the kernel to give each process a certain amount of time to run.

primary key
A column that makes the rows in the table unique and that is usually an incremental counter.

printer services
Let you set up a printer that anyone connected to the network can use.

proactive management strategy
A strategy the project team uses as an objective, measurable process to anticipate and manage any risks.

process
A running application with its own address space and resources.

project
A special MDI application interface that provides a framework whereby objects reside in a window but do not contain child windows.

property
Information that describes an object.

protocol
A set of rules governing data organization and transmission.

queue
A special data structure that processes items in a first in, first out fashion.

reactive management strategy
A strategy that the project team uses to react to consequences of risks as they happen.

Glossary

record
A set of columns or a collection of related data items.

referential integrity
Part of a database application that checks the relationship of data contained in one table to data in other tables.

release candidate
A software release that is, in form, close to the final version.

report
A document that gives the user a printed representation of data.

resource manager
Schedules when the operating system uses hardware components.

risk
The possibility of a product or service suffering a failure.

round-trip engineering
Ability to reverse-engineer Visual C++ or Visual Basic, or to generate Visual C++ and Visual Basic code.

row (tuple)
One part of a table in a database.

security service
Restricts access to the network by unauthorized users.

sequence diagram
A UML diagram that captures the interaction between objects.

server
A specialized computer that supplies resources to the clients through a network.

service
A unit of application logic that defines an operation or function that transforms data.

service standards
The part of the application architecture model that supplies supported business services.

software configuration management
Allows developers to manage versions of products under development.

software development life cycle
The process used to develop a system. It helps managers keep teams organized, stay within budget and time constraints, and deliver products or services that meet business needs.

state
Part of an object that groups the values of all properties.

statechart diagram
A UML diagram that captures the behavior of a class.

stereotype
Allows the UML modeler to classify the links. It includes the behavior of the Authentication use case.

stored procedure
A procedure that defines a task that operates on the database.

string resources
Text that exists on a form, in a graphic, or in messages.

style sheet
A special file that defines the appearance of HTML elements on a page.

synchronous communication
Communication in which the client process and server process need to be running at the same time. When a client requests a service, the client waits until the server responds.

system software
Includes utilities for accomplishing common tasks.

table (relation)
The basic structure of a database. It contains rows (tuples) and columns (attributes).

test cases
Step-by-step instructions for testing a requirement.

test procedures
Special procedures that test a certain function of the system.

theme
A group of style sheets that defines the color, layout, backgrounds, and other visual elements in HTML.

thread
The smallest piece of a program that can be scheduled for execution.

topology
A physical arrangement of network devices.

transaction
(1) A group of statements that are committed all at once or that are all rolled back (uncommitted). (2) A unit of work that the developer defines.

transaction processing
The ability of various components to work in unison with each other.

Unicode
An international character format for localizing the operating system.

usability testing
Testing the software on the basis of different scenarios.

use case
A model used by the systems analyst to document the needs of the user.

use case diagram
A UML diagram that captures the functions of a system from a user's point of view.

user assistance
A way to supply a user with help in an application.

user services
Used when creating the user interface of a traditional GUI application, a Web-based application, or an application embedded in Microsoft Office. They run on the client and are stored on a Web server or on the client. They include VB forms, HTML, DHTML, and ASP.

variable
Stores results for calculations or processing of data within a program.

version
A set of requirements built into a product or service and delivered to the customer.

view
A stored query that allows you to take a snapshot of your data from one or more tables.

virtual communications path
A communications medium that exists logically, but does not exist physically.

WAN (wide area network)
A network of computers and devices that share information among users separated by a long distance. It usually consists of two or more local area networks connected by telephone lines or radio waves.

Glossary

WBS (work breakdown structure)
A hierarchical breakdown of the project
into phases, activities, and tasks.

Web services
Let you use a Web browser and Web server
to access the World Wide Web.

workbook
A type of application interface. It organizes
views of data into sections within the
workbook's primary window, using tabs
instead of child windows.

INDEX

WHAT'S ON THE CD-ROM

The **MCSD Architectures Exam Prep's** companion CD-ROM contains elements specifically selected to enhance the usefulness of this book, including:

➤ Two 35-question practice exams—The practice exam questions simulate the interface and format of the actual certification exams

➤ Answers to end-of-chapter review questions

➤ Answers to end-of-chapter hands-on projects

➤ All the data you will need to complete the steps and projects

System Requirements

Software:

➤ Your Operating System should be Windows 95/98, Windows NT 4.0 Workstation or Windows NT Server 4.0

➤ Windows NT Service Pack 4 is required for users running Windows NT Workstation and Server 4.0

➤ SQL Server 7.0, Standard Edition is required

➤ Microsoft Office is required

➤ Visual Studio 6.0, Enterprise Edition (everything except MSMQ) is recommended to be able to complete most of exercises

➤ Microsoft FrontPage is recommended

➤ A Java-compatible Web browser is needed to view some of the resources on this book's CD-ROM

➤ Internet access is recommended

Hardware:

➤ An Intel (or equivalent) Pentium 100MHz processor is the minimum platform required; an Intel (or equivalent) Pentium 200MHz processor is recommended

➤ 32MB of RAM is the minimum requirement for Windows 95/98, and 64MB is the minimum for NT Workstation and Server 4.0

➤ 2 GB of disk space is the minimum requirement, but 3GB of disk space is recommended for Windows 95/98, and 6GB is recommended for NT Workstation and Server 4.0

➤ An SVGA display type is recommended